STRATEGIES FOR PROBLEM SOLVING WORKBOOK

third edition

BRIAN K. SALTZER

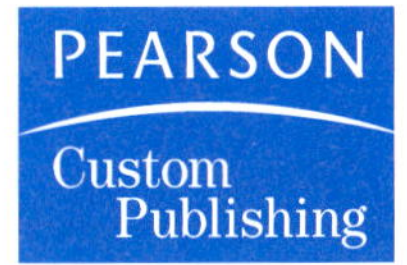

Cover art courtesy of Jerry Blank/Stock Illustration Source, Inc.
Tables on inside front cover and inside back cover taken from *College Physics*, Fourth Edition, by Wilson and Buffa, copyright Prentice-Hall, Inc.

Printed in the United States of America

20 19 18 17

ISBN 0-536-75360-1

BA 998482

JP/KG

Please visit our web site at *www.pearsoncustom.com*

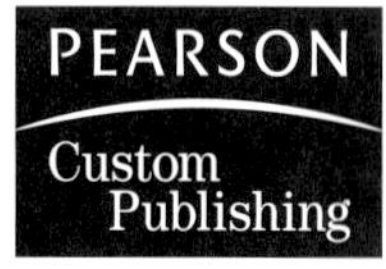

PEARSON CUSTOM PUBLISHING
75 Arlington Street, Suite 300, Boston, MA 02116
A Pearson Education Company

For you Mom.

Contents

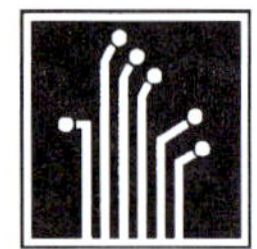

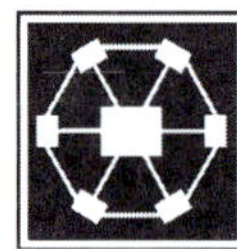

Preface

This text is written specifically for you, a technology student, to be a review of basic math skills as well as an introduction to problem solving—an important skill that you will need to be successful in both your ITT studies and future career. Because technology changes daily, an education that focuses exclusively on memorizing technological facts will not prepare you for long-term success in the job market. What does assure longevity in an ever-changing workplace, however, is the ability to solve problems.

Organization and Purpose

Prelude: An Introduction to Problem Solving

Understanding how to approach a problem and break it down into manageable steps is one of the fundamental challenges most people face—whether they are confronting complex technological problems or the decisions of daily life. Regardless of the topic, all of the projects in this book have one thing in common—they can be approached using Pólya's four-step problem solving strategy.

Pólya's process involves four key steps:

I. Understand the Problem
II. Devise a Plan
III. Carry Out the Plan
IV. Look Back

We introduce this methodology in the *Prelude: An Introduction to Problem Solving,* which sets the stage for the projects that follow.

The main text of this book is divided into four parts:

Baseline Projects
Electronics Application Projects
Drafting/Design Application Projects
Information Technology Projects

Baseline Projects

The twenty-four Baseline Projects cover a wide range of topics and require a variety of different skills. Based on real-world problems, the nineteen Thought Projects provide an interesting context to practice both mathematics and problem solving skills. Each Thought Project is divided into three Skill Levels, which increase in degree of difficulty. The first Skill Level is explicitly broken into the four Pólya steps. Within each step, questions are posed to guide you through the process and to help you develop sound strategies for tackling the problem. In Skill Levels II and III, the Pólya process is not mapped out for you; instead, you must practice what you've learned in order to solve the problems. This structure is intended to give you practice implementing the Pólya process regardless of whether or not you are specifically asked to do so.

Because rote memorization is the enemy of true problem solving, the projects have been constructed in a variety of forms. In some, the problem statement is at the beginning, whereas in others several pages of introductory material must be read before the problem statement is given. The Skill Level structure is designed to allow you to delve deeper into the topic of the project and to extend the math and problem solving techniques being taught.

In addition, there are five Interludes that focus exclusively on key math topics with which you must be very comfortable to be successful in your studies at ITT.

Technical Application Projects

Each of the three Technical Application parts—Electronics, Drafting/Design, and Information Technology—consists of ten projects that focus on problems unique to that discipline. Although the technological problems presented in these projects lend themselves to solution using the Pólya methodology, the steps have not been included, giving you an opportunity for independent practice.

Labs

At the conclusion of each Technical Application Project, you are given the opportunity to gain some basic familiarity with software associated with these fields of study by completing the Labs. Students of electronics will gain experience with MultiSim, while design students will learn the basics of AutoCAD. Information technology students will be introduced to a variety of software programs and hands-on activities that will be useful in their studies. The Appendices at the back of the text provide step-by-step instructions for each of the Labs.

Features

A number of features are built into the text to provide you with help and guidance.

- **Objectives** Each project opens with an Objectives box that lists the math skill(s) to be reviewed in the project, and directs you to the pertinent math coverage in the *Tools for Problem Solving CD.* You will derive the greatest benefit from this text if you develop the habit of referring to your Tools CD whenever you need to review or learn a math skill. The Objectives box tells you which section of the CD will be of most help.

- **Applied Math Skill Checks** Each project concludes with an Applied Math Skill Check set of problems. These exercises provide the opportunity to practice the math skill(s) reviewed in each project. If you have difficulty working these problems, you are strongly encouraged to use the appropriate section(s) from your Tools CD.
- **Margin Boxes** Math Review boxes appear frequently in the margin of the text to provide the timely reviews of important math concepts and formulas that are needed to solve the problem.

  In addition, Hint boxes, Problem Solving Tip boxes, and FYI boxes provide the kind of guidance that teachers might offer were they always available.

Realizing Success in this Course

If you spend time working through each assigned Thought Project and make optimal use of the reference tools provided, you will be on the road to becoming a skilled problem solver, and a highly marketable employee in the technology sector.

Acknowledgments

Thanks to Vikram Savkar, John Pullen, and the entire production team at Pearson Custom Publishing for their work on this third edition.

Thanks also go to the students of ITT Technical Institute for their helpful comments on the second edition of the book.

Prelude: An Introduction to Problem Solving

Most of us use the word "problem" fairly often in our daily conversation. We say things like,

- "I'm having a problem getting on-line."
- "The problem is that we just don't communicate."
- "I had a problem finding a parking space."

Many of the problems that we encounter are easily solved, but others require a more thoughtful approach. The challenge that confronts us in this text is to develop a broad-based problem solving strategy, and a set of skills to accompany it, that will allow us to solve a variety of complex problems. Once we are comfortable with the steps in problem solving, we will see that the process is basically the same, regardless of the nature of the problem.

Pólya's Four-Step Process

George Pólya
Twentieth-century mathematician/educator who formalized a four-step problem solving process.

The problem solving method that we will study is based on the work of the mathematician and educator George Pólya. He formalized a problem solving strategy that is broad enough to encompass all types of problems. This strategy, usually referred to as *Pólya's four-step process,* exploits the underlying similarities shared by all problems.

Pólya's Four-Step Process

I. Understand the Problem
II. Devise a Plan
III. Carry Out the Plan
IV. Look Back

Because our goal is to learn to apply this four-step strategy to real-world problems, it is important to become familiar with each stage in the process.

I. Understand the Problem

The first step is the most important. If we do not understand the problem that confronts us, we have no hope of finding a solution. A lack of understanding can prevent us from beginning the problem—or worse, lead us down a dead-end path.

This first of Pólya's steps has four major components that must be addressed, regardless of the type of problem that confronts us:

(a) Do we understand all of the words/terminology in the problem?
(b) What is the exact problem that we are being asked to solve?
(c) Are we given enough information to solve the problem?
(d) Are we given any information that has nothing to do with the problem, which can be eliminated from the problem solving process?

II. Devise a Plan

During this stage we begin to develop a strategy that will yield the solution to the problem. The following is a list of some useful tactics to employ:

(a) Draw a picture
(b) Make a model
(c) Look for any patterns or trends
(d) Do an experiment
(e) Gather statistics that relate to the problem
(f) Construct an equation that associates quantities that relate to the problem

Because this text focuses mainly on solving problems of a technical nature, we may find the last three items in the list to be the most helpful.

III. Carry Out the Plan

In Step III, we execute the strategy devised in Step II. We must be open to any and all results. The strategy attempted may be 100 percent correct, 0 percent correct, or anywhere in between.

Remember that any result, whether positive or negative, is simply more information for us to feed back into Step II!

Because the strategies of performing an experiment, gathering related statistics, and constructing an equation are so useful in solving problems of a technical nature, let's take some time to discuss what is involved in carrying out each of them.

Do an Experiment The word *experiment* may be slightly misleading and restrictive for our purposes. We do not necessarily mean an experiment in a science lab, with test tubes and bunsen burners. Rather, a better way for us to think about this tactic is "to do something physical" or "to take a physical measurement." The problem solving strategy that we choose may indeed be a chemistry experiment, but it can just as easily be wiring an electronic circuit, or sitting at a computer and using a drafting software package (such as AutoCAD). In other words, when we consider experimentation as a problem solving technique, we must use the word "experiment" as broadly as possible.

Gather Statistics Just as with experimentation, it is advantageous for us to think about statistics and the manner in which we gather them in a broad context. Our statistics might be pages and pages of numerical data that need to be graphed in order to yield effective information, or one or two facts that relate to the problem. Similarly, our methods of acquiring statistics can range from physically taking a survey to obtaining information via the internet. In the simplest form, we can think of statistics as being *facts* that relate to the problem.

Construct an Equation This technique is a very powerful tool for solving technical problems. However, to use this strategy effectively, we must be able to manipulate equations. If we cannot work with an equation, we will not be able to extract the information required to solve the problem. Because the use of equations and mathematics is frequently the most efficient problem solving technique for the projects in this text, we have developed extensive materials to assist you in acquiring the mathematical skills that are necessary.

Every project in this text begins with an Objectives box, which states the goals of the project and provides references to the Tools Book CD. Each section of the Tools CD includes explanations, examples, and exercises to help you gain the mathematical skills you need.

IV. Look Back

The final stage of Pólya's process asks us to evaluate the effectiveness of the problem solving strategy we used. Some of the questions that we must ask are

- Is our answer the full solution or only a partial one?
- Is our answer correct?
- If confronted with this problem (or a problem of a similar type) again, would we use the same problem solving strategy or modify it in some way?

Now let's practice applying Pólya's four steps to the following simple problem statement.

Problem

How many circles with a radius of 1 in. can we fit into a rectangle that is 2-ft long and 1-ft wide?

I. Understand the Problem

This problem statement provides a wonderful example of the importance of understanding the exact question we are being asked to solve. At first glance, this statement seems to present a very simple problem that will not require any elaborate problem solving techniques. However, upon closer analysis, we see that this problem does not lend itself to a single, unique solution!

Upon closer inspection we see that there are at least three different ways that we can interpret this problem:

(a) Because the problem statement does not tell us that the circles cannot overlap, we could literally place an infinite number of them in the rectangle. This would be a perfectly reasonable solution to the stated problem.
(b) Another interpretation would be that we are interested in discovering the number of circles that could be placed into the rectangle if the circles are placed edge to edge, but do not overlap. We could develop a problem solving strategy to approach this problem, the result of which would be a perfectly legitimate solution to the problem statement in its current form.
(c) Finally, we could interpret the problem statement as requesting that we compare the area of the rectangle to the area of the circle. Using mathematics, we could simply divide the area of the rectangle by the area of one circle. In that case our result would probably not be an integer, as it would in interpretation (b).

Because we have several different options for the interpretation of the problem statement, we are now faced with a decision. Do we want to solve the problem in its current form, including all of the different interpretations, or do we want to reword the problem, so that the problem we solve actually has a unique solution?

To further illustrate Pólya's four steps in our example, we will reword this problem so that it will have a unique solution.

Problem

How many circles with a radius of 1 in. can we fit into a rectangle that is 2-ft long and 1-ft wide, if no circles are allowed to overlap or protrude outside of the box?

This new problem statement is now clear and uniquely solvable. Our next task involves Step II of Pólya's process.

II. Devise a Plan

There are several different strategies that we can employ to solve the problem. Some of these strategies are stated in the following list.

(a) Draw a full-sized representation of the problem by hand, and physically draw in the circles.
(b) Draw a smaller version of the problem to scale, and manually insert the circles until we reach the solution.
(c) Use a drafting software package to make a drawing of the problem to scale, and use the same methods as in strategies (a) and (b).
(d) Use mathematical reasoning to decide how many circles will fit, without making a drawing of the problem.
(e) Use a combination of these strategies.

The choice of strategy to implement is largely determined by preference and ability. First, we must evaluate those skills that we already possess or are willing to acquire. Do we have access to the tools needed to make a hand drawing to scale? Do we have access to a drafting software package that will allow us to make the drawing? If we have access to the software, do we have the necessary software skills to solve the problem? Do we have the necessary mathematical background to choose strategy (d)? Will one strategy solve the problem faster than the others?

Once we have decided which problem solving technique is the most efficient to use, we must carry out the strategy.

III. Carry Out the Plan

To illustrate our four-step process most effectively, we will choose a problem solving strategy that does not require a software package or other such tools. To illustrate this third step in the problem solving method, let's choose mathematics as our problem solving approach—that is, strategy (d).

Note that even though we have chosen mathematics as our strategy, it may still be helpful to make a sketch of the problem:

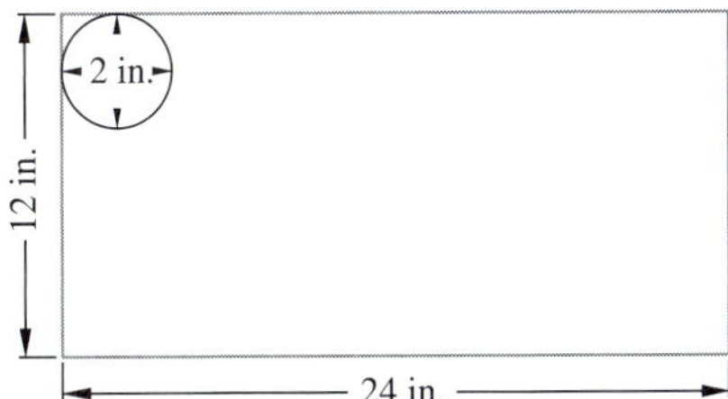

Notice that in the sketch, as an aid to solving the problem, we have expressed the dimensions of the rectangle in inches so that we can more readily compare it to our circles. Using mathematics, we also see that because our circles have a radius of 1 in., they are 2 in. across at their widest points. Using mathematical reasoning and our drawing, we see that we can place 6 rows of 12 circles in the rectangle. We can now find the number of circles in the rectangle either by adding them, or by multiplying 12×6. We conclude that 72 circles can fit in the rectangle.

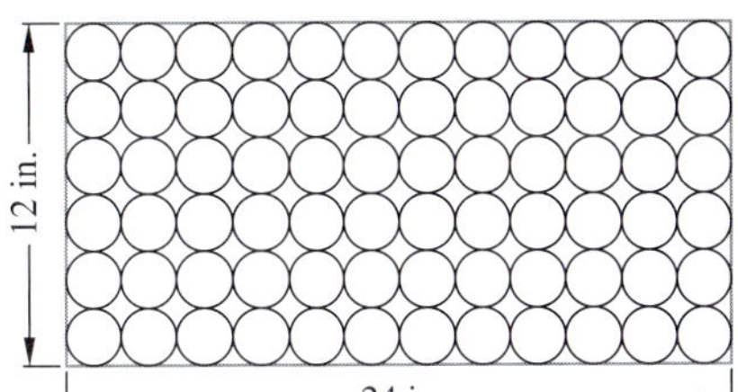

IV. Look Back

During the last phase of Pólya's method, we evaluate the effectiveness of our strategy. Some of the questions that we should ask include:

a) Is our answer a correct solution to the problem?
b) Can this strategy be applied to other problems of similar type?

c) Can this strategy be extended to the original problem statement that we reworded?
d) Is there any error associated with our solution? If so, is there a way to quantify this error?
e) If confronted with this problem again, would we use the same strategy, a modified version of it, or choose a totally different one?

Now it's your turn! This book contains Thought Projects from a variety of real-world situations. Because rote memorization is the enemy of true problem solving, the projects are written in a variety of forms and include many different reading and skill levels. Sometimes the problem to solve is given at the beginning of the project. Other times you will need to read several pages of background material to prepare for solving the problem. In some cases, only the required information is given; in others, excess information is given and you must sift through it to extract what is necessary and applicable. You may choose to do research on the internet, perform a physical experiment, use mathematics, or employ a number of other strategies to solve the problem. As you become more adept at problem solving, you may not consciously think about each of Pólya's steps; however, they are always at work in the background. At the end of the course, you should have acquired problem solving that will help you excel at ITT Technical Institute and in your future career.

Completion Chart

Baseline Projects Enter the date you submit each Skill Level

	Skill Level I	Skill Level II	Skill Level III
1. Fractions and Construction			
2. Density			
3. Ages			
4. Distance, Rate, and Time			
5. Colors			
6. Thermodynamics			
7. The Speed of Light			
8. The Motion of Fluids			
9. Michael's Budget			
10. Computer Repair Calls			
11. Ratios and Proportions			
12. Temperature Scales			
13. Sports and Statistics			
14. Interlude: Bases and Exponents			
15. The Behavior of Astronomical Masses			
16. Interlude: Unit Analysis			
17. Global Warming and the Ozone Layer			
18. Interlude: Polynomials and Factoring			
19. Simultaneous Equations and the Physical World			
20. Interlude: Simplifying Radicals, Exponents, and Negative Exponents			
21. Projectile Motion			
22. Radiocarbon Dating			
23. Interlude: Trigonometry			
24. Billboards			

Electronics Projects Enter the date you submit each Skill Level

	Skill Level I	Skill Level II	Skill Level III
1. Ohm's Law			
2. Wiring Resistors in Series and Parallel			
3. The Power Dissipated by a Resistor			
4. Transformers			
5. Capacitors in DC/AC Electronics			
6. Working with Capacitors			
7. Inductors			
8. RLC Circuits			
9. Semiconductors			
10. Independent Electronics Research			

Drafting/Design Projects Enter the date you submit each Skill Level

	Skill Level I	Skill Level II	Skill Level III
1. Columns and Beams			
2. Two- and Three-Dimensional Visualization			
3. Thermal Expansions of Materials			
4. Gear Systems			
5. Center of Mass			
6. Fluids and Piping			
7. Strength of Materials			
8. Elevations			
9. Torque			
10. Independent Drafting/Design Research			

Information Technology Projects Enter the date you submit each Skill Level

	Skill Level I	Skill Level II	Skill Level III
1. Prime Numbers and Computer Encryption Codes			
2. Converting Binary to Decimal			
3. Permutations and Combinations			
4. Logical Reasoning			
5. Tracking Profits			
6. Corporate Optimization			
7. Memory and Matrices			
8. Fiber-Optic Cables			
9. The Next Generation of Computing			
10. Independent Information Technology Research			

BASELINE PROJECTS

1. Fractions and Construction
2. Density
3. Ages
4. Distance, Rate, and Time
5. Colors
6. Thermodynamics
7. The Speed of Light
8. The Motion of Fluids
9. Michael's Budget
10. Computer Repair Calls
11. Ratios and Proportions
12. Temperature Scales
13. Sports and Statistics
14. Interlude: Bases and Exponents
15. The Behavior of Astronomical Masses
16. Interlude: Unit Analysis
17. Global Warming and the Ozone Layer
18. Interlude: Polynomials and Factoring
19. Simultaneous Equations and the Physical World
20. Interlude: Simplifying Radicals, Exponents, and Negative Exponents
21. Projectile Motion
22. Radiocarbon Dating
23. Interlude: Trigonometry
24. Billboards

THOUGHT PROJECT 1

Fractions and Construction

Whether you are thinking about a small home remodeling project or the construction of a skyscraper, one fact of construction is the same: builders must be comfortable in manipulating fractional expressions so that they may use the appropriate tools and find essential measurements. In this Thought Project, we use the topic of building construction to illustrate how to add, multiply, and divide fractions.

Objectives

1. Add, subtract, multiply, and divide fractions
2. Work with both improper and mixed fractions

Tools Book CD: R.2, R.3D

Skill Level I 

Installing new, energy efficient windows correctly requires careful measurement and calculation.

Courtesy of Omni-Photo Communications, Inc.

Problem

You are working on a home improvement project in which you are installing new, energy-efficient windows in your home. In preparation, you have borrowed tools from a friend. There are two wrenches in the toolbox and their sizes are given in fractions. You need to select the largest wrench available.

One of the wrenches has a measurement of $7/16''$ and the other has a size of $3/8''$. Which one is larger?

I. Understand the Problem

(a) What are the critical pieces of information in this problem statement, and what is the specific problem you are being asked to solve?

II. Devise a Plan

(b) Identify some ways in which the sizes of the two wrenches can be effectively compared.

(c) How can you use the language of fractions to express the sizes of the two wrenches so that they can be effectively compared? Explain.

(d) Find a common denominator that can be used to express the size of both wrenches.

(e) How can you use decimals instead of fractions to express the size of each wrench?

III. Carry Out the Plan

(f) Use fractions to determine which wrench is larger. Show your work.

IV. Look Back

(g) Although you were instructed to use mathematics to solve this problem, other problem solving strategies would also have been effective. If no instructions were given, would you have chosen mathematics as the best strategy to solve the problem? Explain.

Skill Level II 

MATH REVIEW

A mixed fraction includes both a whole number and a fractional part.

Problem

A construction worker is using two pieces of pipe to form an L-joint for a section of piping that connects a water source to a showerhead. Pipe 1 is $6'4''$ and Pipe 2 is $8'1''$. Use this information to answer the following questions.

(h) Express the length of each pipe in feet using mixed fractions.

MATH REVIEW

A proper fraction is one in which the numerator is smaller than the denominator.

In an improper fraction, the numerator is equal to or larger than the denominator.

(i) Express the length of each pipe in feet using improper fractions.

(j) Using improper fractions, find the length of the L-joint by adding together the lengths of the pipes. Show your work.

(k) Express your answer from step (j) as a mixed fraction and as a decimal.

Skill Level III ♦♦♦

Problem

The kitchen floor of your home is 12′6″ in width and 10′4″ in length. You have decided to put in a new tile floor. The tiles that you have selected are 5″ on each side.

1. Express the area of the kitchen floor, in square feet, as an improper fraction.
2. Express the area of each tile in square feet.
3. How many tiles are required to tile the floor?
4. Explain how your answer relates to the real world.

Record your answers in the space provided.

Applied Math Skill Check

1. Add/subtract the following fractions.

(a) $\frac{2}{3} + \frac{5}{7}$

(b) $\frac{3}{4} + \frac{7}{12}$

(c) $\frac{4}{9} - \frac{1}{8}$

2. Express the following fractions as decimals.

   (a) $\frac{3}{5}$

   (b) $\frac{2}{7}$

   (c) $\frac{43}{100}$

3. Multiply the following fractions.

   (a) $\frac{2}{3} \cdot \frac{5}{7}$

   (b) $\frac{1}{3} \cdot \frac{5}{9}$

   (c) $\frac{7}{5} \cdot \frac{11}{6}$

4. Divide the following fractions.

   (a) $\dfrac{\frac{2}{5}}{\frac{4}{7}}$

   (b) $\dfrac{\frac{5}{9}}{\frac{2}{7}}$

   (c) $\dfrac{\frac{6}{5}}{\frac{13}{8}}$

5. In your opinion, when would it be advantageous to record a fractional answer in each of the following forms?

   (a) A mixed fraction

   (b) An improper fraction

   (c) A decimal

THOUGHT PROJECT 2

Density

The physical concept of *density* provides an interesting scientific setting to examine the basic parts of a fraction.

Objectives

1. Identify the three basic parts of a fraction—numerator, denominator, and fraction bar
2. Convert a fractional expression into a decimal expression
3. Acquire internet research skills

Tools Book CD: R.2A, B; R.3A, D

Skill Level I 

Did you know that diamonds and the graphite in your pencil are made of the same material? Even though they look very different and have very different physical properties, they are both made of carbon. How tightly the atoms of carbon are packed together determines the physical characteristics of the object. We call this atomic tightness *density*.

The density of a material (usually expressed using the lower case Greek letter rho, ρ) is defined as the mass of the material divided by its volume. The equation for density is:

$$\rho = \frac{m}{V}$$

Math Review

Remember that the *numerator* of a fraction is the portion above the fraction bar and the *denominator* of a fraction is the portion below the fraction bar.

Problem

Find the density of a material that has a mass of 10 kg and a volume of 0.5 m^3.

Problem Solving Tip

With simple problems such as this one, steps in the problem solving process may be combined.

In this problem you need not devise a plan, since the strategy "use an equation" is given to you. Therefore you may go directly to solving the problem.

I. Understand the Problem

(a) What is the numerator of this expression?

(b) What is the denominator of this expression?

II. Carry Out the Plan

(c) What is the density of the material?

(d) How are the units of the density found?

III. Look Back

(e) How is the density affected by increasing the mass while holding the volume constant?

(f) How is the density affected by increasing the volume while holding the mass constant?

Skill Level II ♦♦

The example of finding the density of a material illustrates the inherent mathematical operation of division implied by the fraction bar, and suggests a built-in method for converting from fractional to decimal notation. A fraction such as 3/10 can be converted into its decimal equivalent by performing the division implied by the fraction bar:

$$\frac{3}{10} = 10\overline{)3} = 0.3$$

Problem

Find the density of a material that has a mass of 2 kg and a volume of 5 m^3. Express your answer in both fractional and decimal form.

Record your answers in the space provided.

Skill Level III ♦♦♦

The concept of density can be applied to situations other than those involving mass and volume. For example, if we compare the number of people who live in a five-square-mile region of rural Montana to the number of people who live in an area of the same size in the Silicon Valley of California, we see that the Silicon Valley has a much higher *population density*. In this case, the density is expressed as the number of people per square mile.

As another example, if we look at the universe as a whole, astronomers tell us that the *density* of the stars in the nighttime sky is constant in all directions. By "constant," we mean that if we sample equal volumes of space in any direction, the number of stars in these volumes will be approximately equal.

Thus, a better way for us to think about density is as the ratio of the amount of some thing (mass, people, electrical charge, etc.) to the size of the spatial region occupied by the thing. This spatial region can be one-, two-, or three-dimensional. In other words, density is simply a measurement of how tightly packed a quantity is in a particular spatial region.

Problem

Use the internet or another resource to find the information required to calculate the population density of your state. Express your answer in people per square mile.

Record your answer in the space provided.

Applied Math Skill Check

1. (a) Write a fraction with a numerator of 6 and a denominator of 20.

   (b) Express this fraction in decimal form.

2. (a) Which of the following terms is larger?

   $\frac{2}{3}$ 0.7

   (b) Explain the method you used to arrive at your answer.

3. For each fraction described below, state the relationship of the fraction to the number 1.

   (a) The numerator of the fraction is larger than the denominator of the fraction.

   (b) The denominator of the fraction is larger than the numerator of the fraction.

   (c) The numerator and the denominator of the fraction have the same value.

Ages

Looking at the age relationships among family members provides an opportunity to review simple equations.

Objectives

1. Use a variable to represent an unknown quantity in an equation
2. Interpret a mathematical relationship expressed in words, and write it as an equation

Tools Book CD: 1.1B, 1.2D

Skill Level I 

Problem

An eight-year-old boy named Nathan wants to compare his age with that of his mother and grandfather. His mother is exactly four times his age and his grandfather is exactly seven times his age. How old is Nathan's mother? How old is his grandfather?

I. Understand the Problem

(a) Underline the key pieces of information contained in the problem statement.

II. Devise a Plan

(b) Can you rewrite the problem statement in the form of an equation? If so, what is required for you to write it?

(c) Can the mother's age be found using the same problem solving strategy as the one used to find the grandfather's age? Explain.

III. Carry Out the Plan

(d) Solve the equations. How old is Nathan's mother? How old is his grandfather?

(e) One year from now, will the same relationship exist between Nathan's age and that of his mother and grandfather? Use numbers to illustrate your answer.

IV. Look Back

In this Thought Project, the relationships between the ages of various family members could have been found without using equations and variables. Describe a situation in which it would be necessary to employ the more formal mathematical techniques of variables and equations rather than simple reasoning.

Skill Level II 

Problem

Nathan has two brothers, Conner and Josh. If we add 2 to Conner's age, it is exactly 1/2 the age of their older brother Josh, who is 12. How old is Conner?

Show your work.

Skill Level III 

Problem

How many years will it be until Conner's age is 1/2 of Josh's age?

Show your work.

Applied Math Skill Check

1. Write out, in words, what each of the following equations says mathematically.

   (a) $ab = cd$

   (b) $3x + 5y = 2z$

   (c) $x + 4 = \frac{t}{7}$

2. Translate each of the following into an equation.

   (a) If the variable x is multiplied by 6, the product is equal to 4 times the variable y.

   (b) If 8 is added to the variable t, the sum is equal to the variable B.

   (c) If 9 is subtracted from the variable R, the difference is equal to the variable x divided by 5.

THOUGHT PROJECT 4

Distance, Rate, and Time

Many problems, from simple concerns of travel time to more complex situations involving the rate at which the moon orbits the earth, require us to work with the algebraic relationships of distance, speed, and time.

Objectives

1. Set up an equation for one variable
2. Solve for a variable using algebraic manipulations
3. Carry out effective internet research

Tools Book CD: 1.2B, 2.3A, 2.6A

Skill Level I 

Problem

Bob Rodriguez, the Albany, NY sales representative for Advanced Drafting Software, Inc., must attend the regional sales meeting in New York City. Unfortunately, his car is in the shop so he must make other travel arrangements to reach his destination. One option is to take a train that departs at 8:00 A.M. Alternatively, he could ride to the meeting with another sales rep.

Bob has an important presentation to deliver at the meeting and needs to arrive as early as possible. He knows that the train travels at 80 miles per hour, but has a 30-minute layover halfway through the 156-mile trip. He also knows that his friend cannot depart before 8:00 A.M. and will adamantly refuse to drive any faster than 55 miles per hour.

If both methods of transportation leave at the same time (8:00 A.M.), will the train or the car allow him to reach the regional sales meeting sooner?

HINT

Distance = Rate × Time

I. Understand the Problem

(a) What are the key pieces of information in this problem?

II. Devise a Plan

(b) Is there a way to make a drawing of this problem? If so, how?

(c) Is it possible to break this problem into smaller pieces in order to solve it? How?

(d) Discuss your strategy for solving this problem.

III. Carry Out the Plan

(e) Execute your strategy and determine which method of travel will allow Bob to reach the meeting in the shortest amount of time.

IV. Look Back

(f) How efficient was the strategy you used? Would your strategy be useful for solving other types of problems? Explain.

Skill Level II 

Problem

A businessman drives from Washington, D.C. to Boston, a distance of 442 miles, and then makes the return trip. On the way to Boston, he drives 65 miles per hour, taking a 1-hour rest stop during the drive. After finishing his business in Boston, he makes the return trip driving at 60 miles per hour and takes a 45-minute rest stop halfway through the trip.

Which leg of the journey, Washington, D.C. to Boston, or Boston to Washington, D.C., takes the longer time?

Show your work.

Skill Level III 

Hint

The average distance between the earth and the moon is 382,000,000 meters.

Problem

Find an approximate value for the rate at which the moon orbits the earth. Assume that the moon's orbit is circular.

Show your work.

Applied Math Skill Check

1. If $x = yz$, find the value for x given that $y = 2$ and $z = 5$.

2. Given that $T = RV$, find R if $T = 4$ and $V = 8$.

3. Given that $w = xyz$, find w if $x = 2$, $y = 3$, and $z = 6$.

4. If $C = ab$, find C if $a = 0.65$ and $b = 1.9$.

Colors

It's almost impossible to pick up a current newspaper or magazine without encountering a graph. From weather trends, to the ups and downs of the stock market, to the results of scientific research, complex information is routinely summarized in graphical form. In this Thought Project, we use the study of the effects of color on behavior as a setting to develop our ability to read and interpret graphs.

Objectives

1. Read a two-dimensional graph
2. Extract important information from a graph and apply it to a real-world setting
3. Interpret the information contained in a graph and draw inferences based on it

Tools Book CD: 1.8, 3.1A

Skill Level I ♦

Do you have a favorite color? Are there colors that you find unattractive and would never consider wearing or using in your home? Do you ever think about the impact color has on your moods and your impressions of things? Believe it or not, color plays such a significant role in our society that entire branches of scientific research are devoted to the study of this phenomenon.

One of the interesting characteristics of color is that each color is produced by an electromagnetic wave of a different length.

For example, whereas the wave for one color may look like this:

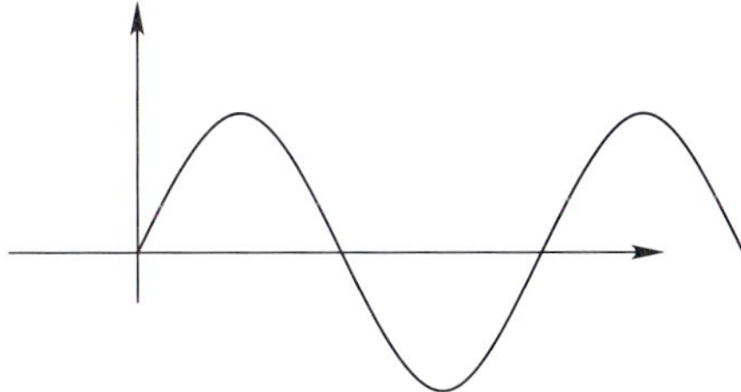

Figure 5.1

another takes this form:

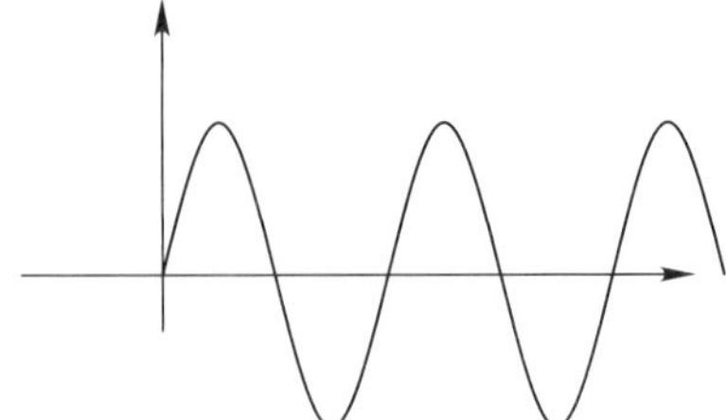

Figure 5.2

Because there are many different colors with varying wavelengths, we need to find a convenient method for summarizing this information. One method is to display the information in a *graph*. In simple terms, a graph is a picture of quantitative information.

Let's graph the colors in the rainbow. The colors red, orange, yellow, green, blue, and violet represent the color spectrum. Look at the graph that lists the various colors of this spectrum according to their wavelengths:

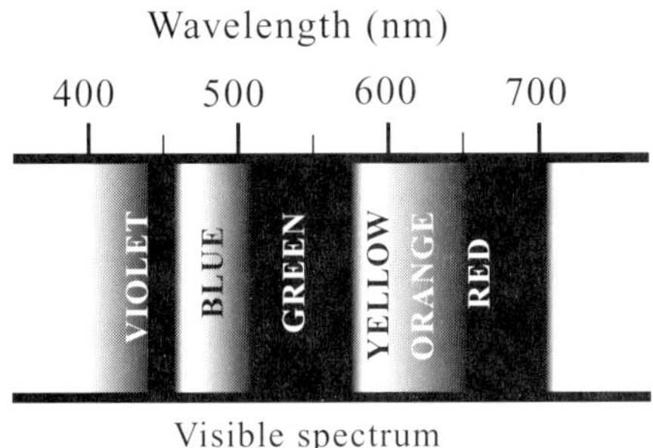

Figure 5.3

There are many different ways to graph data, and to interpret the data in the graph. The next graph compares the wavelengths of various colors to the sensitivity of the human eye:

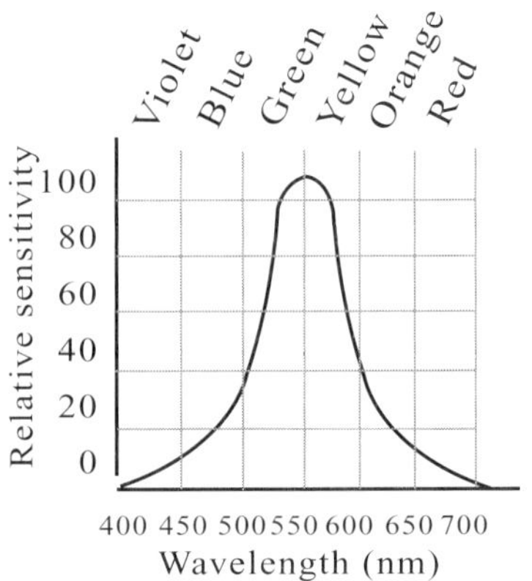

Figure 5.4

The human eye responds differently to various colors. For example, the peak of the graph corresponds to yellow-green. Our eyes are capable of discerning subtle differences in shades of green more easily than in those colors on the edges of the graph (red and blue). Studies have also shown that green is far less stressful on the human eye than either red or blue.

Use these graphs to develop a strategy for solving the following problem.

Problem

Design an experiment that uses color to modify human behavior.

I. Understand the Problem

(a) Discuss how the graph of wavelengths versus eye sensitivity relates to this problem.

(b) Write down a hypothesis for this problem.

II. Devise a Plan

(c) Identify some possible strategies to test your hypothesis.

(d) Are all the strategies that you listed in step (c) equally viable? Might any of them yield a solution to the problem more readily than others? If so, why?

(e) In addition to the graphs given in this Thought Project, are there any additional data that would be useful or necessary to solve this problem using your strategy?

(f) If you answered yes to the question in step (e), what are some possible sources for this data?

(g) For assistance in testing your hypothesis, do you feel that the data given in the graphs could be displayed more effectively? In other words, would a bar chart, pie chart, or other form of display be a better way to graph this data?

III. Look Back

(h) Discuss your opinion of graphing as a problem solving tool. When can it be used as an effective tool?

(i) Discuss the outcome that you think would result if your problem solving technique were applied to the problem in this Thought Project.

Skill Level II 

Problem

Execute any research necessary to support your explanation for why bullfighters' capes are red.

Record your answer in the space provided.

Skill Level III 

HINT

Begin by considering where *ultra*violet and *infra*red would be on the graph, compared to the visible colors violet and red.

Problem

Discuss how the graphs presented in this Thought Project help to explain why humans cannot see colors that fall in the ultraviolet or infrared part of the electromagnetic spectrum.

Record your answer in the space provided.

Applied Math Skill Check

Use the graph in Figure 5.5 to answer questions 1 and 2.

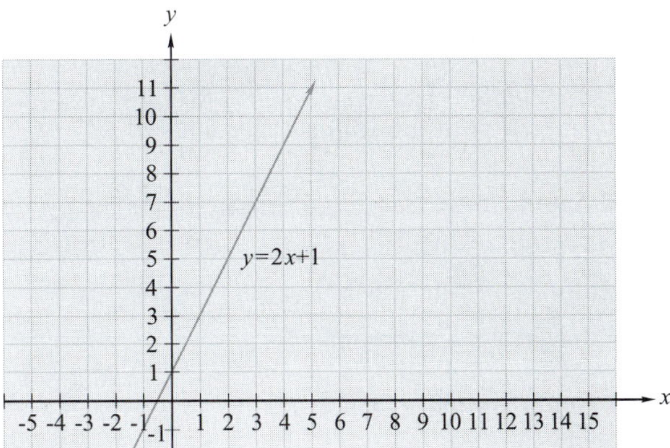

Figure 5.5

1. What value of the variable y is associated with the following values for the variable x?

   (a) $x = 1$

   (b) $x = 3$

   (c) $x = 0$

2. What value of the variable x is associated with the following values for the variable y?

   (a) $y = 1$

   (b) $y = 5$

Use the graph in Figure 5.6 to answer questions 3–5.

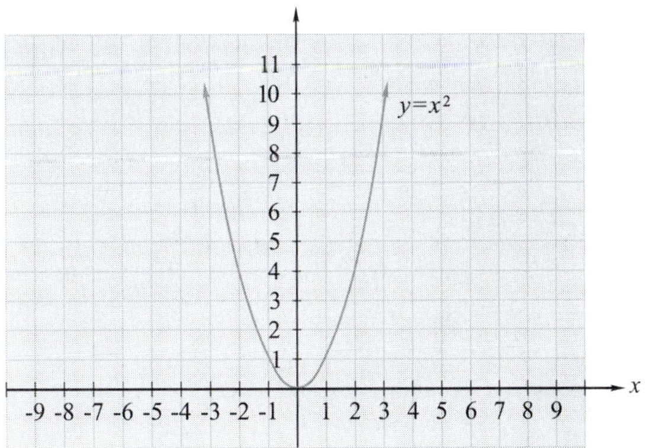

Figure 5.6

3. What value of y is associated with $x = 0$?

4. What value of y is associated with the following values of x?

   (a) $x = 2$

   (b) $x = 3$

   (c) $x = -2$

5. What value(s) of x are associated with the following values of y?

   (a) $y = 0$

   (b) $y = 1$

Thermodynamics

An important topic of study in science is thermodynamics. The underlying physics of changes in both state and temperature provides an interesting setting for reviewing the algebra skill of solving for a variable in an equation with several variables.

Objectives

1. Manipulate an algebraic equation and solve for one of the equation's variables
2. Practice the careful reading of text to determine which pieces of information are pertinent to finding a solution

Tools Book CD: 2.3A, 2.6B

Have you ever sat and watched ice melt on a hot summer day? Although it may not appear very active, the process of ice changing into water requires a great deal of activity at the molecular level. Solids, such as ice, are held together by the electrostatic attraction between their molecules. Although invisible to our eyes, the molecules in a solid are actually oscillating (moving around) at rapid speeds inside the solid. This movement, or velocity, of the molecules is directly proportional to their kinetic energy.

Because heat is equivalent to energy, by adding heat to the ice we actually provide energy to the ice. Most of the energy is transferred to the motion of the molecules, making them move even more rapidly. In general terms, we can say that as we increase the temperature of an object, we increase its kinetic energy. As the kinetic energy increases, the electrostatic bonds that hold the solid together are weakened. Eventually, if we provide enough heat, the kinetic energy of the molecules reaches a level at which the electrostatic bonds between the molecules can no longer sustain the form as a solid. The material then changes into a liquid. In our example, the ice melts.

The equation that tells us how much heat is required to melt a given material is:

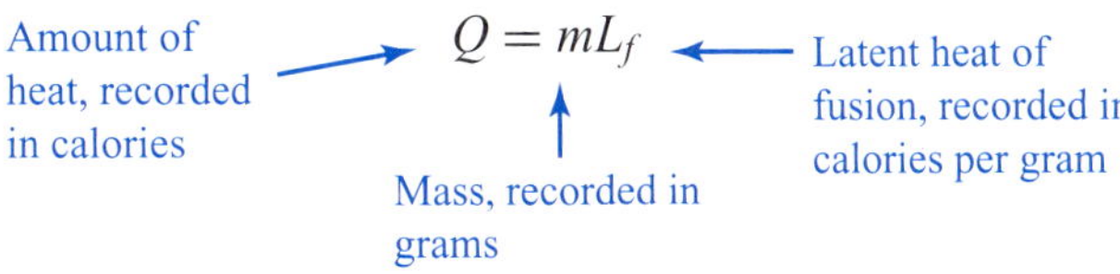

It is logical that the quantity, or mass, of a material affects the amount of heat that is required to melt it. For example, a large block of ice melts much more slowly than does a single ice cube. Thus, mass enters into the equation and is directly proportional to the amount of heat. However, the term L_f, the latent heat of fusion, may be unfamiliar. This variable represents the measurement of how easily a material moves between the solid and the liquid state. It is a number that varies dramatically from material to material.

Skill Level I 

Problem

The latent heat of fusion for ice is 79.8 cal/gram. How much ice can we melt with 1000 calories of heat?

I. Understand the Problem

(a) Read the introduction carefully. Underline the key pieces of information that are required to solve this problem.
(b) Identify the extraneous information in the background reading.

II. Devise a Plan

(c) Explain your strategy for solving this problem.

III. Carry Out the Plan

(d) Solve the problem. How much ice can you melt with 1000 calories of heat?

Skill Level II 

A different equation allows us to find the amount of heat required to move between the liquid state of matter and the gaseous state (for example, for boiling water to turn into steam).

The equation is given by

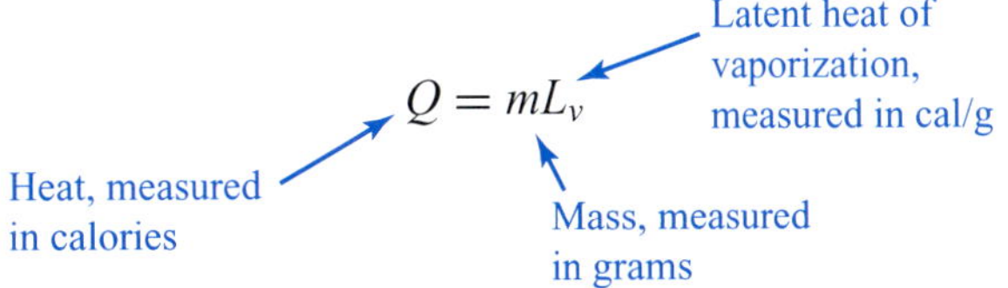

The latent heat of vaporization is a measurement of how easily a material moves between the liquid and the gas state.

Hint

Water freezes at 0°C, boils at 100°C, and the L_v of water is 539.6 cal/g.

Problem

Which would require more heat, melting 500 g of 0°C ice or turning 500 g of 100°C water into steam?

Show your work.

Skill Level III ♦♦♦

Within certain temperature ranges, a change in temperature will not result in a change in the state of a given material. For example, if heat is applied to water at 20°C, the temperature of the water increases, but the water does not change into steam until it reaches a temperature of 100°C.

The equation that is used to calculate the amount of heat required to cause a temperature change is:

$$Q = mc\Delta T \tag{1}$$

where

- Q is the amount of heat required to cause the temperature change (expressed in calories)
- m is the mass of the material experiencing the temperature change (expressed in grams)
- c, called the specific heat capacity, is a measurement of the material's ability to retain heat (expressed in cal/g°C)
- ΔT is the change in the temperature of the material (expressed in °C)

Problem

A 500 g sample of an unknown material requires 750 calories of heat to raise its temperature by 50°C. Use Equation (1) and Table 6.1 to identify the material.

Table 6.1 Specific Heats of Various Substances (at 20°C and 1 atm).

Substance	Specific heat (cal/g°C)
Air (50°C)	0.25
Alcohol, ethyl	0.58
Aluminum	0.22
Copper	0.093
Glass	0.20
Ice (−5°C)	0.50
Iron or steel	0.11
Lead	0.031
Soil (average)	0.25
Steam (110°C)	0.48
Water (15°C)	1.00
Wood (average)	0.40

Show your work.

Applied Math Skill Check

Solve the following equations for the variable x.

1. $4x = y$

2. $xyz = t$

3. $4xz = P$

4. $y = xtz$

5. $3.5tpx = R$

The Speed of Light

The light from the supernova that initiated the formation of the Crab Nebula, as well as the light generated by a laser, provides a fascinating setting to examine the mathematical concepts of variables and equations.

Objectives

1. Manipulate an equation with several variables
2. Evaluate the information acquired during internet research

Tools Book CD: 2.6

Skill Level I 

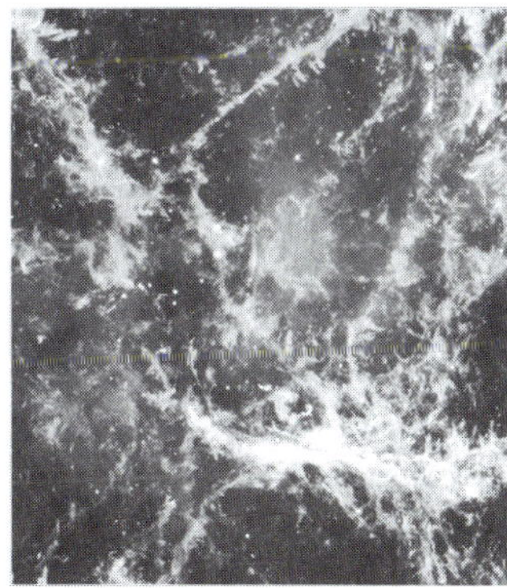

The Crab Nebula formed from the supernova documented by Chinese astronomers in 1054.

Courtesy of NASA/Johnson Space Center

You may have heard the expression "faster than the speed of light," but have you ever thought about how fast that might be? Although light travels very quickly, it does not move from point to point instantaneously. In other words, although the light seems to appear instantaneously when you flick on a light switch, it actually takes a little time for the light rays to move from the light source to your eyes. So, you may be wondering, just how fast does light travel? Very fast! The velocity of a light ray moving through a vacuum (space) is 186,000 miles per second.

Problem

In A.D. 1054, Chinese astronomers observed the light from a supernova in the night sky. This supernova was the incredibly powerful origin of what is now the Crab Nebula.

Using the velocity of light, devise and execute a strategy for finding out when the supernova actually occurred, relative to when the Chinese astronomers saw the explosion.

HINT

Not all problems have precise numerical solutions. However, it is often possible to place an upper and lower boundary on the *possible* solutions to a problem.

I. Understand the Problem

(a) Read the problem statement carefully to be sure you understand what problem you are being asked to solve. Identify the pertinent pieces of information.

II. Devise a Plan

(b) What are some possible strategies for solving this problem?

(c) Of the strategies that you listed in step (b), discuss the advantages/disadvantages of each.

(d) What additional information, if any, is necessary to solve the problem?

(e) If you listed any items in step (d), identify some possible sources for finding this information.

There may be several useful approaches to finding a solution to this problem. Two of these methods follow:

1. Use the algebraic relation

$$\text{Distance} = \text{Rate} \times \text{Time}$$

together with information found from independent research.

2. Execute the research necessary to find the solution directly.

(f) To use the algebraic relationship described in the first strategy, you must first express it using variables. Rewrite the algebraic relationship, Distance = Rate × Time, using variables.

(g) Although you can use any variable to represent a physical quantity, some variables are better than others. Why do you think that is the case?

(h) Use the equation you wrote in step (f) to solve for the variable that represents the rate.

(i) Use your equation to solve for the variable that you used to represent time.

(j) Which strategy do you think is best for finding a solution to this problem? Explain your decision.

III. Carry Out the Plan

> **HINT**
>
> Regardless of the strategy that you choose to solve the problem, it may be helpful to learn about a measurement taken by Edwin Hubble early in the twentieth century.

Devise a third option of your own, or use one of the two given strategies to solve the problem. Show your results and explain the methods you used to find the solution.

IV. Look Back

(k) How effective was the strategy that you chose? If confronted with a similar problem, would you use the same strategy? If not, why not?

(l) After carrying out your strategy, did you find that the problem solving strategies of mathematics and internet research could be executed independently of one another? Explain.

(m) If you followed the Hint and researched the measurement taken by Edwin Hubble, how did this information affect your solution and/or approach to the problem? Explain.

> **HINT**
>
> Although we do not necessarily know the historical rate of the expansion of the universe, we do know that it has expanded.

(n) Why is it impossible to find a precise answer to the problem, but possible to place a boundary on the possible answers?

Skill Level II 

Problem

The average distance between the earth and the sun is 93 million miles. Using the velocity of light given at the beginning of this Thought Project, find an approximate value for the amount of time it takes a light ray to travel from the sun to the earth.

Show your work.

Skill Level III 

Problem

Lasers, which use light rays of set wavelengths (colors), are in constant use in our world, in everything from surgery to supermarket checkout scanners.

Execute the necessary research to determine whether the color of a laser affects the velocity of the light wave projected by the laser.

Cite the sources you used and record your answer in the space provided.

Applied Math Skill Check

1. Solve $x = yz$

   (a) for the variable y

   (b) for the variable z

2. Solve

   $$v = \frac{d}{t}$$

   for the variable d.

3. Solve

   $3x = wyz$

   (a) for the variable x

   (b) for the variable w

   (c) for the variable y

   (d) for the variable z

4. Find t in the following equations.

   (a) $Rt = F$
   if $R = 6$ and $F = 18$.

   (b) $\frac{t}{p} = D$
   if $p = 4$ and $D = 5$.

   (c) $Bt = 2y$
   if $B = 2$ and $y = 6$.

The Motion of Fluids

One important area of study in the fields of physics and engineering is fluid mechanics. In this Thought Project, we examine the motion of fluids to illustrate the importance of manipulating an equation with several variables.

Objectives

1. Manipulate an algebraic equation that contains several variables
2. Execute independent research and apply the findings to solve a problem

Tools Book CD: 2.3A, 2.6B

Skill Level I 

Problem

One evening, a husband and wife are working in their garden. While watering the grass, the wife holds the hose horizontally and the water flows from the end of the hose. She twists the nozzle of the hose to partially close it and suddenly the water shoots farther from the end of the hose. This seems odd to her husband, who wonders, "Why does the stream of water travel farther, since it appears that less water is flowing from the end of the hose?"

Your challenge is to give a scientific explanation for this seemingly unnatural phenomenon.

I. Understand the Problem

(a) Reread the problem statement, to be sure you understand what problem you are asked to solve. You may want to draw a picture to help you visualize the problem.

II. Devise a Plan

(b) Discuss possible problem solving strategies for solving this problem.

(c) For this Thought Project, which strategy (physical experimentation, information research, or mathematics) would be most likely to generate a successful solution? Why?

(d) Why do you think that the strategies that you eliminated would not be viable problem solving options for this situation?

III. Carry Out the Plan

Although various problem solving strategies might be used, the most efficient approach is to use mathematics, specifically a principle called the *Continuity Equation.* This equation is written as:

$$A_1 v_1 = A_2 v_2$$

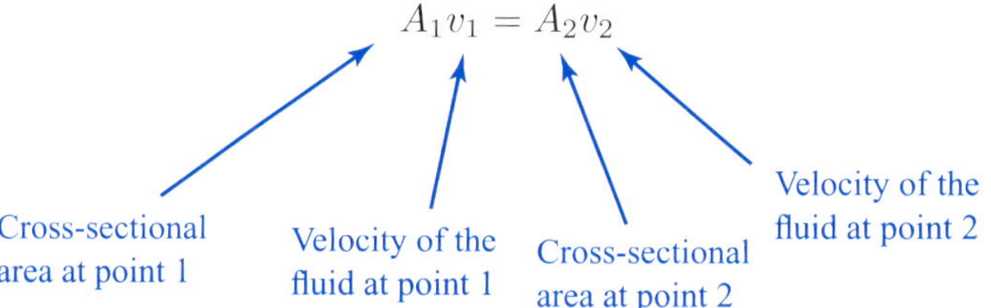

The *cross-sectional* area of a figure is the two-dimensional surface area of the shape that is generated by slicing through the figure. In this problem, the cross-sectional areas are areas of circles.

It may be helpful to view an illustration, as in Figure 8.1.

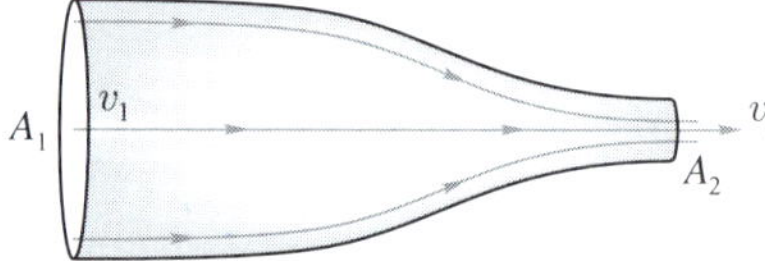

Figure 8.1

(e) Does the introduction of the Continuity Equation modify your interpretation of the original problem, or your strategy for solving it? If so, how?

(f) Choose some real numbers and show how this equation provides an answer to the husband's apparent problem. What does this equation suggest about the relationship between velocity and area?

(g) Write out a detailed explanation of your solution to this Thought Project.

(h) Suggest some other situations in which the Continuity Equation would come into play.

Skill Level II ♦♦

Problem

Use the Continuity Equation to explain how jet engines provide a forward thrust for an airplane.

Record your answer in the space provided.

Skill Level III ♦♦♦

Problem

The Continuity Equation is related to a powerful equation from fluid dynamics called Bernoulli's Equation. Do the research and answer the questions listed below.

(i) Do the research necessary to find Bernoulli's Equation.

(j) Identify what each term in Bernoulli's Equation represents.

(k) Reread the problem statement given in Skill Level I of this Thought Project. What assumption is built into the wording of the problem that becomes unnecessary if you use Bernoulli's Equation?

(l) Discuss how the Continuity Equation and Bernoulli's Equation might relate to one another.

Applied Math Skill Check

Solve the following equations for the variable x.

1. $xy = wt$

2. $ab = cx$

3. $axc = by$

4. $8xp = tyz$

5. $3.7xy = 7.4fp$

Michael's Budget

An ITT student's examination of his monthly expense budget provides a practical setting to review several basic arithmetic skills.

Objectives

1. Perform basic addition, subtraction, and multiplication
2. Calculate a percentage
3. Carry out independent research

Tools Book CD: 2.7A, B

Skill Level I 

Problem

Upon completion of his degree, Michael is hired as a technician at the rate of $900 every two weeks (after taxes). His monthly bills, payable on the first of the month, are:

Rent	$500
Electricity	80
Gas (heat)	65
Car payment	300
Car insurance	70
Fuel for car	80
Groceries	150
Credit cards	200

Given Michael's current expenses, how much money is available weekly for leisure spending?

I. Understand the Problem

(a) Do you have all of the information you need to solve this problem? If not, what additional information do you need or what assumptions must you make?

II. Devise a Plan

(b) What steps must you take to solve this problem?

(c) Is mathematics an appropriate strategy to use in solving this problem? Explain.

(d) Do you need to find an equation to solve this problem? Explain your reasoning.

III. Carry Out the Plan

(e) Solve the problem. How much money will Michael have left each week after paying his bills?

(f) Suppose that Michael's electric and home gas bills were due on the fifteenth of the month instead of the first. How does this new information affect the problem?

(g) What effect, if any, does the different payment date have on your answer?

IV. Look Back

Evaluate the strategy that you used to solve this problem. If confronted with a similar problem, would you take any different steps in finding the solution? Explain.

Skill Level II 

Problem

Instead of spending his additional earnings each month, Michael chooses to open a savings account offering 3% interest, accrued monthly. Calculate the amount of money Michael will have in his savings account at the end of each of the following periods.

(a) three months
(b) six months
(c) one year

Show your work.

Skill Level III

Problem

Many people choose to invest some of their surplus income in *municipal bonds*. Carry out the necessary research and give your opinion of the value of investing in municipal bonds versus earning 3% interest every month in a savings account, as Michael is doing.

Record your answer in the space provided.

Applied Math Skill Check

1. Perform the following additions. (Do not use a calculator.)

(a)
$$\begin{array}{r} 6 \\ 8 \\ +9 \\ \hline \end{array}$$

(b)
$$\begin{array}{r} 143 \\ +258 \\ \hline \end{array}$$

(c)
$$\begin{array}{r} 12 \\ 247 \\ +\quad 8 \\ \hline \end{array}$$

2. Perform the following subtractions. (Do not use a calculator.)

(a)
$$\begin{array}{r} 52 \\ -16 \\ \hline \end{array}$$

(b)
$$\begin{array}{r} 800 \\ -457 \\ \hline \end{array}$$

(c)
$$\begin{array}{r} 1024 \\ -695 \\ \hline \end{array}$$

3. With the aid of your calculator, calculate the following percentages.

(a) 20% of 30 (b) 42% of 57 (c) 35% of 89

Computer Repair Calls

Whether applied to time, money, grades, or any of a number of practical problems, the concept of percentage is one of the most important mathematical concepts we will encounter in daily life. In this Thought Project, we see how understanding percentages helps a manager assess employee performance to resolve a promotion decision.

Objectives

1. Calculate a simple percentage
2. Use information in the form of a percentage to make a decision
3. Solve an equation containing a percentage

Tools Book CD: 2.7A, B

Skill Level I ♦

The personnel manager for a large computer company is planning to promote one of two outside computer repair technicians. Unfortunately, she has limited data on which to base the decision. The only quantitative information that is available for the last year is summarized in the following tables.

Technician 1	Jan	Feb	Mar	Apr	May	Jun	Jul	Aug	Sep	Oct	Nov	Dec
Number of calls	42	65	57	39	41	55	62	38	45	52	47	61
Successful repairs	29	43	38	22	28	48	50	27	30	39	31	40

Technician 2	Jan	Feb	Mar	Apr	May	Jun	Jul	Aug	Sep	Oct	Nov	Dec
Number of calls	30	25	28	32	22	21	31	29	35	33	26	32
Successful repairs	18	19	22	20	15	12	19	20	30	17	20	18

Problem

Devise and execute a strategy that will allow the personnel manager to compare these two candidates in an objective manner.

I. Devise a Plan

(a) Using the data in the tables, identify some possible ways to compare these two candidates.

II. Carry Out the Plan

(b) Execute your strategy and discuss your findings.

III. Look Back

(c) In your opinion, how valid are the summary results you derived from the data? Is there a way to increase the validity of your findings? If so, how?

(d) If you were the personnel manager, what other information would you like to have before making the promotion decision between these two candidates?

(e) For the information that you listed in step (d), detail a plan how you might acquire this information.

Skill level II

Problem

To help make the promotion decision, the personnel manager decides to use the data she has found to project the likely number of successful repairs that each candidate might make if sent on an identical number of calls in a month. Based on the average yearly percentage of successful repair calls for each candidate, how many successful repairs would each candidate make on 50 calls?

Show your work.

(f) Discuss the validity of this type of projection.

Skill level III 

Problem

If technician 1 made five fewer calls in the month of March and five more calls in the month of April, what effect, if any, would there be on his yearly completion percentage? Show a calculation that supports your argument.

Record your answer in the space provided.

Applied Math Skill Check

1. What is 20% of 15?
2. Which is larger, 25% of 90 or 27% of 85?
3. What percentage of 70 is 5?
4. What number is 20% of 500?
5. 57.8 is 17% of what number?
6. Find 33% of the following sum.

$$\begin{array}{r} 231 \\ 643 \\ +357 \\ \hline \end{array}$$

Ratios and Proportions

In this Thought Project, we use a computer science class as a setting to review the concepts of ratios and proportions.

Objectives

1. Set up a basic ratio/proportion equation
2. Solve for an unknown quantity in a ratio/proportion statement

Tools Book CD: 2.7C, D

Skill Level I 

Problem

The instructor of an introductory computer course wants to make a wall chart of a computer desktop for her students. To make it as realistic as possible, she would like the desktop icons to be proportional to the size of her $6' \times 6'$ chart. If the icons on her $15'' \times 15''$ PC screen are $3/8'' \times 3/8''$, how large should they be on her wall chart?

I. Understand the Problem

(a) Explain, in your own words, what the terms “desktop” and “icon” mean.

II. Devise a Plan

(b) What are some of the strategies that you might use to solve this problem?

(c) Discuss any particular skills or materials that would be required to execute the strategies that you listed in step (b).

III. Carry Out the Plan

(d) Execute your strategy and find the dimensions of the desktop icon on the wall chart.

IV. Look Back

(e) Having used mathematics to solve the problem, is there an alternative problem solving strategy that you would suggest? Explain.

(f) Identify situations in which one problem solving strategy would be more advantageous than another.

Skill Level II 

Problem

In her morning class, the computer teacher has 20 students, 8 of whom are women and 12 of whom are men. If her afternoon class has 30 students, how many of them must be women so that both classes have the same ratio of women to men?

Show your work.

Skill Level III ♦♦♦

Problem

The instructor has learned that for the 30 students in her afternoon class, the ratio of students who do not own a computer to those who do is 2 to 1. How many students in the class own their own computer?

Show your work.

Applied Math Skill Check

1. Express the proportionality statement

   $$\frac{1}{2} = \frac{5}{10}$$

   in a different way.

2. Express the proportionality statement

   $2 : 5 = 4 : 10$

   as a fraction.

3. Solve for x in the following proportion.

   $$\frac{3}{5} = \frac{x}{25}$$

4. Solve for x in the following proportion.

   $4 : 10 = x : 40$

5. In the following proportion, if y is larger than 8, what statement can be made about the size of x?

   $$\frac{y}{4} = \frac{x}{3}$$

Temperature Scales

"It's seventy-five degrees outside and a beautiful day." In the United States, we use the Fahrenheit scale to measure temperature. However, most of the world uses the Celsius scale. A comparison of the various possible temperature scales used in both daily life and the technological community provides a setting for finding the slope of a line on a graph.

Objectives

1. Given the coordinates of two points on a line, find the slope of the line
2. Use the point-slope form of a line to construct an equation of a line
3. Given the equation of a line, expressed in terms of the independent variable, manipulate the equation to solve for the independent variable

Tools Book CD: 3.2; 3.3; 3.4A, B, C; 7.2A, B

Skill Level I ♦

Although residents of the United States are familiar with the Fahrenheit scale, the Celsius scale is actually much easier to use, because it is an evenly divided metric scale that establishes the freezing point of water at 0° and the boiling point at 100°. In contrast, the span of temperatures between the freezing and boiling point of water on the Fahrenheit scale is from 32° to 212°.

Problem

You are an American exchange student planning to study in Florence, Italy, during the winter term. In preparation for your trip, you consult the Italian school's Web site to find out what the temperature is likely to be. However, the daily weather is given in the Celsius scale. Use the table to find a way to convert temperatures from the Celsius to the Fahrenheit scale.

Water	Fahrenheit Scale	Celsius Scale
Freezes	32°	0°
Boils	212°	100°

I. Understand the Problem

Read the problem carefully. It may be helpful to underline the key pieces of information that you need to solve the problem. Be sure that you understand exactly what problem you are asked to solve.

II. Devise a Plan

(a) What are some of the strategies you might use to find a solution to this problem?

(b) Graph the information by drawing coordinate axes with degrees Fahrenheit, T_F, along the y-axis and degrees Celsius, T_C, on the x-axis. Plot the information on freezing and boiling temperatures as points on the graph.

(c) Devise a plan for how to use your graph to determine a relationship between T_F and T_C that can be used to convert Celsius into Fahrenheit measurements. Explain your strategy.

III. Carry Out the Plan

(d) Execute your strategy and find a relationship between these two temperature scales.

(e) Explain what the straight line on the graph tells us about the relationship between the two temperature scales.

(f) In pure mathematics, when we draw a straight line through two points, we put an arrow on each end of the line to indicate that it continues infinitely in both directions. Would it be accurate to add arrowheads to the ends of the lines in your graph? Explain.

(g) Is there a way to find the coordinates of the point on your graph that would be halfway between the freezing point and the boiling point of water? If so, how?

IV. Look Back

(h) After implementing your strategy, would you do anything differently if you were confronted with the same problem again? Explain.

Skill Level II ♦♦

Problem

Find a relationship that will allow you to go from a Fahrenheit measurement to a Celsius measurement in two ways:

1. By graphing the data in the chart drawn in Skill Level I.
2. By taking the relationship that you found in Skill Level I and algebraically manipulating it so that T_C is isolated.

Show your work.

(i) Discuss any advantages or disadvantages that you believe one of these strategies has over the other.

Skill Level III

Another scale that is widely used by the scientific community is known as the Kelvin scale. This scale is based on absolute zero and thereafter is incremented in the same way as the Celsius scale. The temperature on the Kelvin scale can be found from the temperature in degrees Celsius by the formula

$$T_K = T_C + 273.15$$

FYI

Unlike the other measurement scales, temperatures on the Kelvin scale are recorded using K, *not* °K.

Problem

If the temperature graph of a certain experiment formed a straight line when recorded on the Celsius scale, discuss what a graph of the same experiment on the Kelvin scale would look like.

Record your answer in the space provided

Applied Math Skill Check

1. Find the slopes of the lines that pass through the following pairs of points.

   (a) (1,2) (3,5)

   (b) (0,0) (4,6)

   (c) (−1,2) (4,5)

   (d) (−2,−5) (−3,−9)

2. Given the slope of the line and a point on the line, find an equation for each line.

   (a) A line of slope 4 passing through the point (0,2)

   (b) A line of slope −5 passing through the point (3,4)

   (c) A line of slope 0 passing through the point (1,2)

3. Sketch an example of each of the following.

   (a) A line with a positive slope

   (b) A line with a negative slope

   (c) A line with a slope of 0

   (d) A line with an undefined slope

4. If a line has a slope of 0, what can you say about the vertical coordinates of each of the points on the line?

5. If a line has an undefined slope, what can you say about the horizontal coordinates of each of the points on the line?

Sports and Statistics

Baseball is said to be the "great American pastime." For many baseball fans, one of the most entertaining aspects of the game is keeping track of the many different statistics that are generated. In this project we will use statistics from baseball and other sports, to illustrate how different types of graphs can be used most effectively to summarize different kinds of information.

Objectives

1. Read statistical data and summarize it using a graph
2. Carry out independent research
3. Determine which type of graphing technique is most useful to summarize a given set of data

Tools Book CD: 1.8, 3.1

Skill Level I 

Mark McGwire
In 1998, St. Louis Cardinals' first baseman, Mark McGwire's 70 home runs broke Roger Maris's longstanding record for the most home runs in a single season. McGwire's accomplishment was short lived, as Barry Bonds hit 73 home runs in 2001.

Courtesy of Getty Images

During the 1998 baseball season, the daily sports news was dominated by the home run race that unfolded between Mark McGwire of the St. Louis Cardinals and Sammy Sosa of the Chicago Cubs. The data generated in this home run derby gives us an opportunity to analyze a number of variables, and to contrast the recent statistics with history. For example, how do we compare the performance of Mark McGwire, who grabbed the record for the most home runs in a season in 1998, with performances by Hank Aaron or Babe Ruth? Is it possible to compare the careers of these three athletes in an objective manner that yields useful information?

Problem

Acquire the necessary data, and compile it in an effective format, to compare the batting careers of Babe Ruth, Hank Aaron, and Mark McGwire.

I. Understand the Problem

(a) In your opinion, what are the difficulties involved in making such a comparison?

(b) What data do you need to compare the performances of these athletes in an objective manner?

> **MATH REVIEW**
>
> A *graph* is a table or picture in which mathematical information has been summarized.

When there is a wealth of information, it is helpful to compile the data in a manner that summarizes the information and allows you to look for patterns in the data. These summaries frequently take the form of *graphs*.

II. Devise a Plan

(c) Identify some resources for acquiring the data that you need.

(d) What type of graph do you think would be most effective at showing patterns in your data?

III. Carry Out the Plan

(e) With the help of your instructor, construct a graph to summarize your data.

(f) Now that you have graphed your data, do you think you need to do any additional research to make an objective comparison of Mark McGwire's, Hank Aaron's, and Babe Ruth's batting careers? If so, what is it?

(g) Does your graph show any patterns and/or trends? If so, discuss these patterns.

(h) If you answered yes to step (g), what inferences can you make based on the patterns you observed?

IV. Look Back

(i) What method, if any, do you believe would be more effective than using a graph to summarize this type of data?

(j) What types of problems might be most receptive to graphing as a problem solving technique?

Skill Level II 

Problem

Whereas batters are often judged by the number of home runs they hit, pitchers are judged by statistics such as the number of games they win, their earned run average (ERA), and the number of no-hitters they throw.

1. Execute the necessary research to identify the winning pitcher in the final game of three World Series of your choice.
2. For each of the three pitchers, find the number of games they won during the entire season, their ERA, and the number of no-hitters (if any) they threw during the baseball season in which they won the World Series.
3. Construct one graph that summarizes the data for all three pitchers.

Draw your graph in the space provided.

Skill Level III 

Problem

One of the most difficult challenges faced by sports analysts is identifying the best athlete in a given year or era, because it requires them to compare the careers of athletes from different sports. For example, it is not a trivial exercise to compare baseball's Barry Bonds to basketball great Michael Jordan, or to tennis player Pete Sampras.

1. Choose three athletes representing *three different* sports.
2. For your chosen athletes, decide on a set of statistics that you think could be used to evaluate the careers of all three athletes.
3. Construct a graph that summarizes your statistics.

Draw your graph in the space provided.

Applied Math Skill Check

1. Use the graph to identify the percentage of employees of Alpha Corporation who are women.

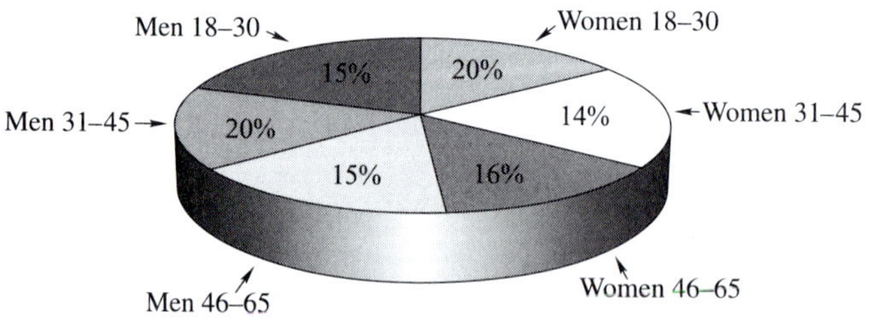

Employees of Alpha Corporation

2. Read the graph to determine the gross sales of Advanced Technological Ideas in March.

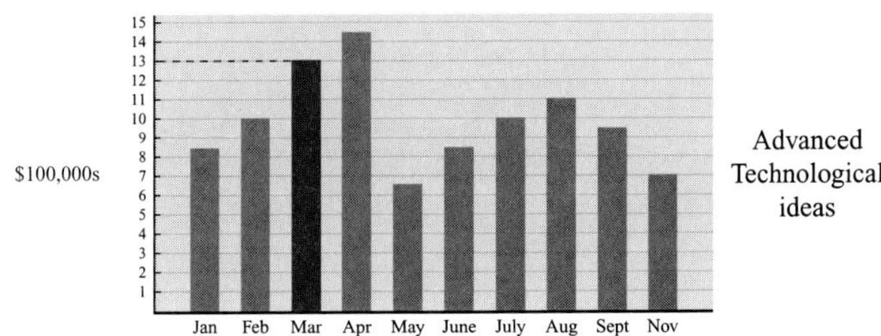

3. The following three graphs summarize the number of hits that a baseball player had in June, July, and August. What do these graphs tell you about the batter's hitting record, and where he might end up for the season if the season is over at the end of September?

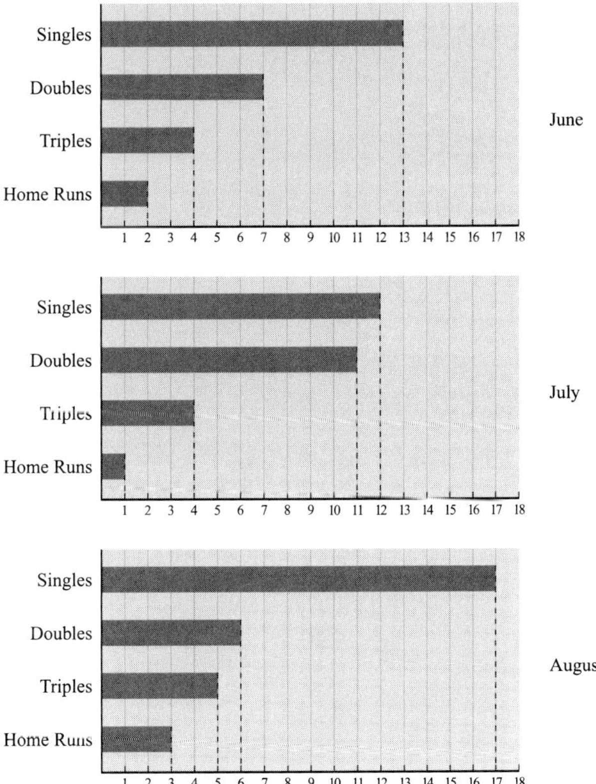

Interlude: Bases and Exponents

In the fields of science and technology, we encounter the mathematical shorthand of bases and exponents in almost every problem we confront. In this Interlude, we introduce the concepts of bases and exponents, and give examples from a variety of scientific and technological situations in which these mathematical expressions appear.

Objectives

1. Identify the base and exponent in an expression
2. Write out the multiplication indicated by the exponent attached to a variable in an equation

Tools Book CD: 4.1A

Bases and Exponents

Bases and exponents are a shorthand method for expressing repeated multiplication. For example, if we multiply together 3 copies of 2, the result is 8:

$$\underbrace{2 \cdot 2 \cdot 2}_{\text{3 copies}} = 8$$

To avoid writing long strings of numbers, we use bases and exponents to express the repeated multiplication. We call the number that is being multiplied repeatedly the *base*. The name *exponent* is given to the number that indicates how many times the base is being multiplied.

Expressed in the language of bases and exponents, our repeated multiplication becomes:

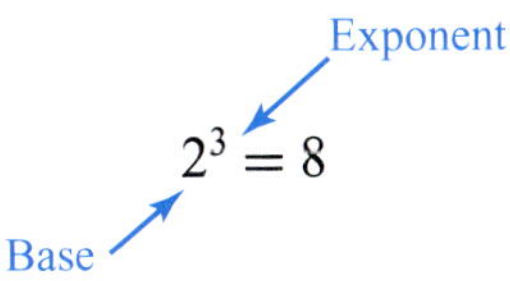

The way we write bases and exponents is to place the exponent at the upper right corner of the base. When stating this equation aloud, we say "two to the third power is equal to eight."

Although it is unnecessary, we can attach an exponent to a number even when there is no repeated multiplication implied. For example, when we write a number such as 5, in actuality we are writing a statement involving bases and exponents. There is an assumed exponent of 1 on the number:

$$5^1 = 5$$

In other words, we have one copy of the number.

Example 1

For each of the following expressions, identify the base and exponent, write out the repeated multiplication indicated by the expression, and give a numerical value for the repeated multiplication indicated by the expression.

(a) 3^2

(b) 4^3

(c) $(0.2)^4$

(d) $\left(\frac{1}{2}\right)^5$

Solution

(a) base $= 3$, exponent $= 2$

$3^2 = 3 \cdot 3 = 9$

(b) base $= 4$, exponent $= 3$

$4^3 = 4 \cdot 4 \cdot 4 = 64$

(c) base $= 0.2$, exponent $= 4$

$(0.2)^4 = (0.2)\,(0.2)\,(0.2)\,(0.2) = 0.0016$

(d) base $= \frac{1}{2}$, exponent $= 5$

$\left(\frac{1}{2}\right)^5 = \left(\frac{1}{2}\right)\left(\frac{1}{2}\right)\left(\frac{1}{2}\right)\left(\frac{1}{2}\right)\left(\frac{1}{2}\right) = \frac{1}{32}$

Variables as Bases

The previous examples used a known number as the base of each expression. We can also use an unknown number, or *variable,* as a base. For example, the expression x^3 indicates that we are to multiply three copies of the variable x:

$$x^3 = \underbrace{x \cdot x \cdot x}_{\text{3 copies}}$$

whereas y^5 indicates that we are to multiply five copies of the variable y:

$$y^5 = \underbrace{y \cdot y \cdot y \cdot y \cdot y}_{\text{5 copies}}$$

Example 2

Write out the repeated multiplication indicated by each of the following expressions.

(a) x^4

(b) t^3

(c) j^8

Solution

(a) $x^4 = x \cdot x \cdot x \cdot x$

(b) $t^3 = t \cdot t \cdot t$

(c) $j^8 = j \cdot j \cdot j \cdot j \cdot j \cdot j \cdot j \cdot j$

Expressions Containing Several Terms

While studying technology, we are often confronted with equations that contain more than one variable, such as

$$P = I^2 R \tag{1}$$

or

$$V = \frac{4}{3}\pi r^3 \tag{2}$$

Consequently, we must have a firm grasp of exactly what repeated multiplications are indicated in multivariable expressions. For example, in Equation (1) we are instructed to multiply two copies of the variable I by the variable R:

$$P = I^2 R = I \cdot I \cdot R$$

MATH REVIEW

Remember that in a formula such as Equation (1), the correct order of operations is to square the variable I first and then to multiply by the variable R.

and in Equation (2) we are instructed to multiply the fraction $\frac{4}{3}$, π, and three copies of the variable r:

$$V = \frac{4}{3}\pi r^3 = \frac{4}{3} \cdot \pi \cdot r \cdot r \cdot r$$

Example 3

Write out the repeated multiplications indicated by each of the following expressions.

(a) x^2y^3

(b) F^4z^5

(c) $\frac{1}{2}Li^2$

(d) $(xy)^4$

Solution

(a) $x^2y^3 = x \cdot x \cdot y \cdot y \cdot y$

(b) $F^4z^5 = F \cdot F \cdot F \cdot F \cdot z \cdot z \cdot z \cdot z \cdot z$

(c) $\frac{1}{2}Li^2 = \frac{1}{2} \cdot L \cdot i \cdot i$

(d) $(xy)^4 = (xy)(xy)(xy)(xy)$

The following exercises contain examples of equations drawn from many different areas of science and technology. These equations illustrate the importance of understanding how to work with bases and exponents.

Applied Math Skill Check

For each of the following equations, identify the exponent attached to each variable, and write out the multiplication(s) indicated by the equation.

Example:

Electronics—The equation used to find the power dissipated by a resistor:

$$P = I^2R$$

Variable	Exponent
P	1
I	2
R	1

Multiplications: $P = I \cdot I \cdot R$

1. Structural analysis—The equation used to find the cross-sectional area of a cylindrical column (area of a circle):

$$A = \pi r^2$$

Variable	Exponent
A	
π	
r	

Multiplications: ________________

2. Physics—The equation used to find the amount of centripetal force on a mass moving in a circle:

$$F = \frac{mv^2}{r}$$

Variable	Exponent
F	
m	
v	
r	

Multiplications: ______________________

3. Electronics—The equation used to find the amount of potential energy stored in a charged capacitor:

$$PE = \frac{q^2}{2C}$$

Variable	Exponent
PE	
q	
C	

Multiplications: ______________________

4. Astronomy—The equation used to find the amount of time required for a planet to execute its orbit:

$$T^2 = \frac{4\pi^2 r^3}{GM}$$

Variable	Exponent
T	
π	
r	
G	
M	

Multiplications: ______________________

The Behavior of Astronomical Masses

Some philosophers and scientists claim that the same technology that appears to be advancing our culture is actually reducing our creativity. They think that our growing dependence on technology is causing us to lose some of our abstract problem solving abilities. In this Thought Project, you will have the opportunity to demonstrate your abilities to solve abstract problems, involving various astronomical objects, using a number of the algebraic and mathematical skills covered previously in this text.

Objectives

1. Rewrite equations that contain scientific notation, bases, and exponents
2. Isolate and solve for a given variable in an equation and explain the process verbally
3. Execute independent research and critically interpret the information

Tools Book CD: 4.2C, D; 2.6; 4.1A

Skill Level I 

Use your imagination to transport yourself back to an earlier era, when scientists and astronomers used only simple instruments—but great minds—to tackle some of the big ideas of their day. Consider, for example, the work of Johannes Kepler and Isaac Newton in the seventeenth and eighteenth centuries. These gentlemen performed calculations and experiments that first showed the mass of the earth.

The mass of an object, simply put, is a measurement of the amount of "stuff" in the object. The larger the mass of the object, the more stuff it contains. Both Kepler and Newton played major roles in finding that the mass of the earth is

$$5{,}980{,}000{,}000{,}000{,}000{,}000{,}000{,}000 \text{ kg}$$

Working with this very large number is difficult. Fortunately, we can express large numbers in a much simpler way using *scientiÞc notation*. This technique uses the fact that every place in a number corresponds to a different factor of 10. For example, in the number 524, the 2 is in the tens place (10^1) and the 5 is in the hundreds place (10^2). To express the mass of the earth in scientific notation, we move the decimal point (currently on the far right-hand side of our number) to the left. For every space that we move it, we acquire another factor of 10. It is conventional to stop when we are left with a single digit to the left of the decimal point.

Since we need to move the decimal places 24 spaces to the left, the number can be expressed as:

$$5.98 \times 10^{24} \text{ kg}$$

Problem

You and your team know the answer to the question, "What is the mass of the earth?" Your challenge in this Thought Project is to devise a strategy for finding the mass of the earth using only the equations and equipment that were available to scientists in the late seventeenth and early eighteenth centuries.

I. Understand the Problem

(a) Think about the requirement to solve this problem using only seventeenth- and eighteenth-century tools and methodologies. List and discuss some of the constraints that imposes.

(b) What information is necessary for you to solve this problem, given these constraints?

II. Devise a Plan

(c) List some possible strategies for finding the mass of the earth.

(d) Does your team favor a physical experiment or mathematics to address this problem? Explain.

(e) If you favor an experiment, discuss the equipment involved and the data you will attempt to collect. If, however, you think mathematics is the more efficient approach, what is your starting point?

If you research the work of Newton and Kepler, you will find two key equations to help in solving the problem. Newton's *Law of Universal Gravitation* is used to measure the gravitational force between two masses. This equation states:

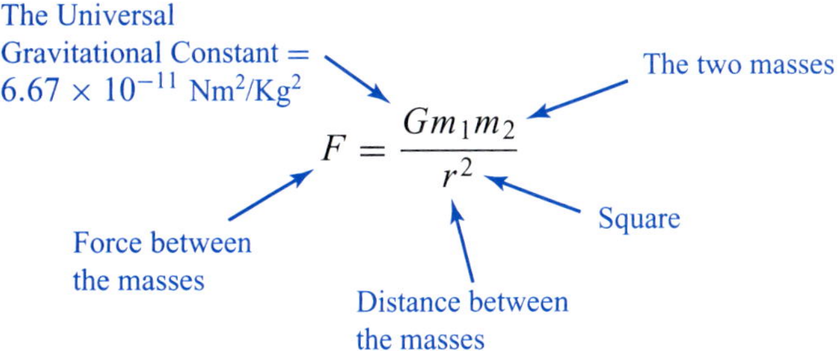

A picture of Newton's Law may be clearer, such as that in Figure 15.1.

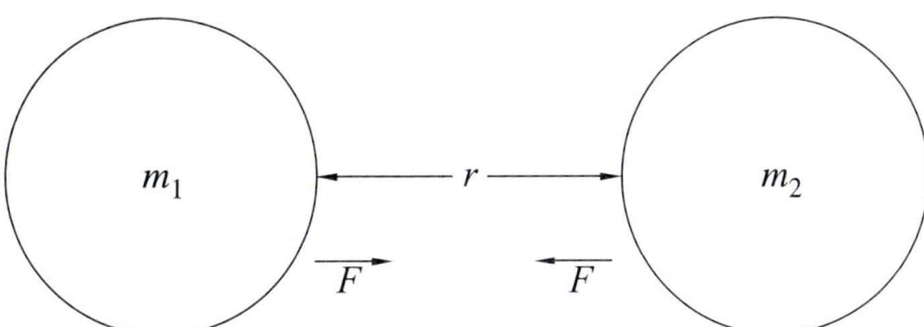

Figure 15.1

Kepler's *Law of Periods* relates how long it takes a satellite (such as a moon or a planet) to orbit a central mass to the distance between the satellite and the central mass:

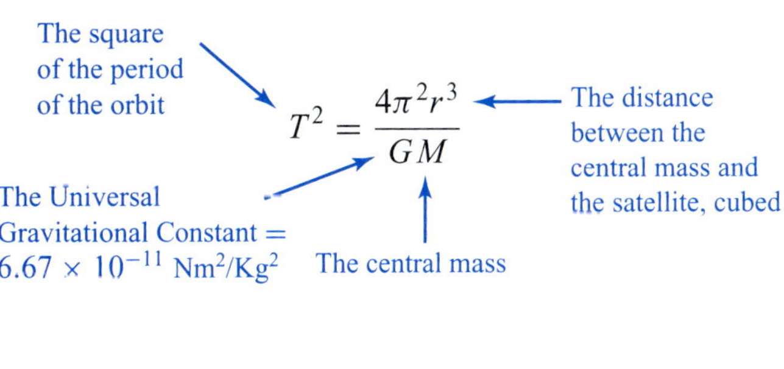

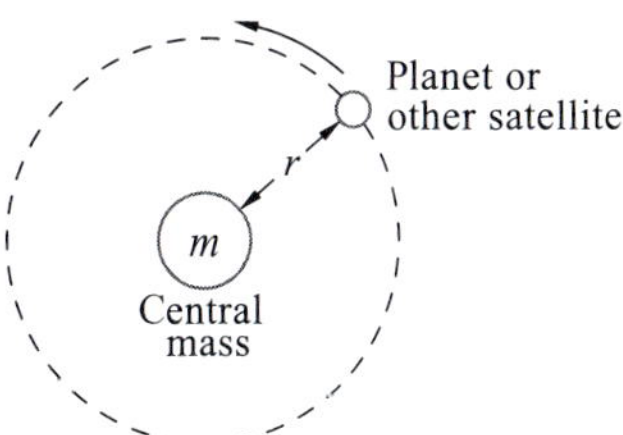

Figure 15.2

(f) Does the knowledge of these formulas suggest that you should change your original problem solving strategy? Why or why not?

III. Carry Out the Plan

(g) Execute your strategy and calculate the mass of the earth.

(h) Did your value differ from the known value? What might be some reasons for this difference?

IV. Look Back

(i) Discuss how the problem solving strategy you employed would have been different with the resources of the twenty-first century at your disposal.

(j) Does the three-hundred-year difference in time impact the two strategies of physical experiment and mathematics equally? Explain.

Skill Level II 

Problem

Given that

- the distance from the earth to the sun is 1.5×10^{11} m, and
- the mass of the sun is 1.9×10^{30} kg,

1. use Kepler's Law of Periods to find the period of the earth's orbit, recorded in seconds;
2. show how to express your answer in years; and
3. if your answer does not agree with the accepted earth orbital period of 365.25 days, explain the discrepancy.

Show your work.

Skill level III ♦♦♦

According to Newton's Law of Gravitation, all objects with mass attract one another. This law implies that all of the atoms that make up a star, such as our sun, are gravitationally attracted to one another. If so, how is it that the sun is able to resist all of this internal attraction between its atoms and not collapse in upon itself?

Problem

Devise and execute a problem solving strategy that will yield a reasonable *physical* explanation for how a star is able to resist collapsing under its own gravitational attraction.

Record your answer in the space provided.

Applied Math Skill Check

1. Express the following numbers using scientific notation.

   (a) 35000000000

   (b) 0.00000000016

2. Solve for T in each of the following equations.

   (a) $T = xh^2$ $\quad x = 2, h = 5$

   (b) $T = \dfrac{v^2 p^3}{c}$ $\quad v = 3, p = 2, c = 4$

   (c) $T = \dfrac{6.23 \times 10^8}{yz}$ $\quad y = 3.8 \times 10^4, z = 2.57 \times 10^3$

   (d) $BT^2 = \dfrac{F^3}{Z}$ $\quad B = 2, F = 3, Z = 4$

3. If you were given the values for y and z, write out, in words, the steps that you would go through to find the value for the variable x in each of the following equations.

   (a) $x = yz$

   (b) $x = y^2 z$

   (c) $x = yz^2$

   (d) $x = y^2 z + y$

   (e) $x = \sqrt{y^2 - 4yz}$

   (f) $x^2 = y(3y - 2z)$

Interlude: Unit Analysis

In this Interlude, we discuss the importance of the units used to describe the measurements and calculations made in real world problems.

Objectives

1. Explain the relationship between the units on the terms in an equation and the units in the solution
2. Find the units on any quantity in an equation given the units on the other terms

Tools Book CD: A.4, A.5

As we have found in the preceding projects, problem solving is often a difficult process. The intuition and practical experience that is helpful in solving non-technical problems is often of no help in working on technical ones. After acquiring experience in the field, technical intuition can be developed, but it takes time and practice to become proficient. As beginning technical problem solvers, we need to acquire as many tools as possible to help us in this endeavor.

One such tool that can give guidance in solving technical problems is *unit analysis*. Analyzing the units in which quantities are expressed gives us access to a wealth of information about the proper setup and correct mathematical execution of the problem.

For example, in Thought Project 7, we worked with the equation $d = rt$. Because the distance is equal to the rate multiplied by the time, the *units* of distance must be the units of rate multiplied by the units of time. If we express the units of rate in meters per second, and the time in seconds, we can find the distance unit by multiplying the other units together:

$$d = rt$$

$$[d] = \frac{\text{meters}}{\text{sec}} \cdot \text{sec}$$

$$[d] = \text{meters}$$

Another example draws on Thought Project 6, in which we learned the equation $Q = mL_f$. Although we were given the units for the latent heat of fusion in the project, we could have found the units ourselves using unit analysis.

If we take the equation and isolate L_f we have

$$Q = mL_f$$

$$\frac{Q}{m} = L_f$$

Multiply both sides by $1/m$

This means that the units of latent heat must be the units of heat (calories) divided by the units of mass (grams):

$$\frac{Q}{m} = L_f$$

$$\frac{[\text{cal}]}{[\text{g}]} = [L_f]$$

By using unit analysis, we reproduced the units of cal/g that were provided to us in the Thought Project.

Although the two preceding examples were straightforward, they do not illustrate the full power of this tool. Its real advantage comes in more complex applications such as geometry, and other, more complicated equations. As an example, let's see how unit analysis can predict the dimensionality of a figure.

By analyzing the units on an expression, we can tell immediately whether the figure is one-, two-, or three-dimensional. Let's calculate some of these, and look at the units that are created.

Using Unit Analysis to Predict Dimension

Volume of an Object

The *volume* of an object is the amount of three-dimensional space that the object occupies. Different geometric forms require different equations for finding their volume. Let's look at two different figures, calculate their volumes, and compare the results.

Example 1—The Volume of a Cube

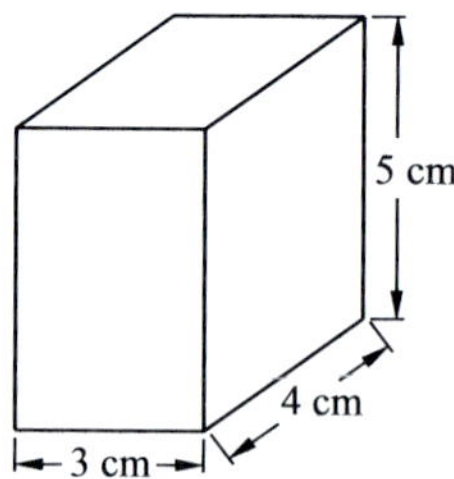

Figure 16.1

We can find the volume of a cubic figure by multiplying its length, height, and width:

$$V = lhw$$

Placing all three variables, *lhw*, adjacent on the right-hand side implies that they are to be multiplied

Because we multiply, the units of volume must be the units of all three sides multiplied together (see Figure 16.1). The key to this calculation is that numbers stay with numbers and units stay with units:

$$V = (3\text{ cm})(4\text{ cm})(5\text{ cm})$$
$$V = (3)(4)(5)\text{ cm}\cdot\text{cm}\cdot\text{cm}$$
$$V = 60\text{ cm}^3$$

Notice that in the final answer, we have replaced cm · cm · cm with its simpler form of cm^3.

Example 2—The Volume of a Sphere

To find the volume of a sphere, we use the equation

$$V = \frac{4}{3}\pi r^3$$

where r is the radius of the sphere. If we apply this equation to the sphere in Figure 16.2,

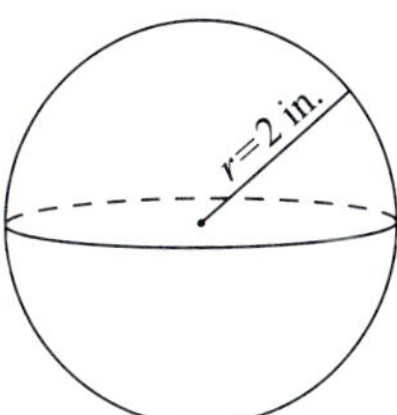

Figure 16.2

we get

$$V = \frac{4}{3}\pi r^3$$
$$V = \frac{4}{3}\pi(2\text{ in.})^3$$

Note that the exponent of 3 on our measurement tells us that we are supposed to multiply 3 identical copies of the radius.

$$V = \frac{4}{3}\pi(2\text{ in.})^3$$
$$V = \frac{4}{3}\pi(2\text{ in.})(2\text{ in.})(2\text{ in.})$$

Once again grouping numbers with numbers and units with units, we have

$$V = \frac{4}{3}\pi(2\text{ in.})(2\text{ in.})(2\text{ in.})$$

$$V = \frac{4}{3}\pi(2)(2)(2)\text{in.} \cdot \text{in.} \cdot \text{in.}$$

$$V = \frac{32\pi}{3}\text{in.}^3$$

If we compare Example 1 and Example 2, we see that the units in both cases are a length unit raised to the third power. This is true of all three-dimensional figures. If the figure is three-dimensional, the units on its volume must be three length units multiplied together.

Area of a Figure

The area of a figure is the amount of two-dimensional space that the figure occupies. Using a similar technique to that used for volumes, let's find the areas of two geometric figures and compare them.

Example 3—The Area of a Rectangle

The area of a rectangle is found by multiplying its length by its width,

$$A = lw$$

If we use this equation to find the area of the rectangle in Figure 16.3,

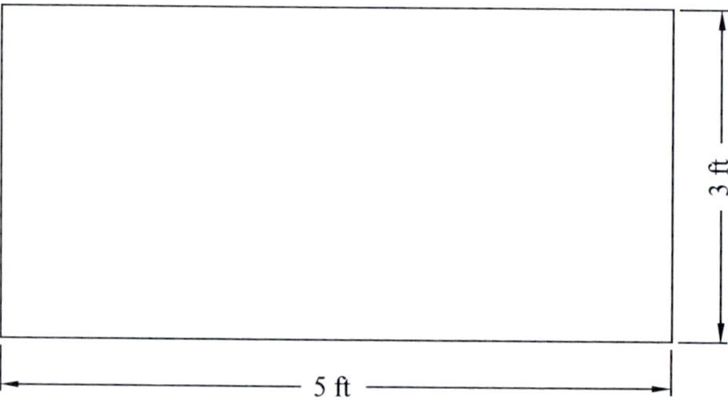

Figure 16.3

we have

$$A = lw$$

$$A = (5\text{ ft})(3\text{ ft})$$

$$A = (5)(3)\text{ ft} \cdot \text{ft}$$

$$A = 15\text{ ft}^2$$

Notice that once again we have replaced the units of ft · ft with ft^2 using the rules of bases and exponents.

Example 4—The Area of a Circle

We can find the area occupied by the circle in Figure 16.4

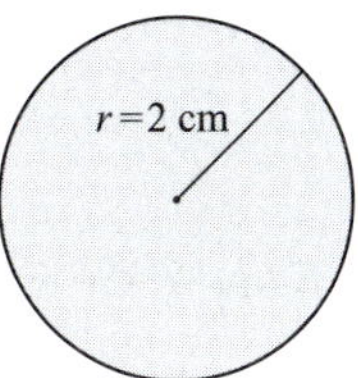

Figure 16.4

by using

$$A = \pi r^2$$

Inserting the value of the radius and being careful to keep track of our units, we see that

$$A = \pi r^2$$
$$A = \pi (2\ \text{cm})^2$$
$$A = \pi (2\ \text{cm})(2\ \text{cm})$$
$$A = \pi (2)(2)\ \text{cm} \cdot \text{cm}$$
$$A = 4\pi\ \text{cm}^2$$

Notice that in Examples 3 and 4, the units on both areas are two length units multiplied together. To calculate the area for any two-dimensional object, we will always multiply two length units.

Realizing that lengths are always measured in units such as inches, centimeters, miles, and so forth, we can now summarize our results.

- The volumes of three-dimensional figures are expressed in length units raised to the third power, such as cm^3, $in.^3$, ft^3, and so on.
- The areas of two-dimensional figures are expressed in length units raised to the second power, such as cm^2, $in.^2$, ft^2, and so on.
- One-dimensional figures are expressed in length units raised to the first power, such as cm, in., ft, and so on.

As a last note in this Interlude, we remember that the technique of unit analysis will also let us move in the other direction. If we were given the dimensions of the area of a circle, for example, we could take a square root and find the units for the radius. Similarly, were we given the units for the volume of the sphere, we could take a cube root and find the radius of the sphere.

Applied Math Skill Check

1. Identify the units on x in each of the following equations.

   (a) $x = yz$ (both y and z are measured in feet)

   (b) $x = 3y^2$ (y is measured in inches)

   (c) $x = t^3$ (t is measured in seconds)

   (d) $x = 4F^2d$ (both F and d are measured in meters)

2. In the following equation, if x is measured in meters and t is measured in seconds, identify the units on the variable v.

   $x = vt$

3. In the following equation, determine the units on t if S is measured in dollars and p is measured in dollars per year.

   $S = pt$

4. In an exponential expression such as $A = be^{-(t/RC)}$, we cannot attach units to the exponent $-(t/RC)$ because a base, such as e, can only be raised to a pure number. Consequently, if the variable t in this equation is measured in seconds, what does this imply about the units on the product RC?

THOUGHT PROJECT 17

Global Warming and the Ozone Layer

The sensitive environmental issues of global warming and the hole in the ozone layer provide an interesting setting for examining the importance of calculating geometric quantities such as surface area and volume.

Objectives

1. Calculate basic geometric quantities
2. Take geometric measurements and apply them to real-world situations
3. Execute independent research and make decisions based on the information acquired

Tools Book CD: A.4, A.5

Skill Level I 

As we experience a new sense of global community, concerns about our environment and its care continue to grow. Because of political and lobbying efforts on the part of many environmental groups, great strides have been taken in the United States and other parts of the world to combat this problem. Unfortunately, many industrialized countries have not made the necessary effort to protect our fragile environment. Too many nations continue to allow pollutants to be released into the world's atmosphere and water supplies at an alarming rate.

Two environmental issues that have received significant attention during the last fifty years are those of global warming and the hole in the ozone layer. As scientists have investigated these two environmental phenomena, some effort has been made to show that these two effects are somehow related. What do you think? An investigation into possible relationships between these two environmental issues is the focus of this Thought Project.

Global Warming

The rate at which global warming is occurring is a controversial subject among scientists. Because scientists have been studying the earth's weather patterns for only the last century or two, it is difficult to make an accurate comparison of recent weather data to the overall weather patterns of a planet that has existed for millions of years. Consequently, it is hard to know whether rising temperatures are a cyclical phenomenon or a trend that could have devastating effects on our planet.

Very simply, global warming may be thought of as excess heat being trapped near the surface of the earth. Think about how hot a car becomes while parked in the sun on a summer day. The inside of the car is hotter than the surrounding air because the glass of the windshield allows the electromagnetic waves from the sun to pass into the car but does not allow the resultant heat to pass back out. In a similar manner, the burning of fossil fuels (coal, oil, gasoline, etc.) produces a layer of gases (commonly referred to as "greenhouse gases") that acts like the windshield of a car. This layer of gas allows the electromagnetic waves from the sun to pass through, but does not allow the heat from the planet to pass back out into space. Many scientists argue that a prolonged buildup of heat could lead to the melting of the polar ice caps, raised oceanic levels, extensive flooding, and disastrous consequences to life on earth.

The Hole in the Ozone Layer

As we breathe, we take in a mixture of gases that includes life-sustaining oxygen. Actually, the oxygen molecule that our body uses is formed of two oxygen atoms, and is noted in chemical shorthand as O_2.

There is, however, another way for oxygen atoms to form into molecules. When three oxygen atoms bond together they form a molecule we call *ozone* (denoted as O_3). It is this type of molecule that makes up the ozone layer that surrounds the planet. This layer plays an important role in life on earth. Ozone provides a protective layer that shields the earth from the harmful ultraviolet rays of the sun. Without this ozone shield, skin cancer levels would increase dramatically and the world's crop production would suffer devastating consequences.

In the last century, it was discovered that there were holes in the earth's vitally important ozone layer at both the north and south poles. Although the sizes of the holes change during various times of the year, many scientists believe that these holes are being caused, at least partially, by fluorocarbons generated from spray cans and other man-made pollutants.

Problem

To obtain funding for environmental research, you and a group of fellow scientists must develop a strategy for demonstrating a relationship between the two atmospheric effects of global warming and holes in the ozone layer.

The following are possible relationships that might exist:

- The two phenomena share the same cause.
- One phenomenon causes the other.
- The two phenomena produce the same effect.

I. Understand the Problem

(a) In your opinion, is there any sort of clarification that this problem requires in order to be solvable? Rewrite the problem, if desired.

II. Devise a Plan

(b) Discuss your initial problem solving strategy, using your interpretation of the problem.

(c) Do you think that taking actual physical measurements would yield helpful data? If so, what measurements would they be?

(d) How does your strategy compare to others in your class?

PROBLEM SOLVING TIP

Draw a picture or diagram.

One way to obtain some useful data about how to relate these two effects is to examine where each exists in the atmosphere. Is the layer of gas that may be causing global warming close to the layer of ozone gas that protects us from the ultraviolet radiation? What does the word "close" mean in this situation? Also, how much total gas is in each layer? What is the total area that each layer occupies?

(e) Would such physical measurements benefit your proposed problem solving strategy? Why, or why not?

(f) Identify some sources for finding the data necessary to calculate the quantities that you think are beneficial to your problem solving strategy.

III. Carry Out the Plan

(g) After you have done any necessary research, use the following chart to record your calculations and summarize your data.

	Average distance from the surface of the earth	**Average distance from the center of the earth**	**Surface area of sphere generated**
Greenhouse gases			
Ozone layer			

IV. Look Back

(h) In the process of researching and making your calculations, were there any surprises? If so, what?

(i) What corrections to your initial problem solving strategy would you make if you were confronted with this problem again?

Skill Level II 

Problem

Find the names of the levels of our atmosphere and their respective distances from the surface of the earth. Record your data in the following table. If the layer has a substantial thickness, record the distance range that corresponds to the layer.

Name of layer	Average distance

(j) Calculate the surface area *and* the volume of the sphere that correspond to the outermost edge of each layer of the atmosphere.

HINT

Consider whether or not the radius of the earth is important to this problem.

Name of layer	Surface area	Volume

Skill Level III ♦♦♦

The volume between two spheres such as that in Figure 17.1

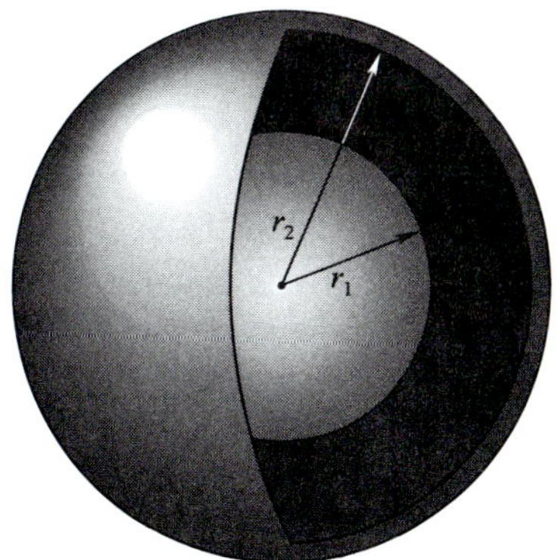

Figure 17.1

can be found from the equation

$$V = \frac{4}{3}\pi\left(r_2^3 - r_1^3\right)$$

Using this equation, find the volume of each of the layers in the table in Skill Level II.

Name of layer	Inner radius	Outer radius	Volume

Applied Math Skill Check

1. What is the volume of a sphere of radius 4 meters?

2. What is the surface area of the sphere in Exercise 1?

3. Find the area of the shaded region in the following figure.

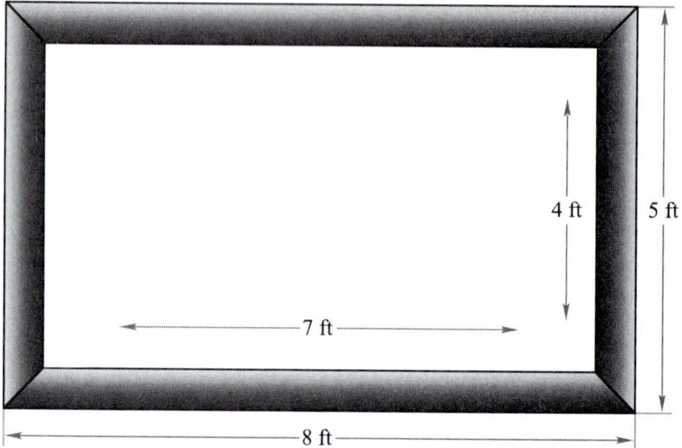

4. Find the volume between the two spheres in the following figure.

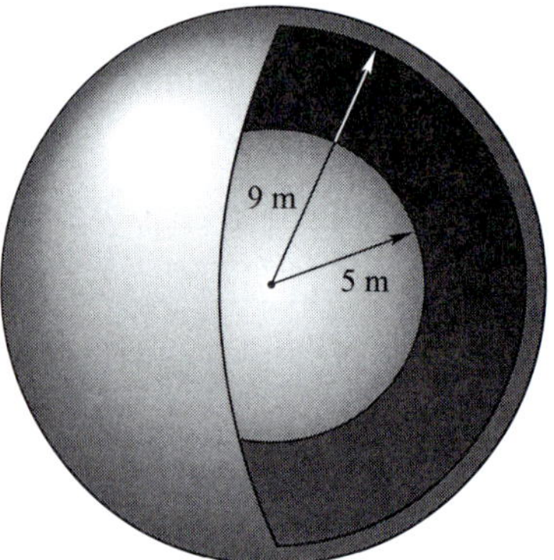

Interlude: Polynomials and Factoring

In this Interlude we discuss how to combine and factor polynomial expressions.

Objectives

1. Combine polynomial expressions
2. Factor polynomial expressions

Tools Book CD: 4.3D; 4.4; 4.5; 4.6; 5.1; 5.5

When solving technical problems, you will encounter equations with expressions that have more than one term. For example,

$$4x^3 + 5x^2 - 7x + 2$$

This type of expression, called a *polynomial* (the prefix *poly-* means "many"), is the subject of this Interlude. The Interlude is divided into two parts. In the first part, we review how to combine polynomial expressions, and in the second part we discuss how to take a polynomial expression and break it into components.

Part 1: Combining Polynomials

Adding and Subtracting Polynomial Expressions

MATH REVIEW

It may be helpful to review Thought Project 14, *Interlude: Bases and Exponents.*

To combine two terms in a polynomial using addition or subtraction, it is necessary for them to have the same *base* and the same *exponent*.

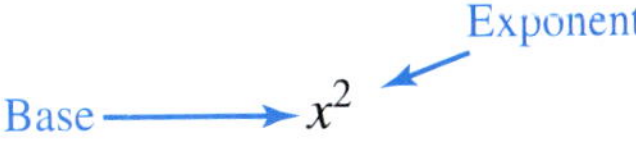

For example, let's add the following two polynomials:

$$(2x^3 + 4x + 3) + (5x^3 + 6x^2 + x + 7)$$

Because we are adding the two terms, removing the parentheses does not alter the signs on any of the terms:

$$2x^3 + 4x + 3 + 5x^3 + 6x^2 + x + 7$$

Having removed the parentheses and verified that any signs on the terms have been retained, we are ready to combine "like terms" (terms that have the same base and the same exponent).

First, let's combine the terms that have been raised to the third power:

$$2x^3 + 5x^3 = 7x^3$$

Then, we'll combine the terms that are raised to the first power:

$$4x + x = 5x$$

Although the "x" term does not include the number 1, we interpret "x" as having a coefficient of 1 and therefore the addition of $4 + 1$ yields 5.

Next we add together the constant terms:

$$3 + 7 = 10$$

Finally we see that only one term is raised to the second power, so it cannot be combined with any of the other terms.

Thus,

$$(2x^3 + 4x + 3) + (5x^3 + 6x^2 + x + 7) = 7x^3 + 6x^2 + 5x + 10$$

By convention, we arrange the terms in order of decreasing exponents to yield an answer in the simplest form.

Example 1

Add/subtract each of the following.

(a) $(5x^2 + 6x + 3) + (2x^3 + 7x^2 + 5)$

(b) $(9x^4 + 8x^3 + 5x) - (5x^4 + 6x^2 - 3x + 2)$

(c) $3(2x^3 + 5x^2 - 8) + 5(7x^2 + 4x + 3)$

Solution

(a) First remove parentheses,

$$(5x^2 + 6x + 3) + (2x^3 + 7x^2 + 5) = 5x^2 + 6x + 3 + 2x^3 + 7x^2 + 5$$

and then combine like terms:

$$(5x^2 + 6x + 3) + (2x^3 + 7x^2 + 5) = 2x^3 + 12x^2 + 6x + 8$$

(b) First we must remove the parentheses on the expressions. When doing this, we must be careful to change the signs on each of the terms in the second expression:

$$(9x^4 + 8x^3 + 5x) - (5x^4 + 6x^2 - 3x + 2)$$
$$= 9x^4 + 8x^3 + 5x - 5x^4 - 6x^2 + 3x - 2$$

Combining like terms,

$$(9x^4 + 8x^3 + 5x) - (5x^4 + 6x^2 - 3x + 2) = 4x^4 + 8x^3 - 6x^2 + 8x - 2$$

(c) First, we distribute the numerical coefficients in front of each set of parentheses:

$$\begin{aligned} &3(2x^3 + 5x^2 - 8) + 5(7x^2 + 4x + 3) \\ &\quad = (6x^3 + 15x^2 - 24) + (35x^2 + 20x + 15) \end{aligned}$$

Dropping the parentheses and combining like terms,

$$3(2x^3 + 5x^2 - 8) + 5(7x^2 + 4x + 3) = 6x^3 + 50x^2 + 20x - 9$$

Multiplying Polynomials

Multiplication of polynomials is based on the distributive property. Each of the terms in the first polynomial must be multiplied by each of the terms in the second polynomial. For example, if we have two terms in the first polynomial and three terms in the second polynomial, we will have six multiplications to execute.

As an example, let's carry out the following polynomial multiplication:

$$(2x^2 + 5x)(4x^3 + 5x^2 + 3)$$

Multiplying polynomials requires us to work with expressions that have different exponents, such as $2x^2 \cdot 4x^3$.

Thus,

$$\begin{aligned} &(2x^2 + 5x)(4x^3 + 5x^2 + 3) \\ &\quad = (2x^2 \cdot 4x^3) + (2x^2 \cdot 5x^2) + (2x^2 \cdot 3) + (5x \cdot 4x^3) + (5x \cdot 5x^2) + (5x \cdot 3) \\ &\quad = 8x^5 + 10x^4 + 6x^2 + 20x^4 + 25x^3 + 15x \end{aligned}$$

Once the multiplication is completed, we can simplify the expression by adding together the like terms, those terms that have the same base and the same exponent, and expressing the answer in descending order. Expressed in simplest form, the resulting polynomial is

$$(2x^2 + 5x)(4x^3 + 5x^2 + 3) = 8x^5 + 30x^4 + 25x^3 + 6x^2 + 15x$$

Raising a Polynomial to a Power

Having discussed how to multiply two polynomials, we will now review how to raise a polynomial to a power. Remember that an exponent on an expression tells us how many times we are to multiply that expression by itself. If we have a polynomial expression of the form

$$(3x^2 - 4x)^2$$

we take the expression $(3x^2 - 4x)$ and multiply it by itself:

$$\begin{aligned} (3x^2 - 4x)^2 &= (3x^2 - 4x)(3x^2 - 4x) \\ &= 9x^4 - 12x^3 - 12x^3 + 16x^2 \\ &= 9x^4 - 24x^3 + 16x^2 \end{aligned}$$

Part 2: Factoring Polynomials

In this section, we reverse the techniques of polynomial multiplication discussed in the last section. Instead of multiplying two polynomials together to form a new polynomial:

$$(x+2)(x-2) = x^2 - 4$$

we start with the solution and determine what two polynomials must be multiplied together to get it:

$$x^2 - 4 = (x+2)(x-2)$$

This method of breaking a polynomial such as $x^2 - 4$ into a product of terms is called *factoring*.

Factoring

When we factor an expression, we break it down into the terms that compose it. For example, we can break down the number 6 into the product of the numbers 2 and 3:

$$6 = 2(3)$$

MATH REVIEW

To check the answer when factoring, simply multiply the factors together to see if they yield the original expression.

Using the language of mathematics, 2 and 3 are called the *factors* of the number 6.

This procedure can be applied to expressions that contain variables as well as to those with numbers. When we perform this technique, we say that we have *factored* the polynomial. However, when factoring polynomials, it is not always easy to determine what types of terms must be multiplied together. The following four factoring techniques are the most common.

Factoring Technique 1—Finding Common Factors

MATH REVIEW

For a review of the distributive property, see section 1.7B of the Tools Book CD.

This factoring technique is simply the distributive property in reverse. Recall that to carry out a multiplication such as

$$2xy(x^3 + 3y)$$

the $2xy$ term must be distributed to each of the terms inside the parentheses:

$$\begin{aligned} 2xy(x^3 + 3y) &= (2xy \cdot x^3) + (2xy \cdot 3y) \\ &= 2x^4y + 6xy^2 \end{aligned}$$

Because $2xy$ is a part of each of the two terms on the right side of the equation, we call it a *common factor*.

Consequently, if we want to factor the expression $2x^4y + 6xy^2$ using the method of common factors, we simply remove the largest common term, $2xy$, from both terms:

$$2x^4y + 6xy^2 = 2xy(x^3 + 3y)$$

Example 2

Factor each of the following expressions by removing the largest common factor.

(a) $a^2b + 5b$

(b) $3t^3 + 12ct$

(c) $7xz^4 + xz$

Solution

(a) The only term that each of the terms in the expression has in common is b. Thus,

$$a^2b + 5b = b(a^2 + 5)$$

(b) Since we can think of the number 12 as being 3 times 4,

$$12 = 3(4)$$

the terms have $3t$ in common. Factoring out this common term yields

$$3t^3 + 12ct = 3t(t^2 + 4c)$$

(c) There are two issues to consider in this problem. First, the largest common term is xz. Second, there is an assumed 1 in front of the xz term, thus,

$$7xz^4 + xz = xz(7z^3 + 1)$$

Factoring Technique 2—The Difference of Two Squares

HINT

Recall that the word "difference" implies subtraction.

The next-simplest method of factoring involves situations in which the expression is the difference of two expressions that have each been raised to the second power. We call this technique the *difference of two squares*. The technique for factoring this type of expression can be found by looking at the following two polynomial multiplications:

$$(x + 2)(x - 2) = x^2 - 2x + 2x - 4$$
$$= x^2 - 4$$
$$(x + 5)(x - 5) = x^2 - 5x + 5x - 25$$
$$= x^2 - 25$$

Notice that in each case the middle terms in the multiplication cancel one another. If we now write these equations in the language of factoring, we have

$$x^2 - 4 = (x + 2)(x - 2)$$
$$x^2 - 25 = (x + 5)(x - 5)$$

The algorithm, or recipe, for factoring this type of expression becomes even more apparent if we rewrite the left-hand side of both equations:

$$x^2 - 2^2 = (x + 2)(x - 2)$$
$$x^2 - 5^2 = (x + 5)(x - 5)$$

Therefore, if the expression asks us to find the difference of two quantities that have been raised to the second power, generalized as $a^2 - b^2$, it may be factored as

$$a^2 - b^2 = (a + b)(a - b)$$

Example 3

Factor the following expressions that are differences of two squares.

(a) $x^2 - 100$

(b) $t^2 - 1$

(c) $4x^2 - y^2$

Solution

(a) Since we can think about 100 as being 10 squared,

$$100 = 10^2$$

we can rewrite the expression as the difference of two squares:

$$x^2 - 100 = x^2 - 10^2$$

therefore we can factor it as

$$\begin{aligned} x^2 - 100 &= x^2 - 10^2 \\ &= (x + 10)(x - 10) \end{aligned}$$

(b) At first glance this expression does not appear to be the difference of two squares. However, when we realize that 1 squared is still 1, we can rewrite the expression in the required form:

$$t^2 - 1 = t^2 - 1^2$$

Thus,

$$\begin{aligned} t^2 - 1 &= t^2 - 1^2 \\ &= (t + 1)(t - 1) \end{aligned}$$

(c) Since

$$4x^2 = (2x \cdot 2x)$$
$$4x^2 = (2x)^2$$

the expression can be rewritten as

$$4x^2 - y^2 = (2x)^2 - y^2$$

and then can be factored into

$$4x^2 - y^2 = (2x + y)(2x - y)$$

Factoring Technique 3—The Difference of Two Cubes

This factoring technique is similar to the difference of two squares, but can be applied to expressions that contain the difference of two terms that have been raised to the third power. An example of this type of expression is

$$a^3 - b^3$$

which factors according to the algorithm

$$a^3 - b^3 = (a - b)(a^2 + ab + b^2)$$

To test the validity of this algorithm, we can do the multiplication indicated on the right-hand side of the equation and verify that it yields the expression on the left-hand side:

$$\begin{aligned} a^3 - b^3 &= (a - b)(a^2 + ab + b^2) \\ &= a^3 + a^2b + ab^2 - a^2b - ab^2 - b^3 \\ &= a^3 - b^3 \end{aligned}$$

Example 4

Factor the following expressions that are differences of two cubes.

(a) $x^3 - 8$

(b) $y^3 - 64$

(c) $p^3 - 1$

Solution

(a) Since 8 is 2 raised to the third power, the expression can be written:

$$x^3 - 8 = x^3 - 2^3$$

which factors into

$$x^3 - 2^3 = (x - 2)(x^2 + x(2) + 2^2)$$

Thus,

$$x^3 - 8 = (x - 2)(x^2 + 2x + 4)$$

(b) First we must realize that 64 is 4 cubed:

$$y^3 - 64 = y^3 - 4^3$$

This expression then factors into

$$y^3 - 4^3 = (y - 4)(y^2 + y(4) + 4^2)$$

which may be simplified as

$$y^3 - 64 = (y - 4)(y^2 + 4y + 16)$$

(c) Since 1 to the third power is still 1, the expression factors into

$$p^3 - 1^3 = (p-1)(p^2 + p(1) + 1^2)$$

which may be simplified as

$$p^3 - 1 = (p-1)(p^2 + p + 1)$$

Factoring Technique 4—The Sum of Two Cubes

HINT

Recall that the word "sum" implies addition.

This factoring technique is similar to the previous factoring method. It is used when the expression is the *sum* of two terms that have each been raised to the third power:

$$a^3 + b^3$$

The algorithm used to factor this type of expression is

$$a^3 + b^3 = (a+b)(a^2 - ab + b^2)$$

Again, to verify that this algorithm will produce the original expression, we need only execute the multiplication on the right-hand side of the equation:

$$\begin{aligned} a^3 + b^3 &= (a+b)(a^2 - ab + b^2) \\ &= a^3 - a^2b + ab^2 + a^2b - ab^2 + b^3 \\ &= a^3 + b^3 \end{aligned}$$

Example 5

Factor the following expressions that are sums of two cubes.

(a) $x^3 + 27$

(b) $a^3 + 125$

(c) $x^3 + y^3$

Solution

(a) Since 27 is 3 cubed,

$$27 = 3^3$$

the expression factors into

$$\begin{aligned} x^3 + 27 &= x^3 + 3^3 \\ &= (x+3)(x^2 - x(3) + 3^2) \end{aligned}$$

which can be simplified as

$$x^3 + 27 = (x+3)(x^2 - 3x + 9)$$

(b) Since 125 is 5 cubed,

$$125 = 5^3$$

the expression factors into

$$\begin{aligned} a^3 + 125 &= a^3 + 5^3 \\ &= (a+5)(a^2 - a(5) + 5^2) \end{aligned}$$

which may be simplified as

$$a^3 + 125 = (a+5)(a^2 - 5a + 25)$$

(c) $x^3 + y^3 = (x+y)(x^2 - xy + y^2)$

Applied Math Skill Check

1. Combine the like terms in the following expressions.

   (a) $8x^2 + 6x^3 + 2x + 5x$

   (b) $3x + 7x^2 + 9x$

   (c) $4x^3 - 3x^3 + 9x + 2x$

   (d) $(5x^2 + 6x + 8) + (6x^3 + 2x^2 - 4x)$

   (e) $(10x^3 + 6x^2 + 4x) - (8x^3 + 2x^2 - 3x)$

2. Execute each of the indicated multiplications.

   (a) $x(a + b)$

   (b) $3x^2(7x + 8y)$

   (c) $(3x + 2)(8x + 5)$

   (d) $(4x - 6)(2x + 1)$

   (e) $(5x^2 + 7x + 3)(8x + 2)$

   (f) $(x + 1)(x - 1)$

   (g) $(x - 2)(x^2 + 2x + 4)$

3. Factor the following expressions using the method of common factors.

   (a) $6a + 6c$

   (b) $8x^2 + 2xb$

   (c) $x^3y^2 + xy$

4. Factor the following differences of two squares.

   (a) $x^2 - 81$

   (b) $t^2 - 4$

   (c) $b^2 - 144$

5. Factor the following sums or differences of two cubes.

   (a) $b^3 - 8$

   (b) $x^3 + 8$

   (c) $m^3 - n^3$

   (d) $c^3 + f^3$

Simultaneous Equations and the Physical World

Beginning with an examination of why we see the light from a lightning strike before we hear the thunder associated with it, and moving through a variety of other physical examples, this Thought Project illustrates the need for the ability to solve simultaneous equations.

Objective

Solve simultaneous equations using the substitution method

Tools Book CD: 8.2, 8.3

Although it appears that the lightning in this photo originates from a cloud formation, the beginning of this weather phenomenon actually starts on the ground.

Courtesy of Jeffrey M. Hamilton/ Liason Agency, Inc.

It is not uncommon to see something happen and only afterward hear the sound from the event. A familiar example is that of seeing lightning strike, but not hearing the thunder for an appreciable amount of time. Why is it that the sight is not "in sync" with the sound?

We can explain this strange phenomenon with the science of waves. Whether it is a wave in the ocean, a wave on a rope, or an electromagnetic wave (such as the light from our sun), all waves take a certain time period to move from point A to point B.

Problem

1. Construct a physical explanation for why the sound of thunder from a lightning strike appears after the actual bolt of lightning is observed.
2. Devise and execute a strategy that would allow you to determine the distance to a lightning strike, given a five-second time difference between seeing the lightning and hearing the thunder.

Skill Level I ♦

HINT

Distance = Rate × Time

I. Understand the Problem

(a) What are the key pieces of information in the two parts of the problem statement? If desired, rewrite them in your own words.

(b) In your opinion, would it be better to approach these two problems separately, or as one large problem? Explain your reasoning.

(c) Do you have all of the information you need to solve the two parts of the problem? If not, what additional information or clarification do you need? After recording the additional information that you think is necessary, research any missing information and then proceed.

HINT

The following facts may be helpful in solving the second part of the problem.

- The velocity of light is approximately 3.0×10^8 meters per second.
- The velocity of sound depends upon the temperature of the air through which the sound wave moves. With the temperature expressed in Celsius, the velocity of sound (in meters per second) can be found using the formula

$$v = 331 + 0.6T_c.$$

II. Devise a Plan

(d) For the first part of the problem, state your explanation for the difference in time between when lightning is observed and the thunder is heard. How does it compare to that of others near you in the class?

(e) For the second part, describe your problem solving strategy for finding the distance from your position to the lightning strike.

(f) Do the facts in the Hint, about the speed of light and the formula for calculating the speed of sound, suggest that you should modify your initial problem solving strategy? If so, how?

III. Carry Out the Plan

(g) Implement your strategy, and find the distance from your position to the lightning strike.

IV. Look Back

(h) How effective was your method? Do you believe that your approach is the best strategy to solve the problem?

Skill Level II 

Simultaneous equations can also be used to solve a problem associated with a physical system, such as the hanging traffic light shown in Figure 19.1.

> **FYI**
>
> cos 30° = 0.866
> sin 30° = 0.5
> cos 40° = 0.766
> sin 40° = 0.643

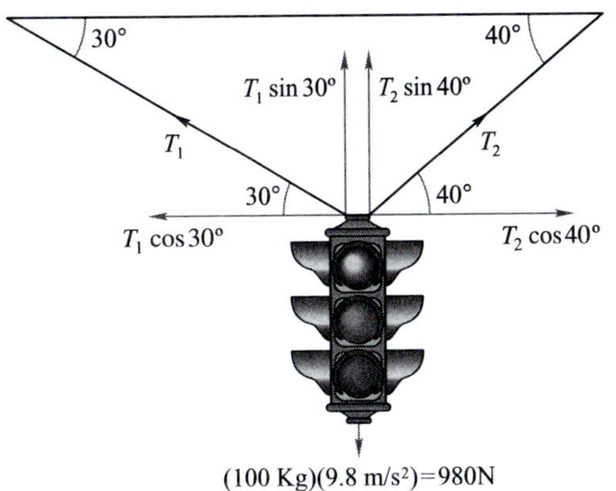

Figure 19.1

Given the weight of the traffic light and the angles of the cables, the following two equations can be constructed:

$$0.866T_1 - 0.766T_2 = 0$$
$$0.5T_1 + 0.643T_2 = 980$$

Using the methods of simultaneous equations, it is possible to solve for the tension in the first cable (T_1) and the tension in the second cable (T_2).

Problem

Solve for the tension in each of the cables attached to the traffic light.

Show your work.

Skill Level III 

Problems involving simultaneous equations are also frequently encountered when working with electrical circuits. The ability to solve such problems is of critical importance to students of electronics, and to computer engineering and computer drafting students who will use computers in their chosen vocations.

Problem

Consider the following direct current (DC) circuit:

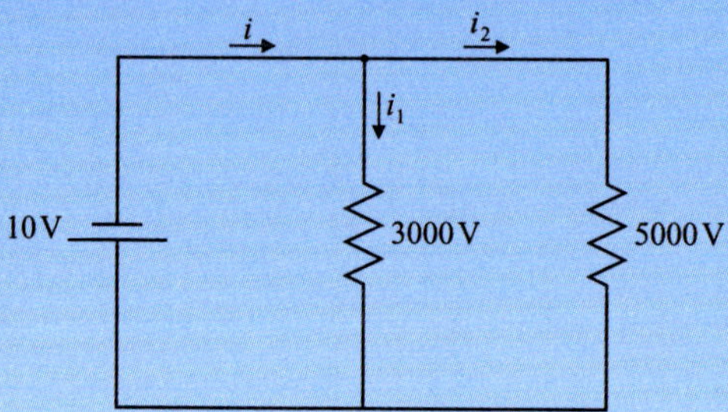

The following simultaneous equations can be constructed from this circuit:

$$i = i_1 + i_2$$
$$10 - 3000i_1 = 0$$
$$10 - 5000i_2 = 0$$

Solve for i, i_1, and i_2.

Show your work.

Applied Math Skill Check

Solve for x and y in each of the following systems of equations.

1. $2x + 3y = 7$
   $5x - y = 9$

2. $3x = 4y - 10$
   $y = x + 2$

3. Solve for x, y, and z in the following system of equations.

$$x + 2y + z = 2$$
$$5x = z$$
$$y = -2x$$

Interlude: Simplifying Radicals, Exponents, and Negative Exponents

In this Interlude, we review the topics of radicals and exponents, and discuss methods by which these types of expressions may be simplified.

Objective

Simplify expressions containing radical signs and integer, fractional, and negative exponents

Tools Book CD: 9.1–9.4A

Multiplying and Dividing Two Radical Expressions

When we have an expression such as

$$\sqrt{4} \cdot \sqrt{25}$$

in which we are taking the square root of both terms, we can combine them by placing them inside one radical sign. Since the expressions ask for the two square roots to be multiplied, we will multiply the two terms inside the radical:

$$\sqrt{4} \cdot \sqrt{25} = \sqrt{4 \cdot 25} = \sqrt{100}$$

Let's verify that this algebraic manipulation works, by solving the problems separately and comparing our answers:

$$\sqrt{4} \cdot \sqrt{25} = \sqrt{100}$$
$$2 \cdot 5 = 10$$
$$10 = 10$$

This step of algebraic simplification holds true regardless of the terms that are inside the radical. Provided that the same type of root is being taken, we can always combine the two expressions under one radical symbol.

Example 1

Simplify the following expression.

$$\sqrt[3]{5x} \cdot \sqrt[3]{4yz}$$

Solution

Since both terms in the multiplication are cube roots, we can combine the terms under a single radical sign:

$$\sqrt[3]{5x} \cdot \sqrt[3]{4yz} = \sqrt[3]{(5x)(4yz)}$$

Simplifying,

$$\sqrt[3]{5x} \cdot \sqrt[3]{4yz} = \sqrt[3]{20xyz}$$

This method of combining radicals of the same type can be extended to expressions involving radicals that are divided by one another, such as

$$\frac{\sqrt{100}}{\sqrt{25}} = \sqrt{\frac{100}{25}} = \sqrt{4} = 2$$

Again, let's verify that this technique yields the same numerical answer as if we had worked each step independently:

$$\frac{\sqrt{100}}{\sqrt{25}} = \sqrt{\frac{100}{25}} = \sqrt{4} = 2$$

$$\frac{10}{5} = 2$$

$$2 = 2$$

In other words, we get the same numerical result if we calculate the square roots first and then divide the results, or combine the two square roots into one. As with the technique for multiplication, the technique for division can be applied even if we are taking a root other than a square root, or if the terms inside the radicals are not numbers.

Example 2

Simplify the following expression.

$$\frac{\sqrt[3]{x}}{\sqrt[3]{y}}$$

Solution

Since both terms involve a cube root, we can combine the two expressions under a single radical:

$$\frac{\sqrt[3]{x}}{\sqrt[3]{y}} = \sqrt[3]{\frac{x}{y}}$$

Because the two variables in the expression are different, no further simplification is possible.

Adding and Subtracting Two Radical Expressions

Unlike multiplication and division, the rules for combining expressions using addition or subtraction require that the radical expressions be identical. We must take the same root *and* have the same terms inside the radicals to be able to combine radical expressions that are being added or subtracted.

Example 3

Simplify the following expressions, if possible.

(a) $\sqrt{xy} + \sqrt{xy}$

(b) $\sqrt{x^2y} + \sqrt{xy}$

(c) $7\sqrt[3]{x} - 2\sqrt[3]{x}$

Solution

Notice that while the expressions in (a) and (c) can be combined, the expression in (b) cannot, because the terms inside the two radicals are not identical.

Adding the two terms in part (a) yields

$$\sqrt{xy} + \sqrt{xy} = 2\sqrt{xy}$$

Subtracting the two terms in part (c) yields

$$7\sqrt[3]{x} - 2\sqrt[3]{x} = 5\sqrt[3]{x}$$

An Alternative Method of Writing Radical Expressions

In this section of the Interlude, we will discuss an alternative manner in which to express radicals. Although the method is different, the results from multiplying radical expressions will be the same as we have learned previously.

This technique requires us to rewrite the radical expressions in terms of fractional exponents. The fractional exponent contains both the information that is inside the radical and the type of root that is being taken (square root, cube root, etc.).

> To write a radical expression using a fractional exponent, use the power that is on the term inside the radical as the numerator of the fraction and the root that is being taken as the denominator of the fraction.

Let's practice this technique by rewriting several different examples.

Example 4

Express

$$\sqrt[3]{x^2}$$

using fractional exponents.

Solution

In this case, we are taking a cube root (or third root), and the x inside the radical has been raised to the second power. Thus, we can rewrite the expression as

$$\sqrt[3]{x^2} = x^{2/3}$$

Example 5

Express

$$\sqrt{x}$$

using fractional exponents.

Solution

For many students, working with a square root is more difficult than higher roots because, by convention, we do not include the 2 that alerts the reader that it is a "2nd" root that is being taken. Furthermore, we do not include the assumed 1 that is the exponent, x^1, in this example. If we use these two pieces of information, we can rewrite the expression as

$$\sqrt{x} = x^{1/2}$$

Before we move on to the next example, let's briefly discuss an algebraic technique that is useful in simplifying algebraic statements. It is possible to move terms between the numerator and the denominator of a fraction by changing the sign of the exponent on the term. For example,

$$\frac{3}{x^2}$$

can be rewritten as $3x^{-2}$.

Note that we did not change the sign on the entire term, only on the exponent. Let's use this technique in our next example.

Example 6

Express

$$\frac{2}{\sqrt[4]{x^3}}$$

using a fractional, negative exponent.

Solution

First, we express the denominator in terms of a fractional exponent,

$$\frac{2}{\sqrt[4]{x^3}} = \frac{2}{x^{3/4}}$$

We then move the denominator into the numerator, yielding

$$\frac{2}{\sqrt[4]{x^3}} = 2x^{-3/4}$$

We can now compare these two techniques for expressing radicals by multiplying the expression

$$\sqrt{x} \cdot \sqrt{x}$$

and comparing our results.

Lets begin by multiplying the two expressions expressed as radicals. Because both terms have a square root, we know that we can combine the two expressions:

$$\begin{aligned} \sqrt{x} \cdot \sqrt{x} &= \sqrt{x \cdot x} \\ &= \sqrt{x^2} \\ &= x \end{aligned}$$

Now, let's use fractional exponents to solve the same problem. Beginning with the expression, we can rewrite each radical using fractional exponents:

$$\sqrt{x} \cdot \sqrt{x} = x^{1/2} \cdot x^{1/2}$$

Because the two terms have the same base, we can combine them by adding their exponents:

$$\begin{aligned} \sqrt{x} \cdot \sqrt{x} &= x^{1/2} \cdot x^{1/2} \\ &= x^{1/2+1/2} \\ &= x^1 \\ &= x \end{aligned}$$

Thus, we see that in both cases, we arrived at a final answer of x.

In summary, we see that it is advantageous to know as many mathematical tools as possible to become effective problem solvers. The techniques discussed in this Interlude are only a few of the many mathematical tools that are available to help us in problem solving.

Applied Math Skill Check

1. Simplify the following expressions by combining as many terms as possible.

   (a) $3xy + 5xy$

   (b) $9x^2t - 7x^2t$

   (c) $2xy + 6y + 8xy$

   (d) $4\sqrt{x} + 3\sqrt{xy} + 7\sqrt{xy} - \sqrt{x}$

2. Simplify the following expressions by performing the indicated operations.

   (a) $\sqrt[3]{x} \cdot \sqrt[3]{x}$

   (b) $\sqrt{t} \cdot \sqrt{t}$

   (c) $\dfrac{\sqrt[3]{R}}{\sqrt[3]{x}}$

3. Express each of the following radical expressions using fractional exponents.

   (a) $\sqrt[4]{x^3}$

   (b) $\sqrt{t}$

   (c) $\sqrt[4]{x^7}$

   (d) $\dfrac{1}{\sqrt[5]{x^2}}$

4. Write each of the following using only positive exponents.

   (a) $\dfrac{x^2}{y^{-3}}$

   (b) x^3y^{-5}

   (c) $x^2y^{-4}z^4$

   (d) $\dfrac{x^2}{y^{-1/2}}$

   (e) $x^2y^3t^{-4}z^{-6}w$

THOUGHT PROJECT 21

Projectile Motion

An examination of the motion of objects provides an interesting setting for reviewing the importance of solving quadratic equations.

Objectives

1. Insert numerical values into a second-order equation using the correct order of operations
2. Discern which of the two possible solutions of a quadratic equation are physically possible
3. Use the quadratic formula
4. Execute effective independent research

Tools Book CD: 4.1A, 10.1A, 10.2A

Skill Level I 

In the physical sciences, we must often distinguish between those equations and relationships that can be derived mathematically and those that are purely *empirical*. By empirical we mean that the terms in the equation are included because they predict what we see in an experiment. Through trial and error, we have found the equation that will work. There is no profound mathematical basis for the equation.

An example of an empirical equation is the *displacement equation* from Newtonian physics:

$$y = v_0 t + \frac{1}{2}at^2$$

This rather formidable equation is used to predict the motion of projectiles. Before we move on, let's examine each term in the equation:

- y is the total vertical *displacement* of the object. In this Thought Project, we will use meters to measure how far an object moves, or the displacement of the object.
- v_0 is the initial velocity of the object. This velocity, measured in meters per second (m/s), is how fast the object is moving at the beginning of the problem.
- t is the time that corresponds to the displacement. If we know where the object is located, it is possible to solve for the time when the object is at

this location. Conversely, if we know the time of interest, we can insert it into the equation and find the displacement.

- a is the acceleration of the object. Accelerations change the velocities of objects. If the acceleration is in the same direction as the velocity of the object, the object will move faster. If the acceleration is applied in the direction opposite to that of the object's velocity, the object will slow down. When dealing with vertical problems, we normally must consider the acceleration caused by gravity. Gravitational acceleration is directed straight downward and is given by 9.8 m/s^2.

Problem

Devise and execute an experiment that will yield the time that it takes a marble (or some other object) to drop from a table to the floor. Compare your experimental result with that predicted by the displacement equation.

I. Understand the Problem

(a) Read the problem statement carefully. How many steps are required to solve this problem?

Step I: Performing an Experiment

II. Devise a Plan

(b) Write down the steps in your experimental procedure and identify the equipment that will be necessary to carry it out.

(c) Do you see any potential problems with your experimental setup? Explain.

III. Carry Out the Plan

(d) Conduct five trials of your proposed experiment. Record your results and their average in the table below.

	Time (to hit the floor)
Trial 1	
Trial 2	
Trial 3	
Trial 4	
Trial 5	
Average	

Math Review

To find the average of a set of figures, the sum of the figures is divided by the number of figures. For example, the average of the three numbers 2, 4, and 6 is:

$$\text{Avg} = \frac{2+4+6}{3} = \frac{12}{3} = 4$$

IV. Look Back

(e) How successful was your experiment? Would you modify it in any way? Explain.

Step II: Using the Displacement Equation

Problem Solving Tip

You have been given the strategy of using the displacement equation. The critical steps are to Carry Out the Plan and Look Back to understand what you have learned.

III. Carry Out the Plan

(f) Using your own words, explain what each of the terms in the displacement equation represents.

(g) If the object is dropped (as opposed to thrown) straight downward, what is the initial velocity of the object?

(h) Identify the total distance that your object will travel.

(i) If you incorporate the information from steps (g) and (h), what form does the displacement equation take?

(j) Execute the algebra necessary to solve your equation from step (i) for the time that it would take for your object to hit the ground.

IV. Look Back

(k) In the process of solving your equation, you should have found two solutions. Are both solutions reasonable physically? Explain.

(l) If your experimental result did not agree with your mathematical result, discuss possible reasons for this discrepancy.

Skill Level II 

As a continuation of Skill Level I, let's see what happens if we reverse the direction of the object's motion. As we will observe, this simple reversal of the direction adds considerable complexity to the problem.

Problem Solving Tip

Note that in this Skill Level you are not actually required to *execute* your experiment, only to design it. Consequently, Step III, *Carry Out the Plan*, is eliminated.

Problem

An object is shot straight upward with an initial velocity of 6 m/s. Design an experiment that will allow you to measure how long it takes for the object to reach a height of 1 m.

I. Understand the Problem

(m) Review the problem statement. In your own words, write out what you think the problem is asking.

II. Devise a Plan

(n) Explain, as completely as possible, the structure of your experiment. If possible, make a sketch of your experimental setup.

(o) What equipment would you need to conduct your experiment?

(p) Do you think that your experiment will yield an exact result? Why or why not?

Hint

To solve step (q), remember that if an object is shot upward, the acceleration due to gravity is opposite to the direction of the displacement. Consequently, these two terms would get different signs in the displacement equation.

(q) Use the displacement equation to find the time at which the projectile would reach a height 1 m above its initial position.

III. Look Back

(r) After thinking through your proposed experiment, would you suggest a physical experiment as the appropriate problem solving strategy for this situation? Why or why not?

Skill Level III ♦♦♦

When dealing with projectile motion, we must realize that real-world effects can often modify the results that we find from pure mathematics. This Skill Level is therefore designed to introduce you to two of the effects that can often affect the motion of objects on earth.

Problem

Execute the research necessary to answer each of the following questions.

1. When does the mass/size of an object affect the time of its free fall?
2. What is the terminal velocity of an object?

Record your answers in the space provided.

Applied Math Skill Check

1. Find y in each of the following equations.

   (a) $y = 4x^2$ $\quad\quad x = 3$

   (b) $y = x^2 + 3x$ $\quad\quad x = 2$

   (c) $y = vx^2 + vx$ $\quad\quad x = 4,\ v = 3$

2. Solve the following quadratic equations.

   (a) $4x^2 = 100$

   (b) $3x^2 + 2x - 10 = 0$

   (c) $4t^2 = 3t + 12$

3. In general, how many distinct solutions are there to a quadratic equation?

4. Explain the conditions under which a quadratic equation can be solved using simple rearrangement, versus using the quadratic formula. Is there a way to decide, from the structure of the equation being solved, when each approach is appropriate?

Radiocarbon Dating

In this Thought Project, we use the archaeological tool of radiocarbon dating to illustrate how the function of the natural logarithm is used in our everyday world.

Objectives

1. Insert numerical values into an exponential expression
2. Solve an exponential expression for a single variable
3. Insert a percentage into an equation
4. Solve an exponential equation using the natural logarithm

Tools Book CD: 11.6, 11.7

Skill Level I 

In 1997, scientists discovered the frozen remains of a long-extinct animal, the wooly mammoth. The body of the animal was so well-preserved by ice that scientists believe they will be able to extract a sample of DNA from it and clone a replica. If they are successful, a long-extinct animal will once again appear. To identify the age of the remains of this amazing animal, scientists used the process of *radiocarbon dating*. For us to understand radiocarbon dating, we must explore the central portion of the atom, known as the *nucleus*.

The nucleus of an atom contains two types of particles—protons and neutrons. The number of each of these particles conveys the information that we need to understand this archaeological dating technique.

The number of *protons* inside the nucleus determines the *element*. For example, all atoms that have a total of eight protons inside their nucleus are called oxygen; all atoms that have a total of six protons are called carbon.

Whereas the number of protons determines the element, the number of *neutrons* determines the version (or *isotope*) of the element. An example of this isotope concept is the element carbon. The atom that has six protons and eight neutrons is called carbon-14, whereas the atom that has six protons and six neutrons is called carbon-12. The number that is attached to the name comes from adding the number of protons and the number of neutrons. Since they both have a total of six protons, each is a kind of carbon. The differing numbers of neutrons classify them as different isotopes of the element carbon.

In addition to having different numbers of neutrons, the two carbon isotopes behave very differently. The nucleus of a carbon-12 atom is very stable, whereas the nucleus of a carbon-14 atom is not. The nucleus of the carbon-14 atom radiates energy and mass as a result of its instability, and therefore *decays* and is no longer carbon-14. The decay of carbon-14 is the basis of radiocarbon dating.

All living things, such as trees, people, and woolly mammoths, contain this radioactive isotope of carbon. By finding the amount of carbon-14 left in an archaeological discovery, scientists are able to backtrack and calculate when the animal, tree, and so forth, was alive.

The basic decay equation that the scientists use is

$$N = N_0 e^{-\lambda t} \tag{1}$$

where N is the amount of a material that is left after a certain amount of time, t; N_0 is the initial amount of the material before it began to decay into other materials; λ is the decay constant of the material; and t is the time at which you are looking at the sample.

Notice that the negative sign on the exponent has the mathematical meaning that we will have less and less of a radioactive sample as time goes along. This agrees with what we expect *physically* in this Thought Projcct.

Example

One-half of a 2000 gram sample of radioactive material remains after the material decays for 500 seconds. How much of the material remains after 100 seconds?

FYI

The amount of time required for one-half of a decaying substance to remain is called the *half-life* of the substance.

Solution

First we find the decay constant of the material. Representing one-half of the initial amount as $\frac{1}{2}N_0$, and inserting the time required to reach this amount, 500 seconds, Equation (1) takes the following form.

$$\begin{aligned} N &= N_0 e^{-\lambda t} \\ \frac{1}{2}N_0 &= N_0 e^{-\lambda(500)} \\ \frac{1}{2} &= e^{-500\lambda} \end{aligned}$$

Taking the natural log of both sides of the last equation and solving for λ, we get

$$\begin{aligned} \frac{1}{2} &= e^{-500\lambda} \\ \ln\left(\frac{1}{2}\right) &= \ln(e^{-500\lambda}) \\ -0.693 &= -500\lambda \\ 0.0014 &= \lambda \end{aligned}$$

Now, using the decay constant for the material to find the amount of the material that remains after 100 seconds, we have

$$N = N_0 e^{-\lambda t}$$
$$N = 2000e^{-(0.0014)(100)}$$
$$N = 2000e^{-0.14}$$
$$N = 2000(0.869)$$
$$N = 1738$$

Thus, 1738 grams of the radioactive material remain after 100 seconds.

Problem

If we have 5000 g of a radioactive substance and it has a half-life such that we will have half of the original material left after 100 seconds, how much will we have left after 50 seconds?

HINT

To solve the problem we must first find the decay constant, λ, of the radioactive substance.

(a) The problem statement requires us to know one-half of the original amount of the radioactive substance. What is this amount?

(b) Inserting the information from both the problem statement and step (a), what form does Equation (1) take if we want to solve for the decay constant λ?

(c) Use the natural logarithm to solve your equation from step (b) for the decay constant λ.

(d) Rewrite Equation (1) using the decay constant from step (c) and the relevant information from the problem statement.

(e) Solve your equation from step (d) for the amount of the radioactive substance that remains after 50 seconds.

(f) In the problem statement, you were given that the starting amount of the material was 5000 grams and that one-half of the substance remained after 100 seconds. In your opinion, if we are given the amount of time required for only one-half of the original amount to remain, is the initial amount of the substance required to solve for the decay constant, λ? Explain.

Skill Level II 

Problem

For the radioactive material in the preceding problem, how long would we have to wait until 99% of the original material had decayed?

Solve the problem and show your work.

Skill Level III 

Problem

Work with a partner to compose a list of important objects from the past. The criterion for an object to be included in your list is that its date is of critical importance to our current understanding of the world. In other words, if we can attach a date to these objects, it will aid us in understanding our physical world. For each of the objects on your list, give a strategy for how you might attach a reliable date to it. Remember, an important object might be one year old, or 500 million years old!

Object	Why its date is significant	Dating technique

I. Understand the Problem

(g) In your own words, write out what you interpret the problem statement to be asking. Compare your interpretation with that of others in your class.

(h) In your interpretation, what are the key terms in the problem statement?

II. Devise a Plan

(i) Explain by what criteria you and your partner are judging the "importance" of an object.

(j) For which historical objects would a determination of the age add significantly to our understanding of our world? Defend your choices.

III. Carry Out the Plan

(k) For the objects that you listed in step (j), explain how you might attach a reliable date to each.

IV. Look Back

(l) For each of the methods that you listed in step (k), is there a way to quantify the error associated with your dating technique? Explain.

Applied Math Skill Check

1. Calculate each of the following.

   (a) e^1

   (b) $e^{2.5}$

   (c) $e^{-0.653}$

   (d) e^0

2. Calculate each of the following.

   (a) $\ln 3$

   (b) $\ln 0.763$

   (c) $\ln 1$

   (d) $\ln 0$

3. Solve for x in each of the following equations.

   (a) $e^{2x} = 5$

   (b) $0.6 = e^{-5x}$

   (c) $e^{6x+1} = 1$

Interlude: Trigonometry

In this Interlude, we introduce the basic concepts of right-triangle trigonometry.

Objectives

1. Use the Pythagorean Theorem to solve for a given unknown in a right triangle
2. Find the sine, cosine, and tangent of a given angle

Tools Book CD: A.6

Part I – The Pythagorean Theorem

Recall that a triangle is a closed polygon that has three sides and three interior angles. Although a triangle can have an infinite variety of interior angles and side lengths, in this Interlude we are interested only in those triangles with a 90° angle, as illustrated in Figure 23.1.

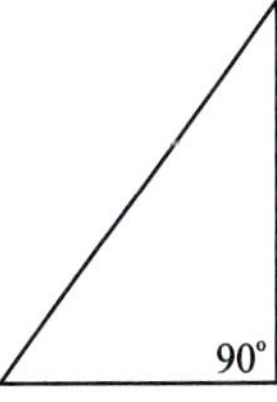

Figure 23.1

By convention, we insert a small box in the appropriate corner of the triangle (as shown in Figure 23.2), to alert the reader that it is a 90° angle:

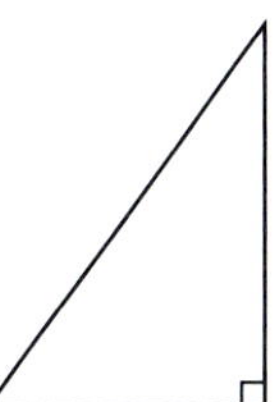

Figure 23.2

Because the leg on the right makes a right angle with the leg at the bottom, this type of triangle is called a *right triangle.*

Our understanding of right triangles can be traced directly back to the work of a Greek mathematician named Pythagoras, who showed that the lengths of the sides of any right triangle can be related to one another. He was able to show a mathematical relationship between the lengths of the legs a and b to the length of the longest side c (see Figure 23.3).

Pythagoras (sixth century, B.C.) Greek mathematician who studied the relationships between numbers and the sides of right triangles.

Courtesy of Pearson Education

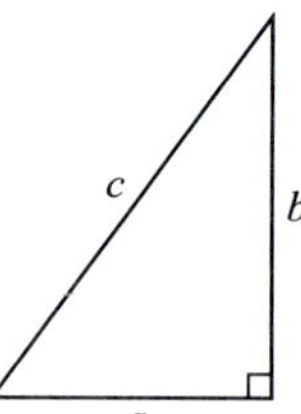

Figure 23.3

The longest side, c, is always located directly across the triangle from the right angle, and is called the *hypotenuse* of the triangle.

The mathematical theorem that Pythagoras found, referred to as the *Pythagorean Theorem,* states that if we square the lengths of each of the shorter legs, a^2 and b^2, and add them, $a^2 + b^2$, we will always get the length of the hypotenuse squared. In equation form, we have:

> *Pythagorean Theorem*
>
> $$a^2 + b^2 = c^2$$

Example 1

Find the hypotenuse of the right triangle in Figure 23.4.

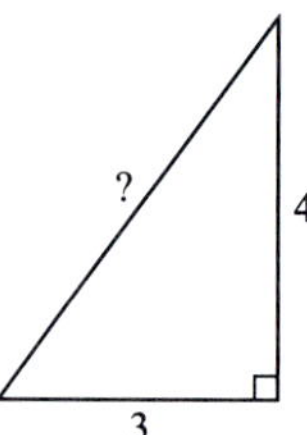

Figure 23.4

Solution

The hypotenuse can be found by employing the Pythagorean Theorem:

$$\begin{aligned} a^2 + b^2 &= c^2 \\ 3^2 + 4^2 &= c^2 \\ 9 + 16 &= c^2 \\ 25 &= c^2 \\ 5 &= c \end{aligned}$$

Note that we ignore the other answer to $\sqrt{25}$, namely -5, since a negative length would have no meaning in this context.

Example 2

Find the length of the base leg of the right triangle in Figure 23.5.

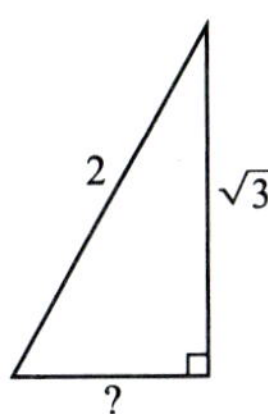

Figure 23.5

Solution

By inserting the lengths of the side and the hypotenuse into the Pythagorean Theorem, we get:

$$a^2 + b^2 = c^2$$
$$a^2 + (\sqrt{3})^2 = 2^2$$
$$a^2 + 3 = 4$$
$$a^2 = 1$$
$$a = 1$$

Problem

1. Find the length of the hypotenuse of the following right triangle:

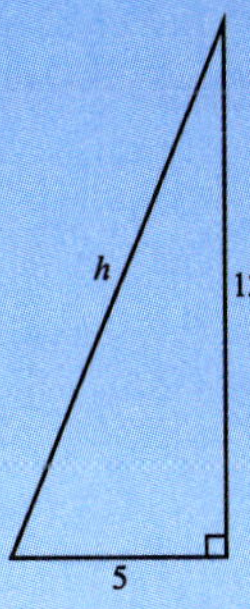

2. Find the length of the base side of the following right triangle:

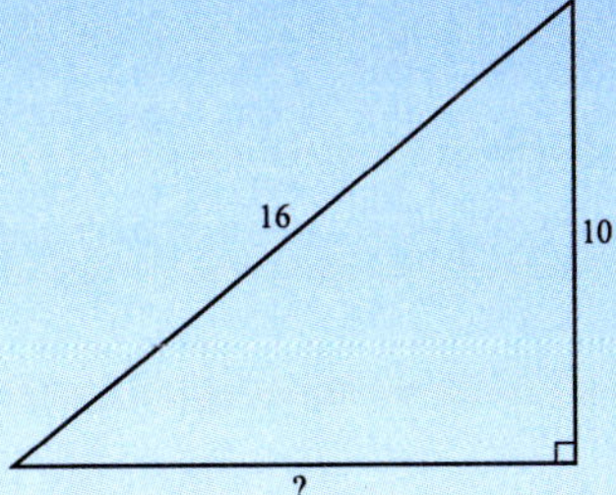

Show your work.

Part II – The Three Trigonometric Functions Sine, Cosine, and Tangent

Future courses at ITT Technical Institute will make use of a set of remarkably powerful problem solving tools that can be found by relating the three sides of a right triangle to one another. This area of mathematics is known as *trigonometry*.

Let's look again at the right triangle shown in Figure 23.4.

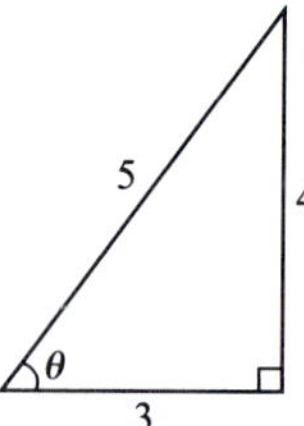

Figure 23.6

Notice that this time we place a symbol to represent the angle at the bottom corner of the triangle. This symbol is the Greek letter theta, θ, and is the variable that is most often used to represent an unknown angle.

Next we assign names to the sides of the triangle. We already know the side of the triangle across from the right angle is called the hypotenuse. All that remains is to name the two legs of the right triangle.

The side of the triangle across from the angle of interest is called the *opposite side*. The remaining side of the triangle is called the *adjacent side* to our angle (see Figure 23.7).

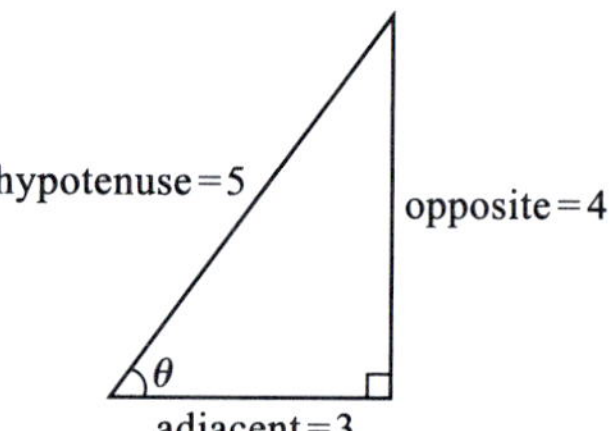

Figure 23.7

Now that we have named the sides of the triangle, we can define ratios of one side to another. We will assign names to each of the ratios we create.

1. The *sine* of the angle θ, written $\sin\theta$, is the ratio of the length of the opposite side to the length of the hypotenuse. In equation form:

$$\sin\theta = \frac{\text{opp}}{\text{hyp}}$$

2. The *cosine* of the angle θ, written $\cos\theta$, is the ratio of the length of the adjacent side to the length of the hypotenuse. In equation form:

$$\cos\theta = \frac{\text{adj}}{\text{hyp}}$$

3. The *tangent* of the angle θ, written tan θ, is the ratio of the length of the opposite side to the length of the adjacent side. In equation form:

$$\tan\theta = \frac{\text{opp}}{\text{adj}}$$

Example 3

Using the triangle from Figure 23.7, find the sine, cosine, and tangent of the angle θ.

Solution

By inserting the lengths of the three sides of the right triangle into the equations, we see that the three trigonometric ratios are

$$\sin\theta = \frac{4}{5}$$

$$\cos\theta = \frac{3}{5}$$

$$\tan\theta = \frac{4}{3}$$

Two additional important points must be made about trigonometry.

The Dependence of the Sine, Cosine, and Tangent on the Angle of Interest

Notice that if we focus our attention on the top angle of the triangle (see Figure 23.8), the sides of the triangle that we identified as the opposite and the adjacent change names (see Figure 23.9).

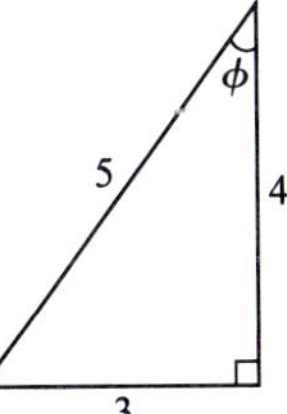

Figure 23.8

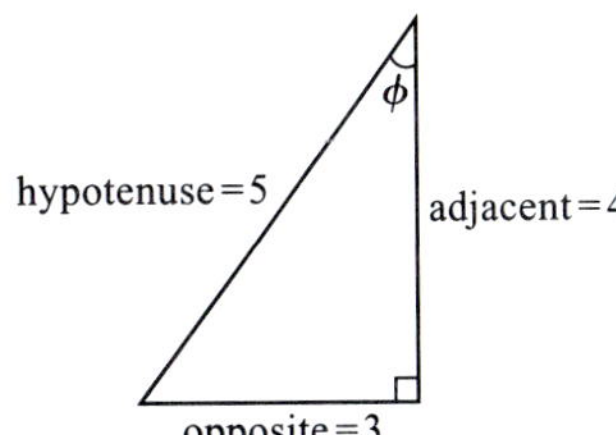

Figure 23.9

Consequently, for the angle ϕ,

$$\sin\phi = \frac{3}{5}$$

$$\cos\phi = \frac{4}{5}$$

$$\tan\phi = \frac{3}{4}$$

Note that we used a different variable, the Greek letter phi, ϕ (pronounced "fie"), to represent the top angle of the triangle. We must use a different variable than in the previous example because the two angles of a triangle will almost always have different values.

The Boundary on the Sine and Cosine

Since the hypotenuse of a right triangle is always the longest side of the triangle, and is in the denominator of both the sine and cosine definitions,

$$\sin\theta = \frac{\text{opp}}{\text{hyp}}$$

$$\cos\theta = \frac{\text{adj}}{\text{hyp}}$$

the sine and the cosine of any angle will always be less than or equal to 1.

Applied Math Skill Check

1. Find the length of the hypotenuse of a triangle that has a base length of 3, and a side length of 8.

2. Find the sine, cosine, and tangent of the angle θ in the following right triangle:

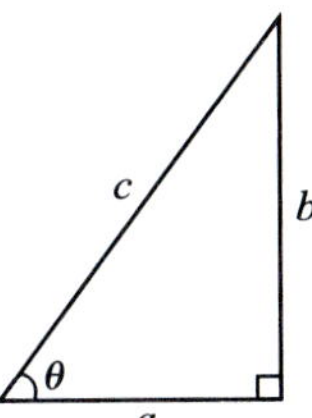

3. Find the sine, cosine, and tangent of the angle θ in the following right triangle:

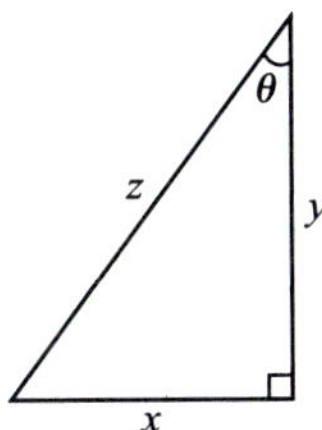

4. For the following right triangle, find
   (a) the length of the hypotenuse of the triangle
   (b) the sine, cosine, and tangent of the angle θ
   (c) the sine, cosine, and tangent of the angle ϕ

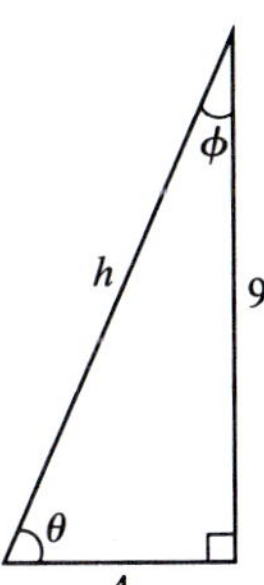

Billboards

Examining the challenge faced by a painter as she prepares a new freeway billboard sign provides an opportunity to use the Pythagorean Theorem in a real-world setting. As an extension of this theorem, we also look at the measurement technique of parallax as an applied example of right-triangle trigonometry.

Objectives

1. Use the Pythagorean Theorem to solve for a given unknown in a right triangle
2. Find the length of the side of a right triangle given an angle and the length of another side

Tools Book CD: A.6

Skill Level I ♦

A billboard painter has been assigned the task of changing the advertisement on a 20-ft billboard, the bottom of which is 15 ft off the ground.

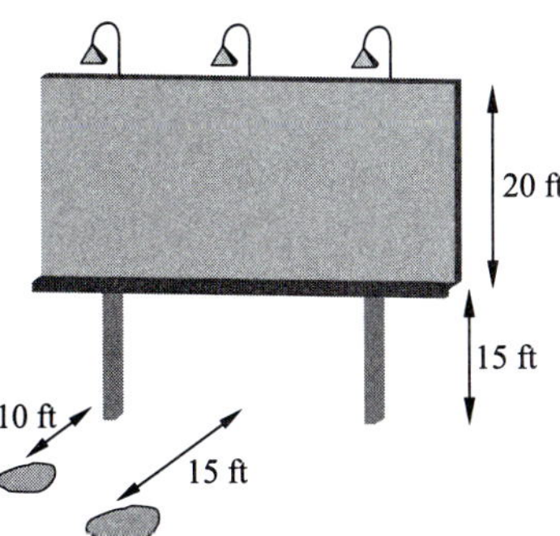

Figure 24.1

After examining the site, she identifies two areas on the ground under the sign that are sturdy enough to support her ladder. One area is 10 ft from the base of the billboard and the other is 15 ft from the base.

Problem

If the painter uses the patch of ground that is 10 ft from the base of the billboard,

1. What length of ladder is required for her to reach the bottom of the sign?
2. What length of ladder is required for her to reach the top of the sign?

If she uses the patch of ground that is 15 ft from the base of the billboard,

3. What length of ladder is required for her to reach the bottom of the sign?
4. What length of ladder is required for her to reach the top of the sign?

I. Understand the Problem

(a) Draw a diagram of the problem. In your opinion, is it better to make one diagram of all four problems, or several diagrams?

II. Devise a Plan

(b) Discuss a strategy for solving these problems.

III. Carry Out the Plan

(c) Execute your strategy and solve the problems.

(d) What is the difference in the length of ladder needed to reach the bottom of the sign if she places her ladder 10 ft from the base of the sign, versus placing it 15 ft from the base of the sign?

IV. Look Back

(e) In terms of the *physical* setup of the problem, is there anything that the painter should be aware of as she sets up her workspace? Explain.

Skill Level II

Problem

Suppose that on the second day of the project, the painter brings a ladder that is 25 ft in length.

1. If the patch of ground 10 ft from the base of the sign is used, at what point will the ladder touch the sign? Record your answer in two ways: first, indicate the length if measured from the ground; second, if measured from the bottom of the sign.
2. If the patch of ground 15 ft from the base of the sign is used, at what point will the ladder touch the sign? Again, record your answer measured from both the ground and the bottom of the sign.

Show your work.

Skill Level III ♦♦♦

One of the mathematical tools most widely used by astronomers is known as *parallax*. This tool is a method by which the distances between stars, galaxies, and other celestial bodies are estimated without having to leave the surface of the earth. This simple technique is based on the same trigonometric principles discussed in the Interlude on Trigonometry.

Problem

Execute the necessary research and explain the principles behind, and the uses of, the technique of parallax. Please be as detailed as possible in your discussion of both the theory and its uses.

Record your answer in the space provided.

Applied Math Skill Check

1. Find the hypotenuse of each of the following right triangles, given the lengths of the two legs.
   (a) $a = 3, b = 5$
   (b) $a = 10, b = 25$
   (c) $a = 5.2, b = 6.7$
2. Find the length of the missing leg of each of the following right triangles, given the length of the hypotenuse, c, and the length of the other leg, a.
   (a) $a = 6, c = 15$
   (b) $a = 4, c = 10$

ELECTRONICS APPLICATION PROJECTS

1 Ohm's Law
2 Wiring Resistors in Series and in Parallel
3 The Power Dissipated by a Resistor
4 Transformers
5 Capacitors in DC/AC Circuits
6 Working with Capacitors
7 Inductors
8 RLC Circuits
9 Semiconductors
10 Independent Electronics Research

Ohm's Law

For students of electronics, Ohm's Law is a fundamental mathematical equation that will be used on a regular basis. In this Electronics Project, we introduce Ohm's Law and use it to practice manipulating variables in mathematical equations.

Objectives

1. Use a variable to represent a physical quantity
2. In a given equation, insert numerical values for the variables
3. Solve for a single unknown in an equation

Tools Book CD: 2.6

Skill Level I 

Georg Ohm (1787–1854) German physicist who formulated a law relating voltage, current, and resistance. "Ohm's Law" is central to the study of electricity.

Courtesy of the Library of Congress

Electricity plays such an important role in our society that it is hard to imagine life without it. Amazingly, electricity and its everpresent companion, magnetism, is a very recent discovery considering the length of time that human beings have walked on the earth. Although we have evidence that the ancient Egyptians used lodcstoncs (a natural form of magnct), our modcrn undcrstanding of clcctricity and magnetism traces its roots to the work of such eighteenth- and nineteenth-century scientists as André Ampère and Georg Ohm. It was their thoughtful and creative experiments that led to our current understanding of electrical circuits and electronics.

At the heart of electricity and electronics is the concept of the *circuit.*

A ***circuit*** is a complete, closed path that allows electricity to flow. If there is a break in the path, there will be no flow of electricity.

This flow of electricity is usually referred to as *electric current*. Electrical current can be pictured in the same way that we picture the current in a stream. Just as a greater current in the stream implies that more water is passing by a certain point on the shore, more electrical current implies that more electricity is passing by a certain point in the circuit. Because of his major contributions to this field of study, electrical current is named for André Ampère. The unit of amperes is usually shortened to the simpler form of *amps*.

André Ampère (1775–1836) French physicist and mathematician who helped to lay the foundations of modern electromagnetic theory.

In the same way that some force, like gravity, must cause water to flow in the first place, something must cause the electricity to flow. All circuits have a battery or some other device that exerts a pressure that causes the current to flow. This electrical pressure is known as *voltage* after Alessandro Volta (1745–1827).

> ***Voltage,*** or voltage source, can be thought of as electrical pressure. It is this electrical pressure, or voltage, that causes the current to flow when the switch is closed in the circuit. Voltage is measured in volts.

However, the current flow that is caused by the voltage source does not appear without opposition. The amount of this opposition depends upon the type of material through which the current must flow. Some materials allow electricity to flow more readily than others. Those materials that allow for a large current flow are known as *conductors,* while those materials that inhibit flow are known as *insulators*. This opposition to current flow is known as *resistance* and is measured in ohms. This unit is usually expressed using the capital Greek letter omega: Ω.

Ohm's Law

Using the language of mathematics, it is possible to write a mathematical sentence that relates current, voltage, and resistance. This mathematical sentence takes the form of an *equation*. An equation is a mathematical statement that says, "Even though the left side of the equation and the right side of the equation may look different, they have the same value."

Using the language of equations, we can express the relationship between the three quantities in a circuit as:

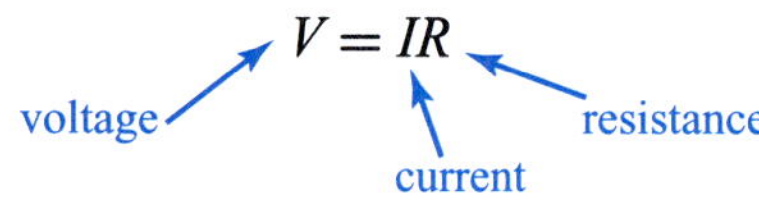

MATH REVIEW

Recall that even though no multiplication sign appears between the I and the R in the equation, their placement next to one another implies that they are to be multiplied.

This equation is commonly called "Ohm's Law." In words, Ohm's Law says:

"The voltage is equal to the current multiplied by the resistance."

Problem

Use Ohm's Law to find the amount of voltage required to cause 0.005 amps of current to flow through a 1 kΩ resistor.

MATH REVIEW

Remember that the letter k (representing the prefix "kilo-") represents a factor of 1000. Thus, a resistance of 1 kΩ is actually 1000 Ω.

(a) Read the problem statement carefully. Do you understand all of the terms used?

(b) Write Ohm's Law with the given values inserted into the equation.

(c) Execute the indicated multiplication and find the voltage required to generate the required current flow.

(d) Since both sides of an equation must be identical in terms of both the numbers and the units, use Ohm's Law to give an alternative set of units that could be used to designate voltage.

Skill Level II ♦♦

Problem

Use Ohm's Law to find the amount of current that would flow in a circuit that contains a 10 (V) source and a 4 kΩ resistor.

(e) Can this problem be solved in the same way as the problem in Skill Level I? Explain.

(f) Do the terms in Ohm's Law need to be manipulated to solve the problem? Explain.

(g) In your opinion, would it be simpler to manipulate Ohm's Law to solve for the unknown variable and then insert the given values, or to insert the given values and then manipulate the equation to solve for the unknown? Explain.

(h) Find the amount of current flow that would be generated by the given voltage source.

(i) Given that a lower case *m* (representing the prefix "milli-") is often used to represent a factor of 10^{-3}, express your answer from step (h) in milliamps (mA).

Skill Level III ♦♦♦

The conductance, σ, of an object is defined as the reciprocal of the object's resistance:

$$\sigma = \frac{1}{R}$$

Problem

Using Ohm's Law, express conductance in terms of current and voltage.

Show your work.

Applied Math Skill Check

Solve for y in each of the following equations.

1. $y = xz$ $\quad$ $x = 2$, and $z = 5$
2. $y = rt$ $\quad$ $r = 1.5$, and $t = 0.78$
3. $y = pc$ $\quad$ $p = 100$, and $c = \frac{1}{100}$
4. $y = xb$ $\quad$ $x = 2$, and $b = 0$

Solve for x in each of the following equations.

5. $y = xz$ $\quad$ $y = 10$, and $z = 2$
6. $t = rx$ $\quad$ $t = 50$, and $r = 5$
7. $v = px$ $\quad$ $v = 1.5$, and $p = 0.5$
8. $y = xs$ $\quad$ $y = 0$, and $s = 10$

MultiSim Project—Ohm's Law

The MultiSim software package can be used to find both voltage and current measurements in a circuit. In this project, you will draw a simple circuit, like the one discussed in this Electronics Project, and take both voltage and current measurements.

Hint

See Appendix B-1 for step-by-step instructions on using MultiSim to complete this project.

Problem

1. Use MultiSim to construct a working circuit that contains a 10 V source and a 4.7 kΩ resistor.
2. Use the MultiSim voltmeter to take a voltage measurement across the resistor. Your meter should read 10 V.

Wiring Resistors in Series and in Parallel

In the first Electronics Project, we were introduced to Ohm's Law and learned how to use it to solve the problem of a circuit with one resistor. In this project, we expand our understanding of electronics by confronting circuits that have more than one resistor. An examination of series and parallel wiring provides an opportunity to manipulate fractions in equations.

Objectives

1. Identify the basic parts of a fraction
2. Add fractions by finding a common denominator
3. Find the reciprocal of both sides of an equation
4. Insert numerical values into an equation and solve for a single unknown

Tools Book CD: R.2, 1.2, 2.1, 2.3A

Skill Level I ♦

Given a single voltage source, we may choose one of two ways in which to wire two resistors into a circuit. The two possible arrangements are:

1. wiring the resistors in series, or
2. wiring the resistors in parallel.

Series Wiring

When we say that two circuit elements (such as resistors) are wired in series, we mean that all of the electric current that passes through the first circuit element also passes through the second. An example of two resistors wired in series is given in Figure 2.1.

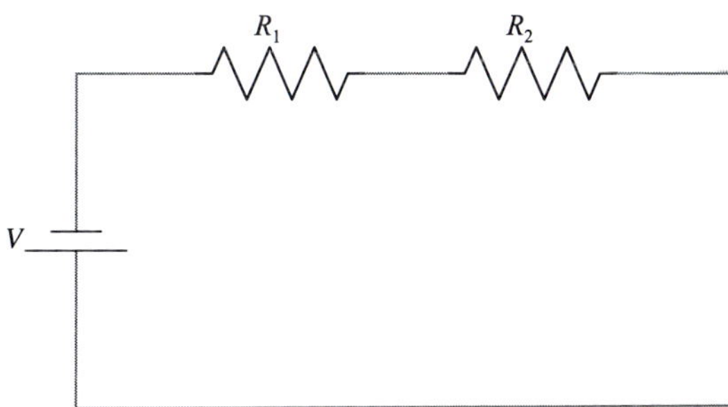

Figure 2.1

To find the total resistance of two resistors wired in series, we need only add the two resistances:

$$R_{\text{total}} = R_1 + R_2$$

Example 1

Find the total resistance of a series circuit that contains a $5\,\text{k}\Omega$ and a $7\,\text{k}\Omega$ resistor.

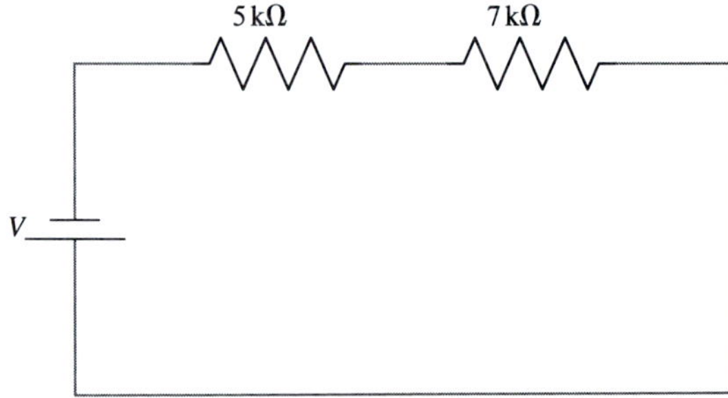

Figure 2.2

Solution

Because the resistors are wired in series, we simply add the two resistances to find the total resistance:

$$R_{\text{total}} = R_1 + R_2$$
$$R_{\text{total}} = 5\,\text{k}\Omega + 7\,\text{k}\Omega$$
$$R_{\text{total}} = 12\,\text{k}\Omega$$

Parallel Wiring

An alternate way to arrange two resistors is to place them such that the electric current may flow through one resistor or the other. The point at which the current (I) splits and becomes two currents (I_1 and I_2) is called a *junction* or a *node*. An example of two resistors wired in parallel is given in Figure 2.3.

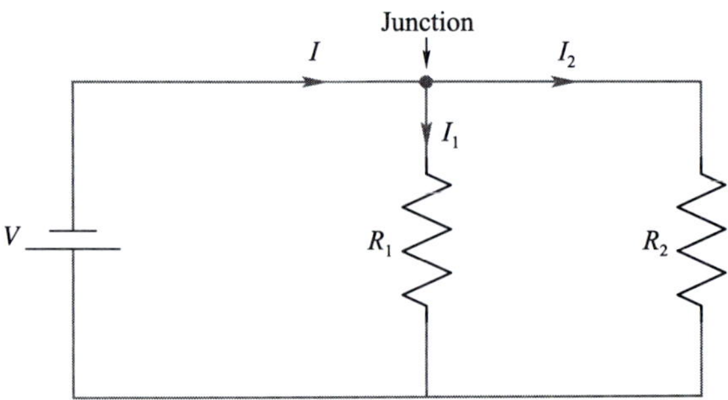

Figure 2.3

To find the total resistance of two resistors wired in parallel, we must use an equation slightly more difficult than that used when the resistors are wired in series:

$$\frac{1}{R_{\text{total}}} = \frac{1}{R_1} + \frac{1}{R_2}$$

Example 2

Find the total resistance of a parallel circuit that contains a 2 kΩ and a 3 kΩ resistor.

Solution

First, we insert the values of the two resistors into the equation for parallel resistors:

$$\frac{1}{R_{\text{total}}} = \frac{1}{R_1} + \frac{1}{R_2}$$

$$\frac{1}{R_{\text{total}}} = \frac{1}{2} + \frac{1}{3}$$

MATH REVIEW

Remember that when we express the fractions in a problem using a common denominator, we do not change the size of the fractions, only the manner in which they are expressed.

Because we need to add the two fractions on the right side of the equation, we must express each fraction using a common denominator. A common denominator of 6 can be found by multiplying the denominators of the two fractions. Expressing both fractions using this common denominator, the equation for the total resistance becomes

$$\frac{1}{R_{\text{total}}} = \frac{1}{2} + \frac{1}{3}$$

$$\frac{1}{R_{\text{total}}} = \frac{3}{6} + \frac{2}{6}$$

$$\frac{1}{R_{\text{total}}} = \frac{5}{6}$$

Notice that one more step of algebra is required to find R_{total} since it is contained in the denominator on the left side of the equation. Taking the reciprocal of both sides of the equation yields

$$\frac{1}{R_{\text{total}}} = \frac{5}{6}$$

$$R_{\text{total}} = \frac{6}{5}$$

$$R_{\text{total}} = 1.2$$

Finally, since both resistors in the circuit are expressed in *kilo*-ohms, the total resistance in the circuit is

$$R_{\text{total}} = 1.2\,\text{k}\Omega$$

Problem

Find the current flow in the following series circuit.

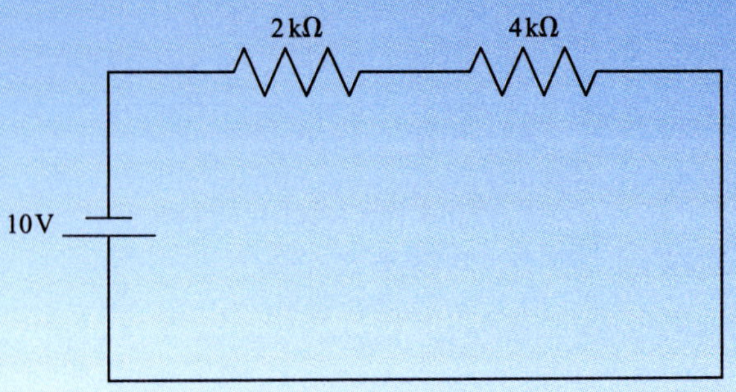

(a) What is the total resistance in the circuit?

Hint

It may be helpful to review Electronics Project 1, *Ohm's Law*.

(b) Using Ohm's Law, what is the total current flow in the circuit?

Problem

Find the total current flow in the following parallel circuit.

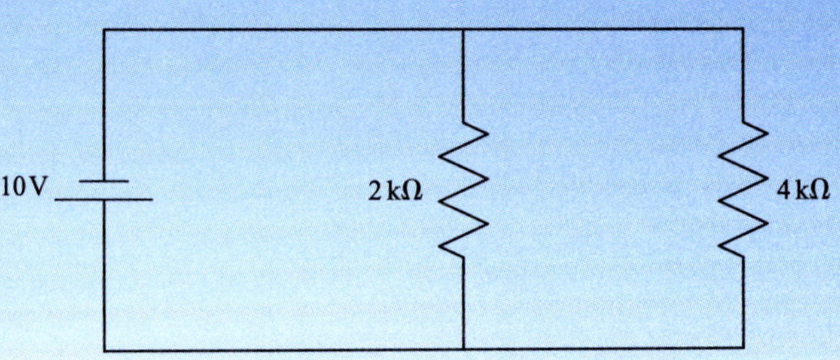

(c) What is the total resistance in the circuit?

(d) Using Ohm's Law, what is the total current flow in the circuit?

Skill Level II ♦♦

Series-Parallel Circuits

Circuits that contain a combination of both series and parallel wiring are called *series-parallel* circuits. An example of this type of circuit is given in Figure 2.4.

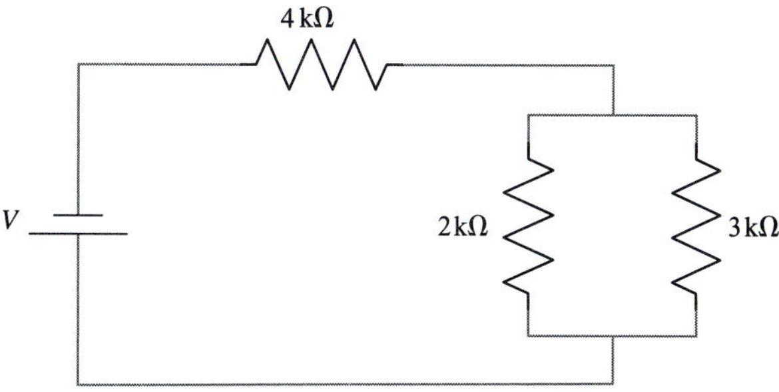

Figure 2.4

Notice that in this circuit the 4 kΩ resistor is wired in series with the parallel combination of the 2 kΩ and 3 kΩ resistors.

Example 3

Find the total resistance of the circuit in Figure 2.4.

Solution

First, we find the total resistance of the 2 kΩ and 3 kΩ resistors that are wired in parallel:

$$\frac{1}{R_{\text{total}}} = \frac{1}{2} + \frac{1}{3}$$

$$\frac{1}{R_{\text{total}}} = \frac{3}{6} + \frac{2}{6}$$

$$\frac{1}{R_{\text{total}}} = \frac{5}{6}$$

$$R_{\text{total}} = \frac{6}{5} = 1.2$$

Replacing the parallel combination with its equivalent resistance, the circuit becomes:

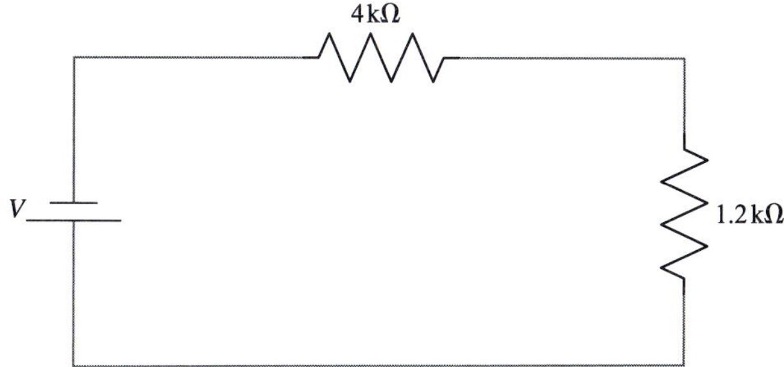

Figure 2.5

Since the combination is wired in series with the 4 kΩ resistor, we find that the total resistance in the circuit is

$$R_{\text{total}} = R_1 + R_2$$
$$R_{\text{total}} = 4\,\text{k}\Omega + 1.2\,\text{k}\Omega$$
$$R_{\text{total}} = 5.2\,\text{k}\Omega$$

Problem

Find the total current flow in the following series-parallel circuit.

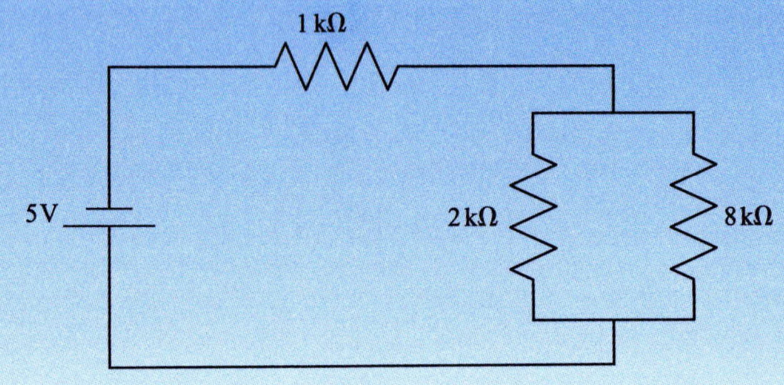

(e) What is the total resistance of the parallel resistors in the circuit?

(f) What is the total resistance in the circuit?

(g) Using Ohm's Law, what is the total current flow in the circuit?

Skill Level III ♦♦♦

Problem

Find the total current flow in the following series-parallel circuit.

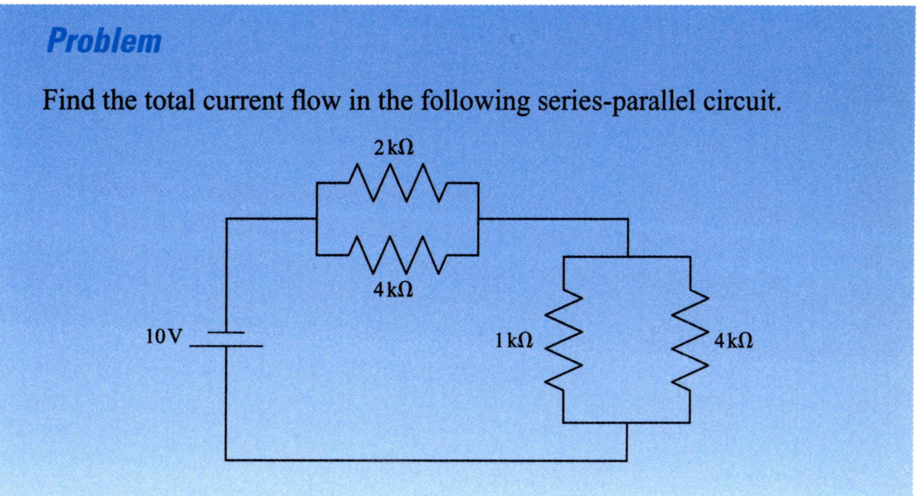

Show your work.

Applied Math Skill Check

Add or subtract the following fractions.

1. $\frac{2}{3} + \frac{4}{5} =$

2. $\frac{7}{8} - \frac{2}{3} =$

3. $\frac{1}{5} + \frac{1}{25} =$

Find y in each of the following equations.

4. $y = x + z$ $\quad$ $x = 2$, and $z = 7$

5. $y = u + v$ $\quad$ $u = 5.67$, and $v = 2.38$

6. $y = \frac{1}{x} + \frac{1}{z}$ $\quad$ $x = 2$, and $z = 5$

7. $y = \frac{2}{x} + \frac{3}{p}$ $\quad$ $x = 5$, and $p = 7$

8. $\frac{1}{y} = \frac{1}{x} + \frac{1}{z}$ $\quad$ $x = 3$, and $z = 5$

MultiSim Project—Wiring Resistors in Series and Parallel

HINT

See Appendix B-2 for step-by-step instructions on using MultiSim to work this project.

Problem

1. Use MultiSim to construct a series circuit that contains a 10 V source, a 3.3 kΩ resistor, and a 4.7 kΩ resistor. Using two multimeters, measure the voltage across each of the two resistors. If you add the readings from the two multimeters, you should get 10 V.
2. Construct a circuit with a 10 V source, and one 3.3 kΩ and one 4.7 kΩ resistor wired in parallel. Using two multimeters, measure the voltage across each of the two resistors. The readings on both meters should be 10 V.
3. Construct a circuit with a 10 V source, and a 4.7 kΩ resistor wired in series with the parallel combination of a 2.2 kΩ resistor and a 3.3 kΩ resistor. Using a single multimeter, measure the voltage across the combination of all three resistors. Your meter should read 10 V.

The Power Dissipated by a Resistor

In this Electronics Project, we use the power dissipated by a resistor as a setting to review the mathematical concepts of bases, exponents, order of operations, and substitution of variables.

Objectives

1. Identify the base and exponent in an expression and explain the relationship between them
2. In a given equation, substitute numerical values and solve for an unknown using the correct order of operations
3. Given two equations, substitute variables between the two equations

Tools Book CD: 4.1A, 8.2

In the first Electronics Project, we introduced the concepts of voltage, current, and resistance. These three concepts provide an essential foundation for the study of electronics and warrant a quick review:

FYI

For an introduction to voltage, current, and resistance, refer to Electronics Project 1, *Ohm's Law*.

Voltage is the quantity that causes electrical current to flow. It can be thought of as the electrical pressure in the circuit and is measured in units of volts.

Current is a measurement of the rate at which electricity flows through the circuit. It is analogous to the current flowing in a stream and is measured in units of amps.

Resistance measures how much opposition the electric current encounters as it flows through a type of material or device. Resistance is measured in ohms.

The goal of this electronics project is to use the physical results of this electrical current opposition, such as heat, energy loss, and power dissipation, to review several basic tools from algebra.

The Power Dissipated by a Resistor

Heat and Energy

James Joule was one of the first people to do experiments illustrating that heat and energy are the same thing. In other words, if you add heat to a physical system, you add energy to the system. Conversely, if you subtract heat from a system, you subtract energy from the system. This interplay between heat and energy has a direct impact on our discussion of resistors.

James Prescott Joule (1818–1889) was a British physicist who established experimentally that heat is a form of energy.
Courtesy of the Library of Congress

MATH REVIEW

To understand the bases and exponents used in the power equation, it may be helpful to review Thought Project 14, *Interlude: Bases and Exponents,* or your Tools Book CD.

Although there are other factors involved, the main source of a resistance is the friction caused inside the resistor as the electrical current attempts to pass through it. As anyone who has ever slid down a gym rope can tell you, *friction produces heat!* This heat generated inside the resistor is dissipated into the air (and other material) surrounding the resistor.

Power

Because the resistor gives off heat, it gives off energy. Consequently, the circuit loses energy because of the heat lost by the resistor. In electronics, we are often more interested in the *rate* at which the energy is being lost than the actual amount of energy lost. In other words, we often focus on the *power* dissipated by the resistor.

Power (measured in watts) is the rate at which the energy of a system is changing. In equation form:

$$\text{power} = \frac{\text{the change in the energy}}{\text{the change in the time}}$$

$$P = \frac{\Delta E}{\Delta t}$$

Using the definition of power, we can derive an equation that will allow us to find the amount of power dissipated by a resistor in terms of two familiar electronics quantities, current and resistance. Using these two electronics quantities, the power dissipated by a resistor can be found from the equation

$$P = I^2 R$$

Skill Level I 

Problem

Find the power dissipated by an 8.2 kΩ resistor if a current of 0.005 amps is passing through the resistor.

(a) Write the power equation using the given current and resistance in the problem statement.

(b) In your own words, write out the correct order of operations required to solve for the power dissipated by the resistor.

(c) Using your equation from step (a), find the power dissipated by the resistor.

(d) In the project, you were told that watts are the units attached to the physical quantity of power. Use your equation from step (a) to find an alternative set of units that can be used to measure power.

Substituting Variables

When working in the field, speed and efficiency are desirable qualities. Consequently, it is advantageous to use equations that are as simple as possible. If an equation can be found that allows for direct numerical substitution to find the required solution, the job can be completed more quickly. One way of constructing such a "plug and chug" equation is by substituting variables between equations.

For example, suppose that we are given the equations

$$ab = c \tag{1}$$

$$y = mb \tag{2}$$

and we want to express Equation (2) using only the variables m, a, and c. We can accomplish this objective by using Equation (1) and Equation (2) together.

First, we solve Equation (1) for the variable b:

$$ab = c$$

$$b = \frac{c}{a} \tag{3}$$

Since Equation (3) says that b is the same as $\frac{c}{a}$, we can retain the equality in Equation (2) by substituting $\frac{c}{a}$ for the variable b:

$$y = mb$$

$$y = m\frac{c}{a}$$

After making this substitution, we see that Equation (2) is expressed using only the variables m, a, and c.

Skill Level II ♦♦

Problem

Using the equation for the power dissipated by a resistor given in this Electronics Project, and Ohm's Law,

$$V = IR$$

find an expression for power that involves only current and voltage.

(e) Using the method of substitution of variables, find a solution to the problem statement.

(f) Using your solution, find an alternative set of units that could also be used to express power.

Skill Level III 

Problem

Using the power equation,

$$P = I^2R$$

Ohm's Law,

$$V = IR$$

and the method of substitution, find the following.

1. An expression for power that involves only voltage and resistance.
2. An expression for current that involves only power and voltage.
3. An expression for voltage that involves only power and resistance.

Show your work.

Applied Math Skill Check

Solve for y in each of the following equations.

1. $y = x^2 z$ $x = 2$, and $z = 3$
2. $y = x^2 z^3$ $x = 3$, and $z = 4$
3. $y = t^2 + c^4$ $t = 2$, and $c = 1$
4. Use the following two equations to construct an equation for y that involves only the variables a, b, and c.

$$y = cx$$

$$ax = b$$

5. Use the following equations to construct an equation for w that involves only the variables a and b.

$$xw = yt$$

$$\frac{x}{a} = b$$

$$a^3 y = b$$

$$a^2 = tb$$

MultiSim Project—The Power Dissipated by a Resistor

HINT

See Appendix B-3 for step-by-step instructions on using MultiSim to work this project.

Problem

1. Wire a resistor with a 12 V DC voltage source.
2. Use a multimeter to measure the voltage across the resistor and current flow through it.
3. Use these measured values, and the appropriate equations, to calculate the power dissipated by the resistor.

Transformers

In this Electronics Project, we use transformers as a setting to reinforce the mathematical concepts of fractions, equations, and variables.

Objective

Manipulate equations containing both fractional and variable expressions

Tools Book CD: 2.7D

In the first three Electronics Projects, we examined circuits that had a direct current. However, many circuits, such as those used in homes, have an alternating current in which the current switches direction with a set frequency. This current alternation gives rise to some interesting electronic effects and devices, one of which is the transformer.

Alternating Current and Power

Let's begin our study of alternating current and transformers by looking at the power generated by electric companies. Even though we are now concerned with alternating current, we can still express the power generated by the power plant as $P = IV$. However, in this situation, we must be careful to use average quantities.

In Electronics Project 3, we learned that the power dissipated by a resistor is given by $P = I^2R$. This equation continues to hold, even though we are now using an alternating current. Because the transmission lines that carry the power sent by the electric companies have resistance, power will be lost during the transmission process. These losses, which are dependent on the amount of current flow and the resistance of the transmission lines, are called *ohmic losses*.

Although some power loss is inevitable, the power equation $P = IV$ provides a way to minimize these losses. Because the power generated by the plants is equal to the current flow produced, multiplied by the voltage produced, we can make the current flow very small by making the voltage very large. Having a small current will result in small ohmic losses. A device that takes an existing voltage and either increases or decreases it is called a *transformer*.

NOTE

As we saw in Electronics Project 3, there are many ways to express equations. Using the power equation

$$P = I^2R$$

and Ohm's Law, we can arrive at the power equation

$$P = IV.$$

FYI

You will learn what it means to find the average value versus the *root mean square* (or rms) value of quantities in later coursework.

Transformers

To create a transformer, we take two sets of wire and wind them around an iron (or similar material) core, as in Figure 4.1.

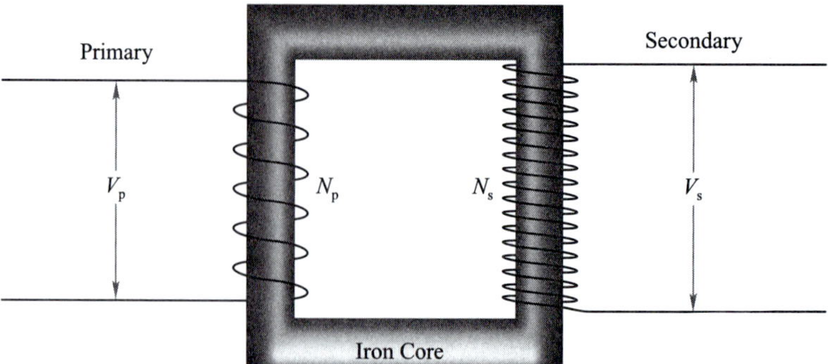

Figure 4.1

The left-hand side, called the *primary,* is the original voltage. The *secondary* is the new voltage that is created after the primary voltage is modified by the transformer. This secondary voltage is induced because of the alternating current in the primary. The alternating current in the primary causes an ever-changing magnetic field to appear inside the primary windings.

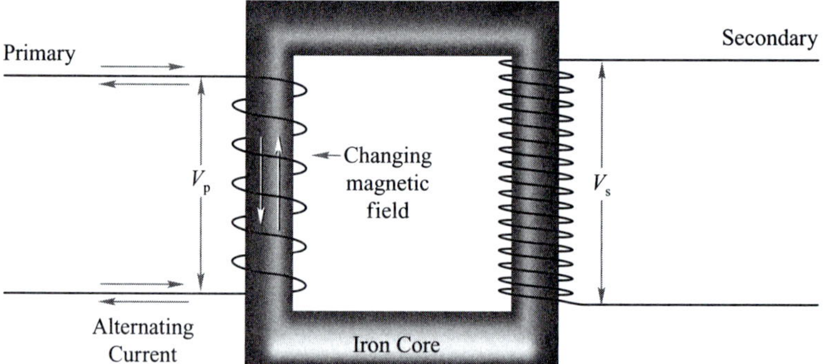

Figure 4.2

This changing magnetic field inside the primary windings causes the magnetic field to change throughout the iron core. Specifically, the changing magnetic field inside the secondary windings induces an alternating current in the secondary windings, as well as a secondary voltage.

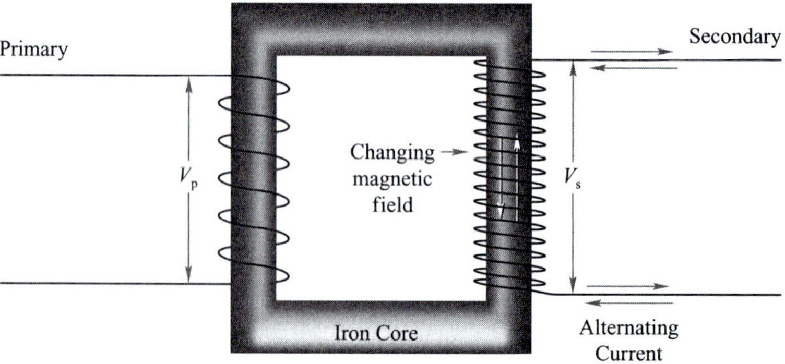

Figure 4.3

The primary voltage, the number of turns in the primary, the secondary voltage, and the number of turns in the secondary can all be related by the equation

$$\frac{V_{\mathrm{p}}}{V_{\mathrm{s}}} = \frac{N_{\mathrm{p}}}{N_{\mathrm{s}}} \tag{1}$$

Notice from the equation that if $N_{\mathrm{s}} > N_{\mathrm{p}}$, the new, secondary voltage will be larger than the original, primary voltage. Because the voltage has been increased, this is called a *step-up transformer*.

Conversely, if $N_{\mathrm{s}} < N_{\mathrm{p}}$, the secondary voltage is forced to be less than the primary voltage. This is known as a *step-down transformer*.

Skill Level I 

Problem

A transformer has 20 primary windings and 100 secondary windings. If the secondary voltage is 25 V, find the primary voltage.

(a) Write out Equation (1) using the values given in the problem statement.

(b) What mathematical operation must be performed on your equation to solve for the primary voltage?

(c) Solve your equation for the primary voltage.

(d) Is the transformer in the problem statement a step-up or a step-down transformer?

Skill Level II ♦♦

Problem

A transformer has 200 primary windings and 20 secondary windings. If the primary voltage is 10 V, find the secondary voltage.

(e) Write out Equation (1) using the given values from the problem statement.

(f) Write out, in words, the correct order of operations necessary to solve for the secondary voltage.

(g) Solve your equation for the secondary voltage.

(h) Is the transformer a step-up or a step-down transformer?

Skill Level III ♦♦♦

Problem

Use the following figure to find the number of secondary windings in the transformer.

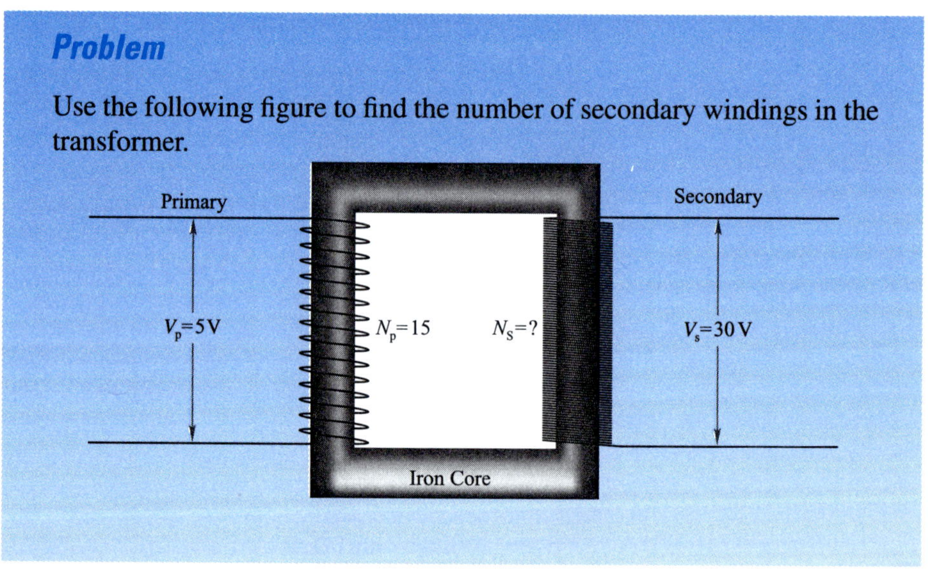

Show your work.

Applied Math Skill Check

Solve for x in each of the following equations.

1. $\frac{x}{4} = \frac{1}{2}$
2. $\frac{2}{3} = \frac{x}{12}$
3. $\frac{2}{x} = \frac{7}{4}$
4. $\frac{t}{y} = \frac{x}{w}$
5. $\frac{R}{x} = \frac{F}{T}$

Optional MultiSim Project—Transformers

HINT

See Appendix B-4 for step-by-step instructions on using MultiSim to work this project.

Problem

1. Construct a circuit that contains an alternating voltage source, a 1:10 step-up transformer, and an 8.2 Ω resistor.
2. Measure the voltage across the resistor. Using the voltage source given in Appendix B-4, your meter should read approximately 20 V.

Capacitors in DC/AC Circuits

One of the most important devices used in the field of electronics is the capacitor. Examining capacitors in both DC and AC circuits provides an ideal setting to review the mathematical concept of how to manipulate variables in equations.

Objectives

1. Use a variable to represent a physical quantity
2. Given an equation, insert numerical values for the variables
3. Solve for a single unknown in an equation
4. Use scientific notation

Tools Book CD: 2.6; 4.2C, D

The Capacitor

A typical capacitor is constructed by placing two conducting surfaces in close proximity to one another, as shown in Figure 5.1.

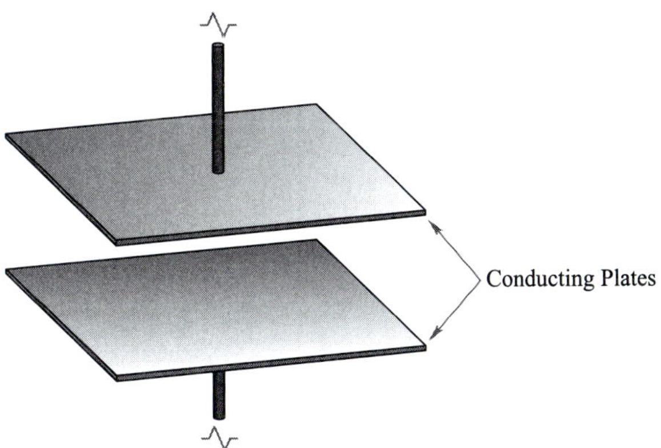

Figure 5.1

Although many different geometric configurations are used in the construction of capacitors, ranging from cylindrical to spherical, we will focus on the simplest arrangement, a parallel-plate capacitor.

When the two plates are connected to a source voltage, charges begin to accumulate on the plates of the capacitor:

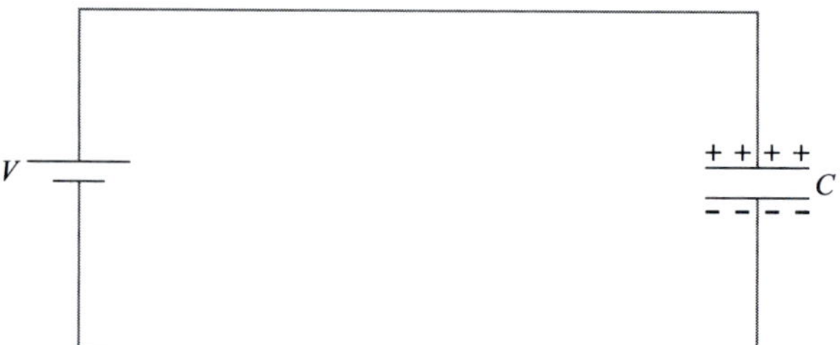

Figure 5.2

These charges cause a potential difference, or *voltage,* to appear across the plates, and an *electric field* to appear between the plates of the capacitor:

> **FYI**
>
> It should be noted that there are "fringing" effects of the electric field around the edges of the capacitor. For our purposes, it is sufficient to ignore these effects and to assume that all electric field lines point straight from the positive plate to the negative plate of the capacitor.

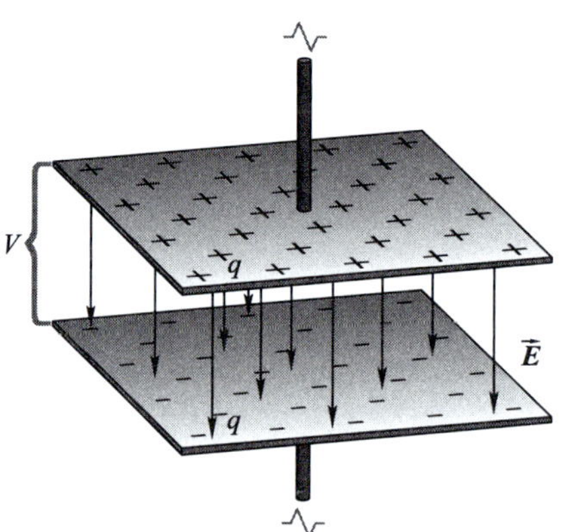

Figure 5.3

The amount of charge stored on the plates of the capacitor, q (measured in coulombs), the voltage across the capacitor, V (measured in volts), and the capacitance of the capacitor, C (measured in farads), are related by

$$C = \frac{q}{V} \tag{1}$$

Skill Level I ♦

Problem

A 5 μF capacitor has 5×10^{-4} coulombs of charge stored on its plates. Find the voltage across the capacitor.

(a) Rewrite Equation (1) substituting the information given in the problem statement.

(b) Solve your equation and find the voltage across the capacitor.

Capacitive Reactance

The electric field between the plates of the capacitor has an orientation that depends upon the polarity of the charges that are stored on the plates of the capacitor. Because electric fields point from positive to negative, we can have one of two possible configurations if the capacitor is wired to a DC source:

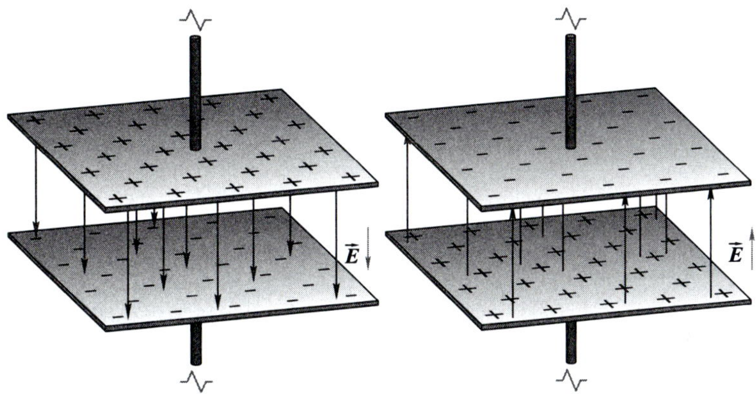

Figure 5.4

However, because the capacitor in the circuit may be connected to an alternating voltage source, it is possible for the polarity of the charges stored on the plates of the capacitor to change at the same frequency as the driving frequency of the source. Consequently, the electric field generated by the stored charges changes its polarity with a regular frequency.

Unfortunately, nature opposes changes in electric fields. This constantly changing electric field inside the capacitor, as well as the imbalance in the stored charge on the plates of the capacitor, produces a quantity known as *capacitive reactance* (X_C). This capacitive reactance acts to oppose the current flow. The capacitive reactance—which depends upon the frequency, f, of the alternating voltage and the size of the capacitor, C is found using the equation

$$X_C = \frac{1}{2\pi f C}$$

Skill Level II 

Problem

A capacitor of unknown capacitance is wired to an alternating voltage source with a frequency of 60 hertz. If the resulting capacitive reactance is 663 Ω, find the capacitance of the capacitor.

Show your work.

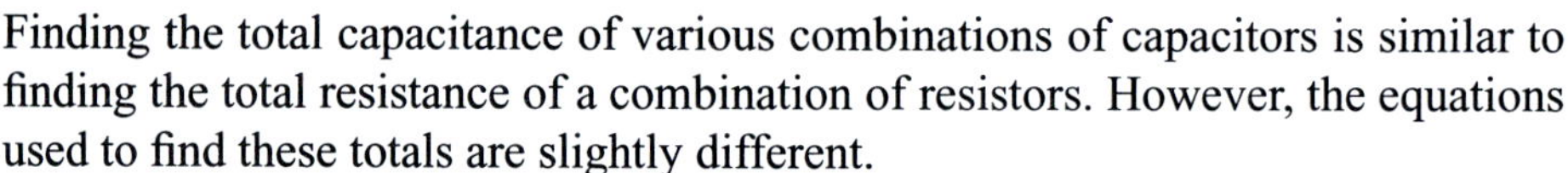

Finding the total capacitance of various combinations of capacitors is similar to finding the total resistance of a combination of resistors. However, the equations used to find these totals are slightly different.

Total capacitance of two capacitors wired in series:

$$\frac{1}{C_T} = \frac{1}{C_1} + \frac{1}{C_2}$$

Total capacitance of two capacitors wired in parallel:

$$C_T = C_1 + C_2$$

Problem

Given a 4 μF capacitor and a 6 μF capacitor, find

1. the total capacitance if the capacitors are wired in series;
2. the total capacitance if the capacitors are wired in parallel.

Show your work.

Applied Math Skill Check

Find x in each of the following equations.

1. $y = \frac{z}{x}$ — $y = 2$, and $z = 10$
2. $y = \frac{2}{3\pi xz}$ — $y = 4$, and $z = 5$
3. $\frac{1}{wzx} = \frac{2}{y}$ — $w = 4 \times 10^{-5}$, $y = 7 \times 10^{-6}$, and $z = \pi \times 10^{8}$
4. $\frac{1}{x} = \frac{1}{R} + \frac{1}{T}$ — $R = 2$, and $T = 7$
5. $\frac{1}{x} = \frac{1}{f} + \frac{1}{g}$ — $f = 3 \times 10^{3}$, and $g = 5 \times 10^{3}$

MultiSim Project—Capacitors in DC/AC Circuits

HINT

See Appendix B-5 for step-by-step instructions on using MultiSim to complete this project.

Problem

Use the Component Editing option in MultiSim to create a capacitor.

Working with Capacitors

In this Electronics Project, we explore the current flow in an RC circuit as a setting to review the mathematical concepts of exponentials and logarithms.

Objectives

1. Insert numerical values into a given exponential expression
2. Solve an exponential equation using logarithms
3. Use scientific notation

Tools Book CD: 11.3B; 11.6C, D

An *RC circuit* is a circuit that contains a resistor and a capacitor, as shown in Figure 6.1.

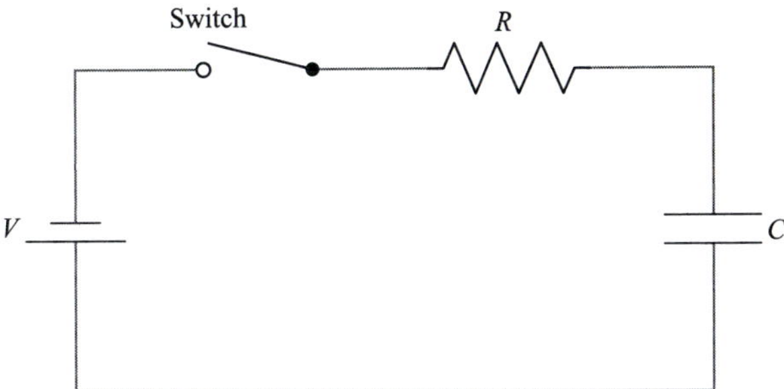

Figure 6.1

In this project, we discuss how the current in this type of circuit behaves once the switch is closed. We begin by reviewing the basic behavior of capacitors, and then introduce and use the exponential equation that is used to find the current flow in this type of circuit.

Capacitors

A *capacitor* is an electronic device that stores potential energy in a circuit. It is usually constructed by placing two conducting surfaces close to one another.

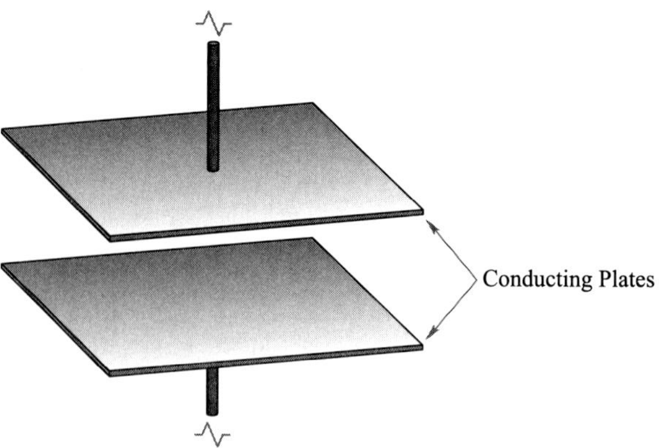

Figure 6.2

When the capacitor is wired with a voltage source, the flow of the current causes electrical charges to be stored on the plates of the capacitor. The result of the storage of charges is that an electric field is generated between the plates of the capacitor.

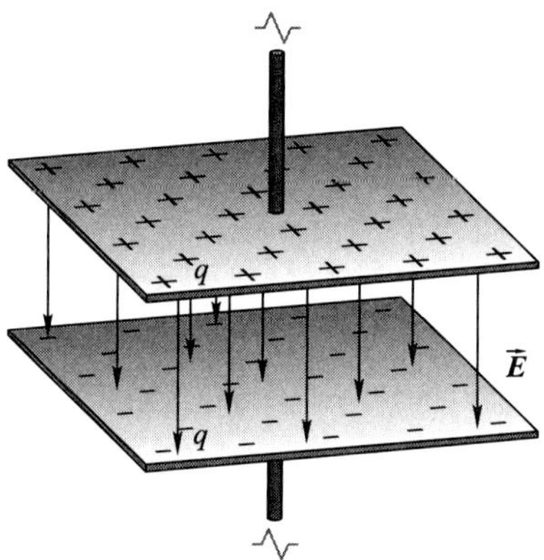

Figure 6.3

In addition, and more importantly for our purposes, a voltage appears across the plates of the capacitor.

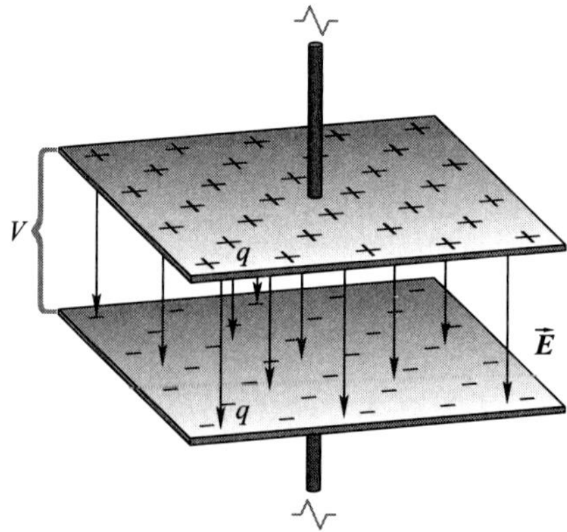

Figure 6.4

Unfortunately, the voltage that appears across the plates of the capacitor is opposite to the orientation (or *polarity*) of the source voltage. This opposing voltage caused by the charging capacitor fights the source voltage and causes the current flow to decrease. Consequently, the maximum current flow, I_{max}, will occur when the switch in the circuit is first closed and the capacitor has not yet begun to charge.

An interesting fact is that the current does not fall off in a linear fashion, but rather in an *exponential* one. The current flow at any time t after the switch in the circuit is closed is given in Equation (1):

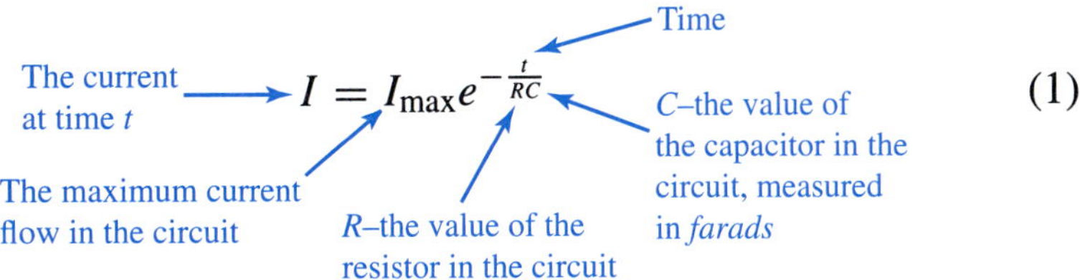

$$I = I_{max} e^{-\frac{t}{RC}} \quad (1)$$

Skill Level I ♦

Problem

If a circuit has a 3.9 kΩ resistor and a 5 μF capacitor, find the current flow in the circuit at 0.005 seconds, if the maximum current flow in the circuit is 1.5 mA.

(a) Express the given values of resistance, capacitance, and current flow using scientific notation instead of the prefixes k, μ, and m.

(b) Rewrite Equation (1) inserting the given values.

(c) Use words to explain the correct order of operations necessary to solve the equation that you wrote in step (b) for the current flow at 0.005 seconds.

(d) Solve your equation for the amount of current flowing at 0.005 seconds.

Skill Level II ♦♦

Using Logarithms to Solve Exponential Equations

To solve equations, it is often necessary to understand the relationship between mathematical operations and their inverses. For example, to solve the equation

$$x + 3 = 5$$

we subtract 3 from both sides of the equation because subtraction is the inverse operation of addition:

$$x + 3 = 5$$
$$x + 3 - 3 = 5 - 3$$
$$x = 2$$

Similarly, if we want to solve the equation

$$3t = 12$$

for the variable t, we must divide both sides of the equation by 3 because division is the inverse operation of multiplication:

$$3t = 12$$
$$\frac{3t}{3} = \frac{12}{3}$$
$$t = 4$$

It follows, then, that we can solve for the variable in exponential expressions such as

$$2^{x+1} = 16$$
$$5^{t-1} = 125$$
$$5 = e^{2x}$$

by performing the appropriate inverse mathematical operation. The formal name we give to this inverse mathematical operation is a *logarithm.*

MATH REVIEW

Before attempting the examples in this section, it may be helpful to review the relationship between logarithms and exponentials in your Tools Book CD.

Example 1

Solve for the variable x in the following equation.

$$2^{x+1} = 16$$

Solution

Because the variable of interest, x, is contained in an expression with a base of 2, we use 2 as the base of the logarithm that will "undo" the exponentiation. We perform this operation by taking the log, base 2, of both sides of the equation:

$$2^{x+1} = 16$$
$$\log_2(2^{x+1}) = \log_2 16$$
$$x + 1 = 4$$
$$x = 3$$

Example 2

Solve for the variable t in the following equation.

$$5^{t-1} = 125$$

Solution

As we did with Example 1, we note that the variable of interest, t, is contained in an expression with a base of 5. Therefore, we use 5 as the base of the logarithm used to solve for the variable of interest:

$$5^{t-1} = 125$$
$$\log_5(5^{t-1}) = \log_5(125)$$
$$t - 1 = 3$$
$$t = 4$$

Example 3

Solve for the variable x in the following equation.

$$5 = e^{2x}$$

Solution

In this example, we follow the same strategy as in the previous two. Because the variable x is contained in an expression with a base of e, we choose e as the base of the logarithm. However, in this case, we have two different choices as to which notation we use. If we follow the approach used in the previous two examples, we would use e as the base of the logarithm and write:

$$\log_e(5) = \log_e(e^{2x}) \tag{2}$$

However, because logarithms of base e are so important to our physical world, they are given a special name, *natural logarithms,* and notation, to indicate their importance:

$$\log_e = \ln$$

Using this notation, Equation (2) can be written as:

$$\ln(5) = \ln(e^{2x})$$

HINT

At this point, you should verify that you can find the natural log of 5 on your calculator.

Just as taking a log base 2 undoes exponentiation using a base of 2, taking the log base e (i.e., taking the natural log) undoes exponentiation using a base of e:

$$\ln(5) = \ln(e^{2x})$$
$$1.609 = 2x$$
$$0.8045 = x$$

Problem

An RC circuit contains a 3.9 kΩ resistor and a 5 μF capacitor. When the switch is first closed in the circuit, a maximum current of 1.5 mA flows in the circuit. Using Equation (1), find the time at which the current flow will have fallen to 1.0 mA.

(e) Rewrite Equation (1), inserting the values from the problem statement into the equation.

HINT

Remember that natural logs "undo" exponentials involving e.

(f) Write out, in words, the correct order of operations necessary to solve the equation that you wrote in step (e).

(g) Solve your equation for the time at which the current will have fallen to 1.0 mA.

Skill Level III

HINT

Remember that 75% of the maximum current I_{max} can be expressed as $0.75I_{max}$.

Problem

An RC circuit contains a 4.1 kΩ resistor and a 6 μF capacitor. Find the time, after the switch is closed, when the current will have fallen to 75% of its maximum value.

Show your work.

Applied Math Skill Check

Solve for y in each of the following exponential equations.

1. $y = 2^x$ $\quad x = 4$
2. $y = 5^{t-1}$ $\quad t = 3$
3. $y = 3^{x/t}$ $\quad x = 10$, and $t = 5$

Solve each of the following exponential equations using logarithms.

4. $2^{x+1} = 32$
5. $10^{3x-1} = 1000$
6. $e^{2x+1} = 1$

Using your calculator, find each of the following natural logarithms.

7. $\ln 2$
8. $\ln 4$
9. $\ln 1$
10. $\ln 0$

MultiSim Project—Working with Capacitors

HINT

See Appendix B-6 for step-by-step instructions on using MultiSim to work this project.

Problem

1. Construct an RC circuit using first a DC and then an AC voltage source, and measure the voltage across both the resistor and the capacitor in each case.
2. Compare these voltage measurements for the two sources.

Inductors

In this Electronics Project, we use inductors as a setting to review the mathematical concepts of variables, equations, bases, and exponents.

Objectives

1. Insert numerical values into an equation with several variables
2. Insert numerical values into an equation involving higher-order exponents
3. Solve higher-order equations for a single variable

Tools Book CD: 2.3A; 2.6A; 4.2C, D, 10.1A

The Inductor

An *inductor* is an electronic device that stores potential energy in the magnetic field produced by a current-carrying wire. As the current flows through the wire, a magnetic field is produced around the wire. The polarity of the magnetic field depends on the direction of the current flow.

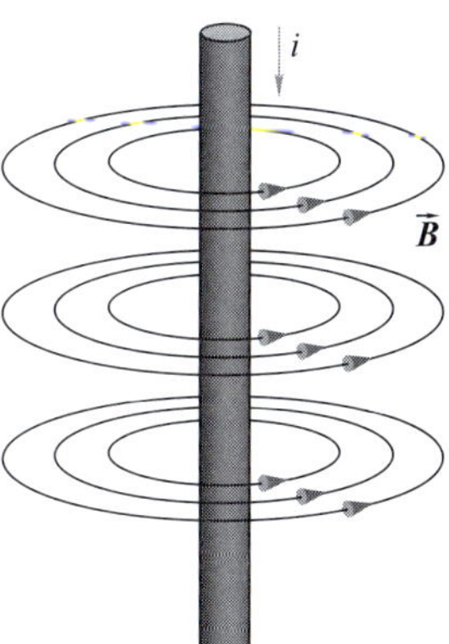

Figure 7.1

If the wire is wound into a coil, or *solenoid,* the magnetic field generated by the current flow takes on a new form. Because the magnetic field lines that surround the wire have a polarity, a cancellation occurs along the edge of the inductor between the windings. Where one wire has magnetic field lines that point outward, the wire immediately adjacent to it has magnetic field lines that point inward:

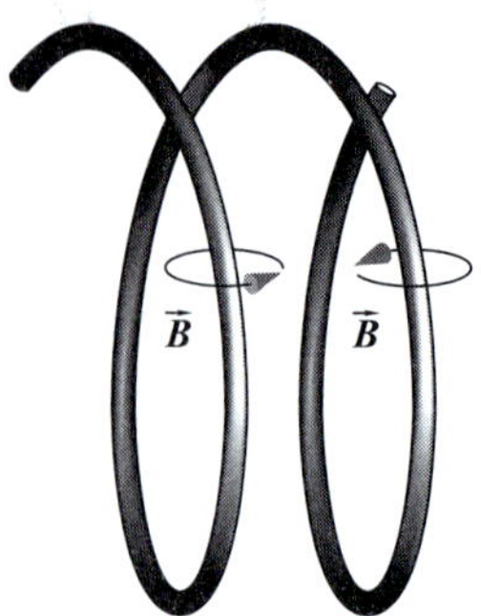

Figure 7.2

The net result is that the only appreciable surviving magnetic field points down the center of the inductor:

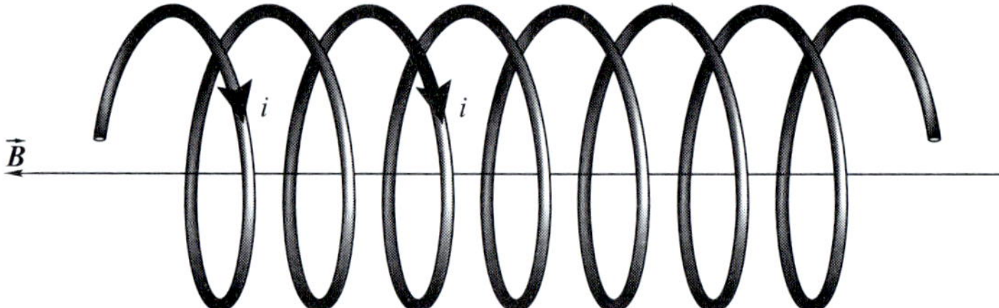

Figure 7.3

It is in this internal magnetic field that the potential energy is stored. To find the amount of stored potential energy, we use the equation

$$\mathrm{PE} = \frac{1}{2}Li^2 \tag{1}$$

where the current i is measured in amps, the inductance L is measured in henries (H), and the potential energy PE is measured in joules (J).

Skill Level I ♦

Problem

1. Solve Equation (1) for the variables L and I.
2. How much potential energy is stored in a 5 μH inductor that has a current of 2 mA flowing through it?

Show your work.

Inductive Reactance

If the inductor is wired to an alternating voltage source, the current flowing through it will alternate with a frequency determined by the source voltage. Consequently, the magnetic field generated by the current flow will also change with a regular frequency. As in the case of the capacitor, nature resists this change in magnetic field polarity. A quantity known as *inductive reactance* (X_L) opposes the current flow. The inductive reactance of an inductor, which depends upon both the size of the inductor and the frequency of the source voltage, is found using:

$$X_L = 2\pi fL$$

Skill Level II 

Problem

1. What alternating source voltage frequency is required to generate an inductive reactance of 10 Ω in a 4 mH inductor?
2. An unknown inductor is wired to a source voltage alternating with a frequency of 120 Hz. Find the inductive reactance of the inductor if there are 240 mA of current flowing through it and 1.44×10^{-4} joules of potential energy stored inside its magnetic field.

Show your work.

Skill Level III ♦♦♦

When two inductors are placed in proximity, they have an effect on one another. This phenomenon is called *mutual induction*.

HINT

It may be helpful to review Electronics Project 4, *Transformers* before beginning this Skill Level.

Problem

1. Execute the necessary research to find and explain the process of mutual induction.
2. Execute the necessary research to explain how the process of mutual induction is related to transformers.

Record your answer in the space provided.

Applied Math Skill Check

Find x in each of the following equations.

1. $y = 3\pi x$ $\qquad y = 6$
2. $y = \frac{1}{3}zx^2$ $\qquad y = 12$, and $z = 2$
3. $\frac{y}{x^2} = z^3$ $\qquad y = 4$, and $z = 2$
4. $y^2 = 0.5x^2z$ $\qquad y = 2.3 \times 10^4$, and $z = 4.7 \times 10^6$
5. $\frac{z^2}{x} = \frac{2}{3}y^4$ $\qquad y = \frac{1}{2}$, and $z = \frac{3}{4}$

MultiSim Project—Inductors

HINT

See Appendix B-7 for step-by-step instructions on using MultiSim to complete this project.

Problem

1. Construct a series circuit containing an alternating voltage source, a resistor, and an inductor.
2. Take voltage measurements across the resistor, the inductor, and the combination of these two circuit elements.

RLC Circuits

The topic of impedance in an RLC circuit is an interesting subject in electronics that serves as a platform for reviewing variables, equations, bases, exponents, and radicals.

Objectives

1. Insert numerical values into an equation with several variables
2. Insert numerical values into an equation involving higher-order exponents and radicals
3. Given a higher-order equation involving radicals, solve for a single variable

Tools Book CD: 9.6A, 10.1A

NOTE

In this Electronics Project, we combine several of the electronic devices discussed in previous projects. Consequently, it may be helpful to review Electronics Projects 1, 5, and 7 before beginning this project.

RLC Circuits and Impedance

An RLC circuit is a circuit that contains a resistor, an inductor, and a capacitor, normally wired to an AC voltage source:

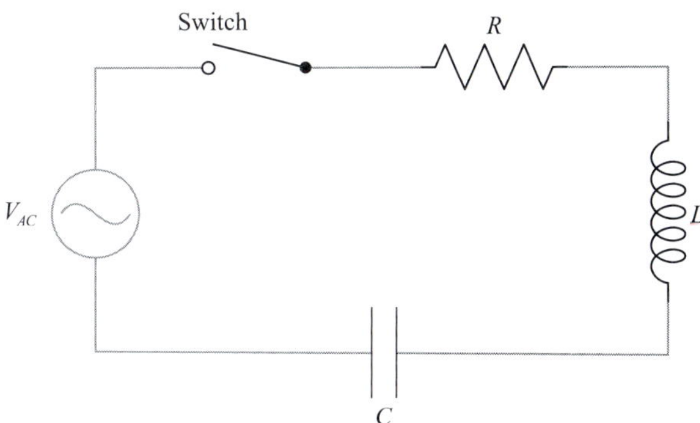

Figure 8.1

From previous Electronics Projects, we know that each of the components in the circuit opposes the current being driven by the AC voltage source. The resistance of the resistor, R, the inductive reactance of the inductor, X_L, and the capacitive reactance of the capacitor, X_C, combine to form a total opposition to the current flow. This total opposition is called *impedance,* and is represented by the variable Z.

To find the total impedance in an RLC circuit, we use the equation

$$Z = \sqrt{R^2 + (X_L - X_C)^2}$$

Skill Level I ♦

Problem

For the RLC circuit in the following figure, find:

1. X_L,
2. X_C,
3. the total impedance in the circuit.

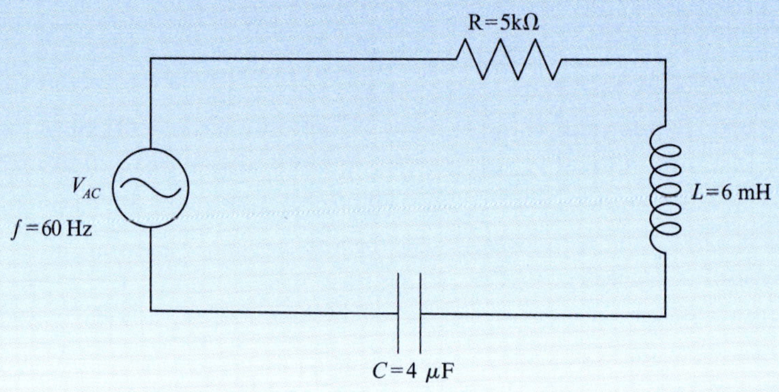

(a) Write out the equations used to find the inductive reactance and the capacitive reactance.

HINT

Capacitive reactance is discussed in Electronics Project 5, *Capacitors in DC/AC Circuits*.

Inductive reactance is discussed in Electronics Project 7, *Inductors*.

(b) Using your equations from step (a) and the values given in the circuit, find the values of the inductive and capacitive reactance in the circuit.

(c) Write out the impedance equation using your known values of resistance, inductive reactance, and capacitive reactance.

(d) Solve your equation from step (c) for the total impedance in the circuit.

(e) Since resistance, inductive reactance, and capacitive reactance are all measured in ohms, what does this imply about the units of impedance?

Skill Level II ♦♦

Problem

Solve the impedance equation

$$Z = \sqrt{R^2 + (X_L - X_C)^2}$$

for each of the following variables.

1. R
2. X_L
3. X_C

Show your work.

Skill Level III

The voltage in the circuit, the current, and the impedance can be related using an equation that is analogous to Ohm's Law from DC electronics. Ohm's Law relates the voltage in the circuit, the current flow in the circuit, and the opposition to current flow (resistance) using the equation

$$V = IR$$

The equation that relates the voltage, current flow, and opposition to current flow (impedance) in our RLC circuit takes the form

$$V = IZ$$

Problem

Find the current flow in the following RLC circuit.

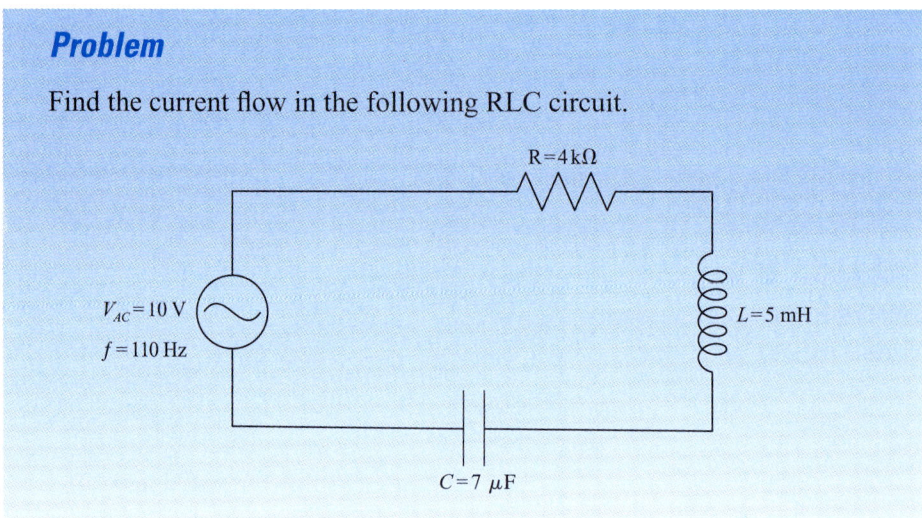

Show your work.

Applied Math Skill Check

Find x in each of the following.

1. $x = \sqrt{y^2 + z^2}$ $y = 6$, and $z = 8$
2. $y = \sqrt{x - z^2}$ $y = 4$, and $z = 3$
3. $c = \sqrt{g^2 + x^2}$ $c = 10$, and $g = 8$
4. $y = \sqrt{x + z^2}$
5. $y = \sqrt{w^2 + (x - z)^2}$

MultiSim Project—RLC Circuits

HINT

See Appendix B-8 for step-by-step instructions on using MultiSim to complete this project.

Problem

1. Construct a series RLC circuit that contains an AC voltage source.
2. Take measurements across each of the circuit elements, and the combination of all three circuit elements.

Semiconductors

In this Electronics Project, we use the topics of conductivity and semiconductors as a setting to review the basics of reading and constructing graphs.

Objectives

1. Construct a one-dimensional graph
2. Read and interpret data from a graph

Tools Book CD: 1.3; 3.2; 3.3C; 7.3A, B

In this Electronics Project, we will look at a different aspect of electronics—namely the *conductivity* of the material through which the current is flowing. After discussing this quantity, we will use it to define and analyze the behavior of both *p*- and *n*-type semiconductors.

Conductors, Semiconductors, and Insulators

The conductivity of a material is simply defined as a measurement of how easily electric current is able to flow through the material. Some materials allow for a large current flow while others do not. By looking briefly at the atomic structure of materials, we can learn some of the reasons for the high or low conductivity of a material.

When the atoms in a material bond together to make a solid, such as copper, silver, rubber, and so on, all of the electrons in the atoms may or may not be necessary for the bonding process. The electrons that are necessary for the bonding process are tightly bound to the atoms and exist at a lower energy level than the electrons that are unnecessary. These low energy electrons are called *valence band* electrons. The term *band* arises from the fact that if we graph the energies of these electrons, they fall within a very narrow range on the graph.

In direct contrast, the electrons that are not needed in the bonding process exist at a higher energy level than the valence band electrons. Once we close the switch in the circuit to provide a voltage, these high-energy electrons are free to move around. Because the number of these free electrons determines how well the material conducts electricity, they are referred to as *conduction band* electrons. Notice that the term "band" appears again. As with the valence band electrons, the energies of the conduction band electrons will fall into a narrow range on a graph.

We are now in the position to discuss whether a particular material is classified as an *insulator,* a *conductor,* or a *semiconductor*.

1. *Insulators* have a large energy gap between the valence band and the conduction band. Consequently, a great deal of energy is needed to cause a valence band electron to move in a solid. Therefore, few conduction electrons exist in the solid and it is difficult to get an appreciable current to flow in the solid.
2. In *conductors,* the electrons at the top of the valence band already have enough energy to move about in the solid if they are exposed to a voltage. A way to interpret this phenomenon visually is to think of an overlap between the conduction and valence bands of this material.
3. *Semiconductors* fall halfway between the other two types. There is still an energy gap between the valence band and the conduction band on the energy graph, but it is not nearly as large as it is in insulating materials. This means that because of temperature increases resulting from the operation of the circuit, some valence band electrons acquire the extra energy needed to jump up and become conduction band electrons.

Skill Level I ♦

Problem

Construct three one-axis graphs to summarize the information given regarding the valence and conduction band relationships in conductors, semiconductors, and insulators.

HINT

Place energy along the vertical axis of each of the three graphs.

(a) Draw your three graphs here.

(b) Review the types of graphs presented in the Tools Book CD, and determine if any of the other graphs would have offered a more efficient means of summarizing this information visually. Explain.

Skill Level II ♦♦

We have learned that the conductivity of a material is often directly related to the number of free, or valence, electrons in the material.

HINT

It may be helpful to begin this Skill Level by first finding the definition of the term *conductivity*.

Problem

1. Execute the necessary research to find the number of valence electrons, and the *conductivity,* for each of the following elements.
   (a) copper
   (b) silver
   (c) gold
   (d) silicon
   (e) gallium
   (f) arsenic
2. Graph the element, the number of valence electrons and the conductivity of each of these elements.

Show your graphs here.

Doping

The conductivity of a semiconducting material, such as silicon, can be increased by adding small amounts of another element to the material. This process is called *doping*. The electronic behavior of the doped semiconductor is determined by the type of doping element that is used. For example, if an element with five valence electrons, such as arsenic, is introduced into silicon, the doped semiconductor gains more mobile *negative* electric charges that are free to move through the solid. This doped semiconductor is referred to as an n-*type semiconductor* (where "*n*" stands for "negative").

Conversely, if silicon is doped with an element that contains three valence electrons, such as gallium, the doped semiconductor gains more mobile *positive* electric charges that are free to move through the solid. In this case, the semiconductor is referred to as a p-*type semiconductor* (where "*p*" stands for "positive").

Interestingly, the energies of these two types of added mobile charges are not identical. The energies of the mobile negative charges in an *n*-type semiconductor lie slightly below the conduction band, whereas the energies of the mobile positive charges in a *p*-type semiconductor are slightly above the valence band.

Skill Level III 

Problem

1. Construct a one-dimensional (one-axis) graph representing the energies of the valence band, the energies of the conduction band, and the additional negative charges in an *n*-type semiconductor.
2. Construct a one-dimensional (one-axis) graph representing the energies of the valence band, the energies of the conduction band, and the additional positive charges in a *p*-type semiconductor.

Draw your graphs in the space provided.

Applied Math Skill Check

1. Using the following graph, find the value of y associated with each of the values of x in the table.

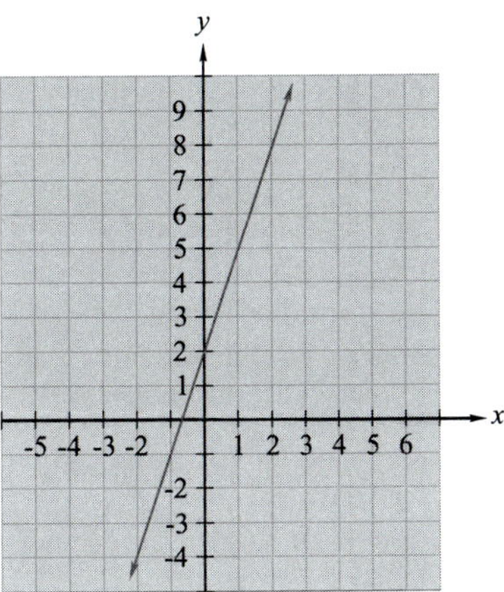

x	y
1	
2	
0	
−1	
−2	

2. If a line is horizontal, what statement can be made about the vertical coordinate of each of the points on the line?

3. If a line is vertical, what statement can be made about the horizontal coordinate of each of the points on the line?

4. In terms of the horizontal coordinate, what statement can be made about the point at which a function intersects the vertical axis on a graph?

5. In terms of the vertical coordinate, what statement can be made about the point at which a function intersects the horizontal axis on a graph?

MultiSim Project—Semiconductors

HINT

See Appendix B-9 for step-by-step instructions on using MultiSim to work this project.

Problem

1. Wire a *pn*-junction diode with a 1 kΩ resistor and an AC voltage source.
2. Use an oscilloscope to measure the voltage across the resistor.
3. Insert a 10 μF capacitor in parallel with the resistor to filter the signal.

Independent Electronics Research

In this Electronics Project, we engage in independent research to acquire an elementary understanding of some of the most important concepts in the field of electronics.

Objective

Complete independent research to describe some of the most important terms and concepts relating to the electronics field

Tools Book CD: No Coverage

One of the factors that determines whether a technician is successful in today's technological workplace is his/her ability and willingness to learn new concepts without the aid of an instructor or trainer. In an educational setting, it is impossible to acquaint a student with every possible circuit configuration and electronics application. Because the technology field changes so rapidly, today's technician must be willing to read journals, textbooks, and so on, to stay abreast of changing terminology, new technology, and myriad other pieces of information. In the workforce, one cannot rely on peers to teach the new developments in the field—self-reliance is required.

In this project, you are challenged to do the independent research necessary to acquaint yourself with a variety of electronics terms and devices, without the aid of an instructor's lecture. In addition to illustrating the necessity of such independent research, this project provides a setting in which you will acquire an introduction to several of the electronic devices and concepts you will be studying at ITT Technical Institute.

The Skill Levels for this project are determined by the number of terms correctly defined.

Skill Level I ♦	15 terms
Skill Level II ♦♦	20 terms
Skill Level III ♦♦♦	25 terms

Problem

Find and write out *in your own words* an explanation for each of the following electronics terms and devices. If it is an electronic device, include the standard way(s) of drawing the circuit element in a schematic. For those terms that are electronic quantities, be sure to include the units on the quantity, and the variable that is used to represent it.

1. Resistor
2. Current
3. Voltage
4. Electric charge
5. Capacitor
6. Switch
7. Inductor
8. Transformer
9. Direct current
10. Alternating current
11. Inductive reactance
12. Capacitive reactance
13. Impedance
14. Conductor
15. Insulator
16. Semiconductor
17. Power
18. *pn*-junction
19. Depletion layer
20. Transistor
21. Operational amplifier
22. Differential amplifier
23. Thevenin's Theorem
24. Kirchhoff's Voltage Law
25. Kirchhoff's Current Law

MultiSim Project—Independent Electronics Research

HINT

See Appendix B-10 for step-by-step instructions on creating these schematic symbols in MultiSim, and then inserting the symbols into a Microsoft Word document.

Problem

1. Draw the schematic symbol (if one exists) for each of the terms and devices you are researching in this Electronics Project.
2. Insert each schematic symbol into a Word document, in which you define each term or describe each device.

(*Note:* Not all of the terms in the project will have schematic symbols.)

DRAFTING/DESIGN APPLICATION PROJECTS

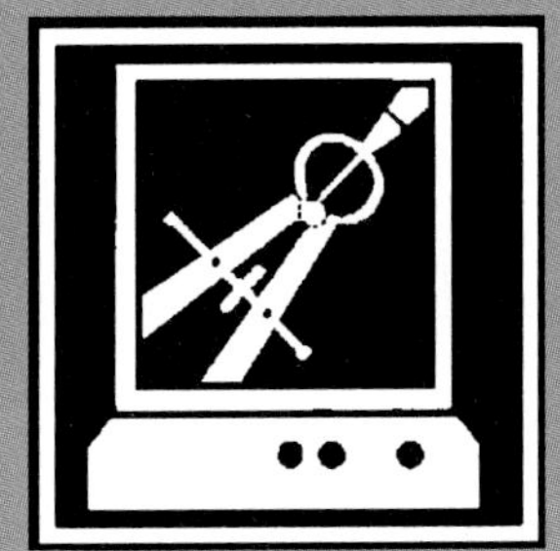

Columns and Beams

Columns and beams are basic components of many architectural designs. To incorporate them correctly into a blueprint, a designer must be able to calculate the size of each element and the type of material from which it should be constructed. The topic of columns and beams provides a context to review various concepts from geometry and algebra.

Objectives

1. Use a variable to represent a physical quantity
2. Given an equation, insert numerical values for the variables
3. Solve for a single unknown in an equation
4. Find the volume of a simple geometric figure

Tools Book CD: A.5, 2.6

Frank Lloyd Wright's Johnson Wax Building (1936)
Columns have intrigued architects from the ancient Greeks to masters of the twentieth century like Frank Lloyd Wright.
Courtesy of S.C. Johnson & Son, Inc.

The Volume of a Column or Beam

Regardless of whether we are working with a vertical column or a horizontal beam, the volume of each structural element is found by means of a geometric formula. For example, the equation for the volume of a cubic shape (horizontal or vertical) is

$$V_{\text{cube}} = lwh$$

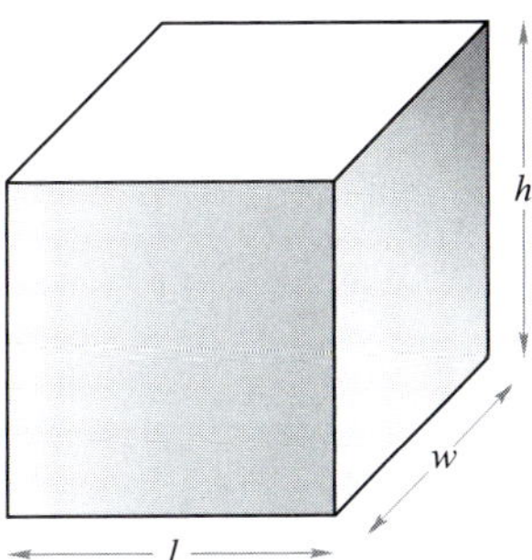

Figure 1.1

and the equation for the volume of a cylindrical column or beam is

$$V_{\text{cyl}} = \pi r^2 h$$

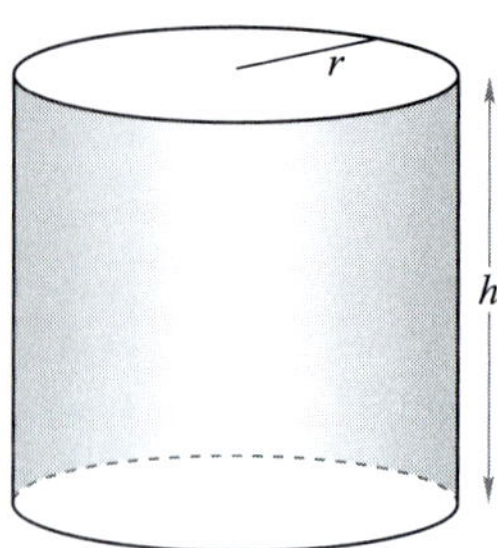

Figure 1.2

Skill Level I ♦

HINT

You will need to use the equation for the volume of a cube to carry out this Skill Level.

Problem

The beam in the following figure has a total volume of 60 ft^3. Find the maximum horizontal gap that the beam can span.

Show your work.

Skill Level II ♦♦

Problem

You are designing a new building and need to compare the amount of structural steel required to construct a beam and a support column. Which would require more steel, a cubical beam with a length of 25 ft, a width of 2 ft, and a height of 3 ft, or a cylindrical column with a height of 10 ft, and a radius of 2 ft?

Show your work.

Skill Level III ♦♦♦

Compressional Stress

The *compressional stress* on a material is defined as the ratio of the downward force (weight) exerted on the column to the cross-sectional area of the column:

$$\text{Stress} = \frac{F}{A}$$

Common sense and experience tell us that some materials are stronger than others, that is, they can tolerate greater amounts of compressional stress before they break. A sample of the maximum compressional stresses for a few materials is given in the following table.

FYI

In this Drafting/Design Project, the compressional strength is measured in the metric units of force (newtons) and area (square meters).

Material	Compressional strength (N/m^2)
Steel	500×10^6
Aluminum	200×10^6
Concrete	20×10^6
Wood (parallel to grain)	40×10^6

Problem

A concrete column has a volume of 565 m^3, and a height of 20 m. What is the maximum weight (expressed in newtons) that the column can tolerate before fracturing?

Show your work.

Applied Math Skill Check

Solve for y in each of the following equations.

1. $y = xz$ $\quad$ $x = 2$, and $z = 5$
2. $y = rt$ $\quad$ $r = 1.5$, and $t = 0.78$
3. $y = p^2c$ $\quad$ $p = 100$, and $c = \frac{1}{100}$
4. $y = xb^3$ $\quad$ $x = 2, b = 0$

Solve for y in each of the following equations.

5. $y = \frac{x}{z}$ $\quad$ $x = 10$, and $z = 2$
6. $y^2 = \frac{t}{g}$ $\quad$ $t = 24.6$, and $g = 8.2$
7. $x = \frac{y}{z^2}$ $\quad$ $x = 4$, and $z = 5$
8. $\frac{y}{p^3} = w^2$ $\quad$ $w = 4.6$, and $p = 2.1$

AutoCAD Project—Columns and Beams

Hint

See Appendix C-1 for step-by step instructions on using AutoCAD to complete this project.

Problem

1. Draw a column using AutoCAD.
2. View it three-dimensionally.

Two- and Three-Dimensional Visualization

Creating objects on a computer in two and three dimensions provides a setting to explore several geometric forms and equations.

Objectives

1. Insert numerical values into a geometric formula
2. Given a geometric formula, solve for a single variable
3. Visualize geometric shapes in two and three dimensions

Tools Book CD: A.4, A.5

When creating a design on the computer, it is important to be able to envision what the design will look like from a variety of angles. In this project, we discuss the relationship between two- and three-dimensional shapes. Specifically, we focus on the two-dimensional projections of three-dimensional shapes, and on the three-dimensional shapes that can be created from the extension of various two-dimensional shapes.

Extending a Two-Dimensional Shape to Three Dimensions

A three-dimensional shape can be created from a two-dimensional shape by continuously translating the two-dimensional shape along a particular axis. For example, if we take a square and translate it along the x-axis, we generate the following cubic shape:

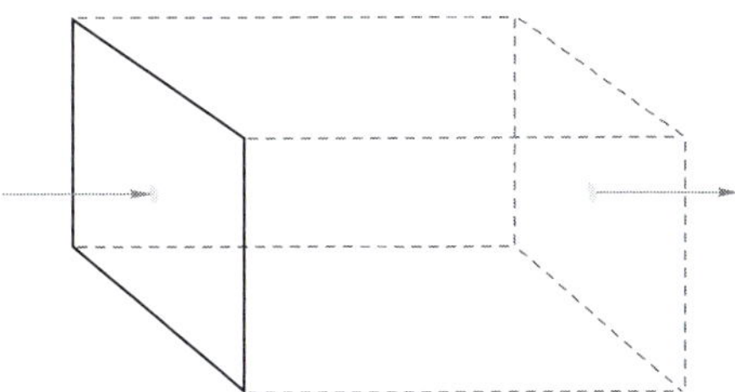

Figure 2.1

Skill Level I ♦

Problem

A circle with a radius of 6 in. is moved vertically 10 in. along an axis drawn through its center, as shown in the following Figure.

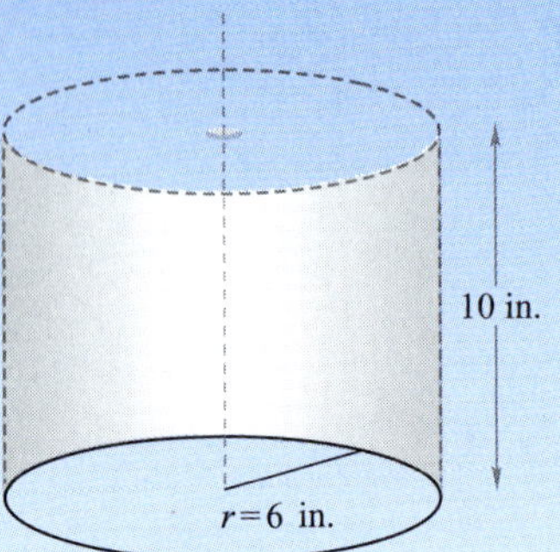

Find the volume of the three-dimensional figure that is generated.

(a) What type of three-dimensional figure is generated in the problem?

(b) What is the equation that is used to find the volume of this type of geometric figure?

(c) Use your equation from step (b) and the information given in the problem to find the volume of the three-dimensional figure.

(d) Since your equation contains three length measurements that are multiplied, what are the correct units for your volume measurement?

(e) Find the area of the circle used to generate the three-dimensional figure in the problem statement. Be sure to attach the correct units to your area calculation.

Skill Level II ◆◆

Two-Dimensional Projections of a Three-Dimensional Shape

When a three-dimensional shape is viewed from one side, we see only a two-dimensional shape. For example, if we view a cube from one side, we see a square. Similarly, the two-dimensional projection of a sphere is a circle.

Problem

Looking straight down along the vertical axis of the right circular cone in the following figure, find the area of the two-dimensional shape that is seen.

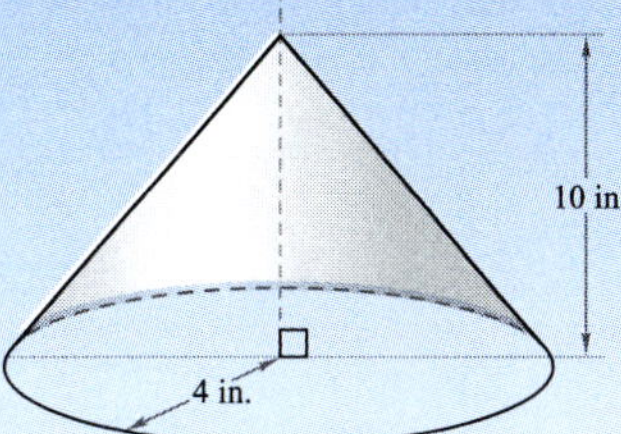

Show your work.

Skill Level III 

Problem

Conic Sections are the set of curves that can be generated by intersecting a plane with a cone. Describe the curve (conic section) that is generated if the plane intersects the cone in each of the following ways.

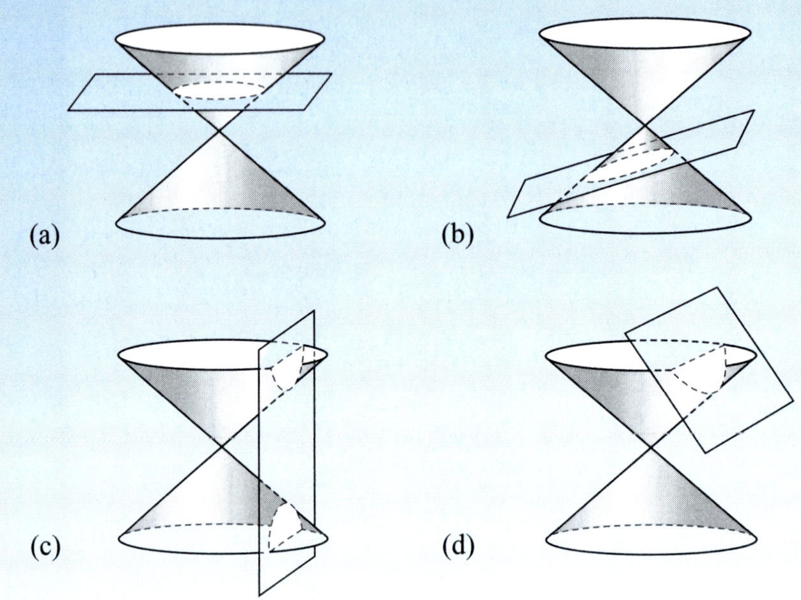

Write your answers in the space provided.

Applied Math Skill Check

Find the area of each of the following figures.

1. A circle of radius 3 in.
2. A square that is 5 cm on each side.
3. A triangle with a base of 3 m and a height of 5 m.

Find the volume of each of the following figures.

4. A sphere of radius 5 ft.
5. A cube that is 6 in. on each side.
6. A cylinder with a radius of 3 cm and a height of 10 cm.
7. A right circular cone with a base radius of 3 ft and a height of 9 ft.

AutoCAD Project—Two- and Three-Dimensional Visualization

HINT

See Appendix C-2 for step-by-step instructions on using AutoCAD to complete this project.

Problem

1. Use AutoCAD to draw a right circular cone.
2. Use the 3D Orbit command to rotate the cone and view its various faces.

Thermal Expansions of Materials

In this project, we explore the effects of heat on structural analysis. When structural designers plan buildings, they must take into account the thermal expansions of materials. This topic also provides a setting to review equations, variables, and scientific notation.

Objectives

1. Insert numerical values into a given equation
2. Given a first-order equation, solve for a given variable
3. Use scientific notation to express very large or very small numbers
4. Find the volume of a figure

Tools Book CD: 2.6; 4.2C, D; A.5

In this project, we explore the effects of heat on structural analysis. As we will see, to build stable structures it is necessary for structural designers to take into account this important physical effect.

One-Dimensional Expansions

When the temperature of an object increases or decreases, the length of the object changes. This phenomenon occurs because the length of an object is related to the amount of vibration of the atoms and molecules that compose it. Because heat and energy are actually the same thing, it is clear that if we raise the temperature of an object we increase the amount of energy inside it. With increased energy comes greater oscillation of the atoms and molecules and the object expands in length. Conversely, if we decrease the temperature of an object, the object will shrink because of the decreased amount of atomic vibration.

The amount of change in the length of an object is found using the equation

$$\Delta L = L_0 \alpha \Delta T \tag{1}$$

where

- ΔL is the change in the length of the object,
- L_0 is the original length of the object before the temperature change,

- α is the coefficient of linear expansion of the material composing the object, and
- ΔT is the change in the temperature of the object.

Notice that because the original length, L_0, and the change in the length, ΔL, are measured in the same units, the units on the coefficient of linear expansion and the change in the temperature cancel one another. Thus, if the change in the temperature is recorded in °C, the units on the coefficient of linear expansion must be recorded in $\frac{1}{°C}$.

Equation (1) is used only to find the *change* in the length of the object. To find the new length of the object after the change in temperature, we must add the change to the original length if the material has increased in temperature ($\Delta T > 0$):

$$L_{\text{New}} = L_0 + \Delta L$$

or subtract the change if the material has decreased in temperature ($\Delta T < 0$):

$$L_{\text{New}} = L_0 - \Delta L$$

Skill Level I ♦

Problem

Using the data in the following table, identify which would experience a greater change in length, an aluminum rod of length 4 m that is raised from 5°C to 40°C, or an iron rod of original length 3.5 m that is raised from 10°C to 35°C.

Values of Linear Expansion Coefficients (α) for Selected Materials at 20°C

Material	Coefficient of linear expansion ($\frac{1}{°C}$)
Aluminum	24×10^{-6}
Brass	19×10^{-6}
Brick or concrete	12×10^{-6}
Copper	17×10^{-6}
Glass, window	9.0×10^{-6}
Glass, pyrex	3.3×10^{-6}
Gold	14×10^{-6}
Ice	52×10^{-6}
Iron or steel	12×10^{-6}

(a) Rewrite Equation (1) for each rod, inserting the pertinent information from the problem statement and the table of coefficients of linear expansion.

(b) Execute the multiplications indicated in your equations and solve for the change in the length of each rod.

(c) Which rod experiences the greater change in length?

(d) What are the units of the change in the length for each rod?

(e) If the aluminum rod started with a length of 4 m at 40°C and dropped to 5°C, what effect would you expect this temperature change to have on the length of the rod?

Skill Level II 

Three-Dimensional Expansions

The idea of an object changing size because of a change in its temperature can be extended to three dimensions. In this case, it is the *volume* of the object that changes, rather than its length.

The equation used to find the change in the volume of an object is similar to the linear expansion equation, and is given by

> **HINT**
>
> The volume of a sphere is
>
> $$V = \frac{4}{3}\pi r^3$$
>
> The volume of a cylinder is
>
> $$V = \pi r^2 h$$

$$\Delta V = V_0 \beta \Delta T \qquad (2)$$

where

- ΔV is the change in the volume of the object,
- V_0 is the original volume of the object,
- β is the coefficient of volumetric expansion of the material, and
- ΔT is the change in the temperature of the object.

As with the coefficient of linear expansion, the units on the coefficient of volumetric expansion are $\frac{1}{°C}$.

HINT

The coefficient of volumetric expansion for aluminum is $72 \times 10^{-6} \frac{1}{°C}$ and for copper is $21 \times 10^{-6} \frac{1}{°C}$.

Problem

Which would experience a greater change in volume, an aluminum sphere with a radius of 0.4 m at 2°C that is raised to 45°C, or a copper cylinder of radius 0.2 m and height 3 m at 14°C that is raised to 35°C.

Show your work.

Skill Level III 

The Relationship Between One-Dimensional and Three-Dimensional Expansions

As we might expect, there is a relationship between the two types of expansions discussed previously in this project. Because a three-dimensional object grows along all three axes during an expansion, we can think of a three-dimensional expansion as being three one-dimensional expansions that occur simultaneously. Consequently, we can express the relationship between the coefficient of linear expansion, α, and the coefficient of volumetric expansion, β, as:

$$\beta = 3\alpha$$

Problem

A rod of length 5 m at 6°C grows to 5.006 m when the temperature is raised to 48°C. Find the coefficient of *volumetric* expansion of the unknown material composing the rod.

Show your work.

Applied Math Skill Check

1. Solve for x.

   $x = rgt$ $\qquad$ $r = 2, g = 5, t = 14$

2. Solve for y.

   $y = 2wxz$ $\qquad$ $w = 4 \times 10^8, x = 3.1 \times 10^{-5}, z = 1.8 \times 10^{-2}$

3. Solve for x.

   $\Omega = 8x\Delta R$ $\qquad$ $\Omega = 4$, and $\Delta R = 10$

4. What value of x must be inserted into the following equation so that y has a value of 5?

   $y = 2x$

5. What must x be so that the difference between y and z is 2.5?

   $y - z = 10x$

AutoCAD Project—Thermal Expansions

HINT

See Appendix C-3 for step-by-step instructions on using AutoCAD to complete this project.

Problem

1. Draw a cube and a cylinder.
2. Attach two different metallic materials to the two figures.

Gear Systems

Almost every machine in use today employs gears and systems of gears. Consequently, today's designer must understand the basic function of a gear and be familiar with how different-sized gears interact in a design. In this project, we use the topic of gears to review equations and variables.

Objectives

1. Insert numerical values into an equation
2. Solve a simple equation for a single variable
3. Use two or more simple equations to solve for a single unknown

Tools Book CD: 2.3, 8.2

Almost every machine in use today incorporates a system of gears to control movement of parts.

Courtesy of Corbis Images

Gears—Linear Versus Angular Velocity

Gears are circular in shape. When a gear of radius r rotates, two distinct velocities are associated with the movement. Understanding the distinctions between these two types of velocities provides a simple way to analyze complex systems of gears that are linked by many different belts and axles.

The first of these velocities is the angular velocity, ω, of the gear. This velocity is a measurement of the angle that the gear moves through in a certain time period.

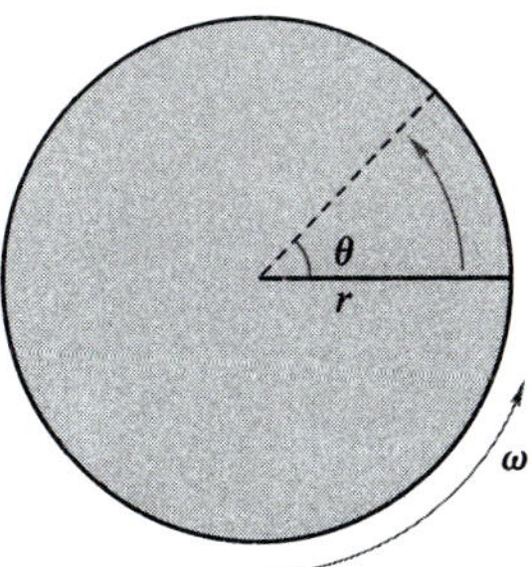

Figure 4.1

The second velocity is the linear velocity, v, which is a measurement of the linear distance that a point on the outside of the gear moves in a certain time period.

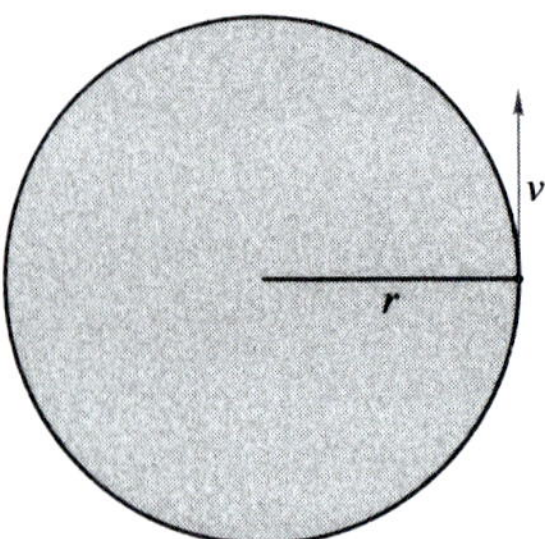

Figure 4.2

These two velocities are related by the equation

$$v = r\omega \tag{1}$$

> **MATH REVIEW**
>
> By convention, we define 1 rad = 1. Consequently, the unit of radians does not appear in the solution to Example 1, but does appear in the solution to Example 2.
>
> In general, units of radians appear in angular solutions, but not in linear ones.

Example 1

A gear of radius 0.2 m is revolving at a rate of 50 rad/s. Find the linear velocity of a point on the edge of the gear.

Solution

Inserting the radius and the angular velocity of the gear into Equation (1), we get

$$v = r\omega$$

$$v = (0.2\,\text{m})(50\,\text{rad/s})$$

$$v = 10\,\text{m/s}$$

Example 2

A point on the edge of a gear of radius 0.4 m is moving with a linear velocity of 14 m/s. Find the angular velocity of the gear.

Solution

Inserting the given values into Equation (1) and solving for the angular velocity

$$v = r\omega$$

$$14\,\text{m/s} = (0.4\,\text{m})\,\omega$$

$$\frac{14\,\text{m/s}}{0.4\,\text{m}} = \omega$$

$$\omega = 35\,\text{rad/s}$$

Skill Level I 

Problem

A gear of radius 0.4 m and a gear of radius 1.2 m are connected by a belt as in the following figure.

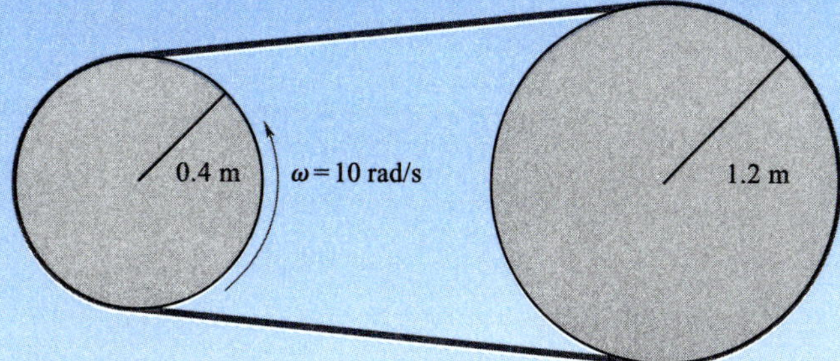

If the smaller gear is rotating with an angular velocity of 10 rad/s, find the angular velocity of the larger gear.

(a) Assuming that the belt does not slip, what can be said about the linear velocity of a point on the edge of gear 1 and the velocity of the belt?

(b) Because it is the movement of the belt that causes gear 2 to turn, what can be said about the linear velocity of a point on the outside of gear 2?

(c) Using the linear velocity of the points on the outside of gear 2, found in step (b), and the radius of gear 2, find the gear's angular velocity.

(d) What is the relationship between the angular velocity of gear 1 and the angular velocity of gear 2?

(e) If two gears are connected by a belt, what can be said about the angular velocity of gear 2 with respect to the angular velocity of gear 1 in each of the following cases?

1. Gear 2 is smaller than gear 1
2. Gear 2 is larger than gear 1
3. Gear 2 and gear 1 are the same size

Skill Level II 

Problem

Two gears of different sizes are attached to the same axle, as shown in the following figure.

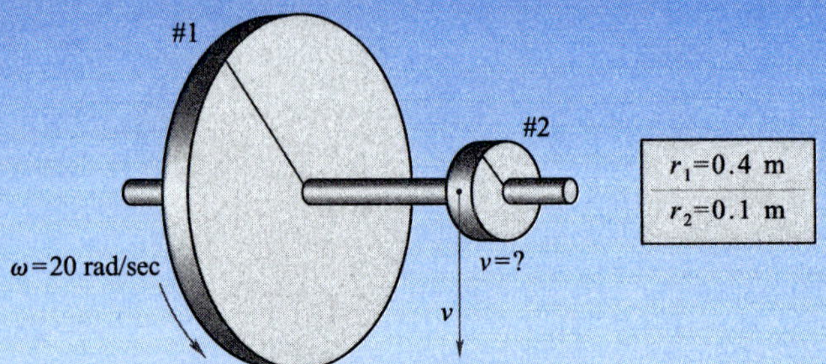

If the angular velocity of gear 1 is 20 rad/s, find the linear velocity of a point on the outside edge of gear 2.

Hint

Since both gears are connected to the same axle, their angular velocities must be the same.

Show your work.

Skill Level III ♦♦♦

Problem

Find the linear and angular velocity of each of the gears in the following system.

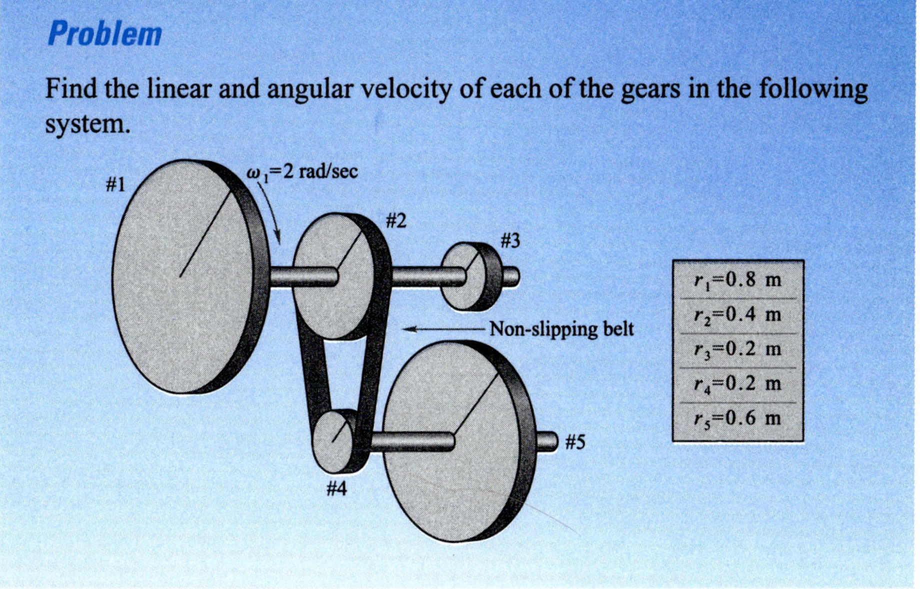

Show your work.

Applied Math Skill Check

1. Solve for y.

   $y = rw$ $\quad\quad$ $r = 2$, and $w = 40$

2. Solve for x.

   $y = xz$ $\quad\quad$ $y = 20$, and $z = 4$

3. Solve for x, given the following information.

   $y = xz$ $\quad$ $y = pr$ $\quad\quad$ $z = 2$, $p = 3$, and $r = 4$

4. Solve for y, given the following information.

   $\frac{x}{y} = z$ $\quad$ $z = tw$ $\quad\quad$ $x = 10$, $t = 1$, and $w = 5$

AutoCAD Project—Gear Systems

HINT

See Appendix C-4 for step-by-step instructions on using AutoCAD to complete this project.

Problem

Draw a three-dimensional gear.

Center of Mass

In this project, we use the topic of a design component's center of mass as a setting to review equations and variables, graphing, and the correct order of operations.

Objectives

1. Substitute numerical values into an equation
2. Use the correct order of operations when carrying out arithmetic calculations
3. Plot points on a number line
4. Plot points on a two-dimensional graph

Tools Book CD: 1.2; 3.2; 4.2C, D

NOTE

Although there is a subtle difference between the two, the *center of mass* is often referred to as the *center of gravity*.

When carrying out a design analysis, we can sometimes simplify the analysis by reducing a design element, such as a strut or a gear, to its center of mass. The center of mass is the point on an object under which a support can be placed for balance to be achieved.

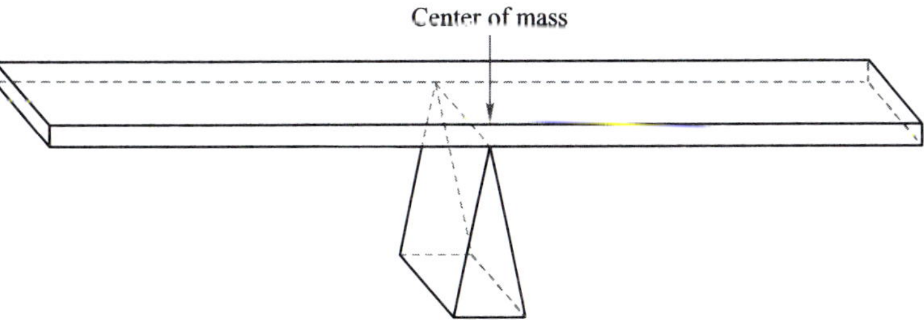

Figure 5.1

We will begin by finding the center of mass of a system of masses placed along one axis. This process requires several steps. After introducing a method for finding the center of mass of a one-dimensional system, we will move on to finding the center of mass of a two-dimensional system, and finally, we will learn how to find the center of mass of a continuous, three-dimensional object.

Skill Level I ♦

The Center of Mass of a One-Dimensional System

Suppose that we have the following three masses placed on the x-axis of a graph, and that we would like to find the center of mass of the system.

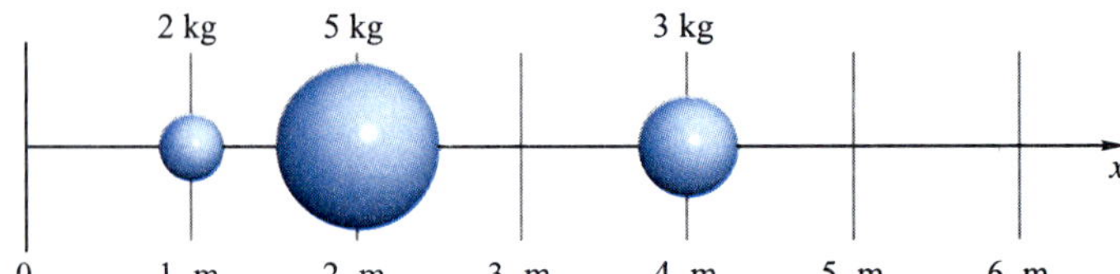

Figure 5.2

To find the center of mass of the system, we first multiply each mass by its distance from zero. We then sum these products and divide by the total mass. In equation form, the center of mass, $\bar{x}$, is found as follows.

$$\bar{x} = \frac{m_1 x_1 + m_2 x_2 + m_3 x_3}{m_1 + m_2 + m_3} \qquad (1)$$

Example 1

Find the center of mass for the system of masses given in Figure 5.2.

Solution

Insert the values of the masses and their respective locations into Equation (1) and solve for $\bar{x}$:

$$\bar{x} = \frac{m_1 x_1 + m_2 x_2 + m_3 x_3}{M}$$

$$\bar{x} = \frac{(2\,\text{kg})(1\,\text{m}) + (5\,\text{kg})(2\,\text{m}) + (3\,\text{kg})(4\,\text{m})}{(2\,\text{kg} + 5\,\text{kg} + 3\,\text{kg})}$$

$$\bar{x} = \frac{2\,\text{kg}\cdot\text{m} + 10\,\text{kg}\cdot\text{m} + 12\,\text{kg}\cdot\text{m}}{10\,\text{kg}}$$

$$\bar{x} = \frac{24\,\text{kg}\cdot\text{m}}{10\,\text{kg}}$$

$$\bar{x} = 2.4\,\text{m}$$

Thus, if a support was placed at $x = 2.4$ m, the system would balance. Notice that because the units of mass cancel between the numerator and the denominator, the units of mass do not affect the calculation. The units attached to the center of mass are determined by the units of the distances from the origin of the various masses.

Problem

Find the center of mass of the following system of masses.

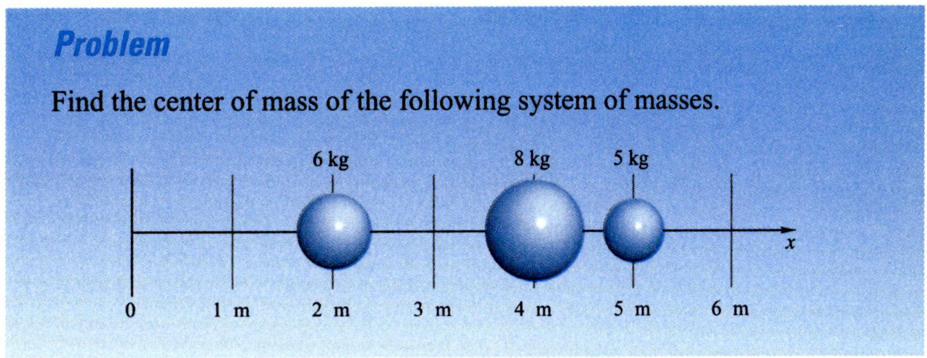

(a) Rewrite Equation (1), inserting the information given in the problem statement.

(b) In words, write out the correct order of operations you would use to solve this problem.

(c) Solve your equation for the center of mass of the system.

(d) If the masses in the problem statement had been expressed in grams and the distances in centimeters, what units would be attached to the center of mass?

Skill Level II 

The Center of Mass of a Two-Dimensional System

To find the center of mass of a two-dimensional system, it helps to understand that the calculation of the horizontal coordinate of the center of mass is independent of the calculation of the vertical coordinate. In other words, we simply need to find the x- and y-coordinates of the center of mass independently, and then add them together to express the two-dimensional coordinates of the center of mass.

Example 2

Find the center of mass of the system in following figure.

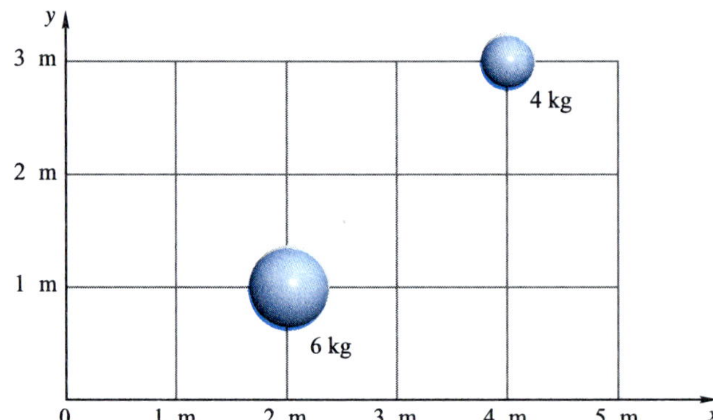

Figure 5.3

Solution

First, we find the x-coordinate of the center of mass by inserting the masses and their respective x-coordinates into Equation (1):

$$\bar{x} = \frac{(6\,\text{kg})(2\,\text{m}) + (4\,\text{kg})(4\,\text{m})}{(6\,\text{kg} + 4\,\text{kg})}$$

$$\bar{x} = \frac{12\,\text{kg}\cdot\text{m} + 16\,\text{kg}\cdot\text{m}}{10\,\text{kg}}$$

$$\bar{x} = \frac{28\,\text{kg}\cdot\text{m}}{10\,\text{kg}}$$

$$\bar{x} = 2.8\,\text{m}$$

The y-coordinate of the center of mass can be found using an equation that is analogous to Equation (1), and that incorporates the y-coordinate of each of the masses:

$$\bar{y} = \frac{m_1 y_1 + m_2 y_2}{m_1 + m_2}$$

Inserting the values given in the problem statement, the y-coordinate of the center of mass becomes

$$\bar{y} = \frac{(6\,\text{kg})(1\,\text{m}) + (4\,\text{kg})(3\,\text{m})}{(6\,\text{kg} + 4\,\text{kg})}$$

$$\bar{y} = \frac{6\,\text{kg}\cdot\text{m} + 12\,\text{kg}\cdot\text{m}}{10\,\text{kg}}$$

$$\bar{y} = \frac{18\,\text{kg}\cdot\text{m}}{10\,\text{kg}}$$

$$\bar{y} = 1.8\,\text{m}$$

Thus, the two-dimensional coordinates of the center of mass of the system of masses are

$$(\bar{x}, \bar{y}) = (2.8, 1.8)$$

Problem

Find the coordinates of the center of mass of the following system. Record your answer using the correct coordinate notation, (x, y).

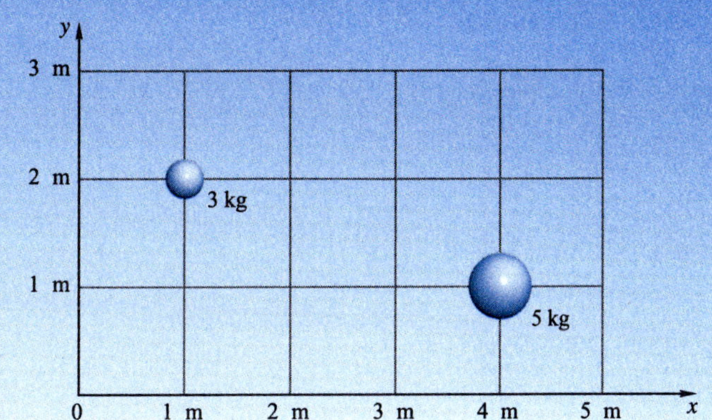

Show your work.

Skill Level III ♦♦♦

The Center of Mass of a Continuous Object

In design, almost all solids are composed of more than one type of material. Consequently, we must be able to find the center of mass of continuous objects that are not uniform in mass.

Finding the center of mass of a continuous object is a two-step process. First, we reduce each section of the solid to its respective center of mass. Then, we treat the object as a system of discrete masses, using the techniques discussed in Skill Levels I and II.

Example 3

Find the center of mass of the solid mass in Figure 5.4.

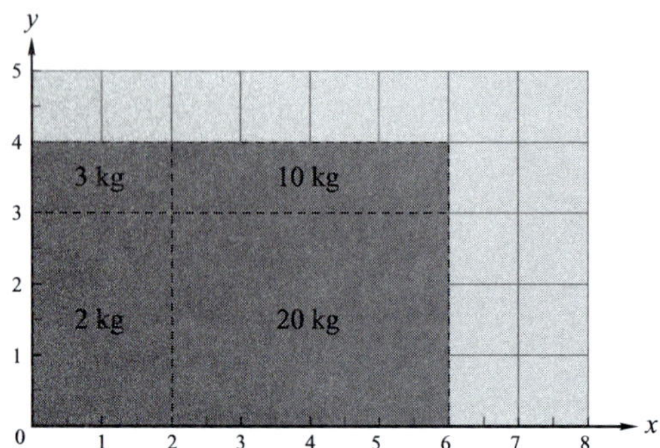

Figure 5.4

Solution

First, since each section of the mass is uniform, we can reduce the solid to the following point masses:

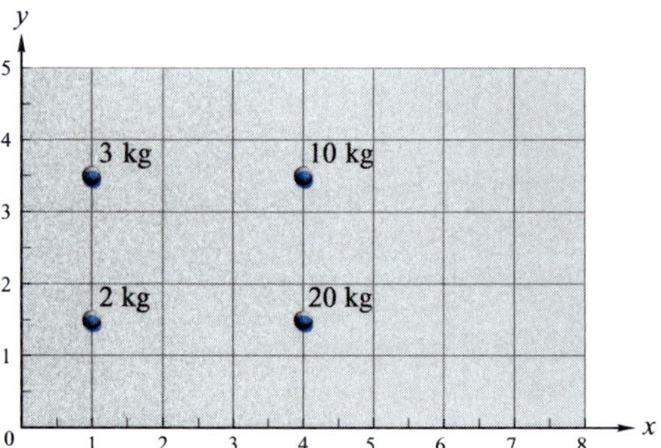

Figure 5.5

Then, we find the x- and y-coordinates of the center of mass:

$$\bar{x} = \frac{(2\,\text{kg})(1\,\text{m}) + (20\,\text{kg})(4\,\text{m}) + (3\,\text{kg})(1\,\text{m}) + (10\,\text{kg})(4\,\text{m})}{(2\,\text{kg} + 20\,\text{kg} + 3\,\text{kg} + 10\,\text{kg})}$$

$$\bar{x} = \frac{2\,\text{kg}\cdot\text{m} + 80\,\text{kg}\cdot\text{m} + 3\,\text{kg}\cdot\text{m} + 40\,\text{kg}\cdot\text{m}}{35\,\text{kg}}$$

$$\bar{x} = \frac{125\,\text{kg}\cdot\text{m}}{35\,\text{kg}}$$

$$\bar{x} = 3.57\,\text{m}$$

$$\bar{y} = \frac{(2\,\text{kg})(1.5\,\text{m}) + (20\,\text{kg})(1.5\,\text{m}) + (3\,\text{kg})(3.5\,\text{m}) + (10\,\text{kg})(3.5\,\text{m})}{(2\,\text{kg} + 20\,\text{kg} + 3\,\text{kg} + 10\,\text{kg})}$$

$$\bar{y} = \frac{3\,\text{kg}\cdot\text{m} + 30\,\text{kg}\cdot\text{m} + 10.5\,\text{kg}\cdot\text{m} + 35\,\text{kg}\cdot\text{m}}{35\,\text{kg}}$$

$$\bar{y} = \frac{78.5\,\text{kg}\cdot\text{m}}{35\,\text{kg}}$$

$$\bar{y} = 2.24\,\text{m}$$

Thus, the coordinates of the center of mass of the solid are

$$(\bar{x}, \bar{y}) = (3.57, 2.24)$$

Problem

Find the center of mass of the following solid.

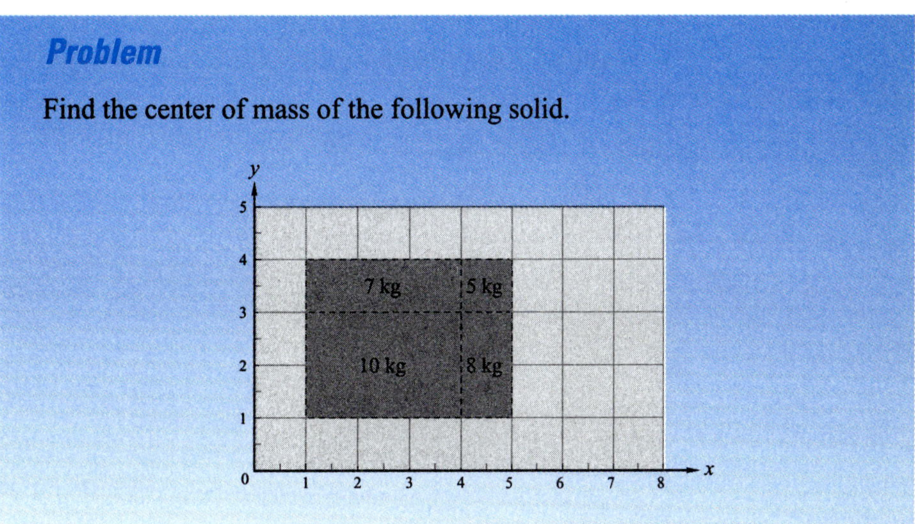

> **HINT**
>
> Begin by reducing each section of the solid to its center of mass.

Show your work.

Applied Math Skill Check

Find x in each of the following equations.

1. $x = \dfrac{yz}{w}$ $\quad y = 2,\ z = 10$, and $w = 4$
2. $x = \dfrac{y_1 z + y_2 b}{8}$ $\quad y_1 = 3,\ y_2 = 4,\ z = 8$, and $b = 1$
3. $x = \dfrac{y_1 z + y_2 z + y_3 z}{2}$ $\quad y_1 = y_2 = y_3 = 4$, and $z = 8$
4. (a) Draw a horizontal number line.

   (b) Represent each of the following numbers with a dot on your number line: 0, 3, −2, 2.7, −4.6, π.
5. Sketch a set of coordinate axes, and plot each of the following points: (1,2), (2,−3), (0,0), (−3,−1), (3.6,4.2).

AutoCAD Project—Center of Mass

HINT

See Appendix C-5 for step-by-step instructions on using AutoCAD to complete this project.

Problem

Use AutoCAD to place three different to-scale masses on a horizontal axis.

Fluids and Piping

In this project, we use the topic of the motion of fluids through piping as a setting to review the solution of equations involving several variables with different exponents.

Objectives

1. Substitute numerical values into an equation
2. In an equation involving several variables with differing exponents, solve for a single variable
3. Factor out like terms

Tools Book CD: 2.6, 5.1

When planning the systems of pipes to be used in a home, office building, or other structures, we must analyze the behavior of the fluids inside the various pipes to decide how many pipes, what kind of pumps that will be required and a host of other design issues. In this project, we will use a special equation for this type of analysis, *BernoulliÕs Equation.*As we work with this equation, we will have an opportunity to review a variety of algebraic topics as we analyze the behavior of fluids in two different architectural situations.

Bernoulli's Equation

Bernoulli's Equation relates the velocity of a fluid through a pipe to the height of the pipe above the ground, and to the pressure of the fluid contained in the pipe.

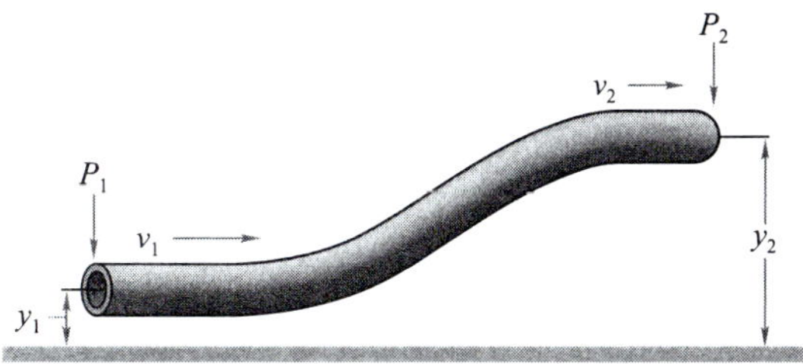

Figure 6.1

Bernoulli's Equation is given by

$$P_1 + \rho g y_1 + \frac{1}{2}\rho v_1^2 = P_2 + \rho g y_2 + \frac{1}{2}\rho v_2^2$$

where

- P_1 and P_2 are the pressures on the fluid at points 1 and 2,
- ρ is the density of the fluid,
- g is the acceleration due to gravity, 9.8 m/s^2,
- y_1 and y_2 are the respective heights of the pipe at points 1 and 2, and
- v_1 and v_2 are the velocities of the fluid at points 1 and 2.

Expressed more simply, Bernoulli's Equation tells us that if the pressure on a fluid remains constant, the fluid will lose velocity if the pipe gains elevation, and will gain velocity if the pipe loses elevation. A good analogy for the gain or loss of fluid velocity in pipes can be understood by thinking about the vertical motion of a baseball.

Just as a baseball gains speed as it falls from a height of y, the molecules of the fluid in the pipe gain speed as they "fall" through a pipe as it loses elevation.

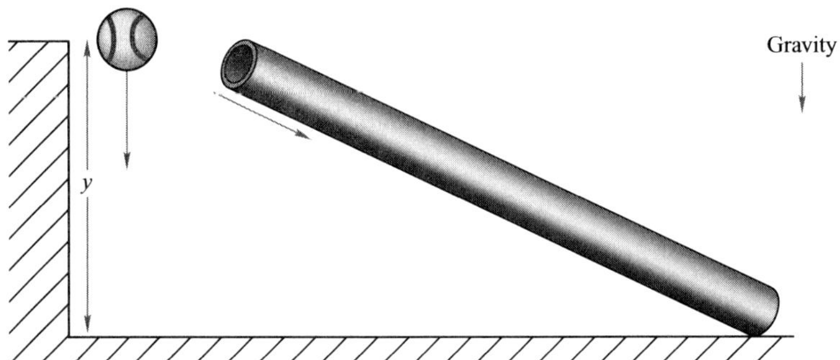

Figure 6.2

Conversely, if a baseball is thrown straight upward, the acceleration due to gravity acts to slow down the ball and eventually cause it to a stop. In a similar way, when the molecules of a fluid gain altitude because of the increase in the elevation of a pipe, the fluid molecules lose speed.

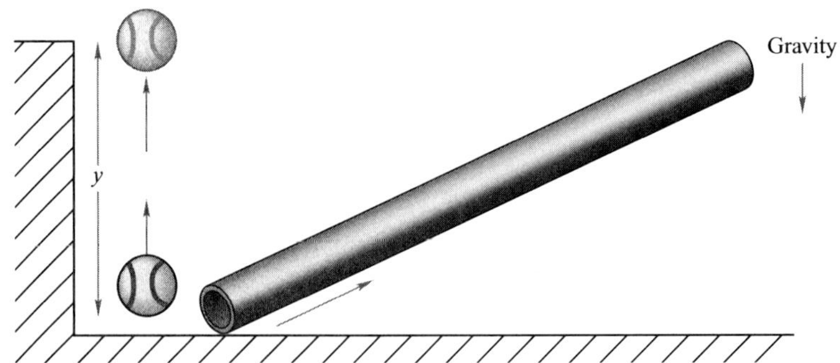

Figure 6.3

Skill Level I ♦

Problem

Assume that water is flowing through a pipe in the first floor of a house, as shown in the following Figure.

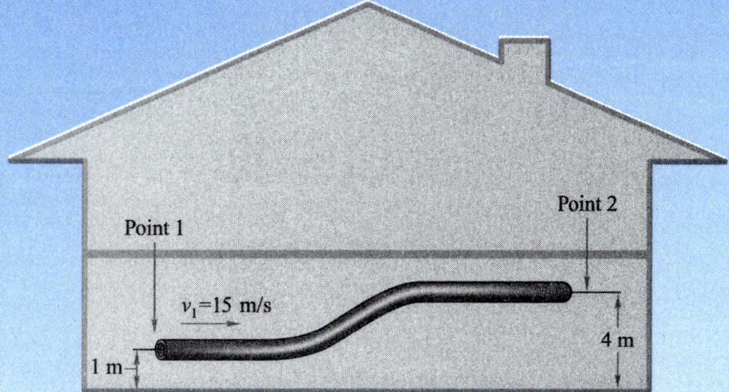

If the pressure on the water is the same at points 1 and 2, find the velocity of the water at point 2. Assume that the cross-sectional area of the pipe is the same at both points.

(a) What form does Bernoulli's Equation take if we use the information in the problem statement that $P_1 = P_2$?

(b) Because the density is the same on all the terms in the equation from step (a), how can the equation be simplified?

(c) Rewrite the equation from step (b), inserting the information given in the figure.

(d) Solve the equation from step (c) for the velocity of the water at point 2.

(e) Because the density of the fluid was cancelled from the equation in step (b), what can we say about the velocity of "hard water" (water with a large amount of iron and other impurities) through the pipe versus the velocity of "soft water"?

(f) If the entire pipe was moved to the second floor of the house, and the velocity of the water remained the same as in the problem statement, what effect, if any, would the added height have on the velocity of the water at point 2?

Skill Level II 

Problem

The water supply for an office building that is being constructed in a valley is drawn from a nearby lake, as shown in the following figure.

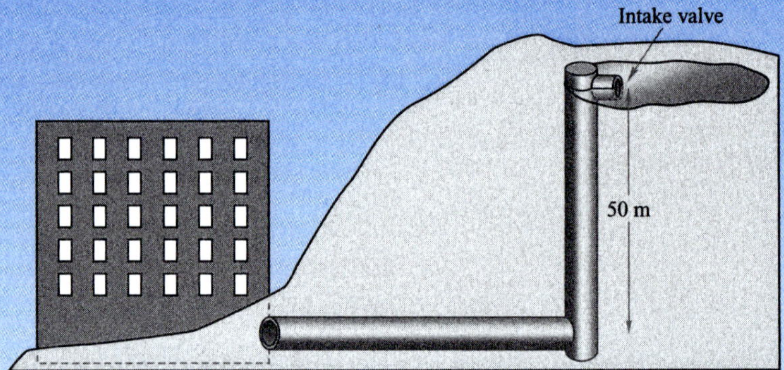

If the intake valve brings the water into the pipe at 3 m/s, find the velocity of the fluid as it enters the building. Assume that no other pumps, precautions, and so on, are working in the system, and that the cross-sectional area of the pipe is the same at the intake point and the point at which the water enters the building.

Show your work.

Skill Level III ♦♦♦

Problem

Solve Bernoulli's Equation for each of the following variables.

1. P_1
2. y_1
3. v_1
4. ρ

Show your work.

Applied Math Skill Check

Solve for y in each of the following equations.

1. $x + \frac{1}{3}y = z^2$
2. $y + \frac{1}{2}x^2z - 8w^2 = t^3 + R^5$
3. $yx^2 + yz^3 = t$
4. $\frac{x}{R} + \frac{2}{3}yz = 4y$
5. $yx^2 + 1 = w^4 - yz^3$ $\quad\quad$ $x = 3, z = 1$, and $w = 2$

AutoCAD Project – Fluids and Piping

HINT

See Appendix C-6 for step-by-step instructions on using AutoCAD to complete this project.

Problem

Draw a three-dimensional piece of pipe that shows both the inner and outer radius.

Strengths of Materials

In this project, we use the topic of material strengths and deformations to review the basic ideas of graphing.

Objectives

1. Read a graph
2. Construct a simple graph
3. Calculate a percentage

Tools Book CD: 1.8, 3.1–3.4

When structural elements are exposed to forces such as heat, cold, wind, and pressure, among others, they tend to experience changes in size and shape. For example, if an external force is applied to the ends of a metal rod, the rod will either increase in length (Figure 7.1(a)), or decrease in length (Figure 7.1(b)) in proportion to the magnitude of the applied force.

Figure 7.1(a)

Figure 7.1(b)

If the applied force is great enough, the rod will not be able to return to its original configuration even when the force no longer acts on the rod. The rod will experience a permanent deformation caused by the applied force. It is not hard to imagine that the application of an even greater force could break the rod. The relationship between the amount of applied force and the resulting behavior of the rod can be summarized by constructing a graph with the applied force on the horizontal axis and the deformation of the rod on the vertical axis.

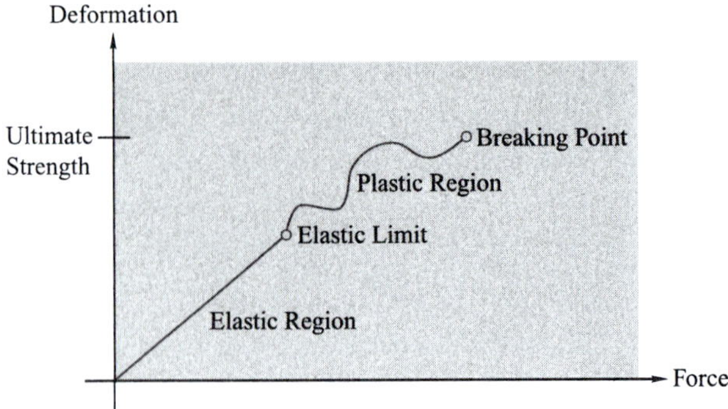

Figure 7.2

For small deforming forces, the deformation of the object is proportional to the amount of applied force. Forces that are too small to cause a permanent deformation correspond to the *elastic region* of the graph. In this region, when the applied force is removed, the object returns to its original size and configuration. Once an object reaches its *elastic limit,* the object will not return to its original size even after the applied force is removed. Forces that are large enough to cause a permanent deformation but not to fracture the material correspond to the *plastic region* of the graph. If the applied force continues to increase, the object reaches its *breaking point*. The maximum force per unit area that a material can tolerate before fracturing is known as its *ultimate strength*.

Skill Level I ♦

Problem

Use the graph in Figure 7.2 to answer the following questions.

1. The relationship between the applied force and the resulting deformation forms a straight line for the forces that lie between 0 and the elastic limit, but does not form a straight line for the forces between the elastic limit and the breaking point. What does the shape of the graph in each of these two regions tell us about the behavior of the material?
2. At the bottom of the graph, the line has a steep slope, and at the top of the graph the curve is close to horizontal. What does this tell us about the rate of change of the deformation as the applied force gets close to the breaking point?
3. Although nearly all materials have an elastic region, a plastic region, and a breaking point, do you think that all materials will have identical graphs of force versus deformation? Explain.
4. In your opinion, are there other types of graphs (bar charts, pie charts, etc.) that could have summarized the same information as Figure 7.2? Explain.

Write out a detailed explanation for your answer to each question.

Skill Level II ♦♦

Problem

An industrial artist submits a proposal for a new sculpture for the local civic park. The park director notes that the proposed sculpture will be built from the following materials in the given amounts.

Material	**Pounds**
Steel	4000
Wood	500
Copper wire	350
Concrete	3000

1. What percentage does each material constitute of the total weight of the sculpture?
2. Construct a pie chart of the total weight to summarize the percentages you found in part 1.

Record your percentage calculations and your pie chart in the space provided.

Skill Level III 

Problem

1. Execute the research necessary to define the *tensile strength, compressional strength,* and *shear strength* of a material.
2. Execute the necessary research and then find the tensile strength, compressional strength, and shear strength for each of the materials used in the sculpture in Skill Level II.
3. Construct a graph that contains all four materials and their respective tensile, compressional, and shear strengths.
4. Explain why you used the type of graph that you did.

Record your answers in the space provided.

Applied Math Skill Check

1. Using the given graph, find the value of y associated with each of the values of x in the table.

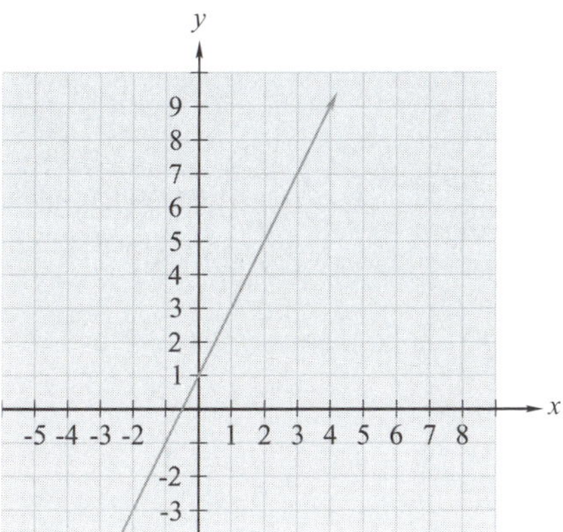

x	y
1	
2	
0	
−1	
−2	

2. If a line is horizontal, what statement can be made about the vertical coordinate of each of the points on the line?

3. If a line is vertical, what statement can be made about the horizontal coordinate of each of the points on the line?

4. (a) In terms of the horizontal coordinate, what statement can be made about the point at which a function intersects the vertical axis on a graph?

   (b) In terms of the vertical coordinate, what statement can be made about the point at which a function intersects the horizontal axis on a graph?

5. Sketch a set of coordinate axes, and plot the following points: (0,4), (1,−3), (0,0), (−4,1), (−3,−3), (4.2,3.1).

6. What percentage of 75 is 20?

AutoCAD Project—Strengths of Materials

In this AutoCAD Project, we illustrate that although AutoCAD is a remarkably useful software package for civil drafting, architecture, and so on, it is not necessarily the easiest software to use when constructing mathematical graphs.

HINT

See Appendix C-7 for step-by-step instructions on using AutoCAD to complete this project.

Problem

1. Create and label a set of coordinate axes.
2. Graph the function $y = 2x + 1$.

Elevations

In this project, we will look at one of the challenges faced by surveyors and drafters as they plan for structures that are built across various elevations. This topic provides an interesting context to review the mathematical concepts of equations, variables, the Pythagorean Theorem, and right-triangle trigonometry.

Objectives

1. Insert given numerical values into equations
2. Manipulate an equation to solve for a single variable
3. Use the Pythagorean Theorem to solve for a given unknown in a right triangle
4. Solve an equation involving the basic trigonometric functions sine, cosine, and tangent
5. Using a calculator, find the sine, cosine, or tangent of a given angle

Tools Book CD: 1.2, A.6

Surveyors use leveling tools to help calculate the different points of elevation involved, before design work begins.

Courtesy of PhotoDisc, Inc.

Finding Points of Elevation

For surveyors, finding the elevation of points requires only basic equipment. Leveling is a process that is normally performed using a transit, tripod, and leveling rod. Several different leveling rods are used for measuring elevations. The Philadelphia rod is the most frequently used. The rod is placed on a known elevation and the instrument is set up approximately halfway to the unknown point. Long distances may require several setups. A reading is taken on the *backsight* or rod location. The value of the measurement is added to the known elevation to give the height of the instrument (H.I.). The rod is then placed on the unknown elevation, called the *foresight,* and a reading is taken. This reading is subtracted from the height of the instrument to give the unknown elevation.

Although various tools and techniques help to simplify the process, it is important that we understand the underlying mathematics involved in finding points at different elevations. In civil drafting, we are often confronted with a variety of elevation measurements. These measurements can be taken from a baseline point, or measured in relation to one another, as in the case of the Philadelphia rod. Regardless of the reference point or the measuring technique, all elevation measurements involve three points:

1. a reference point from which the elevation measurement is being taken (A),
2. the point of elevation being measured (B), and

3. the point that lies directly below the point of elevation being measured and that is on the same plane as the point of reference (C).

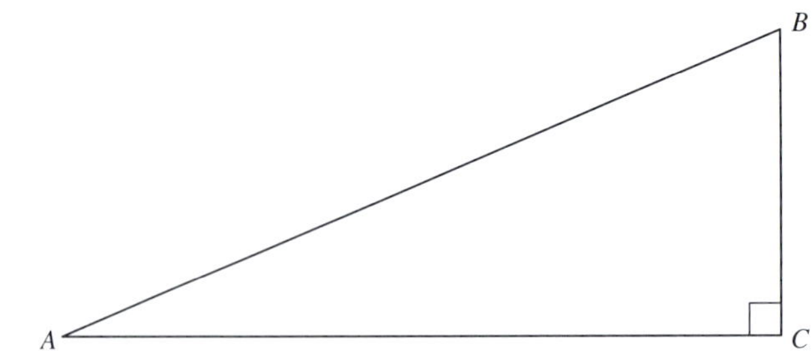

Figure 8.1

As we see in Figure 8.1, regardless of the chosen reference height, elevation surveying requires an understanding of a number of mathematical concepts, including right triangles, the Pythagorean Theorem, and right-triangle trigonometry.

Skill Level I ♦

MATH REVIEW

It may be helpful to review the coverage of the Pythagorean Theorem in Thought Project 23, *Interlude: Trigonometry.*

Problem

A surveyor has made the following measurements:

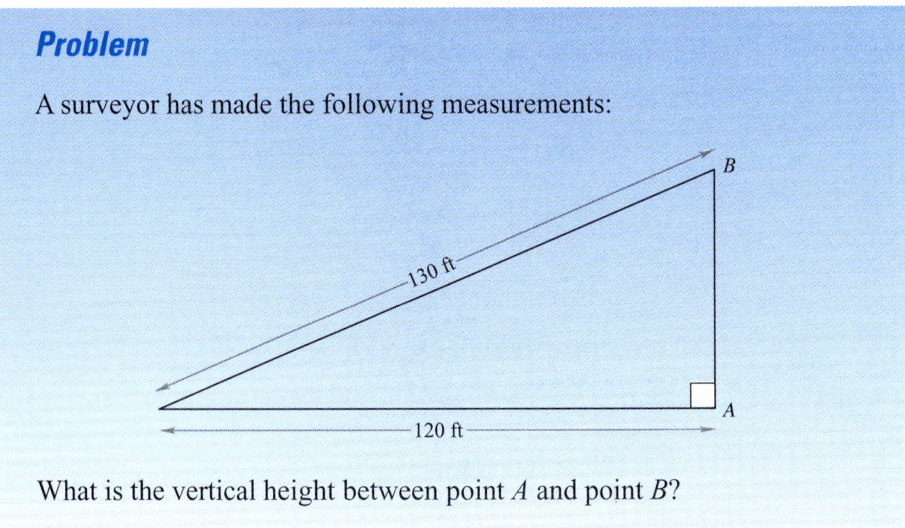

What is the vertical height between point A and point B?

(a) Write out the Pythagorean Theorem.

(b) Using the given values from the problem statement, what form does the Pythagorean Theorem take?

(c) Write out, in words, the correct order of operations required to solve for the unknown in the equation you wrote in step (b).

(d) Solve your equation for the unknown vertical height between A and B.

The rules of algebra dictate that we can solve for an unknown in an equation, provided that we know the values of all the other terms. Stated more simply, we know that we can solve for an unknown value if enough information is given in the problem statement. To solve the problem in Skill Level I, we needed to know the values of two of the three sides in the right triangle. In Skill Level II, we find an unknown side of a triangle, such as a height elevation, given the length of another side and an angle in the triangle.

Skill Level II 

MATH REVIEW

It may be helpful to review the three basic trigonometric functions, sine, cosine, and tangent in Thought Project 23, *Interlude: Trigonometry*, before attempting this Skill Level.

Problem

Find the vertical distance between points A and B in the following elevation diagram.

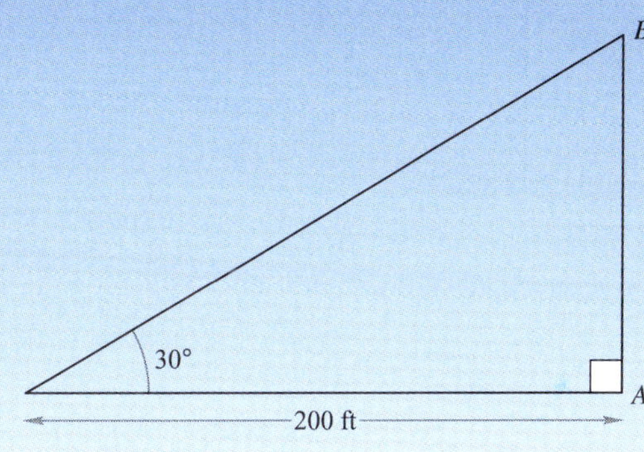

(e) Based on the given information, which of the three basic trigonometric functions—sine, cosine, or tangent—is required to solve this problem?

(f) Using the given information, and the appropriate trigonometric function, write out the exact form of the equation that must be solved to find the unknown height.

(g) Use your equation from step (f) to solve for the unknown height in the problem statement.

The next step in our use of right-triangle trigonometry in surveying is to discuss how to find the angle of elevation when we know two of the lengths in an elevation measurement. To find such an unknown angle, we must draw upon *inverse trigonometric functions*.

Inverse Trigonometric Functions

In technology, we are often confronted with equations in which we are given the value of a particular trigonometric function, such as

$$\sin\theta = 0.53$$
$$\cos\theta = 0.68$$
$$\tan\theta = 2.4$$

However, what we really need to know is the angle that generated this data. As we have seen with other mathematical operations, the three basic trigonometric functions have inverse operations that will "undo" them. These operations are called *inverse sine* ($\sin^{-1}$), *inverse cosine* ($\cos^{-1}$), and *inverse tangent* ($\tan^{-1}$). To find the unknown angle in these equations, we need only apply the appropriate inverse operation *to both sides of the equation*.

HINT

Your calculator is a valuable tool in performing this type of mathematical operation. Make sure that you know how to use your calculator to carry out each of the calculations given to the right.

$$\begin{aligned} \sin\theta &= 0.53 \\ \sin^{-1}(\sin\theta) &= \sin^{-1}(0.53) \\ \theta &= 32.0^\circ \end{aligned}$$

$$\begin{aligned} \cos\theta &= 0.68 \\ \cos^{-1}(\cos\theta) &= \cos^{-1}(0.68) \\ \theta &= 47.16^\circ \end{aligned}$$

$$\begin{aligned} \tan\theta &= 2.4 \\ \tan^{-1}(\tan\theta) &= \tan^{-1}(2.4) \\ \theta &= 67.38^\circ \end{aligned}$$

We'll begin by applying the concept of an inverse trigonometric function to a right triangle, and then practice this technique in an elevation problem.

Example 1

Find the angle θ in the following right triangle.

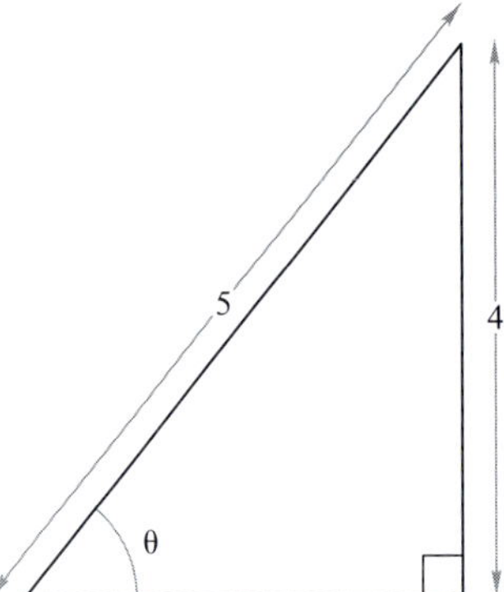

Figure 8.2

Solution

Since we know the hypotenuse and the opposite side for the angle θ, we choose the sine function to solve the triangle:

$$\sin\theta = \frac{4}{5}$$

To solve for the angle θ, we take the inverse sine of both sides of the equation:

$$\sin\theta = \frac{4}{5}$$

$$\sin^{-1}(\sin\theta) = \sin^{-1}\left(\frac{4}{5}\right)$$

$$\theta = 53.13^\circ$$

Example 2

Find the angle θ in the following right triangle.

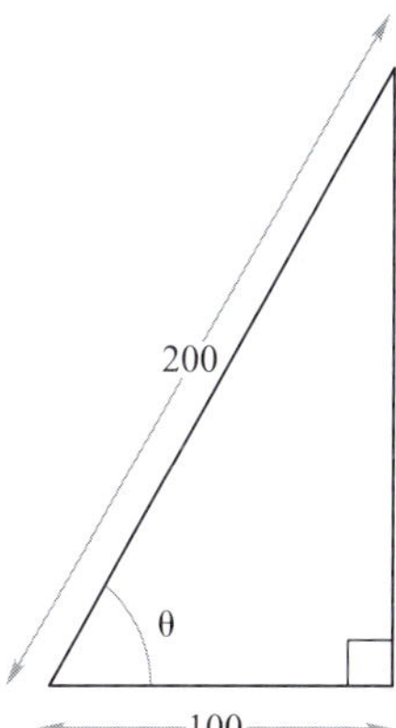

Figure 8.3

Solution

By consulting the figure, we know the values of the adjacent side and the hypotenuse. Consequently, we use the cosine function to solve for the angle θ:

$$\cos\theta = \frac{100}{200}$$

Reducing the fraction on the right-hand side, and employing the correct inverse trigonometric function, gives us

$$\cos\theta = \frac{100}{200}$$

$$\cos\theta = \frac{1}{2}$$

$$\cos^{-1}(\cos\theta) = \cos^{-1}\left(\frac{1}{2}\right)$$

$$\theta = 60^\circ$$

Skill Level III

Problem

A surveyor measured the following distances:

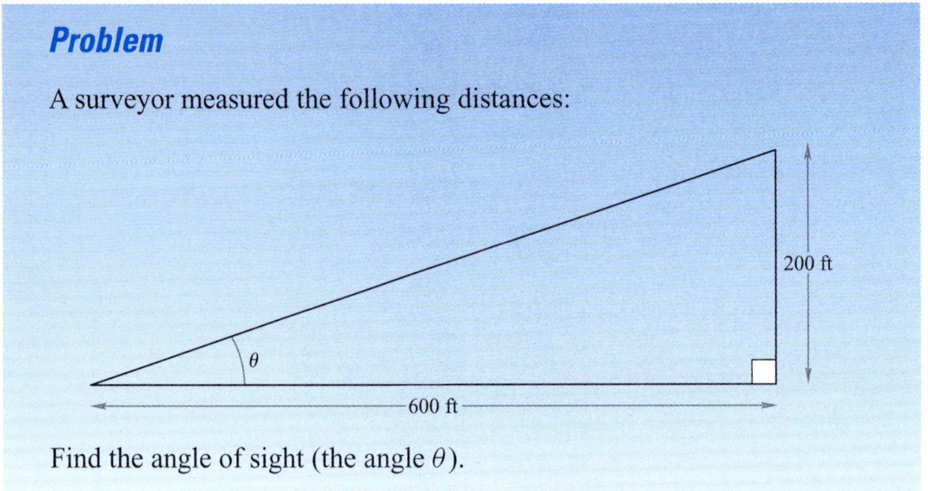

Find the angle of sight (the angle θ).

Show your work.

Applied Math Skill Check

1. Using your calculator, find each of the following quantities.

   (a) $\sin 43^\circ$

   (b) $\cos 48^\circ$

   (c) $\tan 78^\circ$

   (d) $\cos 0^\circ$

   (e) $\cos 90^\circ$

   (f) $\sin 0^\circ$

   (g) $\sin 90^\circ$

   (h) $\tan 45^\circ$

   (i) $\sin 138^\circ$

   (j) $\cos 145^\circ$

2. Find the angle θ, in degrees, in each of the following equations, using the appropriate inverse trigonometric function.

   (a) $\cos\theta = 0.74$

   (b) $\sin\theta = 0.39$

   (c) $\tan\theta = 1.8$

   (d) $\cos\theta = 1$

   (e) $\cos\theta = 0$

   (f) $\sin\theta = 1$

   (g) $\sin\theta = 0$

   (h) $\cos\theta = -1$

   (i) $\sin\theta = -1$

   (j) $\tan\theta = 1$

   (k) $\tan\theta = -1$

   (l) $\tan\theta = 0$

3. Find θ.

   $\sin\theta = \dfrac{x}{y}$ $\qquad\qquad$ $x = 6$, and $y = 12$

4. Find the length of the hypotenuse of the right triangle that has a base of 5 and a side leg of 8.

5. In the following equation, identify the smallest value that y can achieve if $x = 14$. *Hint:* Think about the mathematical boundary on the sine function.

   $\sin\theta = \dfrac{2x}{y}$

AutoCAD Project—Elevations

HINT

See Appendix C-8 for step-by-step instructions on using AutoCAD to complete this project.

Problem

1. Create a right triangle.
2. Reflect the right triangle across both the x and y axis.

Torque

In this project, we use the topic of torque as a setting to review the mathematical concepts of variables, equations, and right-triangle trigonometry.

Objectives

1. Insert numerical values into an equation
2. Manipulate a simple equation and solve for a single variable
3. Calculate the sine, cosine, and tangent of an angle
4. Solve an equation involving a trigonometric function for a single variable

Tools Book CD: 2.6

One of the challenges of design is to consider how all of the various elements interact. For example, when placing a component such as a beam or a strut into a design, it is important to understand the weight distributions that come into play. If the beam or strut is not supported correctly, it might rotate because of torques generated, and weaken the structure. To understand and calculate torque, we must have an understanding of variables, equations, and basic trigonometry.

Torque

A simple way to visualize torque is to look at the rotation of the handle of a wrench when a force is applied to it, as shown in Figure 9.1.

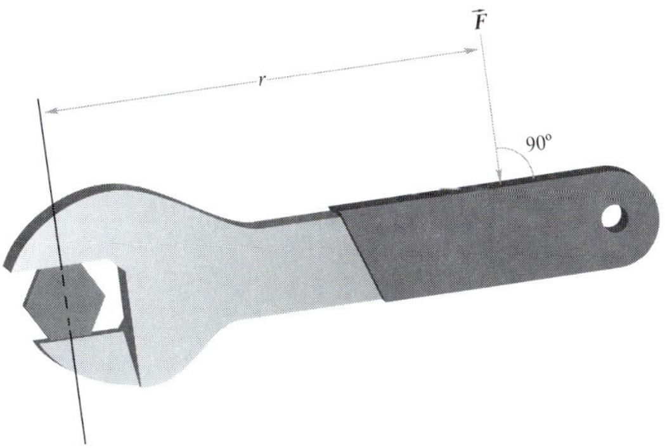

Figure 9.1

Experience tells us that it is easier to rotate the handle of the wrench when we apply the force closer to the outer end of the wrench. Similarly, we know that it is easier to open a door when we push at the handle rather than the hinge. The name for the distance from which the force is applied to the point of rotation (for example, the nut in Figure 9.1) is the *lever arm*.

As you might expect, both the magnitude of the applied force and the length of the lever arm affect the rotation of the handle. The product of the lever arm, r, and the force, F, is called *torque* (τ)

$$\tau = Fr \tag{1}$$

Because weight is a force, it is possible for design elements such as struts and beams to rotate because of the torque caused by their own weight.

Example 1

The horizontal beam in Figure 9.2 weighs 100 lb and is pivoted at the left end. Find the clockwise torque caused by the weight of the beam.

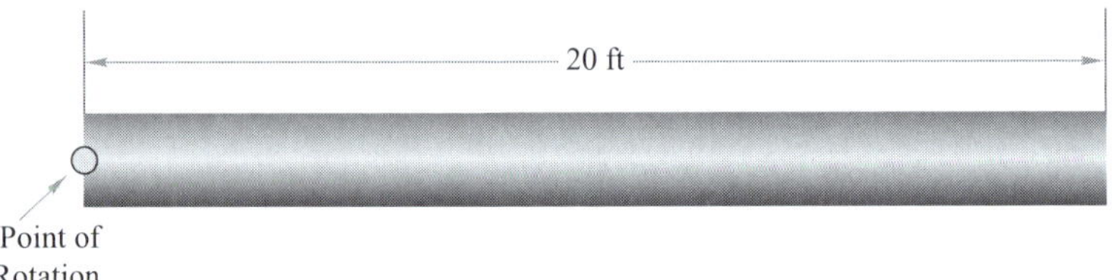

Figure 9.2

Solution

First, if we assume that the beam is uniform, we can assume that the entire weight of the beam acts at its center:

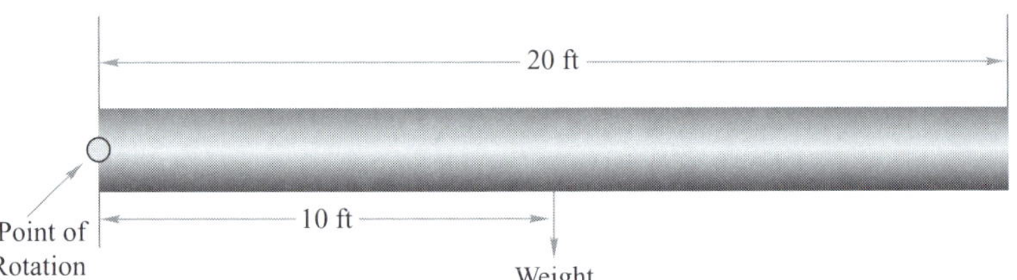

Figure 9.3

Therefore, the force (the beam's weight) is acting at a distance of 10 ft from the point of rotation. This means that 10 ft is the length of the lever arm. Inserting the length of the lever arm and the applied force into Equation (1), we find the torque caused by the beam's weight:

$$\tau = Fr$$
$$\tau = (100\ \text{lb})(10\ \text{ft})$$
$$\tau = 1000\ \text{lb}\cdot\text{ft}$$

Notice that the units of foot-pounds are used to express torque. These units arise from the units attached to the lever arm and the force.

Skill Level I ♦

Problem

A nonuniform beam of length 30 ft and weight 100 lbs has a center of mass 8 ft from the left end.

1. Find the resulting torque caused by the weight of the beam if the beam is supported at its left end.
2. Find the resulting torque caused by the weight of the beam if the beam is supported at its right end.

(a) What is the length of the lever arm in part 1? In part 2?

(b) Using Equation (1), find the solution to both problems in the problem statement. Show your work.

(c) Will the beam rotate in the same direction in both problems? Explain.

Rotational Equilibrium

When the clockwise torques affecting an object are equal to the counterclockwise torques, the object cannot rotate and is said to be in *rotational equilibrium*. This relationship between the clockwise and counterclockwise torques in a nonrotating situation provides a method for finding the amount of vertical support required by a horizontal beam or strut.

Example 2

A uniform horizontal beam 20 ft in length weighs 300 lb and is attached to a wall using a hinge at its left end. How much upward force would need to be applied 3 ft from the right end of the beam to support the beam?

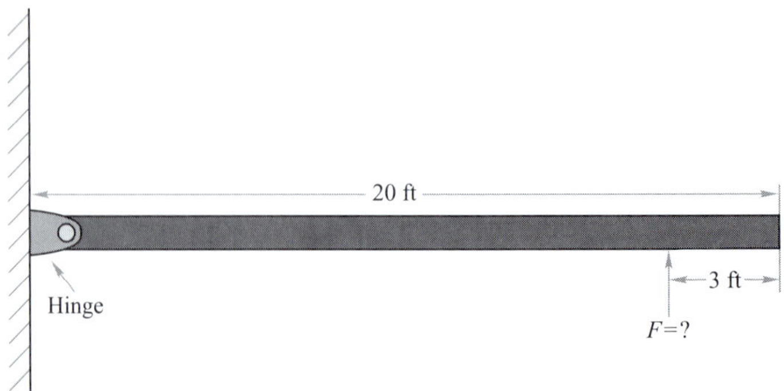

Figure 9.4

Solution

First, we identify that the lever arm for the clockwise torque caused by the beam's weight is 10 ft, and the lever arm for the counterclockwise torque caused by the unknown force is 17 ft. Next, since the beam is not rotating, the clockwise and counterclockwise torques must be equal. Consequently, we can construct the following equation involving the torques:

$$\begin{aligned}
\tau_{CW} &= \tau_{CCW} \\
(300\,\text{lb})(10\,\text{ft}) &= F(17\,\text{ft}) \\
3000\,\text{lb}\cdot\text{ft} &= F(17\,\text{ft}) \\
\frac{3000\,\text{lb}\cdot\text{ft}}{17\,\text{ft}} &= F \\
F &= 176.47\,\text{lb}
\end{aligned}$$

Skill Level II 

NOTE

It may be helpful to review Thought Project 23, *Interlude: Trigonometry* before beginning this Skill Level.

HINT

The maximum force that the support column can withstand is also the upward directed force exerted by the column on the bottom of the beam. It is this upward force that provides the counterclockwise torque balancing the clockwise torque due to the beam's weight.

Problem

A uniform horizontal beam of length 30 ft and weight 400 lb is attached to a hinge at its left end. A vertical support column that can withstand 600 lb of force before fracturing is used to support the beam. How close to the wall can the support column be placed and not fracture?

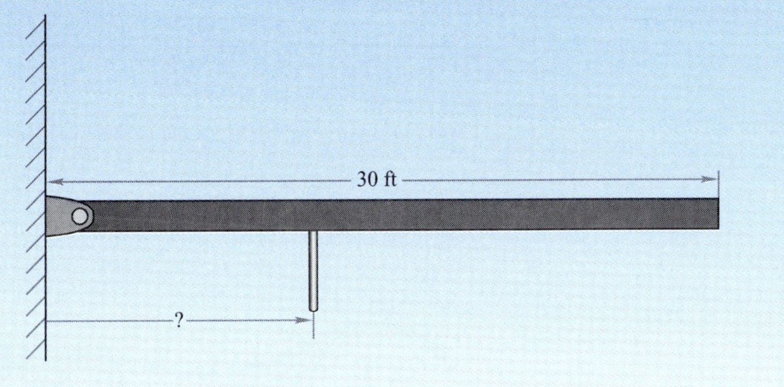

Show your work.

Unfortunately, when analyzing design elements in a structure, the forces are not always exerted at a right angle to the lever arm. Returning to the wrench that we used at the beginning of the project, if the force is instead exerted at an angle of θ with respect to the handle, not all of the force actually causes the handle to rotate.

Figure 9.5

If the applied force is broken into its horizontal and vertical components, we see that only the $F \sin \theta$ portion of the force actually causes the handle to rotate. Consequently, this is the portion of the force that we use to find the amount of torque caused by the force.

We therefore add a $\sin \theta$ term to Equation (1).

$$\tau = Fr \sin \theta \tag{2}$$

Adding this term allows us to isolate the amount of the force that is being exerted perpendicular to the lever arm.

Example 3

Find the amount of torque caused by the force in Figure 9.6.

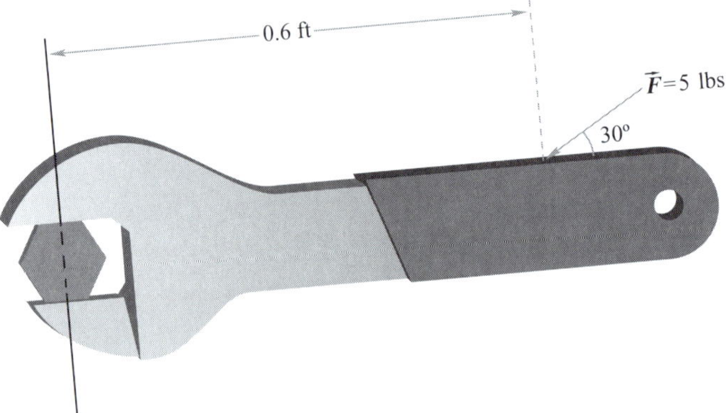

Figure 9.6

Solution

Inserting the given information into Equation (2),

$$\tau = Fr \sin \theta$$

$$\tau = (5 \text{ lb})(0.6 \text{ ft}) \sin 30^\circ$$

$$\tau = 1.5 \text{ ft} \cdot \text{lb}$$

Skill Level III

Problem

How much force must be exerted to support the uniform beam in the following figure?

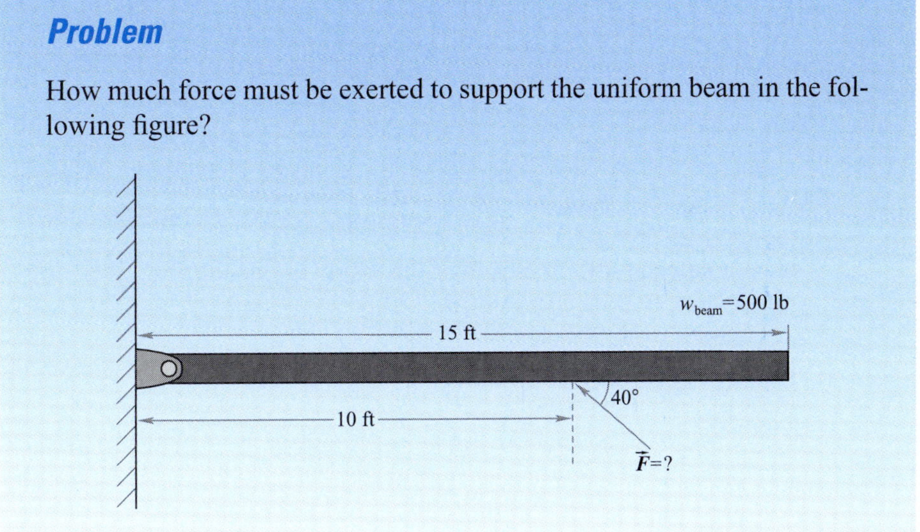

Show your work.

Applied Math Skill Check

Solve for x.

1. (a) $x = yz$ $\quad y = 2$, and $z = 10$

   (b) $a = bx$ $\quad a = 2.8$, and $b = 3.1$

   (c) $\frac{a}{x} = t$ $\quad a = 12$, and $t = 3$

2. Use your calculator to find each of the following quantities.

   (a) $\sin 47°$

   (b) $\cos 79°$

   (c) $\tan 24°$

3. Solve for y.

   (a) $y = ab \sin\theta$ $\quad a = 2, b = 5$, and $\theta = 30°$

   (b) $x = ty \cos\theta$ $\quad x = 15, t = 3$, and $\theta = 45°$

   (c) $\frac{\sin\theta}{y} = G$ $\quad G = 10$, and $\theta = 60°$

AutoCAD Project—Torque

HINT

See Appendix C-9 for step-by-step instructions on using AutoCAD to complete this project.

Problem

Draw a beam, and use the AutoCAD materials utility to add texture to your beam.

Independent Drafting/Design Research

In this project, we engage in independent research to acquire an elementary understanding of some of the most important terms and concepts necessary for a successful career in the technological field of computer drafting and design.

Objective

Complete independent research to describe some of the most important terms and concepts relating to the drafting and design field.

Tools Book CD: No Coverage

One of the factors that determines whether we will be successful in today's technological workplace is our ability and willingness to learn new concepts without the help of an instructor or trainer. In school, it is impossible to learn every drafting and design concept. Because the field changes so rapidly, today's technician must be willing to read journals, textbooks, and other reference materials to stay abreast of changing and new technology.

In this project, you are challenged to do the independent research necessary to acquaint yourself with a variety of design terms, without the aid of an instructor's lecture. In addition to illustrating the necessity of such independent research, this project provides a setting in which you will acquire an introduction to many of the design devices and concepts you will be studying at ITT Technical Institute.

The Skill Levels for this project are determined by the number of terms correctly defined.

Skill Level I ♦	15 terms
Skill Level II ♦♦	20 terms
Skill Level III ♦♦♦	25 terms

Problem

For each of the following design terms, find and write out an explanation *in your own words*.

1. Point
2. Line
3. Plane
4. ANSI
5. Orthographic projections
6. Sectional view
7. Fillet
8. Chamfer
9. MTEXT
10. DTEXT
11. Axonometric
12. Oblique
13. Plus/minus tolerance
14. Absolute, relative, and polar coordinates
15. Contour lines
16. Boolean operation
17. Extruded forms
18. Grids
19. Datums
20. Working drawings/detail drawings
21. Weld symbols
22. Wire frames
23. Surfaces models
24. Thermosetting materials
25. Thermoplastic materials

AutoCAD Project—Independent Drafting/Design Research

Hint

See Appendix C-10 for step-by-step instructions on using AutoCAD to complete this project.

Problem

Become familiar with several AutoCAD commands that are more advanced than those discussed in previous AutoCAD projects.

INFORMATION TECHNOLOGY APPLICATION PROJECTS

1. Prime Numbers and Computer Encryption Codes
2. Converting from Decimal to Binary
3. Permutations and Combinations
4. Logical Reasoning
5. Tracking Profits
6. Corporate Optimization
7. Memory Fields and Matrices
8. Fiber-Optic Cables
9. The Next Generation of Computing
10. Independent Information Technology Research

Prime Numbers and Computer Encryption Codes

The topic of computer encryption codes provides a fascinating setting to review several basic arithmetic concepts, including multiplication, square roots, and prime numbers.

Objectives

1. Solve a multiplication problem by hand
2. Use a calculator to find a square root

Tools Book CD: 9.1B

In today's "information society," the ability to send and receive secure electronic transmissions is of critical importance. Such transmissions are common in areas ranging from the online commerce used by the banking industry to sensitive national security matters. To ensure privacy, electronic transmissions are often encoded or "locked" to prevent tampering. These locks are most commonly in the form of 400-digit numbers that are the products of two prime numbers. To unlock the files being transmitted, the receiver of the transmission must know the two prime number factors that were used to create the 400-digit number. This type of lock is among the most secure against computers, because all computer operations are based on algorithms. While a computer can multiply two prime numbers together with lightning speed, it cannot begin with a 400-digit number and discover the two prime numbers that generated it with the same speed. The algorithm required to find the two prime numbers is slow and tedious. Thus, the electronic file is secure from "hackers" during the transmission process. The focus of this project is one of the algorithms that is often used to identify prime numbers, the Sieve of Eratosthenes.

Skill Level I 

MATH REVIEW

A *prime* number is defined as being evenly divisible only by itself and the number 1. The numbers 5, 7, and 11 are examples of prime numbers.

The Sieve of Eratosthenes

The Sieve of Eratosthenes, created in the third century B.C., is a method for finding the prime numbers that are less than a given number. For example, the sieve can identify all of the prime numbers that are less than 50, less than 200, and so on. Let's see how it works.

Suppose we want to find the prime numbers below a given number, n. We begin by writing out all the numbers from 2 (the lowest prime number) to n. Since 2 is prime, we circle it. Next, we move through the list of written numbers and cross out all multiples of 2. If the number is a multiple of 2, it cannot be prime. After crossing out all multiples of 2, we move to the next number in the list that has not been crossed out, 3. We circle it because it must be prime. We now move through the list and cross out all multiples of 3. After we eliminate multiples of 3, we move to the next number on the list that has not been eliminated, 5. We circle it, identifying it as prime, and then cross off all numbers that are multiples of 5. This process continues until we reach the prime number on the list that is less than or equal to $\sqrt{n}$, and eliminate all of its multiples from the remainder of the list. Circle any numbers on the list that have not yet been circled or eliminated. The circled numbers are now all the prime numbers that are less than n.

 **Example**

Use the Sieve of Eratosthenes to identify the prime numbers that are less than 50.

Solution

We begin by identifying n as being the number 50. According to the algorithm presented, we know that we need to identify $\sqrt{n}$, to determine at which point our process of elimination may end. Because $\sqrt{50} = 7.071$, we must check and eliminate only the multiples of primes up to and including seven. Our first step is to write out all the numbers from 2 to 50. Then we circle 2, identifying it as prime, and cross off all multiples of 2, as shown in Figure 1.1.

	(2)	3	~~4~~	5	~~6~~	7	~~8~~	9	~~10~~
11	~~12~~	13	~~14~~	15	~~16~~	17	~~18~~	19	~~20~~
21	~~22~~	23	~~24~~	25	~~26~~	27	~~28~~	29	~~30~~
31	~~32~~	33	~~34~~	35	~~36~~	37	~~38~~	39	~~40~~
41	~~42~~	43	~~44~~	45	~~46~~	47	~~48~~	49	~~50~~

Figure 1.1

Next, we circle 3, identifying it as prime, and cross off all multiples of 3.

	(2)	(3)	~~4~~	5	~~6~~	7	~~8~~	~~9~~	~~10~~
11	~~12~~	13	~~14~~	~~15~~	~~16~~	17	~~18~~	19	~~20~~
~~21~~	~~22~~	23	~~24~~	25	~~26~~	~~27~~	~~28~~	29	~~30~~
31	~~32~~	~~33~~	~~34~~	35	~~36~~	37	~~38~~	~~39~~	~~40~~
41	~~42~~	43	~~44~~	~~45~~	~~46~~	47	~~48~~	49	~~50~~

Figure 1.2

The next number on the list that has not been crossed off is 5. Therefore, it must be prime. We circle it and then move through the list crossing off multiples of 5.

	(2)	(3)	~~4~~	(5)	~~6~~	7	~~8~~	~~9~~	~~10~~
11	~~12~~	13	~~14~~	~~15~~	~~16~~	17	~~18~~	19	~~20~~
~~21~~	~~22~~	23	~~24~~	~~25~~	~~26~~	~~27~~	~~28~~	29	~~30~~
31	~~32~~	~~33~~	~~34~~	~~35~~	~~36~~	37	~~38~~	~~39~~	~~40~~
41	~~42~~	43	~~44~~	~~45~~	~~46~~	47	~~48~~	49	~~50~~

Figure 1.3

The next number on the list that has not been crossed off is 7, making it prime. We circle it, and move through the list eliminating multiples of 7.

	(2)	(3)	~~4~~	(5)	~~6~~	(7)	~~8~~	~~9~~	~~10~~
11	~~12~~	13	~~14~~	~~15~~	~~16~~	17	~~18~~	19	~~20~~
~~21~~	~~22~~	23	~~24~~	~~25~~	~~26~~	~~27~~	~~28~~	29	~~30~~
31	~~32~~	~~33~~	~~34~~	~~35~~	~~36~~	37	~~38~~	~~39~~	~~40~~
41	~~42~~	43	~~44~~	~~45~~	~~46~~	47	~~48~~	~~49~~	~~50~~

Figure 1.4

We now circle all remaining numbers in the list as shown in Figure 1.5.

	(2)	(3)	~~4~~	(5)	~~6~~	(7)	~~8~~	~~9~~	~~10~~
(11)	~~12~~	(13)	~~14~~	~~15~~	~~16~~	(17)	~~18~~	(19)	~~20~~
~~21~~	~~22~~	(23)	~~24~~	~~25~~	~~26~~	~~27~~	~~28~~	(29)	~~30~~
(31)	~~32~~	~~33~~	~~34~~	~~35~~	~~36~~	(37)	~~38~~	~~39~~	~~40~~
(41)	~~42~~	(43)	~~44~~	~~45~~	~~46~~	(47)	~~48~~	~~49~~	~~50~~

Figure 1.5

Because we need to check for multiples only through 7, we know that the circled numbers are all the prime numbers less than 50.

Problem

Use the Sieve of Eratosthenes to find all the prime numbers less than 100.

(a) What is the largest prime number that you will need to check to solve the problem?

(b) Using the following chart of numbers from 2–100, begin the sieve by circling 2, identifying it as prime, and then crossing off all multiples of 2.

	2	3	4	5	6	7	8	9	10
11	12	13	14	15	16	17	18	19	20
21	22	23	24	25	26	27	28	29	30
31	32	33	34	35	36	37	38	39	40
41	42	43	44	45	46	47	48	49	50
51	52	53	54	55	56	57	58	59	60
61	62	63	64	65	66	67	68	69	70
71	72	73	74	75	76	77	78	79	80
81	82	83	84	85	86	87	88	89	90
91	92	93	94	95	96	97	98	99	100

(c) Use the chart to find all of the prime numbers less than 100.

Skill Level II 

Problem

Use the Sieve of Eratosthenes to find all the prime numbers less than 200.

Show your work.

	2	3	4	5	6	7	8	9	10
11	12	13	14	15	16	17	18	19	20
21	22	23	24	25	26	27	28	29	30
31	32	33	34	35	36	37	38	39	40
41	42	43	44	45	46	47	48	49	50
51	52	53	54	55	56	57	58	59	60
61	62	63	64	65	66	67	68	69	70
71	72	73	74	75	76	77	78	79	80
81	82	83	84	85	86	87	88	89	90
91	92	93	94	95	96	97	98	99	100
101	102	103	104	105	106	107	108	109	110
111	112	113	114	115	116	117	118	119	120
121	122	123	124	125	126	127	128	129	130
131	132	133	134	135	136	137	138	139	140
141	142	143	144	145	146	147	148	149	150
151	152	153	154	155	156	157	158	159	160
161	162	163	164	165	166	167	168	169	170
171	172	173	174	175	176	177	178	179	180
181	182	183	184	185	186	187	188	189	190
191	192	193	194	195	196	197	198	199	200

Skill Level III ♦♦♦

Problem

Find two prime numbers that, if multiplied, would generate a 400-digit number.

Show your work. Discuss your strategy in the space provided.

Applied Math Skill Check

1. Execute the following multiplications by hand.

   (a) $\begin{array}{r} 17 \\ \times\ 19 \\ \hline \end{array}$

   (b) $\begin{array}{r} 257 \\ \times\ 341 \\ \hline \end{array}$

2. Using your calculator, find the following square roots.

   (a) $\sqrt{25}$

   (b) $\sqrt{345}$

   (c) $\sqrt{67.98}$

   (d) $\sqrt{\pi}$

   (e) $\sqrt{0}$

3. Write out all the multiples of 2 that are less than 30.

4. Write out all the multiples of 3 that are less than 50.

5. Identify which of the following numbers are prime.

   (a) 11

   (b) 29

   (c) 33

   (d) 117

Information Technology Project—Prime Numbers and Computer Encryption Codes

Hint

See Appendix D-1 for instructions on completing this project.

Problem

Use Microsoft Word to construct a flowchart for the Sieve of Eratosthenes.

Converting from Decimal to Binary

In this project, we discuss how to convert between the decimal number system we use in daily life and the binary number system used by computers.

Objectives

1. Convert a base 10 number into a base 2 number
2. Convert a base 2 number into a base 10 number
3. Add two binary numbers

Tools Book CD: No Coverage

Computers have become an integral part of our daily lives, helping us with numerous tedious tasks and complex calculations. However, regardless of the complexity of a calculation or application, all of the functions of a computer ultimately reduce to a system of circuits that are either open or closed. We represent these two states by the numbers 0 (for the open state) and 1 (for the closed state). Consequently, calculations inside a computer are done using a base 2 or binary number system rather than the base 10 or decimal system with which we are most familiar. In this project, we will learn how to convert between these two number systems.

Converting a Binary Number into a Decimal Number

First, it is important to remember that the various digits contained in a decimal number correspond to designated powers of 10. For example, the number 3471 contains 3 thousands, 4 hundreds, 7 tens, and 1 one. Expressed in terms of powers of 10, we have

MATH REVIEW

Remember that 10 raised to the zeroth power is 1. Thus, the 10^0 column corresponds to our ones column.

3	4	7	1
10^3 (1000)	10^2 (100)	10^1 (10)	10^0 (1)

In a base 10 system, we have access to the ten digits, 0 through 9, in each column. After 9, we must move into the next column. The number 9,

		9
	10^1 (10)	10^0 (1)

becomes

	1	0
	10^1 (10)	10^0 (1)

if 1 is added.

To express numbers using bases other than 10, we use the same principle. For example, if we use a base of three, the columns are based on powers of 3:

3^4 (81)	3^3 (27)	3^2 (9)	3^1 (3)	3^0 (1)

Just as we have access to ten digits in a base 10 number system, 0 through 9, we have access to three digits in a base 3 system, 0 through 2. An example of a base 3 number is:

2	1	0	0	2
3^4 (81)	3^3 (27)	3^2 (9)	3^1 (3)	3^0 (1)

This number contains two 3s raised to the fourth power, one 3 raised to the third power, and two 3s raised to the zeroth power:

$$\begin{aligned} 2 \times 3^4 &= 2 \times 81 = 162 \\ 1 \times 3^3 &= 1 \times 27 = \ \ 27 \\ 2 \times 3^0 &= 2 \times 1 \ \ = \ \ \ \ 2 \\ \hline & \qquad\qquad\quad 191 \end{aligned}$$

Thus, the number 21002 base 3 is equal to 191 base 10.

As we stated previously, the base 2 or binary number system is the basis for all computer operations. In this system, we have access only to the two numbers 0 and 1.

Skill Level I 

Problem

Find the decimal representation of the following binary number.

1	1	0	1	1	0	0	1
2^7	2^6	2^5	2^4	2^3	2^2	2^1	2^0

Show your work.

Skill Level II 

Converting a Decimal Number into a Binary Number

For many people, converting a decimal number into a binary representation is more difficult than converting a binary number into its decimal representation. Fortunately, a simple algorithm exists for making this conversion. To change a base 10 number into any other base, we simply divide the base into the number and keep track of the remainders.

Example 1

Express the decimal number 245 in base 3.

Solution

To convert the number into base 3, we simply divide 3 into 245, and read the remainders in reverse order:

Division	**Remainder**
3 | 245	
3 | 81	2
3 | 27	0
3 | 9	0
3 | 3	0
3 | 1	0
0	1

Read in reverse order ↑

Thus, 100002 base 3 is the same as 245 base 10.

Problem

Express the decimal number 4693 as a binary number.

Show your work.

Skill Level III ♦♦♦

Adding Binary Numbers

Mathematical operations such as addition, subtraction, multiplication, and division can be performed on binary numbers just as they can be on decimal numbers. Recall that when adding two base 10 numbers, a quantity in excess of the value of 9 in a particular column requires us to move to the next column. For example, when we add 27 and 34, we exceed 9 in the first column and must carry the number 1 into the second column:

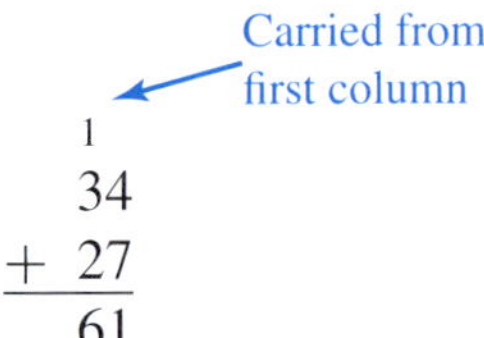

In a like manner, when we add two binary numbers, we must carry values into the next column whenever we exceed the value of 1, since we have access only to the numbers 0 and 1 in the binary system.

Example 2

Find the sum of 1101 and 1011.

Solution

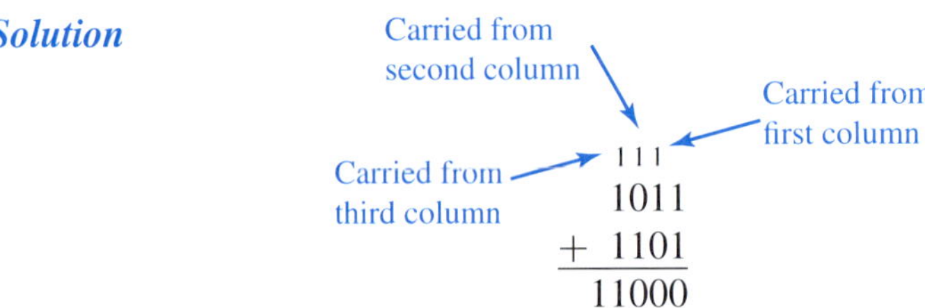

Problem

1. Express the sum of 257 and 431 in decimal form.
2. Convert the two numbers 257 and 431 into their binary representations.
3. Add the two binary numbers from part 2.
4. Show that the decimal version of your answer from part 3 is the same as your answer from part 1.

Show your work.

Applied Math Skill Check

1. Express the following binary numbers in the decimal number system.

   (a) 11

   (b) 101

   (c) 11101

   (d) 100011

2. Express the following decimal numbers in the binary number system.

   (a) 12

   (b) 29

   (c) 143

   (d) 1024

3. Add the following binary numbers.

   (a) $\begin{array}{r} 101 \\ +\ 111 \\ \hline \end{array}$ (b) $\begin{array}{r} 10111 \\ +\ 101111 \\ \hline \end{array}$

Information Technology Project—Converting from Decimal to Binary

HINT

See Appendix D-2 for instructions on completing this project.

Problem

1. Learn the basics of ASCII code.
2. Learn the relationship between binary numbers and ASCII code.

Permutations and Combinations

In this Information Technology Project, we review the topics of factorials, permutations, and combinations, and see how they relate to the information technology field.

Objectives

1. Calculate a permutation
2. Calculate a combination
3. Write the factors for a quantity given in factorial notation

Tools Book CD: No Coverage

Whether we are installing a complex network of computers or determining how to set up a committee of individuals drawn from a workforce, an important skill to acquire is the calculation of *permutations* and *combinations*. We begin this project by discussing the mathematical topic of *factorials,* since such expressions are used extensively when calculating the number of ways that objects can be organized. After this introduction, we move into the main topic of the project and discuss how to calculate permutations and combinations.

Factorials

In the shorthand of mathematics, the expression 5! (read "five *factorial*") means that we multiply all of the numbers from 5 down to 1:

$$5! = 5 \cdot 4 \cdot 3 \cdot 2 \cdot 1$$

$$5! = 120$$

Similarly, the expression 10! is shorthand for the following multiplication.

$$10 \cdot 9 \cdot 8 \cdot 7 \cdot 6 \cdot 5 \cdot 4 \cdot 3 \cdot 2 \cdot 1 = 3{,}628{,}800$$

Most calculators in use today, including the one built into the Accessories menu of the Windows operating system, have a factorial button.

Skill Level I ♦

Problem

Calculate the following factorials.

1. 6!
2. 15!
3. 2!
4. 140!

Record your answers in the space provided.

Permutations and Combinations

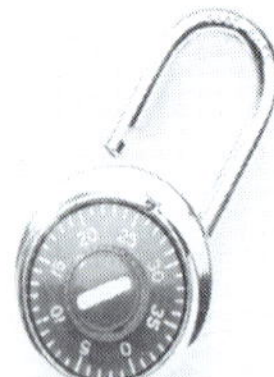

Although locks like the one in this photo are called "combination" locks, they might more accurately be described as "permutation" locks, because the order of the sequence of numbers is important.

Courtesy of PhotoDisc, Inc.

Although many people use the terms *permutation* and *combination* interchangeably, they have distinct meanings from a mathematical standpoint. When considering the possible *combinations* of a set of objects, we are interested only in the objects themselves, without reference to the order in which they appear. In contrast, both the objects and the order in which they appear are important when identifying the possible *permutations* of the objects.

For example, suppose that we want to identify all possible pairs of numbers that may be drawn from the set of numbers 1–3:

$$\{1, 2, 3\}$$

If we identify all possible *combinations*, we find

$$\{1, 2; 1, 3; 2, 3\}$$

However, when we take the order of the pairs of numbers into consideration we see that the pairs 12 and 21 are distinct; therefore, the possible *permutations* are

$$\{1, 2; 1, 3; 2, 1; 2, 3; 3, 1; 3, 2\}$$

If we denote by n the number of objects in the set, and by r the number of objects to be selected from the set, the equations for the number of combinations and permutations can be expressed as follows.

Combinations of n objects chosen r at a time:

$$C(n, r) = \frac{n!}{(n-r)!\,r!}$$

Permutations of n objects chosen r at a time:

$$P(n, r) = \frac{n!}{(n-r)!}$$

Notice that the two equations are the same except for the additional factor of $r!$ in the denominator of the combinations equation. The inclusion of this term means that there will be many fewer combinations than permutations.

Example

Given the set of letters $\{a, b, c, d, e, f\}$, calculate

(a) the number of possible combinations of 4 letters, and
(b) the number of possible permutations of 4 letters.

Solution

(a) Since there are six letters in the set, $n = 6$. Because we are to select four letters at a time, $r = 4$. When we insert these numbers into the combination equation, we find

$$C(n, r) = \frac{n!}{(n-r)!\,r!}$$

$$C(6, 4) = \frac{6!}{(6-4)!\,4!}$$

$$C(6, 4) = \frac{6!}{2! \cdot 4!}$$

$$C(6, 4) = \frac{720}{2 \cdot 24} = \frac{720}{48}$$

$$C(6, 4) = 15$$

(b) Inserting $n = 6$ and $r = 4$ into the permutation equation yields

$$P(n, r) = \frac{n!}{(n-r)!}$$

$$P(6, 4) = \frac{6!}{(6-4)!}$$

$$P(6, 4) = \frac{6!}{2!} = \frac{720}{2}$$

$$P(6, 4) = 360$$

As expected, there are many more permutations of the letters than there are combinations.

Skill Level II 

Problem

Five computers are to be wired in a linear network, as in the following figure.

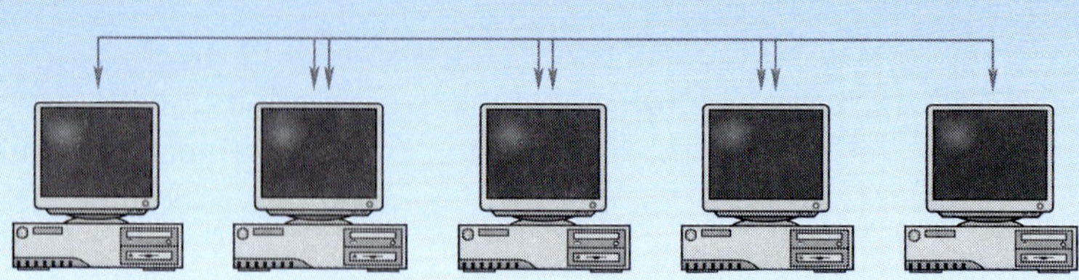

How many permutations of the five computers are possible?

HINT

$0! = 1$

Show your work.

Skill Level III 

Problem

A computer with an old processor locks up if more than 4 applications are running simultaneously. If the owner has 20 applications stored in his program file, how many different sets of 4 can he run, so that his computer does not lock up?

HINT

Does it matter which application is opened first when running the four applications?

Show your work.

Applied Math Skill Check

Calculate each of the following.

1. 20!
2. $\dfrac{15!}{8!}$
3. $C(7, 4)$
4. $P(12, 3)$

Information Technology Project—Permutations and Combinations

HINT

See Appendix D-3 for instructions on completing this project.

Problem

Use the project topic of permutations and combinations as a setting to learn how to insert formulas in Microsoft Excel.

Logical Reasoning

To achieve success in the field of information technology, it is important to hone reasoning and logic skills. This Information Technology Project addresses various problem solving skills associated with logic problems, and reviews equations involving bases and exponents.

Objectives

1. Reason through and solve a logic problem
2. When appropriate, sketch a diagram to help solve a logic problem
3. Identify the number of distinct solutions to a logic problem
4. Use bases and exponents

Tools Book CD: 10.2A

Skill Level I ♦

Problem

A computer technician has been assigned the task of cabling together five computers, numbered 1–5, in a circular network, as shown in the following figure.

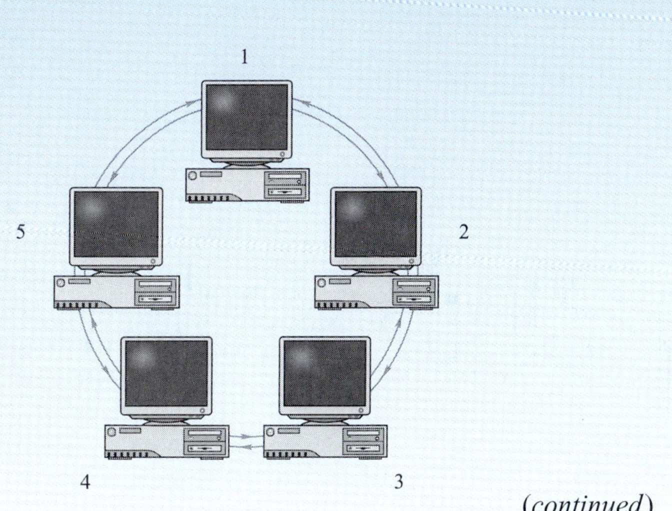

(*continued*)

The technician is given the following pieces of information:

1. Computer 1 must be cabled to computer 3.
2. Computer 2 cannot be cabled to computer 5.

Make a sketch of the *distinct* way(s) that the five computers can be placed in the network.

Show your work.

Skill Level II 

Problem

A server is cabled radially to five computers, each of which is cabled to five more computers, as shown in the following figure.

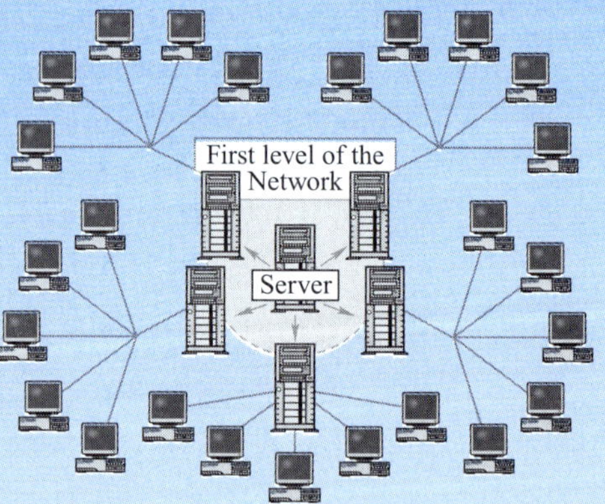

1. If the network continues to expand, with each computer being cabled to five more computers, how many computers will be in the sixth level of the network?
2. Including the server, how many computers would be in the network if it were extended to the seventh level?
3. Using the language of bases and exponents, develop a simple method for predicting how many computers will be in a particular level of the network.

Record your answers in the given space.

Skill Level III ♦♦♦

Zeno's Paradox

The Greek philosopher Zeno of Elea was famous for devising problems, or paradoxes, that have illogical solutions. By placing Zeno's famous "Achilles and the Tortoise" paradox in a modern context, we can examine how imprecise language can affect the solution to a logic problem.

Problem

Zeno's Paradox
Suppose that a man wants to cross to the far wall of a room that is 20-ft across. First, he crosses half of the distance to reach the 10-ft mark. Next, he crosses halfway across the remaining 10 ft to arrive at the 5-ft mark. Dividing the distance in half again, he crosses to the 2.5-ft mark, and continues to cross the room in this way, dividing each distance in half and crossing to that point. Because each of the increasingly smaller distances can be divided in half, he must reach an infinite number of "midpoints" in a finite amount of time, and will never reach the wall.

Explain the error in Zeno's Paradox.

Record your answer in the space provided.

Applied Math Skill Check

1. Identify the base and the exponent in each of the following expressions.

(a) 4^3	base =	exponent =
(b) $(-3)^5$	base =	exponent =
(c) $\left(\frac{2}{3}\right)^4$	base =	exponent =
(d) x^y	base =	exponent =
(e) 1.75^3	base =	exponent =

2. Calculate each of the following quantities.

(a) 2^5

(b) 3^4

(c) 1^8

(d) 0^6

(e) $(-2)^2$

(f) $(-3)^3$

(g) 10^0

(h) 1^0

(i) 0^0

(j) $\left(\frac{1}{2}\right)^3$

(k) $\left(-\frac{1}{4}\right)^2$

(l) $(0.6)^4$

(m) π^5

Information Technology Project—Logical Reasoning

HINT

See Appendix D-4 for instructions on completing this project.

Problem

Learn how to use the basic functions of Boolean logic to increase the effectiveness of your internet searches.

Tracking Profits

In this Information Technology Project, we use the topic of business profits to illustrate how to construct a quadratic equation.

Objectives

1. Read a passage of text and construct an equation based on the information contained therein
2. Rewrite an equation in the standard form of a quadratic equation
3. Solve a quadratic equation using the quadratic formula

Tools Book CD: 10.2A, 10.3A

Regardless of technical specialty, nearly all work in the information technology field is client-driven. Accordingly, technical graduates entering the workplace must be able to interpret information provided by clients and translate it into mathematical symbols and representations that can be encoded for computer use. In this Information Technology Project, we look at the challenges associated with making a profit in a retail business, as an example of how to translate textual information into mathematical symbols and equations.

Skill Level I 

Problem

A retailer spent \$48 to purchase a number of special mugs. Two of them were broken in the store, but by selling each of the remaining mugs for \$3 above the original cost per mug, she made a total profit of \$22.

Construct an equation that will allow us to solve for the number of mugs, denoted by n, that were originally purchased.

(a) If the price for n mugs is \$48, how can we express the cost per mug?

(b) We are told that the retailer, in order to make a specific profit, sells the remaining mugs for \$3 more than the original cost per mug. Using this information, and your answer to step (a), how can we express the selling price per mug?

(c) Since two of the mugs were broken in the store, how can we represent the number of mugs that are available for sale?

(d) Use your answers from steps (b) and (c) to construct an expression for the amount of money made on the sale of the remaining mugs.

HINT

If written correctly, your equation will contain only one variable, n.

(e) The profit on the mugs can be found by subtracting the cost of the mugs from the amount of money made on the sale of the mugs. Write an equation that states this relationship between the money made, the cost, and the profit.

Skill Level II 

Problem

Rewrite the equation that you wrote in step (e) of Skill Level I, in the standard form of a quadratic equation:

$$ax^2 + bx + c = 0$$

Show your work.

Skill Level III ♦♦♦

Problem

Solve your quadratic equation from Skill Level II using the quadratic formula, and answer the following questions.

1. How many mugs were purchased?
2. What was the original cost per mug?
3. What profit was made on each mug?
4. When solving a quadratic equation, there are normally two solutions. Why were you able to discard one of the solutions in this case?

Record your answers in the space provided.

Applied Math Skill Check

Place the following equations in the standard form of a quadratic equation, $ax^2 + bx + c = 0$.

1. $\dfrac{4}{x^2} + \dfrac{3}{x} - 10 = 0$
2. $6 + \dfrac{4}{x-1} = \dfrac{5}{x-3}$
3. $3.5x + \dfrac{4.6}{x} = 1.2$

Use the quadratic formula to solve the following quadratic equations.

4. $3x^2 + 2x - 8 = 0$
5. $5x^2 + 7x = 12$

Information Technology Project—Tracking Profits

HINT

See Appendix D-5 for instructions on completing this project.

Problem

Use Microsoft Excel to calculate the profits of a company.

Corporate Optimization

In this project, we use the topic of corporate optimization as a setting to review the construction of an equation from textual information, and then use the graph of that equation to make predictions.

Objectives

1. Translate written information into an equation
2. Graph an equation that contains a single independent variable
3. Given the equation of a line, find the slope of the line
4. Based on the slope of a line, interpret the response of the dependent variable to a change in the independent variable
5. Given the equations of two intersecting lines, find the point of intersection

Tools Book CD: 3.2, 3.3

To compete in today's economy, businesses must run as efficiently as possible. Managers spend time analyzing how effectively their core resources (including personnel, goods, and capital) are being used. To ensure a "lean, mean" operation, companies work hard to gain the maximum return from their existing resources. This process of using resources in the most effective way is called *optimization*. With the advent of computers, the task of optimization analysis was made easier. *Optimization codes* were constructed that allowed managers to input data and get feedback on the effectiveness of their organizations.

Optimization involves changing one or more variable(s) (personnel schedules, prices, etc.) and monitoring the result of this change on profit or other important outcomes. Expressed in the language of mathematics, optimization involves varying one or more independent variable(s), and monitoring the response of the dependent variable(s). Because today's information technology graduate may encounter these types of optimization codes, it is important to understand the relationship between dependent and independent variables, in both equation and graphical form. As an example of corporate optimization and the relationship between dependent and independent variables, we use a hypothetical sample of data drawn from two fictitious rival trucking companies.

Skill Level I 

Problem

Yellow Trucking Rental Company advertises the following charges.

- One-way rental of a 15-ft truck is $45.00 per day, and 37 cents per mile for every mile driven over 500.
- Round-trip rental for the same truck is $30.00 per day and, 10 cents per mile for every mile driven over 250.

Gray Trucking Rental Company offers the following rates.

- One-way rental of a 14-ft truck is $40.00 per day, and 18 cents per mile for every mile driven over 300.
- Round-trip rental of the same truck is $20.00 per day, and 10 cents per mile driven.

1. For each company, construct an equation that expresses the relationship between the income earned and the miles traveled for a round trip.
2. Graph, separately, both of the equations that you constructed in part 1.

(a) Because the number of *miles* driven determines the *income earned,* which of these quantities is the independent variable and which is the dependent variable?

(b) If we choose y as the dependent variable, and x as the independent variable, what form will the equation for income earned from miles driven take, for each company?

(c) When graphing, we normally place the independent coordinate on the horizontal axis and the dependent coordinate on the vertical axis. In the space provided, sketch two sets of coordinate axes using the axis labels x and y on one set, and the miles driven and the earned income on the other set.

MATH REVIEW

In a graph of the equation

$$y = mx + b$$

m, the coefficient on x, is the slope of the graph.

(d) Sketch a graph of each equation that you wrote in step (b).

(e) What does the fact that the slope of both graphs is the same tell us about the relationship between the vertical coordinate (the earned income) and the horizontal coordinate (the mileage)?

HINT

How will the vertical coordinate change if the horizontal coordinate is varied for each company?

(f) Suppose that the baseline charge was increased for each company, but the price charged per mile driven was held constant. What effect, if any, would this change have on the relationship between earned income and miles driven?

(g) In your opinion, which would have a greater effect on the earned income for each company, increasing the baseline charge, or raising the price for each mile driven? Explain your reasoning.

(h) Using the equations that you constructed in step (b), calculate the rental cost for a 400-mile round trip for each company. Show your work.

Skill Level II 

Problem

1. For each company, construct an equation that represents the mileage driven versus the earned income for a one-way trip.
2. Graph each of the equations that you constructed in part 1.

Sketch your graphs in the space provided.

Skill Level III 

Problem

A corporate analyst is asked to analyze the profitability of the two trucking companies. As a starting point for his analysis, he must find the point at which both companies earn the same amount of money.

1. Using your equations from step (b) of Skill Level I, decide if there is a mileage at which each company earns the same amount of money for a round trip.
2. Find the number of miles that a truck from each company must be driven to earn an identical sum on a one-way trip.

Show your work.

Applied Math Skill Check

Graph the following equations.

1. $y = 2x + 1$
2. $y = \frac{1}{2}x - 3$
3. $y = x + 0.7$

Graph the following horizontal and vertical lines.

4. $y = 3$
5. $x = 5$

Translate the following statements into equations.

6. The variable y is equal to 3 more than 5 times the variable x.
7. If 7 is added to three-fifths of the variable x, the result is equal to the variable y.
8. Identify the slope of each of the following lines.

   (a) $y = 3x - 1$ slope =

   (b) $y = -2x + 5$ slope =

9. Find the value of x at which the two lines $y = 2x + 1$ and $y = -\frac{1}{4}x + 3$ intersect.

Information Technology Project—Corporate Optimization

HINT

See Appendix D-6 for instructions on completing this project.

Problem

Use Microsoft Excel to create a profit and loss balance sheet and graph the results.

Memory Fields and Matrices

In this project, we use the memory fields that store information in a computer as a setting to review the mathematical topic of matrices.

Objectives

1. Add, subtract and multiply two matrices
2. Identify the dimensionality of a matrix

Tools Book CD: No Coverage

When information is entered into a computer, it is recorded in a *field* that behaves in the same way as the mathematical object known as a *matrix*. When the computer manipulates the information in a field, or combines it with the information in another field, the computer is actually performing the same types of calculations that we execute when we manipulate or combine two or more matrices. In this Information Technology project, we discuss how to combine matrices using addition, subtraction, and multiplication in order to gain an understanding of the behavior of the information fields inside a computer

Matrices

In mathematics, a *matrix* is used to store individual numbers, or other pieces of data. The amount of data that can be stored in the matrix depends upon the size of the matrix. Examples of matrices include:

$$\begin{bmatrix} 1 & 5 & -3 \\ -2 & 4 & 11 \\ 7 & 5 & 2 \end{bmatrix} \qquad \begin{bmatrix} a & k \\ b & r \end{bmatrix} \qquad \begin{bmatrix} 2.50 \\ 6.73 \\ -9.02 \\ 4.96 \end{bmatrix}$$

The size of the matrix, and therefore the number of slots for data, is usually expressed in terms of the number of rows and columns in the matrix, and referred to as the *dimensionality* of the matrix. For example, a 2 × 3 matrix has 2 rows and 3 columns:

$$\underbrace{\begin{bmatrix} a & b & c \\ d & e & f \end{bmatrix}}_{\text{3 columns}} \Big\} \text{2 rows}$$

while a 3 × 2 matrix has 3 rows and 2 columns:

$$\underbrace{\begin{bmatrix} 1 & 2 \\ 3 & 4 \\ 5 & 6 \end{bmatrix}}_{\text{2 columns}} \Bigg\} \text{3 rows}$$

Although each of these matrices has six slots for data, they have different shapes and are therefore different matrices. If the number of rows is the same as the number of columns, as in the following two examples, the matrix is referred to as a *square matrix*.

$$\underbrace{\begin{bmatrix} 1.7 & 2.3 \\ 4.5 & 2.8 \end{bmatrix}}_{\text{2 columns}} \Big\} \text{2 rows} \qquad \underbrace{\begin{bmatrix} a & b & 3 \\ t & 5 & 1 \\ 6 & 7 & K \end{bmatrix}}_{\text{3 columns}} \Bigg\} \text{3 rows}$$

Skill Level I ♦

Problem

1. Identify the dimensionality of each of the following matrices. Record the dimensions in row × column form.
2. Identify any square matrices.
3. Record your answers beside each matrix.

(a) $\begin{bmatrix} a & b \\ c & d \end{bmatrix}$

(b) $\begin{bmatrix} 1 & 5 \\ 7 & 3 \\ 2 & 1 \end{bmatrix}$

(c) $\begin{bmatrix} a \\ b \\ c \\ d \end{bmatrix}$

(d) $[1 \quad 3 \quad 5 \quad 8]$

(e) $\begin{bmatrix} 1 & 2 & 3 & 4 \\ 5 & 6 & 7 & 8 \\ 9 & 10 & 11 & 12 \\ 13 & 14 & 15 & 16 \end{bmatrix}$

Skill Level II ♦♦

Adding and Subtracting Matrices

Two or more matrices may be added or subtracted, provided that they have the same dimensionality. For example, a 2 × 3 matrix can be added to another 2 × 3 matrix. However, a 2 × 3 matrix *cannot* be added to a 3 × 2 matrix. To add two matrices of identical dimensionalities, we simply add the components in each of the slots:

$$\begin{bmatrix} a & b \\ c & d \end{bmatrix} + \begin{bmatrix} e & f \\ g & h \end{bmatrix} = \begin{bmatrix} a+e & b+f \\ c+g & d+h \end{bmatrix}$$

To subtract matrices, we subtract each component in the second matrix from its respective partner in the first matrix:

$$\begin{bmatrix} a & b & c \\ d & e & f \\ g & h & i \end{bmatrix} - \begin{bmatrix} 1 & 2 & 3 \\ 4 & 5 & 6 \\ 7 & 8 & 9 \end{bmatrix} = \begin{bmatrix} a-1 & b-2 & c-3 \\ d-4 & e-5 & f-6 \\ g-7 & h-8 & i-9 \end{bmatrix}$$

Problem

Add or subtract each of the following matrices. If the matrices cannot be combined, indicate why.

1. $\begin{bmatrix} 2 & 3 & 4 \\ 6 & 7 & 1 \end{bmatrix} + \begin{bmatrix} 1 & 4 & 9 \\ 3 & 2 & 4 \end{bmatrix}$

2. $\begin{bmatrix} 2 & 1 \\ -4 & 6 \\ 7 & -2 \end{bmatrix} + \begin{bmatrix} 3 & 1 & 7 \\ 4 & -5 & 6 \end{bmatrix}$

3. $\begin{bmatrix} 2 \\ 3 \\ -6 \\ 4 \end{bmatrix} - \begin{bmatrix} -1 \\ 5 \\ -2 \\ -9 \end{bmatrix}$

4. $\begin{bmatrix} 4 & 1 & 2 & 7 \\ 3 & -4 & -5 & 8 \\ 2 & 1 & 4 & -6 \\ 3 & 5 & -8 & -1 \end{bmatrix} + \begin{bmatrix} -1 & 2 & -6 & -5 \\ 3 & -2 & 4 & -9 \\ 4 & -7 & 5 & 2 \\ 3 & 1 & 4 & 6 \end{bmatrix}$

Show your work in the space provided.

Skill Level III ♦♦♦

Multiplying Matrices

Multiplication of matrices takes two forms: multiplying a matrix by a constant, and multiplying two matrices.

Multiplying a Matrix by a Constant

To multiply a matrix by a constant, we distribute the constant to each of the entries in the matrix:

$$3\begin{bmatrix} 2 & 5 \\ -1 & 4 \end{bmatrix} = \begin{bmatrix} 3 \cdot 2 & 3 \cdot 5 \\ 3 \cdot (-1) & 3 \cdot 4 \end{bmatrix} = \begin{bmatrix} 6 & 15 \\ -3 & 12 \end{bmatrix}$$

Multiplying Two Matrices

Multiplying a matrix by another matrix requires more steps than adding or subtracting two matrices, or multiplying a matrix by a constant.

First, we must determine whether it is possible to multiply the two matrices. To make this determination, we check the inner dimensions of the matrices to be multiplied. For example, a 3×2 matrix can be multiplied by a 2×3 matrix, since the inner dimensions of 2 agree.

$$3 \times 2 \qquad 2 \times 3$$

Terms agree

However, a 3×2 matrix cannot be multiplied by another 3×2 matrix since the inner dimensions do not agree (one is 2 and the other is 3):

$$3 \times 2 \qquad 3 \times 2$$

Terms do not agree

The dimensionality of the solution matrix is determined by the outer dimensions. In the case of the 3×2 by 2×3 multiplication that we just learned is possible, the solution matrix would by a 3×3 matrix:

$$3 \times 2 \qquad 2 \times 3$$

Example

Multiply the following two matrices.

$$\begin{bmatrix} 1 & 2 \\ 3 & 5 \end{bmatrix}\begin{bmatrix} 2 & 7 \\ 1 & 4 \end{bmatrix}$$

Solution

First, we verify that the two matrices can be multiplied by checking that the inner dimensions of the desired multiplication agree.

$$2 \times 2 \quad 2 \times 2$$

Since the inner dimensions of both are 2, the matrices can be multiplied. Next, we look at the outer dimensions to determine the expected dimensions of the solution matrix.

$$2 \times 2 \quad 2 \times 2$$

Since the outer dimensions of both are 2, we know that the solution matrix must be 2×2.

To multiply the two matrices, each *row* of the left matrix is multiplied by each *column* of the right matrix. These individual products are then added to get the entries in the solution matrix.

To find the top left entry of the solution matrix, we multiply the top row of the left matrix by the first column in the right matrix, and then add the products:

$$\begin{bmatrix} 1 & 2 \\ 3 & 5 \end{bmatrix}\begin{bmatrix} 2 & 7 \\ 1 & 4 \end{bmatrix} = \begin{bmatrix} 1 \cdot 2 + 2 \cdot 1 & \\ & \end{bmatrix} = \begin{bmatrix} 4 & \\ & \end{bmatrix}$$

To find the top right entry in the solution matrix, we multiply the top row of the left matrix by the second column of the right matrix:

$$\begin{bmatrix} 1 & 2 \\ 3 & 5 \end{bmatrix}\begin{bmatrix} 2 & 7 \\ 1 & 4 \end{bmatrix} = \begin{bmatrix} & 1 \cdot 7 + 2 \cdot 4 \\ & \end{bmatrix} = \begin{bmatrix} 4 & 15 \\ & \end{bmatrix}$$

Notice that the top row of the left matrix generates the top row of the solution matrix. Logically, we then move to the second row of the left matrix to generate the bottom row of the solution matrix. To obtain the bottom left entry in the solution matrix, we multiply the bottom row of the left matrix by the first column of the right matrix:

$$\begin{bmatrix} 1 & 2 \\ 3 & 5 \end{bmatrix}\begin{bmatrix} 2 & 7 \\ 1 & 4 \end{bmatrix} = \begin{bmatrix} & \\ 3 \cdot 2 + 1 \cdot 5 & \end{bmatrix} = \begin{bmatrix} 4 & 15 \\ 11 & \end{bmatrix}$$

Finally, we find the bottom right entry of the solution matrix by multiplying the bottom row of the left matrix by the second column of the right matrix:

$$\begin{bmatrix} 1 & 2 \\ 3 & 5 \end{bmatrix}\begin{bmatrix} 2 & 7 \\ 1 & 4 \end{bmatrix} = \begin{bmatrix} & \\ & 3 \cdot 7 + 5 \cdot 4 \end{bmatrix} = \begin{bmatrix} 4 & 15 \\ 11 & 41 \end{bmatrix}$$

Problem

1. Perform each of the following multiplications.

(a) $3\begin{bmatrix} 2 & 1 \\ 5 & 6 \end{bmatrix}$

(b) $-5\begin{bmatrix} 2 \\ -3 \\ 4 \\ -2 \end{bmatrix}$

(c) $-4\begin{bmatrix} -1 & 2 & -3 \\ 4 & 6 & -2 \\ -5 & 1 & 7 \end{bmatrix}$

(d) $2 \cdot 6\begin{bmatrix} 4.2 & 3.1 & 4.7 \end{bmatrix}$

2. Indicate which of the following matrices can be multiplied. For those that can, indicate the dimensionality of the solution matrix.

(a) $\begin{bmatrix} a & b \\ c & d \end{bmatrix}\begin{bmatrix} 1 & 3 & 4 \\ 2 & 9 & 8 \end{bmatrix}$ (b) $\begin{bmatrix} 2 \\ 4 \\ 8 \end{bmatrix}\begin{bmatrix} 3 & 1 & 7 \end{bmatrix}$

(c) $\begin{bmatrix} 2 & 4 & 9 & -6 \end{bmatrix}\begin{bmatrix} 3 & 2 & -6 & 1 \\ -1 & 4 & 2 & 8 \end{bmatrix}$

(d) $\begin{bmatrix} a & f \\ p & q \end{bmatrix}\begin{bmatrix} 2 & 3 & 5 & 8 \\ 4 & 6 & 2 & 1 \end{bmatrix}$

3. Multiply the following matrices.

(a) $\begin{bmatrix} 3 & 1 \\ 2 & 5 \end{bmatrix}\begin{bmatrix} 6 & 1 \\ 4 & 9 \end{bmatrix}$

(b) $\begin{bmatrix} 2 & 5 & 9 \end{bmatrix}\begin{bmatrix} 1 \\ 5 \\ 4 \end{bmatrix}$

(c) $\begin{bmatrix} -2 & 4 & -6 \\ 1 & -1 & 0 \\ 0 & 2 & 5 \end{bmatrix}\begin{bmatrix} 1 & -1 & 1 \\ 3 & 0 & -2 \\ 4 & -6 & 7 \end{bmatrix}$

Record your answers in the space provided.

Applied Math Skill Check

1. Add/subtract the following matrices.

(a) $\begin{bmatrix} 2 & 3 \\ 4 & 8 \\ 2 & 1 \end{bmatrix} + \begin{bmatrix} 4 & 9 \\ 6 & 3 \\ 2 & 8 \end{bmatrix}$

(b) $\begin{bmatrix} 10 & 8 & 4 \\ -2 & 1 & 5 \\ -6 & 0 & 4 \end{bmatrix} - \begin{bmatrix} 6 & -2 & 1 \\ 5 & 1 & 8 \\ 3 & 4 & -6 \end{bmatrix}$

(c) $\begin{bmatrix} 3 \\ 5 \\ 2 \\ 6 \end{bmatrix} + \begin{bmatrix} 4.7 \\ 3.8 \\ -4.1 \\ 5.6 \end{bmatrix}$

2. Multiply the following matrices by their respective constants.

(a) $4\begin{bmatrix} 3 & 7 & -2 \\ 4 & 6 & 5 \end{bmatrix}$

(b) $-3\begin{bmatrix} 4 & -1 \\ -6 & 2 \end{bmatrix}$

(c) $4.9\begin{bmatrix} 2 & -1 & 0 \\ 3 & 2 & -8 \end{bmatrix}$

3. Multiply the following matrices. Write the dimensionality of the resulting matrix beside each of your solutions.

(a) $\begin{bmatrix} 2 & 1 \\ 4 & 2 \end{bmatrix}\begin{bmatrix} 3 & 6 \\ 5 & -4 \end{bmatrix}$

(b) $\begin{bmatrix} 3 & -1 & 6 \\ 4 & -2 & -1 \\ 5 & 0 & 3 \end{bmatrix}\begin{bmatrix} 6 & 2 & -5 \\ 0 & -3 & 4 \\ 1 & 0 & 1 \end{bmatrix}$

(c) $\begin{bmatrix} -1 & -2 & -3 & -4 \end{bmatrix}\begin{bmatrix} -1 \\ -2 \\ -3 \\ -4 \end{bmatrix}$

Information Technology Project—Memory Fields and Matrices

HINT

See Appendix D-7 for instructions on completing this project.

Problem

1. Execute the necessary research to become acquainted with a variety of the terms associated with computer memory.
2. Summarize your research using Microsoft Word.
3. Perform a disk defragmentation and a disk cleanup.

Fiber-Optic Cables

Fiber-optic cables have become increasingly important to this society, in which we expect instant relay of data and other bits of information. In this project, we use the topic of fiber-optic cables as a setting to review right-triangle trigonometry.

Objectives

1. Use a calculator to find the sine, cosine, and tangent of a given angle
2. Given a trigonometric equation, solve for an unknown quantity
3. Use the inverse trigonometric functions to find an unknown angle

Tools Book CD: No Coverage

To understand fiber optics, we must begin with a discussion of the behavior of light in solids and Snell's Law. Then we will learn how Snell's Law predicts, and places restrictions upon the behavior of fiber-optic cables.

Refraction and Snell's Law

Have you ever noticed that a hand placed beneath the surface of the water in a swimming pool appears to bend at a bizarre angle? This same optical illusion can also be seen if we insert a pencil halfway into a glass of water.

This optical effect is called *refraction* and is the basic principle behind fiber optics. Because a mathematical understanding of refraction is necessary to fully understand fiber-optic cables, we begin by discussing the law that governs refraction—namely, Snell's Law.

Suppose that we aim a ray of light at the surface of a thick piece of glass. If we draw an imaginary dotted line (usually referred to as a *normal line*) perpendicular to the surface of the glass, we can measure the angle of the incoming ray from this line:

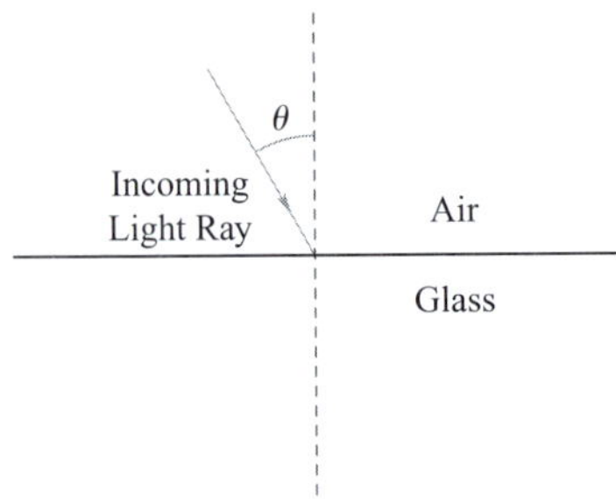

Figure 8.1

If we now follow the light ray into the glass, we see that it bends towards the normal line. The term we use for this bending property is *refraction* (Figure 8.2).

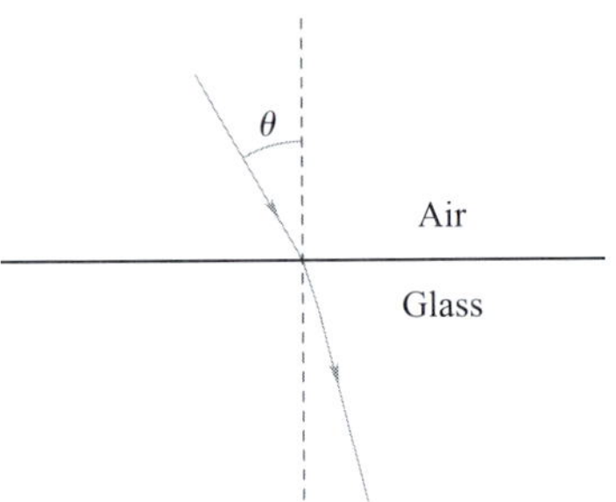

Figure 8.2

Because the material that the light entered (in our example, the glass) was denser than the air from which the light came, the light was refracted toward the normal line. Because materials have different densities, the angle that the refracted ray makes with the normal line varies according to the material. The amount that the ray is refracted is controlled by a property of the material called the *index of refraction*.

The index of refraction of a material (normally assigned the variable n) is the ratio of how fast light travels in a vacuum to how fast light travels in that material:

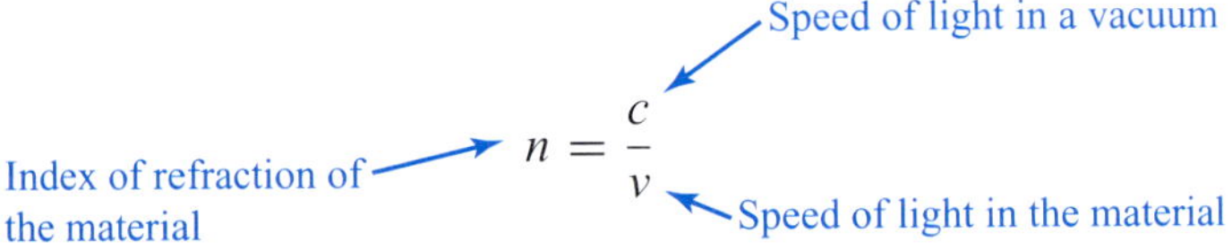

Notice that because both the numerator and the denominator of the right hand side are speeds, they have the same units. Because these units cancel one another, the index of refraction is a pure number with no units. A sample of the indexes of refraction for selected materials is given in Table 8.1.

Table 8.1 Indexes of Refraction for Selected Materials

Material	**Index**
Air	1.00029
Water	1.33
Ethyl alcohol	1.36
Fused quartz	1.46
Glycerine	1.47
Polystyrene	1.49
Oil (typical value)	1.50
Glass (by type)	1.45–1.70
Crown	1.52
Flint	1.66
Zircon	1.92
Diamond	2.42

Source: Wilson/Buffa, *College Physics* 4th ed., Prentice Hall, Upper Saddle River, NJ, 2000.

It is possible to relate the indexes of refraction of our two materials to the incoming angle and the angle of refraction. If we refer to the material in which the light ray starts as material 1, and the material that the light enters as material 2:

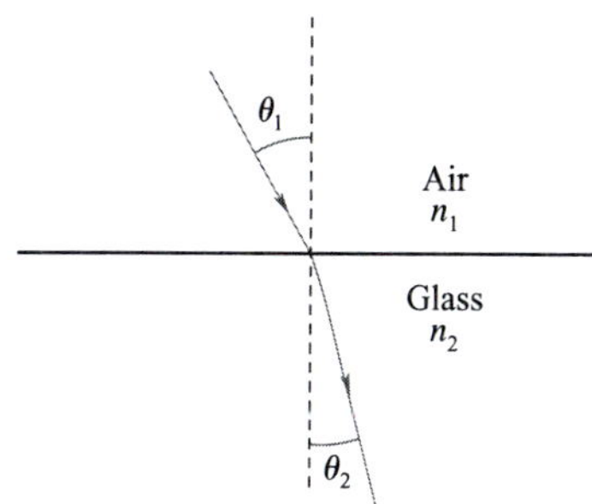

Figure 8.3

we can relate the indexes of refraction, and the angles of the incoming and refracted rays using *Snell's Law:*

$$n_1 \sin\theta_1 = n_2 \sin\theta_2$$

Example 1

A light ray in air ($n = 1.00029$) enters an unknown material at an angle of 30°. If, after being refracted, the light ray makes an angle of 20° with the normal line, find the index of refraction of the unknown material.

Solution

Beginning with Snell's Law and inserting our given values, we get

$$\begin{aligned} n_1 \sin\theta_1 &= n_2 \sin\theta_2 \\ 1.00029 \sin 30^\circ &= n_2 \sin 20^\circ \\ n_2 &= 1.462 \end{aligned}$$

Skill Level I 

Problem

A light ray beginning in fused quartz ($n = 1.46$) makes an angle of 45° with the normal line. Upon entering an unknown material, the light ray is refracted and makes an angle of 22° with the normal line. Find the index of refraction of the unknown material.

(a) Write an equation for the problem, using Snell's Law and the information given in the problem statement.

(b) In words, write out the correct order of operations necessary to find the unknown index of refraction.

(c) Solve your equation from step (a) and find the index of refraction for the unknown material.

Up to this point, we have examined situations in which a ray of light travels from a less dense material into a denser one. Another possibility is for a light ray to begin in a denser material and exit into a less dense material. In this case, the light ray is bent farther away from the normal line:

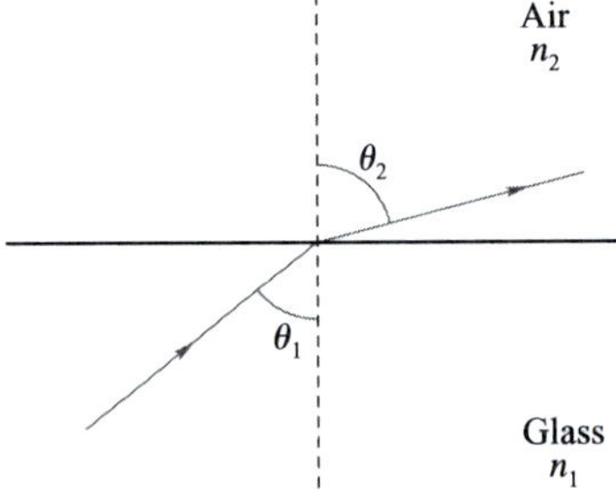

Figure 8.4

Total Internal Reflection and Fiber Optics

With this background on refraction, we are now ready to study the phenomenon at the heart of fiber-optic cables, namely *total internal reflection*. Let's use Snell's Law to conduct a thought experiment. In our experiment, the light ray begins to travel through a denser material (1) and then passes into a less dense material (2). If we continue to increase the angle that the beginning ray makes with the normal line, the refracted ray will move farther away from the normal line, as in Figure 8.5.

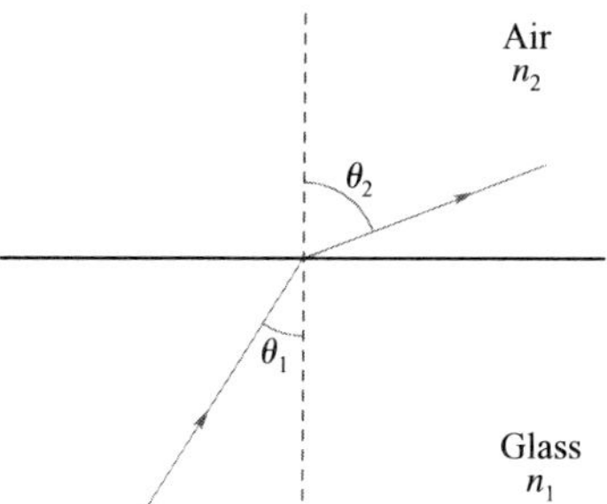

Figure 8.5

Let's continue to increase the initial angle until the refracted ray is bent so far away from the normal line that it is actually along the interface between the two materials:

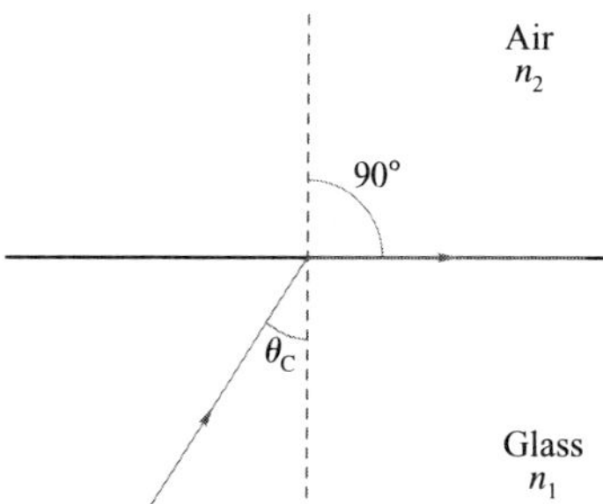

Figure 8.6

The initial angle that causes the refracted ray to move along the interface between the two materials is called the *critical angle,* θ_C. Any angle that is greater than the critical angle will force the refracted ray to be reflected back into material 1. This effect is called *total internal reflection,* and is the basis of fiber optics.

Let's use Snell's Law to describe mathematically the physical situation that we just described in words. If we begin with our initial equation,

$$n_1 \sin\theta_1 = n_2 \sin\theta_2$$

and substitute θ_C (the angle required to cause total internal reflection) for θ_1, and 90° (recall that the refracted ray is measured from the normal line) for θ_2, we get

$$n_1 \sin\theta_1 = n_2 \sin\theta_2$$
$$n_1 \sin\theta_C = n_2 \sin 90^\circ$$

Because the sine of $90^\circ = 1$ (verify this on your calculator),

$$n_1 \sin\theta_C = n_2(1)$$
$$n_1 \sin\theta_C = n_2$$

or, dividing both sides by n_1,

$$\sin\theta_C = \frac{n_2}{n_1} \tag{1}$$

Equation (1) is an example of how mathematics can give us profound physical information. Because the sine function can never be greater than 1, we have the following relationship:

> **MATH REVIEW**
>
> For a fraction to have a value less than one, the denominator of the fraction must be larger than the numerator of the fraction.

$$\frac{n_2}{n_1} \leq 1$$

This means that n_1 must be greater than n_2. In other words, we can only achieve total internal reflection if the material in which the light ray starts has a greater density than the material that the light ray is entering.

Skill Level II 

Problem

Total internal reflection between two materials is seen to occur if a critical angle of 60° is exceeded. If the index of refraction of the material that the light is entering is 1.98, find the index of refraction of the material in which the light is originating.

Show your work.

Skill Level III ◆◆◆

Inverse Trigonometric Functions

In technological contexts, we are often confronted with equations in which we are given the value of a particular trigonometric function, such as

$$\sin\theta = 0.53$$

$$\cos\theta = 0.68$$

$$\tan\theta = 2.4$$

However, what we really need to know is the angle that generated the data. As we have seen with other mathematical operations, the three basic trigonometric functions have inverse operations that will "undo" them. These operations are called *inverse sine* ($\sin^{-1}$), *inverse cosine* ($\cos^{-1}$), and *inverse tangent* ($\tan^{-1}$). To find the unknown angle in the preceding equations, we need only apply the appropriate inverse operation *to both sides of the equation.*

$$\sin\theta = 0.48$$
$$\sin^{-1}(\sin\theta) = \sin^{-1}(0.48)$$
$$\theta = 28.68^\circ$$
$$\cos\theta = 0.37$$
$$\cos^{-1}(\cos\theta) = \cos^{-1}(0.37)$$
$$\theta = 68.28^\circ$$
$$\tan\theta = 1.4$$
$$\tan^{-1}(\tan\theta) = \tan^{-1}(1.4)$$
$$\theta = 54.46^\circ$$

HINT

Your calculator is a valuable tool for performing this type of mathematical operation. Make sure that you know how to use your calculator to carry out each of these calculations.

Problem

1. A light ray attempts to pass from a material with an index of refraction of 2.48 into a material with an index of refraction of 1.74. Find the initial angle of the light ray necessary to achieve total internal reflection.
2. Execute the necessary research to explain how Snell's Law and the process of total internal reflection make it possible for fiber-optic cables to convey data in today's computer-dependent marketplace.

Record your answers in the space provided.

Applied Math Skill Check

1. Using your calculator, find each of the following quantities.

   (a) $\sin 48^\circ$
   (b) $\cos 72^\circ$
   (c) $\tan 38^\circ$
   (d) $\cos 0^\circ$
   (e) $\cos 90^\circ$
   (f) $\sin 0^\circ$
   (g) $\sin 90^\circ$
   (h) $\tan 45^\circ$
   (i) $\sin 138^\circ$
   (j) $\cos 145^\circ$

2. Find the angle θ, in degrees, in each of the following equations, using the appropriate inverse trigonometric function.

   (a) $\cos\theta = 0.49$
   (b) $\sin\theta = 0.73$
   (c) $\tan\theta = 2.5$
   (d) $\cos\theta = 1$
   (e) $\cos\theta = 0$
   (f) $\sin\theta = 1$
   (g) $\sin\theta = 0$
   (h) $\cos\theta = -1$
   (i) $\sin\theta = -1$
   (j) $\tan\theta = 1$
   (k) $\tan\theta = -1$
   (l) $\tan\theta = 0$

3. Find θ.

   $$\sin\theta = \frac{x}{y} \qquad x = 5, \text{ and } y = 10$$

4. Find θ.

   $$\cos\theta = \frac{F}{t} \qquad F = 2, \text{ and } t = 5$$

5. In the following equation, identify the smallest value that y can achieve if $x = 12$. (*Hint:* Think about the mathematical boundary on the sine function.)

   $$\sin\theta = \frac{2x}{y}$$

Information Technology Project—Fiber-Optic Cables

HINT

See Appendix D-8 for instructions on completing this project.

Problem

1. Use the topic of fiber-optic cables as a setting in which to learn how to change the font and page layout in a Microsoft Word document.
2. Learn how to insert images and text boxes into Microsoft Word documents.

The Next Generation of Computing

In this Information Technology Project, we explore current technological developments in computer memory.

Objectives

1. Read and comprehend technical information relating to the computer field and extract relevant information
2. Execute independent research

Tools Book CD: No Coverage

The Computing Challenge

Researchers in the computer industry face myriad challenges. Among the most pressing is the constant demand for faster, more powerful computers that can better handle massive amounts of information and instant communication and analysis. From the early room-sized computers that used relays and transistors, to today's laptops that employ silicon chips with micron-wide logic gates, developers have worked to decrease the size and increase the speed of the processors required for data storage, manipulation, and communication. This race to build better and faster computers has created a new problem for researchers, who must confront objects at the size scale of individual atoms, a scale at which the physics of everyday life (Newtonian physics) no longer applies. In this Information Technology Project, we will explore one of the fascinating areas of research that arises from the new laws of physics that are required in the world of the very small.

The Quantum Problem

At the end of the nineteenth century, experiments were already generating results that were inconsistent with Newtonian predictions. These experiments, conducted at the size scale of atoms and electrons, yielded results that were radically different from those predicted by Newtonian mechanics. For the first time since its formulation, the Newtonian theory of physics was not successful in predicting the location and velocity of the objects to which it was being applied. Because a physical theory must agree with and produce the same results as a physical experiment to be deemed true, the Newtonian theory came into question as the "theory of all objects."

For example, researchers soon observed that the particles being analyzed, such as electrons, did not execute the simple, smooth trajectories familiar from classical physics. Work done by Albert Einstein, Max Planck, and others, led scientists to believe that the energies possessed by the electrons only came in multiples of a certain fundamental, or *quantum*. An electron could have, for example, 5 times an amount of energy or 6 times the amount, but it could not have 5.5 times the amount. It could have 5 times the base amount, or 6, but not a value *between* these integer multiples. This realization, in contrast to the tenets of classical physics, led to the understanding that there is not a continuum of values for the possible amount of energy possessed by an electron. In the language of this new theory, the energy is said to be *quantized*.

Although we know it to exist, this *quantization* is not apparent in the macroscopic world. A useful analogy is to think about how we see a movie as being continuous, even though it is not. A movie actually consists of many individual frames that appear as a smooth image because of the speed at which the frames move.

Niels Bohr (1885–1962) Nobel Prize winner Neils Bohr made numerous contributions to our understanding of atomic structure and quantum mechanics.

Courtesy of Getty Images

NOTE

A centripetal force is a force that is directed toward the center of a circular orbit.

Quantization of Electronic Orbitals

In a related development, researchers found that energy was not the only property of electrons that appeared to come in discrete amounts or *quanta*. Another example of *quantization* arose during an effort to explain electronic orbits. The Danish physicist Niels Bohr put forth a theory incorporating the quantum concept to explain why electrons do not spiral into the atomic nucleus.

According to classical physics, when an electric charge accelerates, energy is released in the form of an electromagnetic wave. Because the electrons appear to execute circular orbits, they should experience a centripetal force and therefore a centripetal acceleration. Since the electrons are constantly being accelerated centripetally, they should release electromagnetic radiation that will decrease their energy and result in their spiraling into the nucleus of the atom. However, we know this scenario is inaccurate because we know that stable atoms exist. Using the concept of quantization, Bohr was able to provide an explanation for this apparent paradox.

In a radical step, Bohr postulated that electrons cannot exist at all locations surrounding the nucleus. Electrons are only allowed to exist in discrete locations called *orbitals*. An electron can exist in one orbital or another, *but not between orbitals*. Thus, as in the case of electron energy, electronic orbitals are also quantized.

The Creation of Quantum Mechanics

Based on such results as the quantizations of energies and electronic orbitals, researchers soon realized that a simple modification of the Newtonian formulation was not sufficient. Because all of the physical properties of the objects being studied appeared to be quantized rather than continuous, a radical new theory was required to describe correctly the world of the very small. This new theory would eventually be called *quantum mechanics*.

Werner Heisenberg (1901–1976) Instrumental in developing the theory of quantum mechanics, Heisenberg was awarded the Nobel Prize for Physics in 1932.

Courtesy of the American Institute of Physics/Emilio Segre Visual Archives

However, the theory of quantum mechanics developed by Werner Heisenberg, Pascual Jordan, and Erwin Schrödinger during the 1920s, which correctly described the quantum behavior of the subatomic world, also made physical predictions that were at once startling and philosophically baffling. One of these predictions took the form of the *principle of superposition.*

Superposition

According to the theory of quantum mechanics, not only are the allowed physical states of a particle quantized, the particle actually exists in several of these states *at the same time*. Amazingly, the theory says that it is possible for a particle such as an electron to exist in a *superposition* of the various possible values of a physically measurable quantity such as energy or position. The act of a person measuring the system causes the electron to "collapse" into one of the possible states.

When first confronted with this concept, a common reaction is that the electron, or other particle, was always in a precise state but that we just had not looked at it yet. In actuality, this simultaneous existence in several states appears to be true, and calculations that ignore this superposition do not agree with experimental results. Interestingly, this strange quantum phenomenon may provide a solution to the problem of creating the next generation of faster computers.

Superposition and Parallel Computing?

In today's digital computers, information is coded using a combination of 1s and 0s. The smallest piece of information, called a *bit,* is specified using either a zero or a one. Thus, a word or other piece of information that contains *n* bits, is expressed using a string of *n* zeros and ones. For example, in a typical digital register, three bits are required to express each of the numbers 1 through 8: 000, 001, 010, and so on.

FYI

The *spin* of an electron is related to its angular momentum.

A new area of research has developed to improve upon the currently used bit concept. Computer researchers are currently attempting to develop a radical new computing entity—the quantum bit, or *qubit*. These qubits may be represented by an atom or particle that possesses one of two states. For example, when measuring the *spin* of an electron, it only has one of two possible values, up or down. In other words, the spin of the electron is quantized like the other physical properties in the microscopic world. These two spin states can be assigned values of 1 and 0 and the electron can now be used as a qubit. Thus, two electrons describe four possible states, and three electrons can describe eight possible states, just as does a classical digital register.

However, unlike the classical register that can only represent one of the numbers between zero and eight at a time, a system of qubits has access to each of the numbers *simultaneously*. Because of the principle of superposition, quantum bits do not exist in a single state, but rather in a superposition of all their possible states. Therefore, in some sense a register consisting of qubits exists in all of the possible states between zero and eight simultaneously. This simultaneity may have a profound impact on parallel computing, since a computer that used qubits would have information about all of the possible states at the same time.

Quantum Entanglement, and "Wiring" a Computer that Uses Qubits

In addition to providing access to huge amounts of information simultaneously, a processor that uses qubits may have a built-in method of "wiring" them together.

This built-in system involves another unusual aspect of the microscopic world, known as *quantum entanglement*.

A visual example of quantum entanglement can be constructed using two quanta of light, or *photons*. Suppose that we construct an experiment in which we use two photons (particles of light) that have opposite polarizations for their electric fields. We then shoot one photon to the left and one photon to the right. Until an observer measures the polarization of one of the photons, the two polarizations remain unknown. However, once the polarization of one of the photons is measured, the polarization of the other photon is immediately known, since we know that the other photon must have a polarization opposite to the one we measure. Amazingly, this relationship between the two photons exists *no matter how great the distance between the photons!* Regardless of the distance between the photons or the length of time that they are separated, a physical connection exists between them.

This type of quantum entanglement could also be applied to qubits. Two or more qubits whose states were known would always maintain a connection with the other qubits with which they were "entangled" at the start of the process, even as they move and carry out their designed behavior.

Conclusion

Although the concept of quantum computing may be far from the point of desktop use, it does provide an example of the exciting research being done in the Information Technology field.

Skill Level I ♦

Problem

Execute the necessary research, and explain how computers are able to take the words entered on a keyboard and translate them into digital information.

Record your answer in the space provided.

Skill Level II 

Problem

Execute the necessary research, and explain what happens when files that contain large amounts of information are "zipped" (compressed).

Record your answer in the space provided.

Skill Level III 

Problem

Execute the necessary research, and explain how information is stored magnetically on hard drives.

Record your answer in the space provided.

Information Technology Project—The Next Generation of Computing

HINT

See Appendix D-9 for instructions on completing this project.

Problem

Use the topic of computer microprocessors as a setting in which to learn the basics of Microsoft Access.

Independent Information Technology Research

In this project, you are challenged to execute the independent research necessary to acquire an elementary understanding of several of the most important concepts necessary for a successful career in this field.

Objective

Complete independent research to describe some of the most important terms and concepts relating to the information technology field.

Tools Book CD: No Coverage

One of the factors that determines whether a technician is successful in today's technological workplace is his/her ability and willingness to learn new concepts without the aid of an instructor or a trainer. In an educational setting, it would be impossible to acquaint a student with every possible information technology concept. Because the technology field changes so rapidly, today's technician must be willing to read journals, textbooks, and so on, to stay abreast of changing terminology and new technology. In the workforce, one cannot rely on peers to teach the new developments in your field; self-reliance is required.

In this project, you are challenged to do the independent research necessary to acquaint yourself with a variety of information technology terms without the aid of an instructor's lecture. In addition to illustrating the necessity of such independent research, this project provides a setting in which you will acquire an introduction to several of the information technology concepts you will be studying at ITT Technical Institute.

The Skill Levels for this project are determined by the number of terms correctly defined.

Skill Level I ♦	15 terms
Skill Level II ♦♦	20 terms
Skill Level III ♦♦♦	25 terms

Problem

For each of the following information technology terms, find and write out an explanation *in your own words*.

1. Information technology
2. Personal computers (Windows/Macintosh)
3. Needs assessment
4. Operating systems
5. High-level language versus machine language
6. Graphic user interface (GUI)
7. Computer network
8. WWW versus internet
9. TCP/IP
10. Ethernet/fast ethernet
11. Bandwidths and speed
12. ISPs (internet service providers)
13. Streaming video
14. MPG
15. AVIs
16. Virtual environments
17. Visual Basic
18. C++
19. Batch files
20. Object oriented programming
21. Browser (IE/Netscape/others)
22. HTML
23. Static Web page
24. Interactive Web page
25. URL

Information Technology Project—Independent Research

HINT

See Appendix D-10 for instructions on completing this project.

Problem

Take the information gathered during your independent research and build it into a Web page using the Hypertext Markup Language (HTML).

Appendix A: Table of Physical Data

TABLE OF PHYSICAL DATA

Multiples and Prefixes for Metric Units*

Multiple	Prefix (and Abbreviation)	Pronunciation
10^{24}	yotta- (Y)	yot'ta (*a* as in *a*bout)
10^{21}	zetta- (Z)	zet'ta (*a* as in *a*bout)
10^{18}	exa- (E)	ex'a (*a* as in *a*bout)
10^{15}	peta- (P)	pet'a (as in *peta*l)
10^{12}	tera- (T)	ter'a (as in *terra*ce)
10^{9}	giga- (G)	ji'ga (*ji* as in *ji*ggle, *a* as in *a*bout)
10^{6}	mega- (M)	meg'a (as in *mega*phone)
10^{3}	kilo- (k)	kil'o (as in *kilo*watt)
10^{2}	hecto- (h)	hek'to (*heck-toe*)
10	deka- (da)	dek'a (*deck* plus *a* as in *a*bout)
10^{-1}	deci- (d)	des'i (as in *deci*mal)
10^{-2}	centi- (c)	sen'ti (as in *senti*mental)
10^{-3}	milli- (m)	mil'li (as in *mili*tary)
10^{-6}	micro- (μ)	mi'kro (as in *micro*phone)
10^{-9}	nano- (n)	nan'oh (*an* as in *an*nual)
10^{-12}	pico- (p)	pe'ko (*peek-oh*)
10^{-15}	femto- (f)	fem'toe (*fem* as in *fem*inine)
10^{-18}	atto- (a)	at'toe (as in an*atomy*)
10^{-21}	zepto- (z)	zep'toe (as in *zep*pelin)
10^{-24}	yocto- (y)	yock'toe (as in *sock*)

*For example, 1 gram (g) multiplied by 1000 (10^3) is 1 kilogram (kg); 1 gram multiplied by 1/1000 (10^{-3}) is 1 milligram (mg).

SI Base Units

Physical Quantity	Name of Unit	Symbol
Length	meter	m
Mass	kilogram	kg
Time	second	s
Electric current	ampere	A
Temperature	kelvin	K
Amount of substance	mole	mol
Luminous intensity	candela	cd

Some SI Derived Units

Physical Quantity	Name of Unit	Symbol	SI Unit
Frequency	hertz	Hz	s^{-1}
Energy	joule	J	$kg \cdot m^2/s^2$
Force	newton	N	$kg \cdot m/s^2$
Pressure	pascal	Pa	$kg/(m \cdot s^2)$
Power	watt	W	$kg \cdot m^2/s^3$
Electric charge	coulomb	C	$A \cdot s$
Electric potential	volt	V	$kg \cdot m^2/(A \cdot s^3)$
Electric resistance	ohm	Ω	$kg \cdot m^2/(A^2 \cdot s^3)$
Capacitance	farad	F	$A^2 \cdot s^4/(kg \cdot m^2)$
Inductance	henry	H	$kg \cdot m^2/(A^2 \cdot s^2)$
Magnetic field	tesla	T	$kg/(A \cdot s^2)$

SI Units of Some Other Physical Quantities

Physical Quantity	SI Unit
Speed	m/s
Acceleration	m/s^2
Angular speed	rad/s
Angular acceleration	rad/s^2
Torque	$kg \cdot m^2/s^2$ or $m \cdot N$
Entropy	J/K or $kg \cdot m^2/(K \cdot s^2)$ or $N \cdot m/K$
Thermal conductivity	$W/(m \cdot K)$
Electric field	N/C or V/m

Conversion Factors

Mass	1 g = 10^{-3} kg 1 kg = 10^{3} g 1 u = 1.66×10^{-24} g = 1.66×10^{-27} kg 1 metric ton = 1000 kg
Length	1 nm = 10^{-9} m 1 cm = 10^{-2} m = 0.394 in. 1 m = 10^{-3} km = 3.28 ft = 39.4 in. 1 km = 10^{3} m = 0.621 mi 1 in. = 2.54 cm = 2.54×10^{-2} m 1 ft = 0.305 m = 30.5 cm 1 mi = 5280 ft = 1609 m = 1.609 km
Area	1 cm^2 = 10^{-4} m^2 = 0.1550 in^2 = 1.08×10^{-3} ft^2 1 m^2 = 10^{4} cm^2 = 10.76 ft^2 = 1550 in^2 1 in^2 = 6.94×10^{-3} ft^2 = 6.45 cm^2 = 6.45×10^{-4} m^2 1 ft^2 = 144 in^2 = 9.29×10^{-2} m^2 = 929 cm^2
Volume	1 cm^3 = 10^{-6} m^3 = 3.35×10^{-5} ft^3 = 6.10×10^{-2} in^3 1 m^3 = 10^{6} cm^3 = 10^{3} L = 35.3 ft^3 = 6.10×10^{4} in^3 = 264 gal 1 liter = 10^{3} cm^3 = 10^{-3} m^3 = 1.056 qt = 0.264 gal 1 in^3 = 5.79×10^{-4} ft^3 = 16.4 cm^3 = 1.64×10^{-5} m^3 1 ft^3 = 1728 in^3 = 7.48 gal = 0.0283 m^3 = 28.3 L 1 qt = 2 pt = 946 cm^3 = 0.946 L 1 gal = 4 qt = 231 in^3 = 0.134 ft^3 = 3.785 L
Time	1 h = 60 min = 3600 s 1 day = 24 h = 1440 min = 8.64×10^{4} s 1 y = 365 days = 8.76×10^{3} h = 5.26×10^{5} min = 3.16×10^{7} s
Angle	1 rad = 57.3° 1° = 0.0175 rad 60° = $\pi/3$ rad 15° = $\pi/12$ rad 90° = $\pi/2$ rad 30° = $\pi/6$ rad 180° = π rad 45° = $\pi/4$ rad 360° = 2π rad 1 rev/min = $\pi/30$ rad/s = 0.1047 rad/s
Speed	1 m/s = 3.60 km/h = 3.28 ft/s = 2.24 mi/h 1 km/h = 0.278 m/s = 0.621 mi/h = 0.911 ft/s 1 ft/s = 0.682 mi/h = 0.305 m/s = 1.10 km/h 1 mi/h = 1.467 ft/s = 1.609 km/h = 0.447 m/s 60 mi/h = 88 ft/s
Force	1 N = 0.225 lb 1 lb = 4.45 N Equivalent weight of a mass of 1 kg on Earth's surface = 2.2 lb = 9.8 N
Pressure	1 Pa (N/m^2) = 1.45×10^{-4} lb/in^2 = 7.5×10^{-3} torr (mm Hg) 1 torr (mm Hg) = 133 Pa (N/m^2) = 0.02 lb/in^2 1 atm = 14.7 lb/in^2 = 1.013×10^{5} N/m^2 = 30 in. Hg = 76 cm Hg 1 lb/in^2 = 6.90×10^{5} Pa (N/m^2) 1 bar = 10^{5} Pa 1 millibar = 10^{2} Pa
Energy	1 J = 0.738 ft·lb = 0.239 cal = 9.48×10^{-4} Btu = 6.24×10^{18} eV 1 kcal = 4186 J = 3.968 Btu 1Btu = 1055 J = 778 ft·lb = 0.252 kcal 1 cal = 4.186 J = 3.97×10^{-3} Btu = 3.09 ft·lb 1 ft·lb = 1.36 J = 1.29×10^{-3} Btu 1 eV = 1.60×10^{-19} J 1 kWh = 3.6×10^{6} J
Power	1 W = 0.738 ft·lb/s = 1.34×10^{-3} hp = 3.41 Btu/h 1 ft·lb/s = 1.36 W = 1.82×10^{-3} hp 1 hp = 550 ft·lb/s = 745.7 W = 2545 Btu/h
Mass–Energy Equivalents	1 u = 1.66×10^{-27} kg ↔ 931.5 MeV 1 electron mass = 9.11×10^{-31} kg = 5.49×10^{-4} u ↔ 0.511 MeV 1 proton mass = 1.673×10^{-27} kg = 1.007 267 u ↔ 938.28 MeV 1 neutron mass = 1.675×10^{-27} kg = 1.008 665 u ↔ 939.57 MeV
Temperature	$T_F = \frac{9}{5} T_C + 32$ $T_C = \frac{5}{9} (T_F - 32)$ $T_K = T_C + 273$
cgs Force	1 dyne = 10^{-5} N = 2.25×10^{-6} lb
cgs Energy	1 erg = 10^{-7} J = 7.38×10^{-6} ft·lb

Mathematical Symbols

$=$	is equal to
$\neq$	is not equal to
$\approx$	is approximately equal to
$\sim$	about
$\propto$	is proportional to
$>$	is greater than
$\geq$	is greater than or equal to
$\gg$	is much greater than
$<$	is less than
$\leq$	is less than or equal to
$\ll$	is much less than
$\pm$	plus or minus
$\mp$	minus or plus
$\bar{x}$	average value of x
Δx	change in x
$\lvert x \rvert$	absolute value of x
Σ	sum of
∞	infinity

The Greek Alphabet

Alpha	A	α	Nu	N	ν
Beta	B	β	Xi	Ξ	ξ
Gamma	Γ	γ	Omicron	O	o
Delta	Δ	δ	Pi	Π	π
Epsilon	E	ε	Rho	P	ρ
Zeta	Z	ζ	Sigma	Σ	σ
Eta	H	η	Tau	T	τ
Theta	Θ	θ	Upsilon	Υ	υ
Iota	I	ι	Phi	Φ	ϕ
Kappa	K	κ	Chi	X	χ
Lambda	Λ	λ	Psi	Ψ	ψ
Mu	M	μ	Omega	Ω	ω

Quadratic Formula

If $ax^2 + bx + c = 0$, then

$$x = \frac{-b \pm \sqrt{b^2 - 4ac}}{2a}$$

Values of Some Useful Numbers

$\pi = 3.141\,59 \ldots$ $\quad$ $\sqrt{2} = 1.414\,21$

$e = 2.718\,28 \ldots$ $\quad$ $\sqrt{3} = 1.732\,05$

Trigonometric Relationships

Definitions of Trigonometric Functions

$\sin\theta = \dfrac{y}{r}$ $\quad$ $\cos\theta = \dfrac{x}{r}$ $\quad$ $\tan\theta = \dfrac{\sin\theta}{\cos\theta} = \dfrac{y}{x}$

$\theta°$ (rad)	$\sin\theta$	$\cos\theta$	$\tan\theta$
$0°$ (0)	0	1	0
$30°$ ($\pi/6$)	0.500	$\sqrt{3}/2 \approx 0.866$	$\sqrt{3}/3 \approx 0.577$
$45°$ ($\pi/4$)	$\sqrt{2}/2 \approx 0.707$	$\sqrt{2}/2 \approx 0.707$	1.00
$60°$ ($\pi/3$)	$\sqrt{3}/2 \approx 0.866$	0.500	$\sqrt{3} \approx 1.73$
$90°$ ($\pi/2$)	1	0	∞

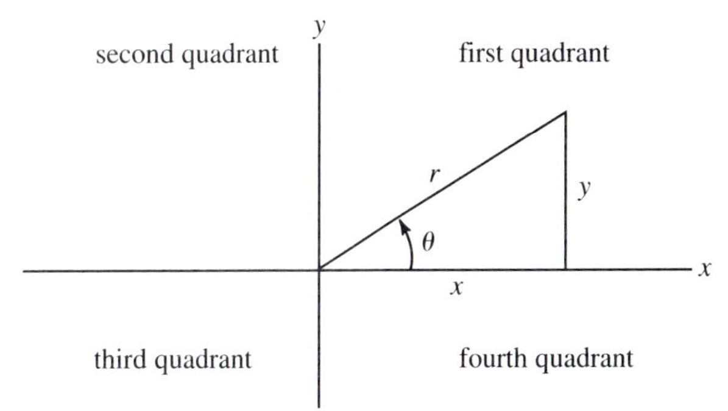

Appendix B: Instructions for Electronics Lab Projects

1 Ohm's Law
2 Wiring Resistors in Series and in Parallel
3 The Power Dissipated by a Resistor
4 Transformers
5 Capacitors in DC/AC Electronics
6 Working with Capacitors
7 Inductors
8 RLC Circuits
9 Semiconductors
10 Independent Electronics Research

Ohm's Law

Drawing a Circuit with a Resistor

Left-click on **Start** and scroll to **Programs.**
From the list, select **Applications CEET.**
Select **MultiSim** and then **MultiSim 2001.**

1. The MultiSim start screen will appear. From the menu of buttons on the left, select the first button, the voltage source symbol, as shown in Figure B1.1. Place your cursor over this symbol until the word "Sources" appears.

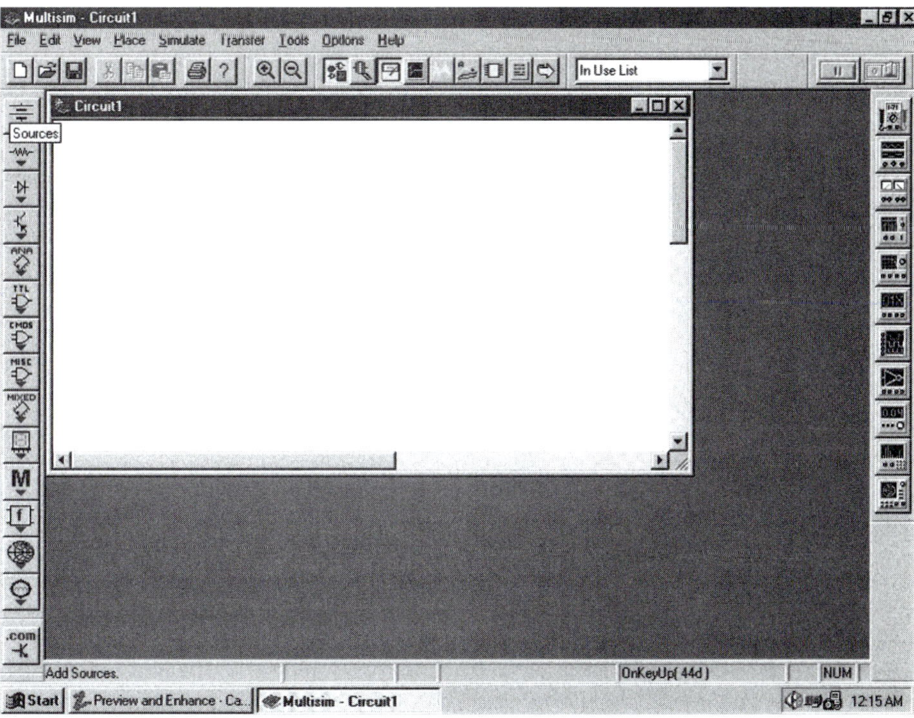

Figure B1.1

2. Left-click on **sources** and a second vertical menu will appear. Left-click on **DC Voltage Source** as indicated in Figure B1.2.

Figure B1.2

3. Drag the DC Voltage Source symbol into the circuit window. It will appear in the window as seen in Figure B1.3.

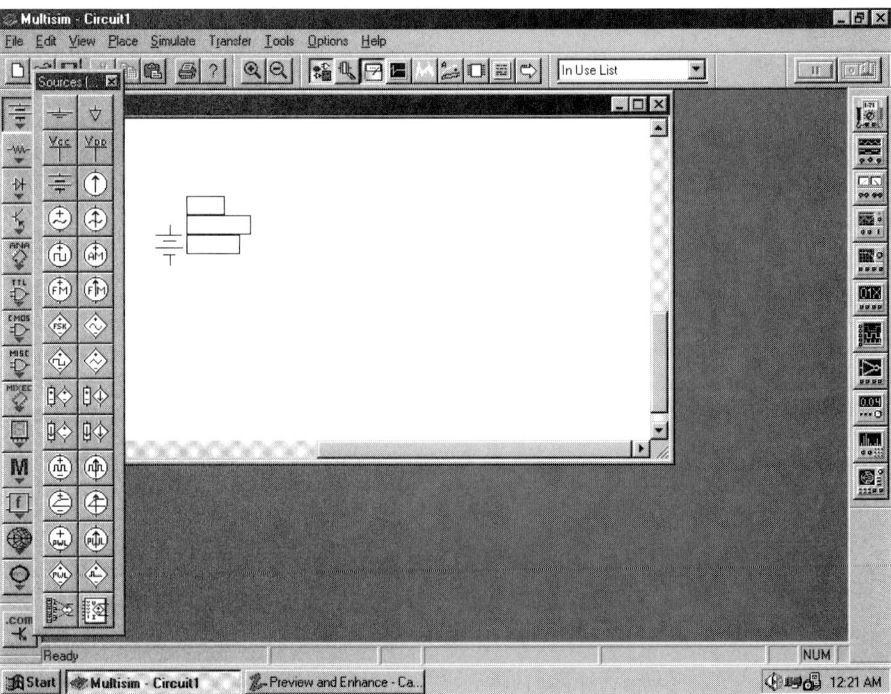

Figure B1.3

4. Left-click on the left side of the window to make the voltage source appear solid.

5. To change the default 12 V setting to a 10 V source, double-click on **12 V** in the voltage source to bring up the battery screen (Figure B1.4). Highlight the **12** and enter 10, then click **OK.**

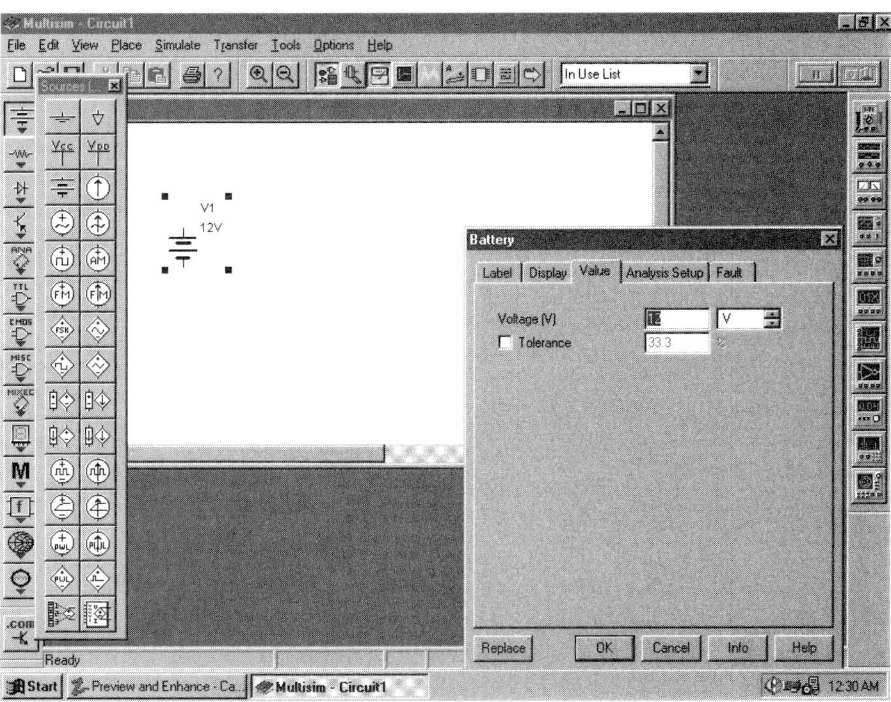

Figure B1.4

6. To add a resistor to the circuit, select the second button from the menu along the left edge of the screen. The **Basic (Mult..** menu will open. Sclect the top left button to open the **Component Browser,** as shown Figure B1.5.

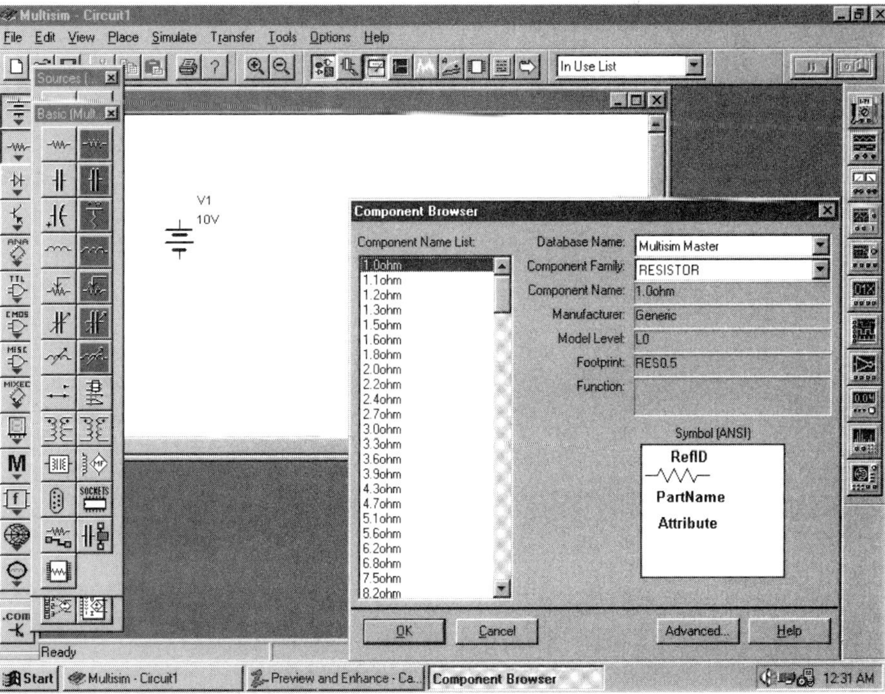

Figure B1.5

7. Scroll down the Component Name List to the **4.7 kohm** resistor and left-click. Click **OK** to add the resistor. The outline of the resistor will now move with the cursor arrow. Left-click on the top, middle of the screen to make the resistor solid.
8. To wire the voltage source to the resistor, left-click on the top of the voltage source and move the cursor. A dotted line, representing wire, will follow the cursor. To make the wire solid, place the cursor at the left end of the resistor and click.
9. To complete the circuit, ground the resistor and the voltage. Left-click the **Ground** symbol in the sources menu, drag it below the voltage source in your schematic, and left-click. Repeat the procedure and place another ground to the right below the resistor. Wire the voltage source and the resistor to their respective grounds as shown in Figure B1.6.

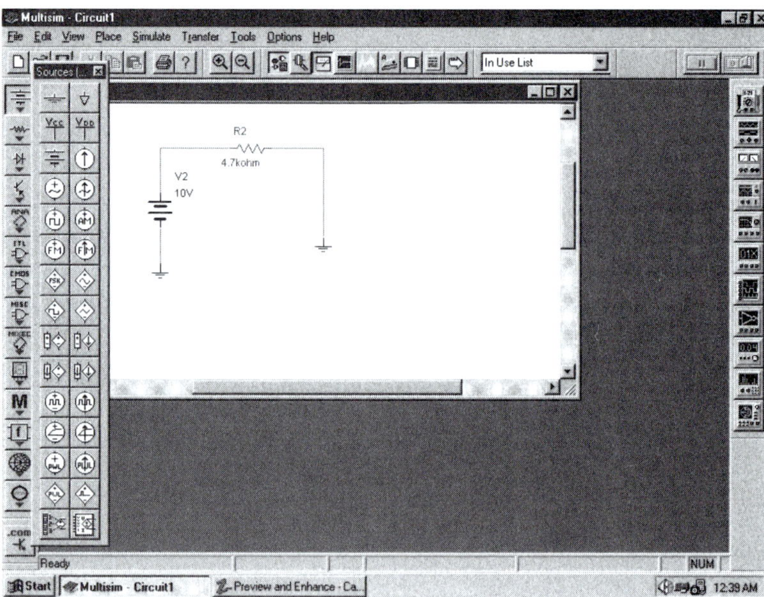

Figure B1.6

Measuring the Voltage Across the Resistor

10. Select a voltmeter from the list of indicators by clicking on the button with the red "8" in the original menu. A small **Indicators** submenu will appear. Left-click on the top left **V** button to open the component browser, as shown in Figure B1.7.

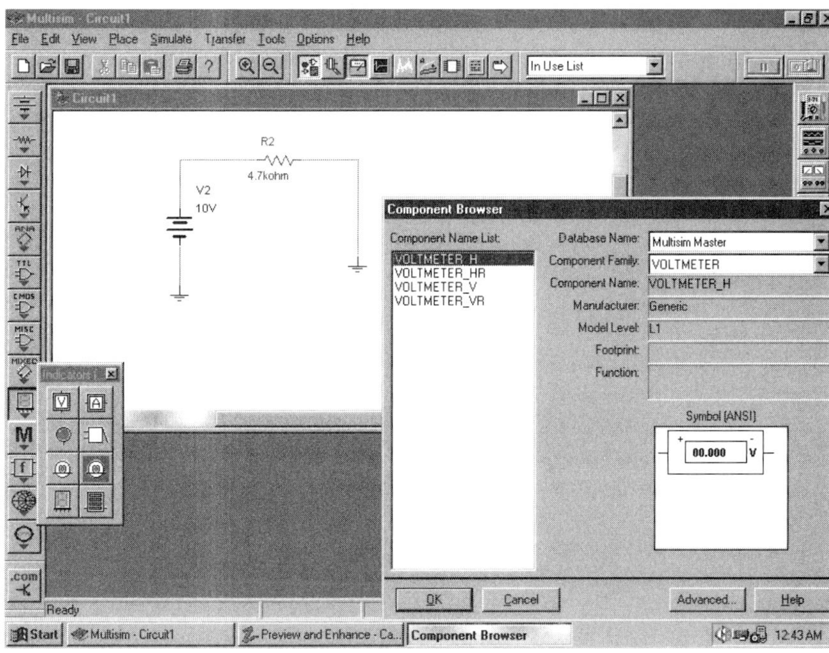

Figure B1.7

11. Click **OK** to choose the default voltmeter. Drag the voltmeter to a position below the resistor. Left-click to turn the voltmeter solid.
12. Wire the ends of the voltmeter to the wires on both sides of the resistor to complete the circuit, as shown in Figure B1.8.

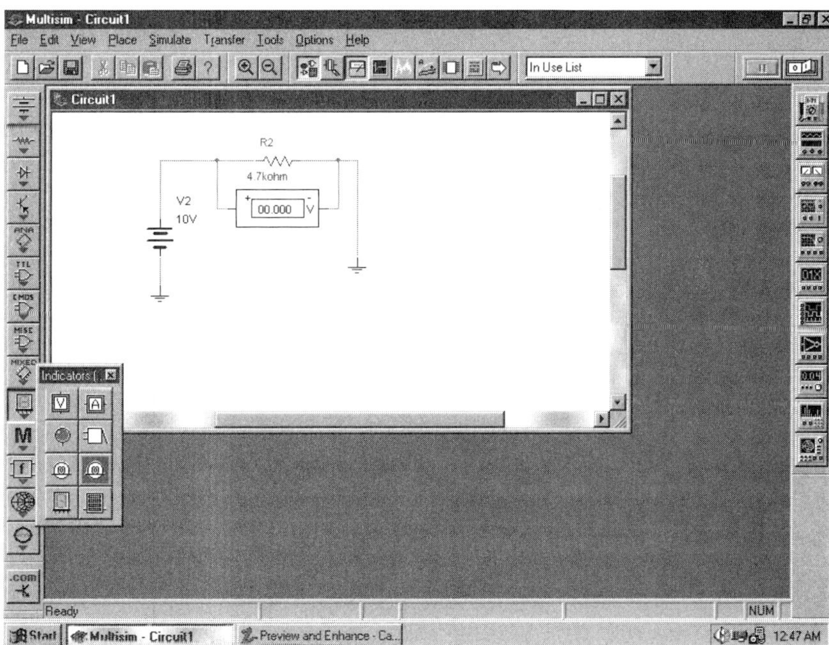

Figure B1.8

13. Your circuit is now complete, and you are ready to run the simulation. To begin the simulation, go to the taskbar at the top of the screen and select **Simulate,** and then **Run.**
14. Your voltmeter should read “10 V”.
15. To stop the simulation, return to **Simulate** in the top taskbar and choose **Pause.**

Wiring Resistors in Series and in Parallel

Series Circuit Simulation

Left-click on **Start** and scroll to **Programs.**
From the list, select **Applications CEET.**
Select **MultiSim** and then **MultiSim 2001.**

1. Maximize the drawing space.
2. Open **sources** in the left menu bar, left-click on **battery** and drag it onto the drawing space. Change the value to 10 V. Move the label and value if desired.
3. Left-click on the **ground** symbol in the sources menu. Drag in a ground and place it below but not touching the negative (lower) end of the battery.
4. Left-click and drag in another ground, place it about two-thirds of the way across the screen to the right of the other ground, as in Figure B2.1.

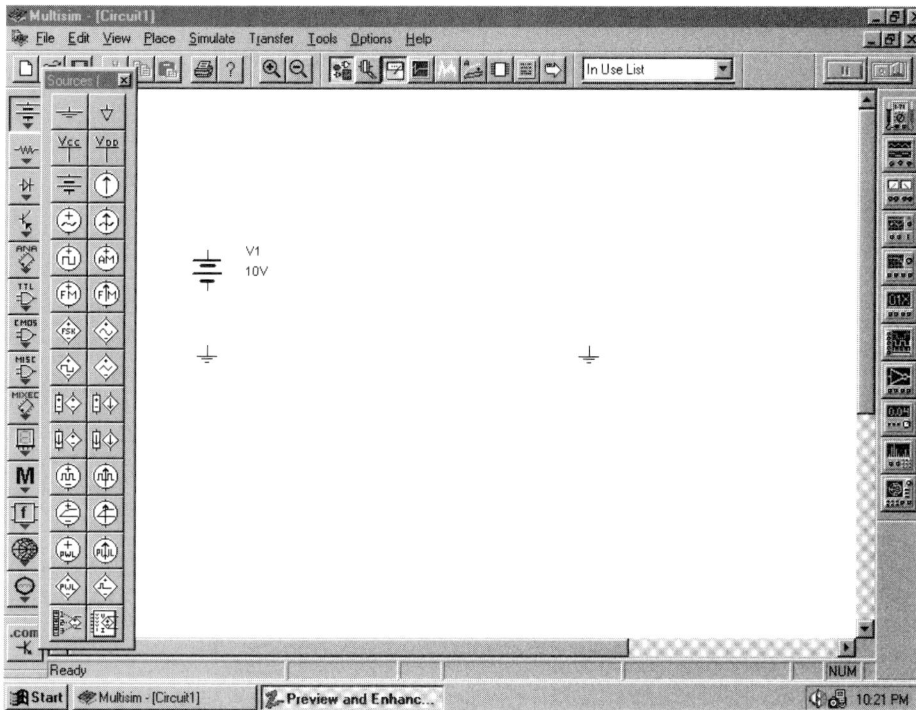

Figure B2.1

5. Close the **sources** menu.
6. Open the **resistors** menu. Open **fixed resistors** (top left icon in the menu), scroll down, select **3.3 kohm,** click **OK** and place above and to the right of the battery. Open the **resistors** menu again, select **4.7 kohm,** click **OK,** and place above the right ground. Right-click, select **ROTATE 90° CW** and move so that the lower end is above but not touching, the ground. Left-click.
7. Connect the wires as indicated in Figure B2.2: V1 to R1, lower end of V1 to ground below it, R1 to R2, R2 to ground below it. (Left-click to start and end wire, right-click while dragging to delete wire.)

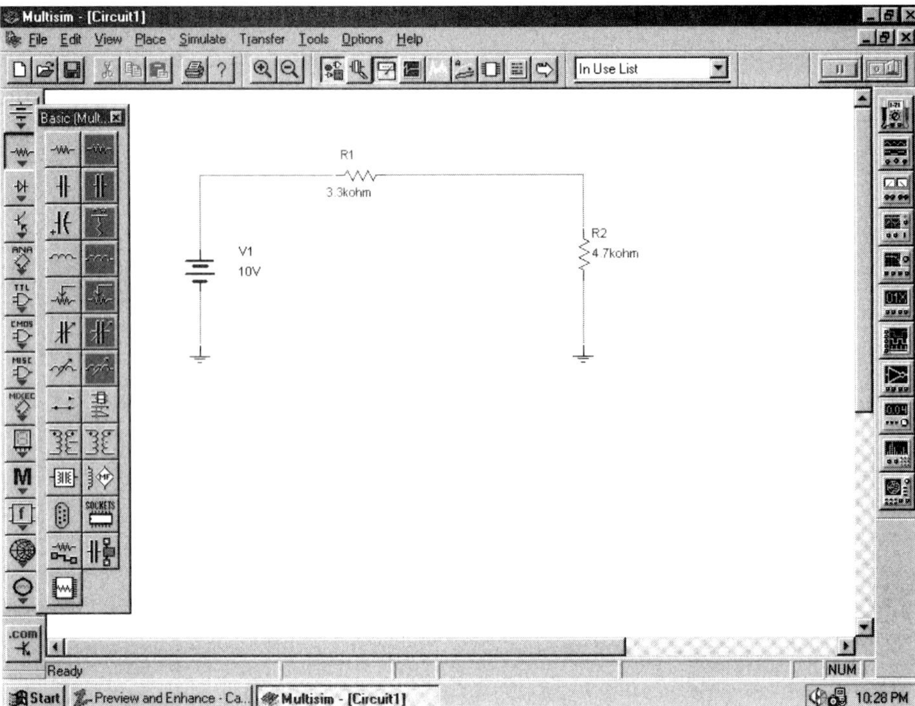

Figure B2.2

8. Close the **resistors** menu.
9. Left-click on top icon in the taskbar on the right-hand side of the window, the multimeter, just below the on/off switch. Place below R1 by dragging and left-clicking. Grab another multimeter and place to the right of R2.
10. Place a wire from the + terminal of XMM1 (below R1) and connect to left side of R1 (anywhere between R1 and V1). Place a wire from the – terminal of XMM1 to the right of R1 (anywhere between R1 and R2). Connect the + terminal of XMM2 above R2 (anywhere between R1 and R2) and connect the – terminal of XMM2 to grounded side of R2, as seen in Figure B2.3. (Left-clicking while drawing wires allows for neat bends.)

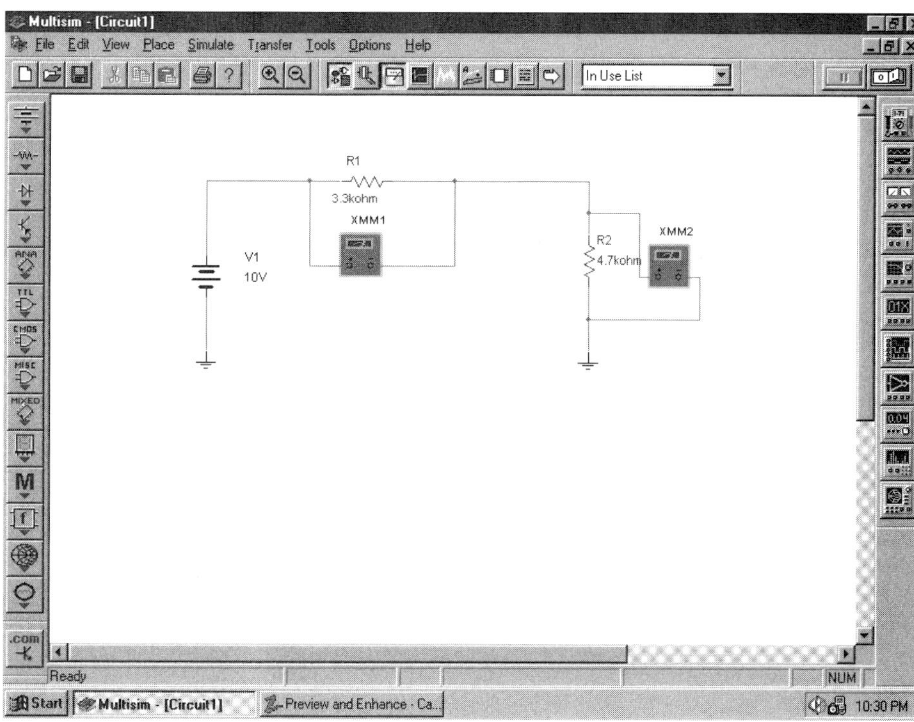

Figure B2.3

12. Double-click on a meter and an instrument face will appear to the lower right of the screen. Repeat for the other meter. They will overlay; left-click and drag faces to a convenient view.

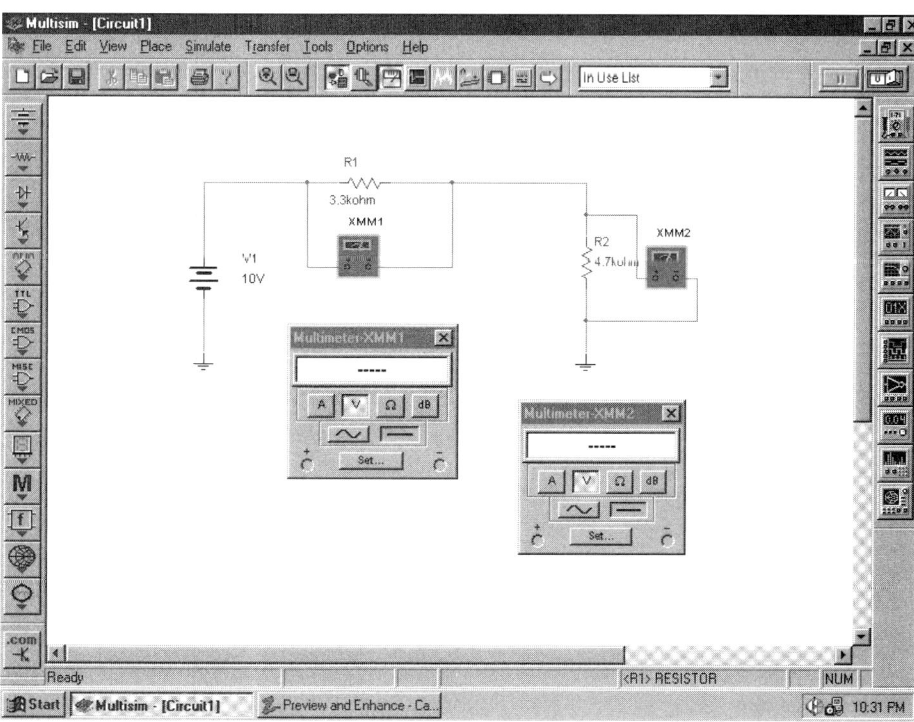

Figure B2.4

13. Begin simulation (click on switch at top right of screen). Both meters should be in volt (V) mode.

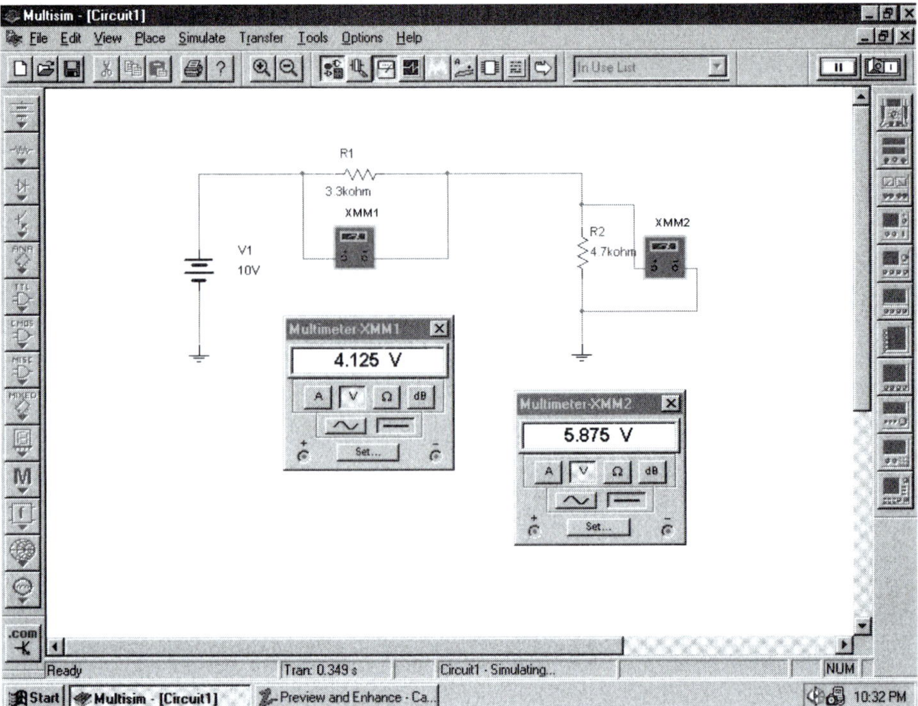

Figure B2.5

Parallel Circuit Simulation

Open **MultiSim2001** and perform the first four steps of the series circuit simulation, placing all the items somewhat lower on the screen. The screen should look similar to Figure B2.1.

1. Close **sources**.
2. Open **resistors** and place a 3.3 kΩ resistor above and to the right of the battery, and then place a 4.7 kΩ resistor below the 3.3 kΩ resistor. Close **resistors**.
3. Connect the right sides of the resistors with a wire, then connect the left sides with another wire. These resistors are now in parallel.
4. Make the following connections with wires: top of battery to left side of parallel resistors, ground at right to right side of parallel resistors, bottom of battery to ground under battery.
5. Place a multimeter above the parallel resistors. Place another multimeter below the parallel resistors. Connect each multimeter to the ends of the resistor closest to it, positive terminal to the left, negative terminal to the right.
6. Double-click on the meters to show meter faces, and left-click and drag the faces to a convenient view (Figure B2.6).

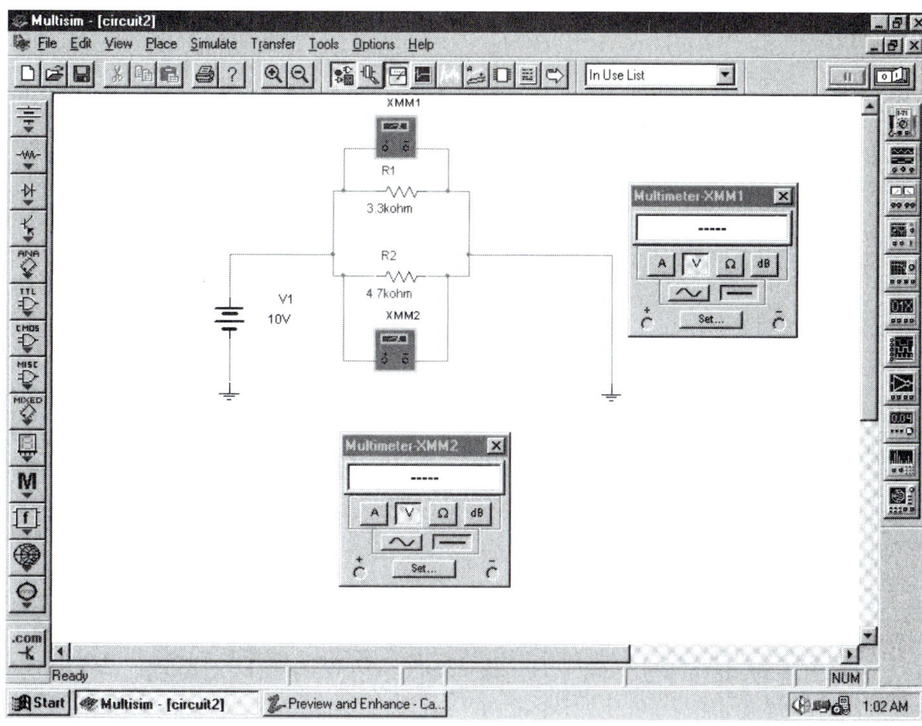

Figure B2.6

7. Start simulation (both meters should read "10 V").

Series Parallel Circuit Simulation

Open **MultiSim2001** and perform the first four steps of the series circuit simulation placing components lower on the screen, with the second ground farther to the right.

1. Close **sources**.
2. Open **resistors** and place a 4.7 kΩ resistor above and to the right of the battery. Leave enough room for other resistors to the right.
3. Place a 2.2 kΩ resistor to the right of the 4.7 kΩ resistor, leaving some space in between. Place a 3.3 kΩ resistor below the 2.2 kΩ resistor.
4. Connect the right side of the 2.2 kΩ resistor to the right side of the 3.3 kΩ resistor with a wire, and then connect the left sides of the same resistors with another wire. These two resistors are now in parallel. Connect the right side of the 4.7 kΩ resistor to the left side of the parallel resistors with a wire. This resistor is now in series with the two parallel resistors. Connect the top of the battery to the left side of the 4.7 kΩ resistor. Connect the bottom of the battery to the ground below it. Connect the ground at the right of the screen to the right side of the parallel resistors. Close resistors.
5. Place a multimeter below the resistors of the circuit. Connect the positive terminal of the meter to the left side of the 4.7 kΩ resistor and the negative terminal of the meter to the right side of the two parallel resistors. Double-click on the meter to show the meter face (Figure B2.7).

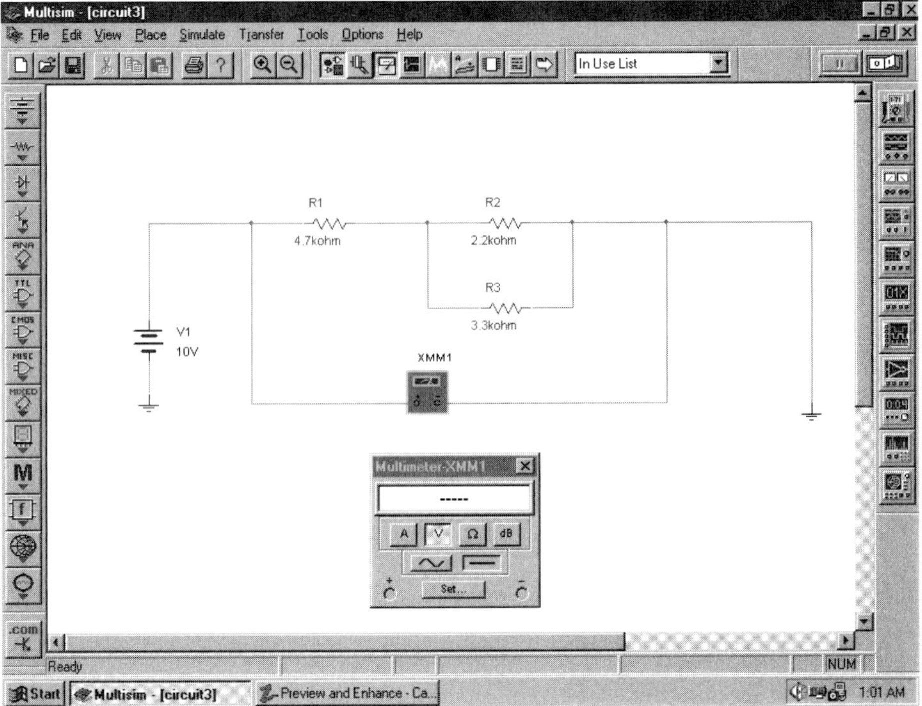

Figure B2.7

6. Start simulation (the meter should read “10 V”).

The Power Dissipated by a Resistor

Power Dissipated Simulation

Left-click on **Start** and scroll to **Programs.**
From the list, select **Applications CEET.**
Select **MultiSim** and then **MultiSim 2001.**

> **HINT**
>
> Review Appendix B-1 if you need detailed instructions on selecting the battery, ground, resistors, and other components.

1. Maximize your workspace.
2. Select a battery, place it on the left side of the screen, and then place a ground below it, being careful not to let them touch. Select and place another ground to the right of the screen. Select a resistor and place it above and to the right of the battery. Connect the top of the battery to the left of the resistor with a wire; connect the right side of the resistor to the ground at right with another wire; and connect the bottom of the battery to the ground at left with a wire.
3. Place a multimeter below the resistor. Connect the left terminal of the multimeter to the left side of the resistor and then connect the right terminal of the multimeter to the right side of the resistor.
4. Place another multimeter to the right of the resistor. Connect both of its terminals to the wire that is connected from the right side of the resistor ground on the right. Leave more space for the right multimeter than the left multimeter (see Figure B3.1). To allow the second multimeter to measure the current, you must break the original circuit by deleting the small segment of wire between the multimeter connections, as shown in Figure B3.1. Make the meter faces appear, and modify the second meter face to read current, by clicking **A** on the face.

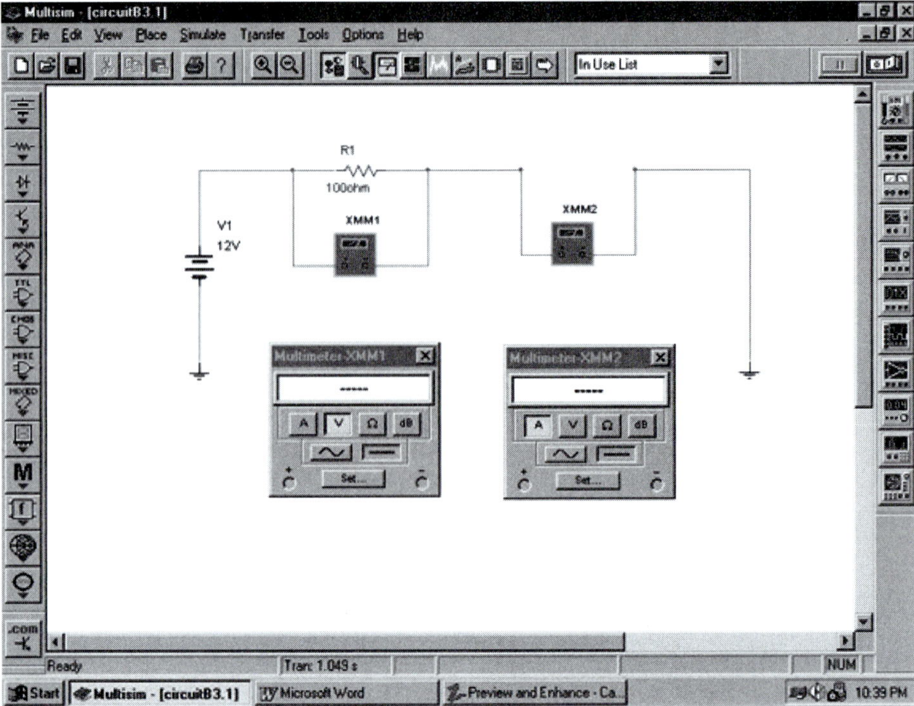

Figure B3.1

5. Start the simulation. The power dissipated can be determined by the voltage reading squared, divided by the resistance (V^2/R), or by the current reading squared, times the resistance (I^2R), or by the product of the voltage reading and the current reading (VI). All three calculations should be very close or exactly the same, in an ideal world. The actual value depends upon the voltage and resistance chosen. (For the circuit shown, $P = 1.44$ W.)

Transformers

Step-up Transformer Simulation

Left-click on **Start** and scroll to **Programs.**
From the list, select **Applications CEET.**
Select **MultiSim** and then **MultiSim 2001.**

1. Maximize the drawing space.
2. Open **components** and find **transformers,** which is the ninth button down in the left column. Click on the icon and observe the types available. The top, highlighted one is a 10:1 audio transformer. Choose this one by clicking **OK** and set it in the center of the screen. Right-click on it and select **flip horizontal** from the pop-up menu. This action will make it act like a 1:10 step-up transformer.
3. Open **sources** and select the **AC source** (fourth down from top on the left). Drag it onto the left side of the screen. Notice that the default value is 1 V_{PEAK}. To obtain a 20 V_{AC} output, you must change it to an amplitude (peak value) of 2.828 V_{PEAK}. (The meter will read the AC value, and the AC or RMS value is 0.7071 times the peak value.) Double left-click on the **source voltage,** click on **value,** and modify amplitude to **2.828.** Notice that the RMS value will become 2.0. Stepping this up by a factor of ten will accomplish the goal.
4. Place a ground below, but not touching, the AC source. Close **sources**.
5. A choice of an 8.2 Ω resistor will closely simulate the value for an audio speaker. Select a resistor and place it to the right of the screen. Right-click on it and then rotate **90° clockwise.** Close **components**.
6. Wire the circuit by attaching the lower part of the source to the ground, the upper part of the source to the top left terminal of the transformer, and the lower left terminal of the transformer to the wire between the source and the ground. Connect a wire from the top of the resistor to the top right terminal of the transformer, and another wire from the bottom of the resistor to the lower right terminal of the transformer.

HINT

Review Appendix B-1 if you need detailed instructions on selecting the ground, resistors, multimeters, and other components.

7. Drag in a multimeter, and place it to the right of the resistor. Connect its + terminal to the wire at the top of the resistor and its – terminal to the wire at the bottom of the resistor. Double-click on the meter face and drag its screen to a convenient viewing location. Set the meter to AC with a single click on the wavy line on its face. Your screen should look like the one in Figure B4.1.

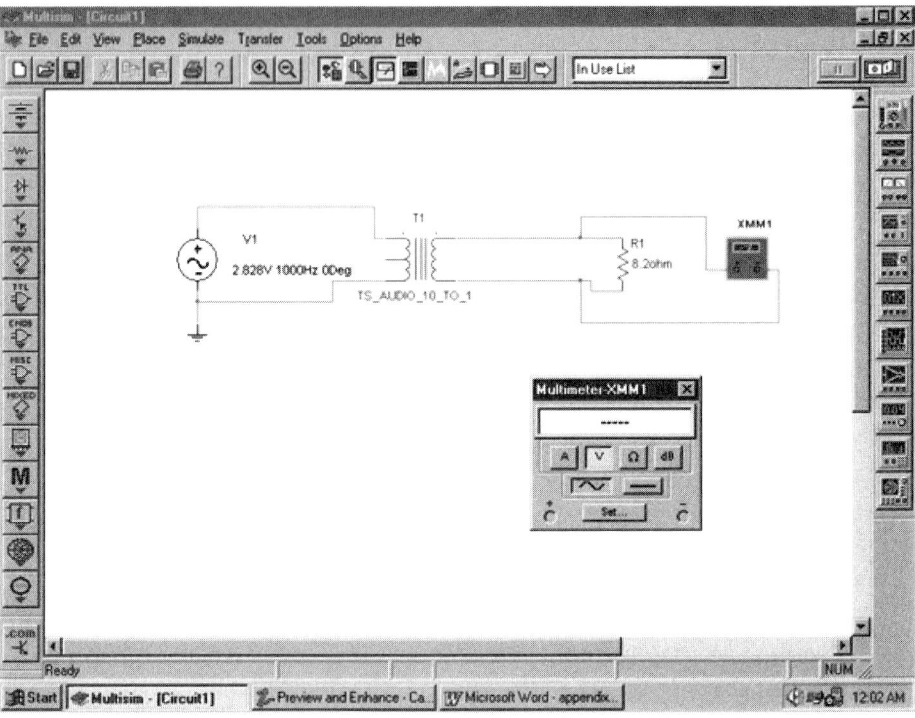

Figure B4.1

8. Start the simulation. The meter should read approximately 20 V_{AC} (19.997 V is a possible reading).

Capacitors in DC/AC Electronics

Defining a New Component

Left-click on **Start** and scroll to **Programs.**
From the list, select **Applications CEET.**
Select **MultiSim** and then **MultiSim 2001.**

1. Open the component wizard by clicking on the **Component Editing** icon located under the Options header (see Figure B5.1).

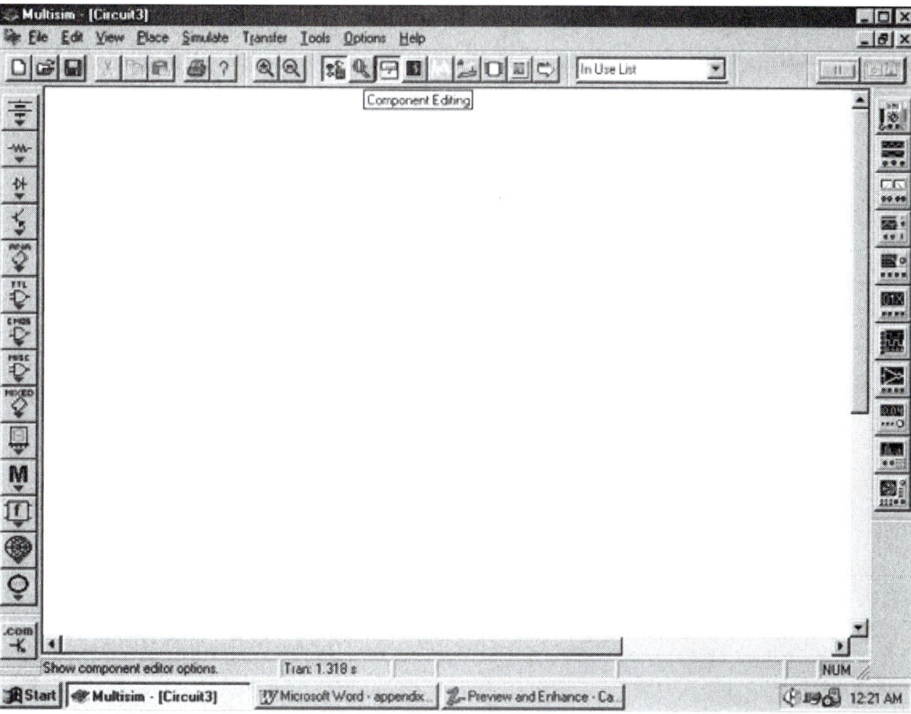

Figure B5.1

2. Enter a component name. Use "mycapacitor," or another name. Click on **next.**
3. Select the package type **cap1.** Click on **next.**
4. Choose the default symbol by clicking on **next** in screen 3 of 6.
5. In screen 4 of 6, enter **left** for "in1" and **right** for "out1," then click on **next.**
6. In screen 5 of 6, select **interdigital capacitor model.** Then specify the general electrical characteristics and linear dimensions, modifying as desired. If you receive a message after selecting **OK,** you may answer **yes** to continue.
7. In screen 6 of 6, click on **finish** and **save,** and then on the next screen, click **OK** and then **EXIT.**
8. Now, click on **components,** select **capacitors** (the second icon down on the left) and change database **to user.** Your ulticap should appear. Click and place your component on screen.

Working with Capacitors

Comparing DC and AC Values Simulation

Left-click on **Start** and scroll to **Programs.**
From the list, select **Applications CEET.**
Select **MultiSim** and then **MultiSim 2001.**

1. Maximize the drawing space.
2. Open **sources.** Click on and drag in a **DC source** (battery). Change the voltage to a convenient value, **10 V.** Place it towards the left side of the screen. Click on and drag in a **ground** and place it slightly below the DC source. Click on and drag in another **ground** and place it about two-thirds of the way across the screen. Repeat this process lower on the screen, this time using an **AC source** (just below the battery icon) and adjusting the RMS value to **10 V** by making it the equivalent amplitude (PEAK value) 14.14 V. Close **sources**. Your screen should look like Figure B6.1.

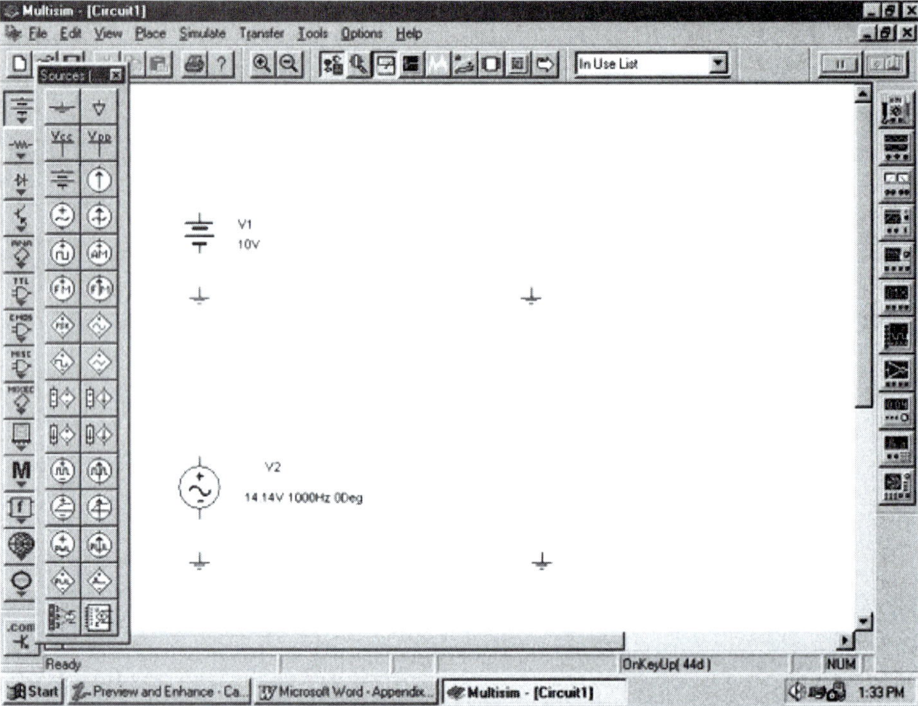

Figure B6.1

3. Open **components**. Locate and click on a **1 kΩ** resistor, select it, click **OK,** and place it above and to the right of the DC source. Right-click and select **Copy.** Move away from R1, right-click and select **Paste.** Move to a corresponding position near the AC source and left-click to place it.
4. Left click on **capacitors** (icon below resistors) and select a **160 nF capacitor.** Click on **OK** and place the capacitor just above the right side ground for the DC circuit. Right-click and select **90° clockwise.** Then select **Copy.** Move away, right-click, and select **Paste.** Place this second capacitor in a similar position in the AC circuit.
5. Connect both circuits with wires.
6. Select multimeters and place in parallel with each component. For all meters, connect the + terminal on the side of the component closest to the source, and the − terminal on the side of the component farthest from the source, so that your screen looks like the one shown in Figure B6.2.

HINT

If you need help on wiring the circuits review Appendix B-1.

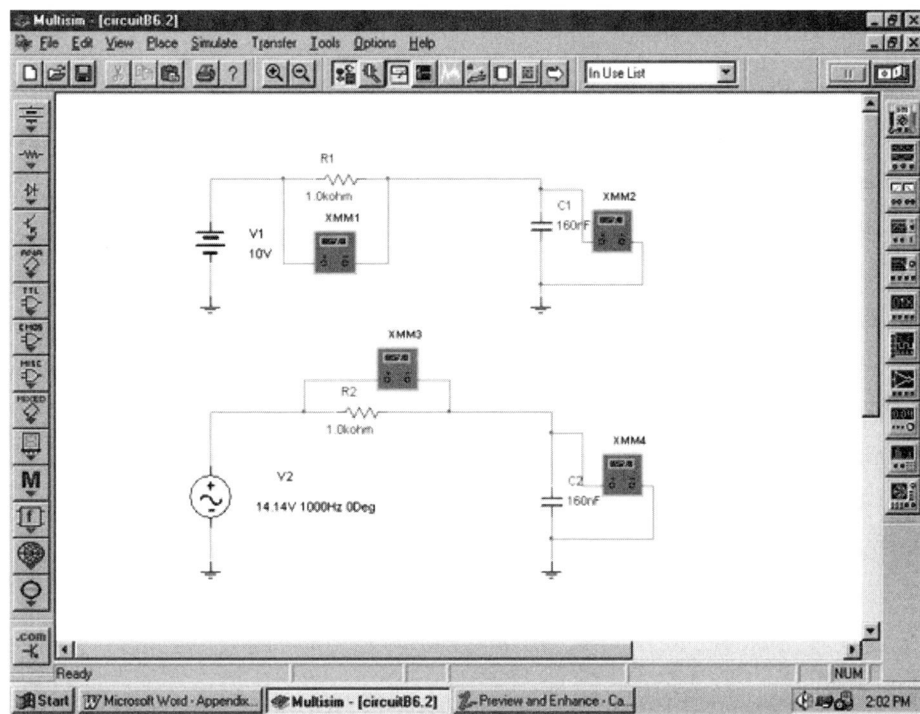

Figure B6.2

MultiSim

7. Double-click on the meters so that the meter faces show, and arrange the meter faces so that they can all be viewed. Make sure all of the meters are reading volts (select **V** on faces). The two meters on the DC circuit should be measuring DC (select flat line on face) and the two meters on the AC circuit should be measuring AC (select wavy line on face).
8. Start the simulation and compare your results to those in Figure B6.3. Notice how similar the values are for the AC circuit and how different they are for the DC circuit. It should be noted that the meters are reading RMS while the source voltage is displayed in PEAK. For further exploration, you may wish to change the frequency of the AC circuit source and determine if any AC readings change.

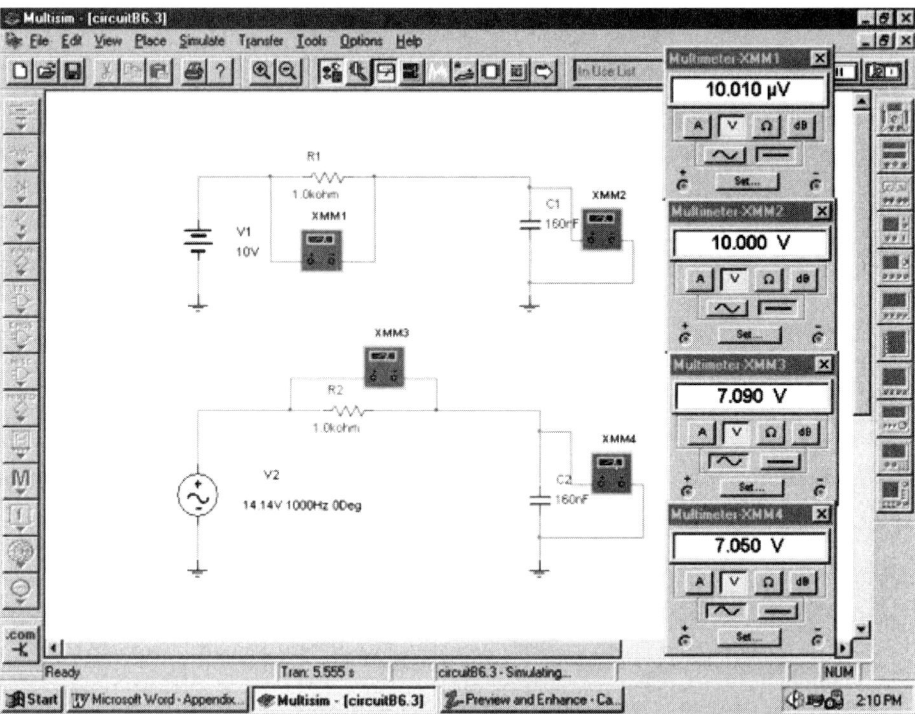

Multisim - [circuitB6.3]
File Edit View Place Simulate Transfer Tools Options Help
R1
1.0kohm
XMM1
V1
10V
C1
160nF
XMM2
XMM3
R2
1.0kohm
V2
14.14V 1000Hz 0Deg
C2
160nF
XMM4
Multimeter-XMM1
10.010 µV
Multimeter-XMM2
10.000 V
Multimeter-XMM3
7.090 V
Multimeter-XMM4
7.050 V
Ready
Tran: 5.555 s
circuitB6.3 - Simulating...
2:10 PM

Figure B6.3

Inductors

Resistor and Inductor Voltage Simulation

Left-click on **Start** and scroll to **Programs.**
From the list select **Applications CEET.**
Select **MultiSim** and then **MultiSim 2001.**

1. Maximize the drawing space.
2. Open **sources**. Click on and drag in an **AC** source (fourth down on the left). Change the voltage to a convenient value of **10** $\mathbf{V_{RMS}}$ (which is equivalent to a PEAK value, or amplitude, of 14.14 V). Click on and drag in a **ground** and place it slightly below the source. Click on and drag in another **ground** and place it about two-thirds of the way across the screen from the first ground. Close **sources**.
3. Open **components.** Open **resistors,** select a 1 kΩ resistor and press **OK.** Place the resistor above and to the right of the AC source. Open **inductors,** select a **160 mH inductor,** click **OK** and place above the right ground. Right-click and select **90° clockwise.** Close **components**.
4. Connect the components with wire segments (your screen should look like the one in Figure B7.1).

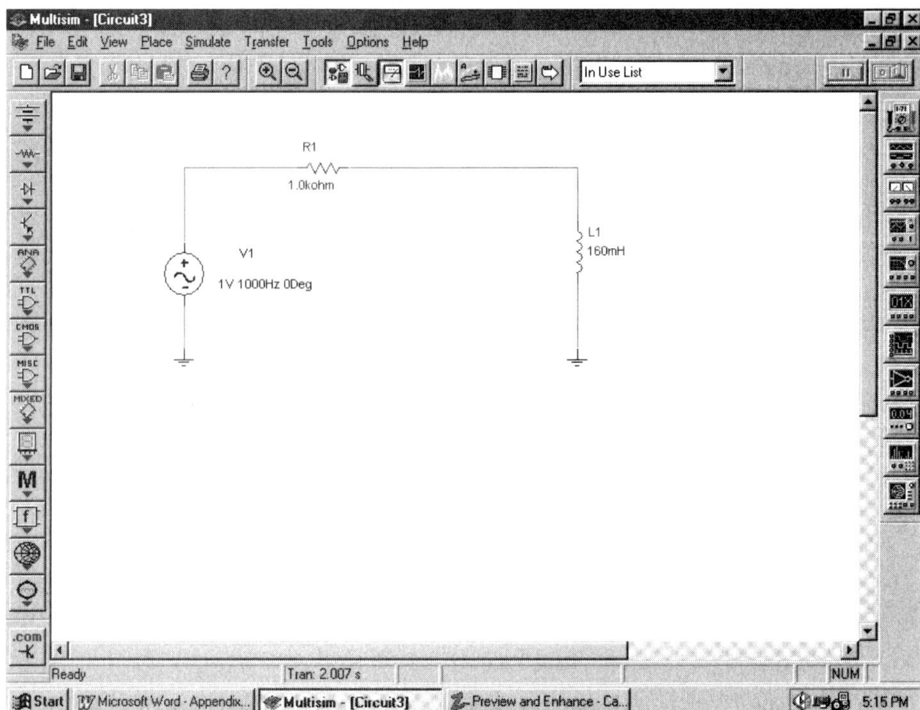

Figure B7.1

5. Grab a **multimeter** and connect it across the resistor (+ terminal of the meter to the left, – terminal of the meter to the right of the resistor). Grab another **multimeter** and connect it across the inductor (+ terminal above and – terminal below the inductor). Grab a third **multimeter** to monitor the total voltage by connecting the + terminal between the source and the resistor and the – terminal between the inductor and the ground just below it.
6. Double-click on the meters and then drag their faces to a convenient location. Make sure that all are on volts (**V**), and AC (select wavy line).
7. Start the simulation. Notice that the total voltage is not the algebraic sum of the AC voltages of the resistor and inductor. Also note that the resistor voltage and inductor voltage are very close. Change the frequency of the source and determine any effect it may have on the readings (see Figure B7.2).

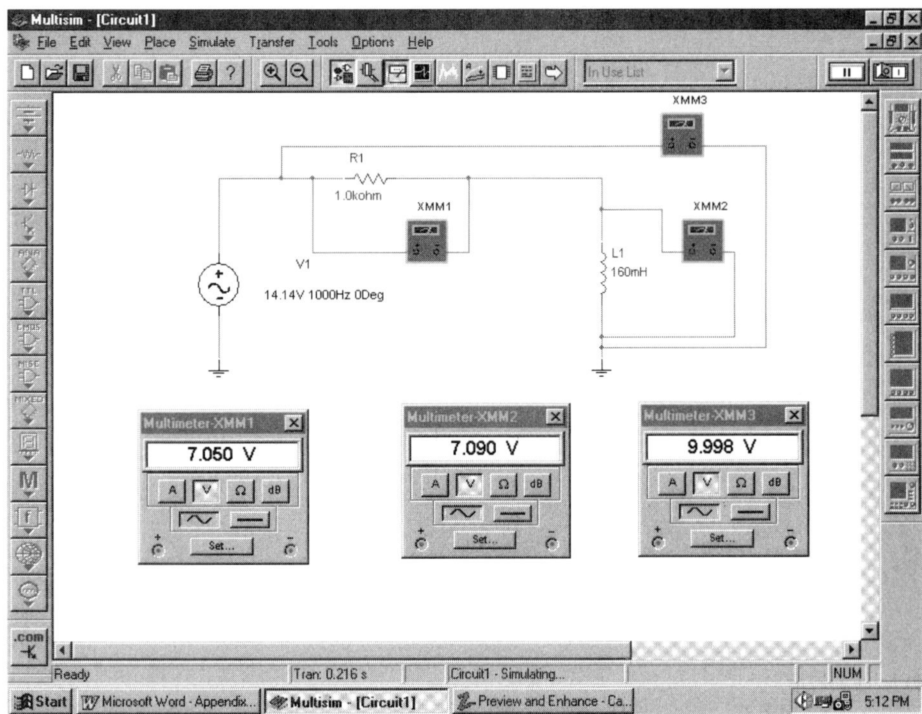

Multisim - [Circuit1]
File Edit View Place Simulate Transfer Tools Options Help
In Use List
XMM3
R1
1.0kohm
XMM1
XMM2
L1
160mH
V1
14.14V 1000Hz 0Deg
Multimeter-XMM1
7.050 V
Multimeter-XMM2
7.090 V
Multimeter-XMM3
9.998 V
A V Ω dB
Set...
Ready
Tran: 0.216 s
Circuit1 - Simulating...
NUM
Start
Microsoft Word - Appendix...
Multisim - [Circuit1]
Preview and Enhance - Ca...
5:12 PM

Figure B7.2

RLC Circuits

An RLC Circuit Simulation

Left-click on **Start** and scroll to **Programs.**
From the list, select **Applications CEET.**
Select **MultiSim** and then **MultiSim 2001.**

1. Click to maximize the drawing space.
2. Open **Sources.** Select the **AC sine wave** source. Place it on the left side of the screen. Select a **ground** and place it slightly under the AC source. Select another **ground** and place it to the right of the first, about two thirds of the way across the screen. Close **sources**. Modify the AC source to a convenient value, **10 V_{RMS}** (14.14 V peak amplitude).
3. Open **components.** Select a 1 kΩ resistor and place it above and to the right of the AC source. Select a **160 mH capacitor** and place it to the right of the resistor (leave space, so that they are not touching). Select a **160 nF capacitor** and place it to the right of the inductor (again, leave some space). Move the right ground if necessary. Close **components**. Connect all items with wires so that your screen looks like Figure B8.1.

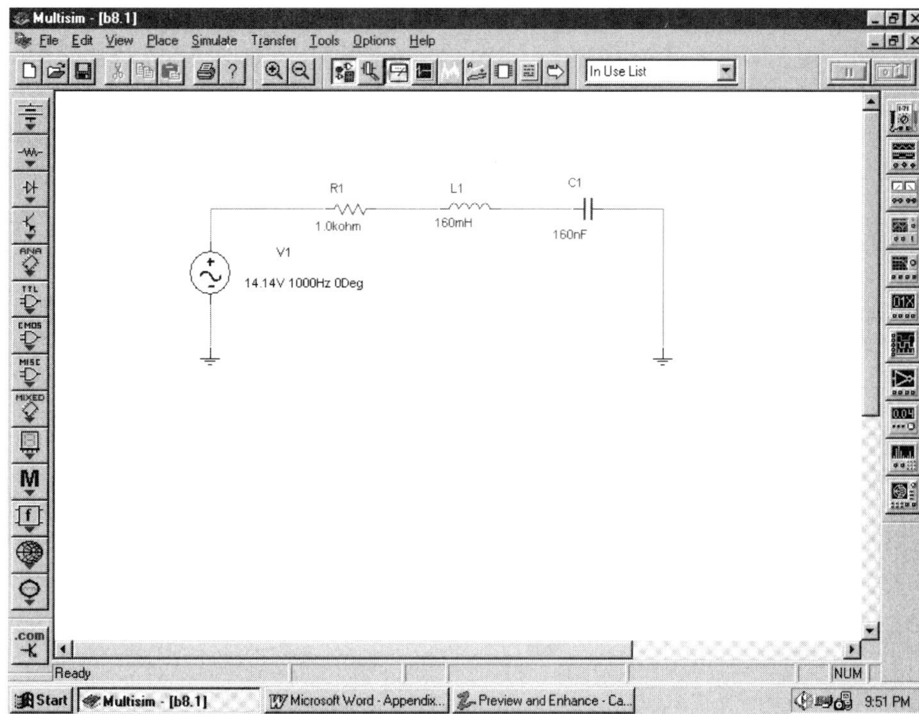

Figure B8.1

4. Select a **multimeter** and place it above the resistor. Select another **multimeter** and place it above the inductor. Select another **multimeter** and place it above the capacitor. Connect each of these meters across the component below it by taking a wire from the + terminal of the meter to the left side of the component and then taking a wire from the − terminal of the meter and connecting it to the right side of the component. Select one more **multimeter** and place it somewhere below the inductor. Connect its + terminal to the left of the left resistor meter connection and its − terminal just above the right side ground. This fourth meter monitors the source RMS voltage. Make sure all of meters are set to measure voltage (**V**) and AC (select wavy line).
5. Start the simulation (see Figure B8.2). Notice how close the readings are for all the meters. Why is this so?

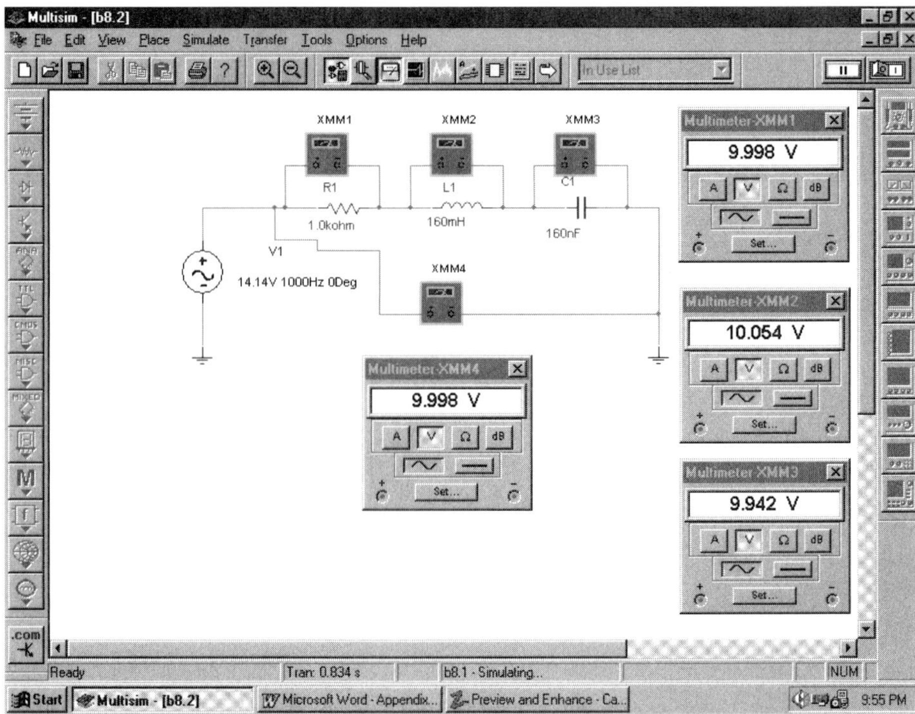

Figure B8.2

6. For further exploration, stop the simulation and change the AC source frequency to a value of **10 kHz.** What change do you expect for the meter readings? Start a new simulation and verify (or modify) your prediction.
7. Again, stop the simulation and change the AC source frequency to **100 Hz.** Predict what the range of readings will now be. Start the simulation. Do the readings correspond to your predictions?

Semiconductors

Semiconductor Simulation

1. Maximize the drawing space.
2. Open **sources.** Select the **AC sine wave** voltage source and place it on the left side of the screen. Select a **ground** and place it slightly below the AC voltage source. Select another **ground** and place it about halfway across the screen. Modify the AC source so that it has an amplitude (peak value) of **10 V.** Close **sources**.
3. Select **diodes** (the icon below resistor in the left taskbar). Click on the upper-left symbol and choose **1N4001GP,** click on **OK,** and place the diode above and to the right of the AC voltage source. Close **diodes**. Open **components** and select a 1 kΩ resistor, click on **OK,** and place it above the right ground. Right-click and select **90° clockwise.** Run wires between all items. Your screen should like Figure B9.1.

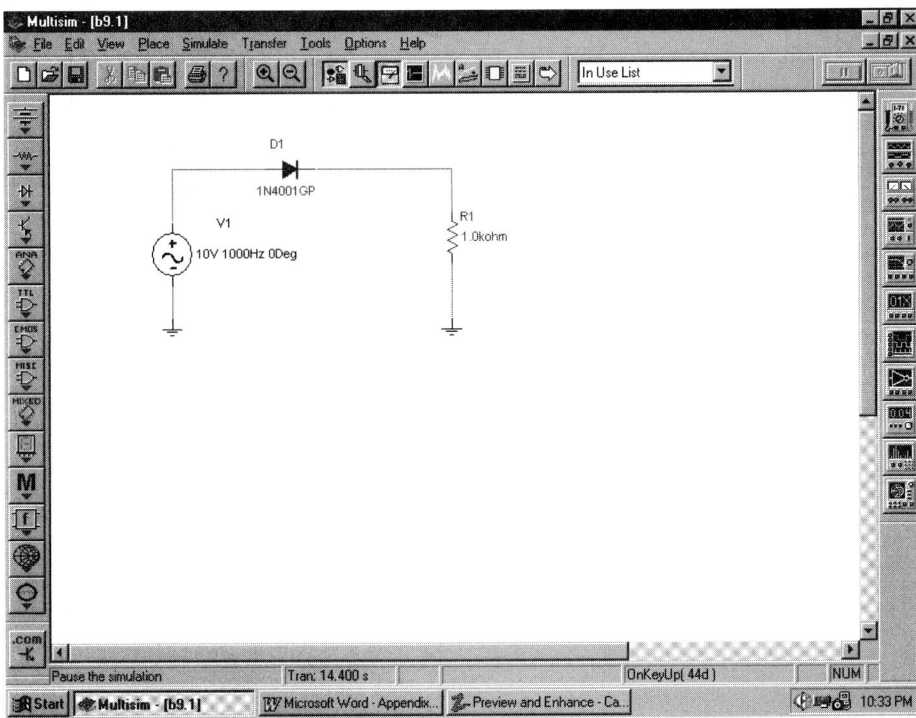

Figure B9.1

4. Select an **oscilloscope.** (Use the fourth icon down in the right taskbar.) Click and drag it to place at the right of the resistor. Connect terminal A above the resistor and connect terminal G to the ground side of the resistor. Double-click on its face and the display will appear. Modify the timebase to **ms/Div** (select and use the decrease down arrow).
5. Start the simulation. Notice that only the upper half of the AC source voltage (minus the diode voltage drop) appears. What does this tell you about the conduction properties of the junction diode?

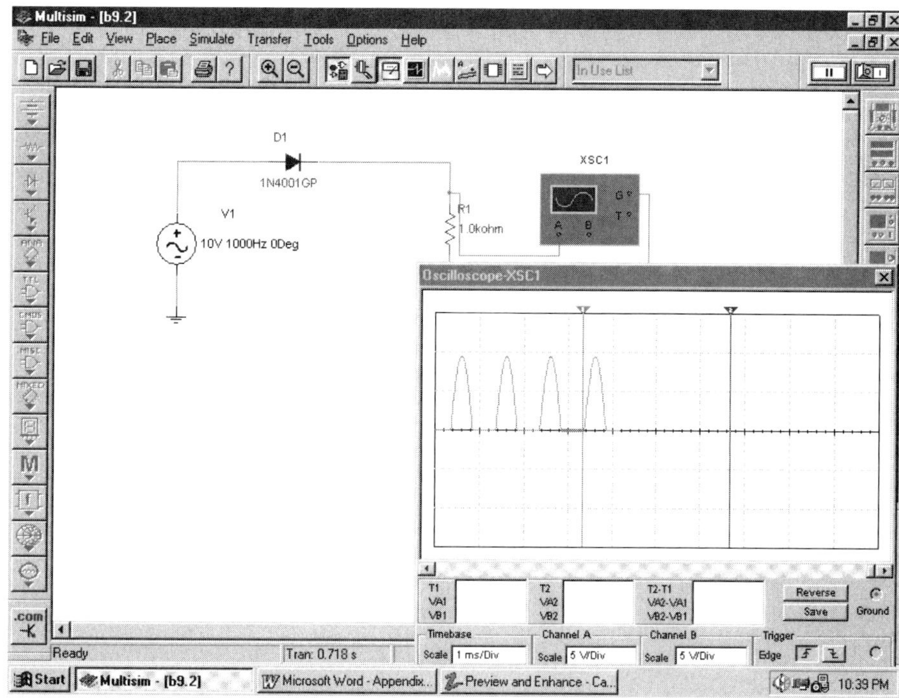

Figure B9.2

6. Stop the simulation. Close the **oscilloscope** display. Open **components** and select **capacitors.** Select a **10 μF capacitor,** click on **OK,** and place it to the left of the resistor. Right click and select **90° clockwise.** Connect the top of the capacitor near the top of the resistor and connect the bottom of the capacitor near to the bottom of the resistor. Double-click on the **oscilloscope** and then start the simulation. Notice how the capacitor "smooths out" or filters the voltage so that it is much more uniform. You have installed a DC filtering cap, and actually made a simple DC power supply that converts the AC input into an unregulated DC output.

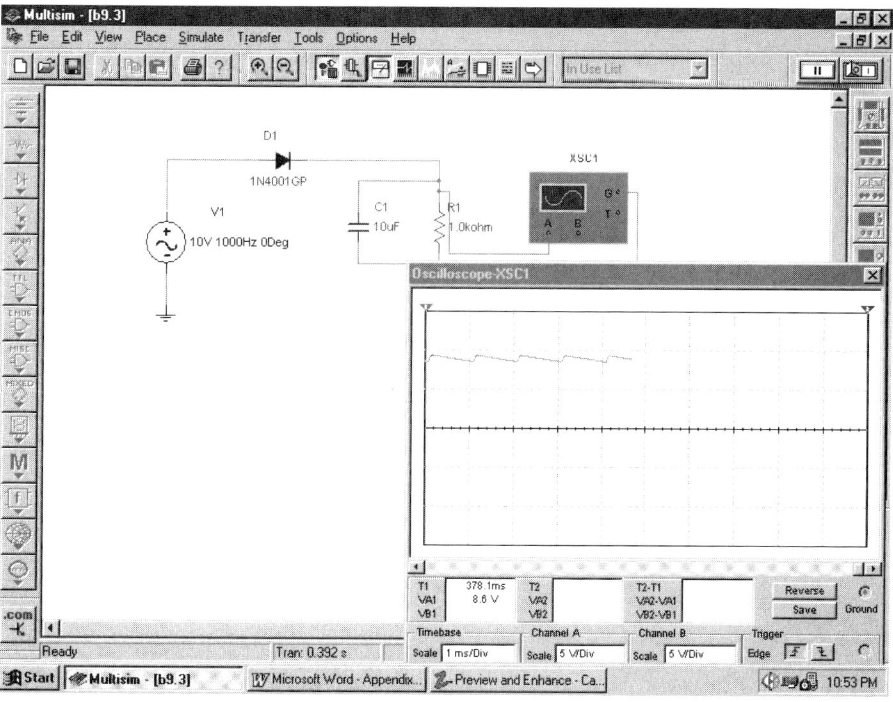

Figure B9.3

Independent Electronics Research

Create Symbols in MultiSim and Import Them into Microsoft Word

1. Open **MultiSim**.
2. Select a **resistor** of any value from components. Minimize the MultiSim workspace by left-clicking on the **underline symbol** at the top right of screen.
3. Open **Microsoft Word** and then open a new document. Enter descriptive text, such as "This is a resistor schematic symbol" and press **enter** several times to leave a blank space in the Word document. Minimize your Word document.
4. Maximize MultiSim by left-clicking on the **MultiSim** tab at the bottom of the screen adjacent to the START icon. Right click on the **resistor** and select **copy.** Minimize the MultiSim workspace.
5. Maximize the Word document by a clicking on its tab in the bottom bar of your screen (it will probably be next to the MultiSim tab). Place the mouse cursor under your text and paste the resistor into the document by right-clicking and selecting **Paste.** By left-clicking on the resistor, you can move it around in the Word document. Experiment with how to fit text around the component. Print the page.
6. Any component can be imported into a Word document in a similar manner. If you want to rotate or change the location of a label or value, this must be done in MultiSim. The copy can be pasted until some other item is copied or cut in the document. Try a transistor next. Open **transistors,** the fourth icon down on the left taskbar. Select **2N2222A,** a common small-signal transistor. Copy it in MultiSim, minimize, reopen Word and paste it in. Move it around and practice building a Word document with MultiSim symbols included.

Appendix C: Instructions for Drafting/Design Lab Projects

1 Columns and Beams
2 Two- and Three-Dimensional Visualization
3 Thermal Expansions of Materials
4 Gear Systems
5 Center of Mass
6 Fluids and Piping
7 Strengths of Materials
8 Elevations
9 Torque
10 Independent Drafting/Design Research

Columns and Beams

Creating Three-Dimensional Columns

HINT

If you press an incorrect button or key at any point during this project, simply press the **escape** key once to clear the current command/action and then enter the correct one.

Start the AutoCAD program:

Left-click on the **Start** button.
Scroll to **Programs.**
From the side menu, select **Applications-CDD.**
Left-click on **AutoCAD 2000** to run the program.
When the Startup box appears, click **OK** to begin the AutoCAD drafting environment.

Step 1: Drawing a Cylindrical Beam

1. Find the **Draw** button in the menu bar at the top of the AutoCAD screen and left-click to access it.
2. Place the cursor over the **Solids** option found at the very bottom of the menu. When the side menu appears, left-click on the **Cylinder** command.
3. First, you will create the base of the cylinder. Using the mouse, locate the AutoCAD crosshairs in the center of the drawing screen and left-click. This point marks the center point of the circular base of the column.
4. The command line (located at the bottom of the AutoCAD screen) asks you to `Specify radius for base of cylinder or [Diameter]`:. At this prompt, type **1** as the radius then press **enter.**
5. AutoCAD will now ask you to `Specify height of cylinder or [Center of other end]`: (look at the command line). Ignore the part of the command in brackets and type **20** and then **enter** to set the height of the cylinder.
6. Your screen should be similar to the one shown in Figure C1.1. AutoCAD has calculated the cylinder for you but it is hard to visualize in this view.

Figure C1.1

Step 2: Changing the View Orientation

1. Click on the **View** button at the top of the AutoCAD window. Scroll down the pull-down menu until you reach **3D Views.** From the side menu, choose **SW Isometric.** (Selecting this view establishes a three-dimensional angle. Viewing the depth, width, and height of the object simultaneously gives you a better feel for the object's true dimensions.)
2. However, even though your shape has dimension, it doesn't look very solid. To make the column look more realistic, type **hide** then press **enter.** Your column now appears ready to handle the compressional stress discussed in the project (Figure C1.2).

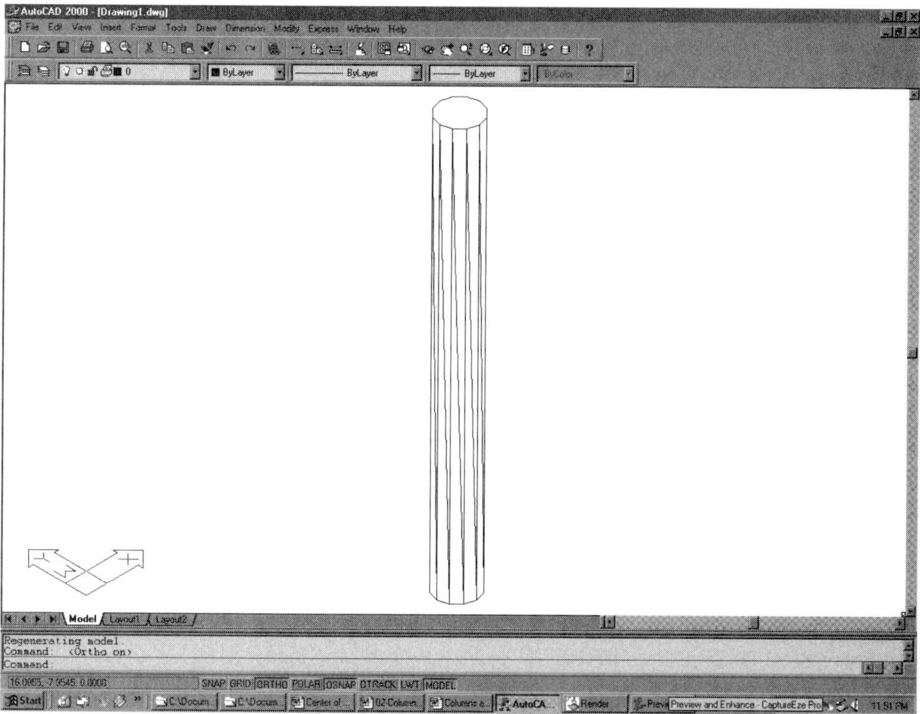

AutoCAD 2000 - [Drawing1.dwg]
File Edit View Insert Format Tools Draw Dimension Modify Express Window Help
ByLayer
ByLayer
ByLayer
Model
Layout1
Layout2
Regenerating model.
Command: <Ortho on>
Command:
SNAP GRID ORTHO POLAR OSNAP OTRACK LWT MODEL
Start

Figure C1.2

Two- and Three-Dimensional Visualization

Drawing and Viewing a Three-Dimensional Cone

HINT

If you press an incorrect button or key at any point during this project, simply press the **escape** key once to clear the current command/action and then enter the correct one.

Start the AutoCAD program:

Left-click on the **Start** button.
Scroll to **Programs.**
From the side menu, select **Applications-CDD.**
Left-click on **AutoCAD 2000** to run the program.
When the Startup box appears, click **OK** to begin the AutoCAD drafting environment.

Step 1: Drawing a Cone

1. Using the mouse, left-click on the **Draw** button at the top of the AutoCAD screen. When the pull-down menu appears, scroll down to the last option on the menu, **Solids.** From the side menu left-click on the **Cone** option.
2. AutoCAD will ask you to indicate where on the screen you want to start drawing the cone. Using the mouse, move the crosshairs to the center of the drawing screen and left-click.
3. The command line, located at the bottom of the AutoCAD window, asks for you to `Specify radius for base of cone or [Diameter]`:. Type in a value of **2** and press **enter.**
4. To give your cone a dimension of height, type **5** and **enter.** AutoCAD will draw the cone for you but seen from an overhead view it doesn't yet look like a cone (see Figure C2.1). The next step will focus on presenting the cone in a three-dimensional manner.

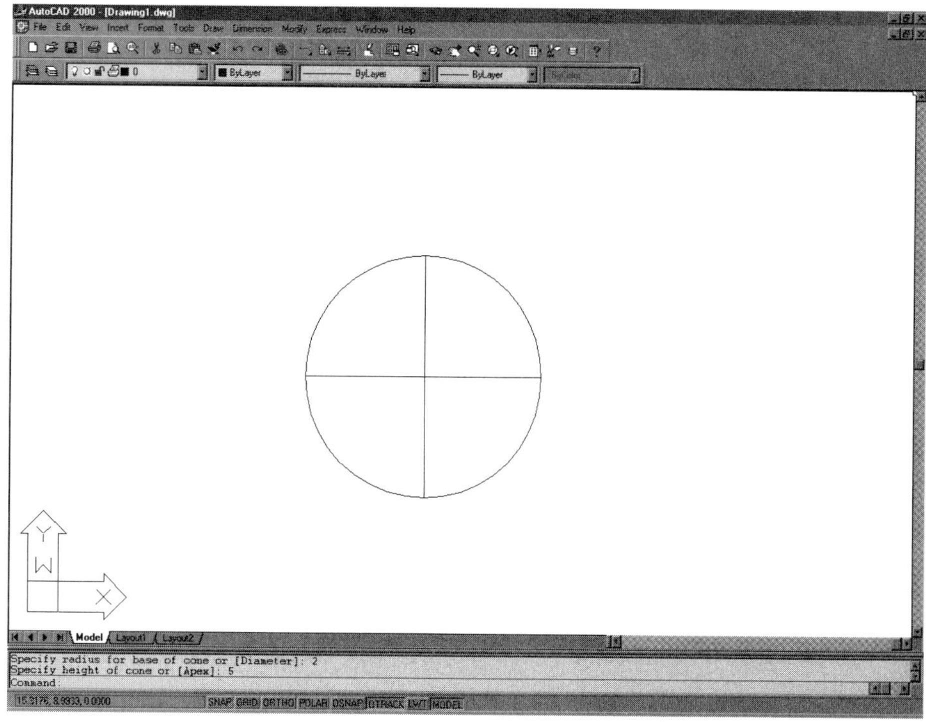

Figure C2.1

Step 2: Orbiting the Cone

1. Left-click on the **View** button at the top of the window. Scroll down to the **3D Orbit** option about halfway down the menu and left-click.
2. When this window appears you need to note some changes. First, the drawing crosshairs have changed into a small symbol. This symbol is the orbit cursor that you will use to change the viewing angle of your object. Second, a green circle has appeared on the screen with smaller circles at the quadrants, as seen in Figure C2.2. These components will help you to orbit the object.

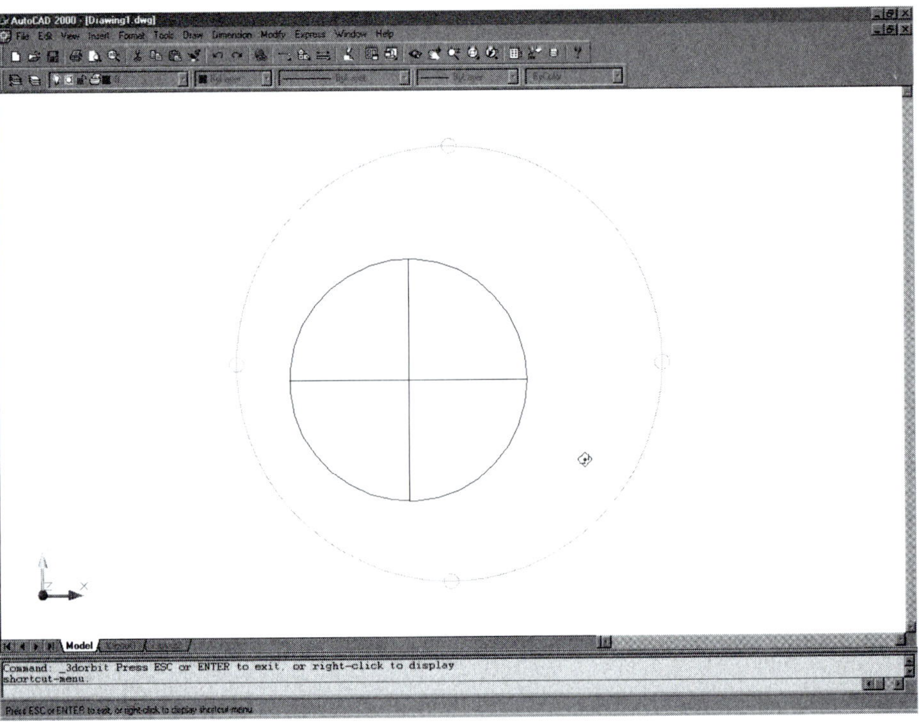

Figure C2.2

FYI

Although the object appears to rotate and flip randomly, it is actually moving along a set circular path. With more time and experience with AutoCAD, you will be able to predict the movement.

3. Place the orbit cursor inside the large green circle. Hold down the left mouse button and move the cursor around in the drawing screen. *Note:* The left mouse button must be held down, not just clicked, the entire time you are orbiting the object.
4. Release the mouse button to stop the object from orbiting in tandem with your mouse movements. Place the cursor in another spot within the circle, hold down the button, and orbit the object some more. Repeat these steps until you can easily see an upright cone. Press **enter** to leave the 3d orbit command.
5. To make your cone appear larger, type **zoom** and press **enter.** Then type **all** and press **enter** again. This command will cause the program to zoom in on the cone so that it fills more of the drawing window.
6. Type **hide** and press **enter**. Your screen should be similar to Figure C2.3.

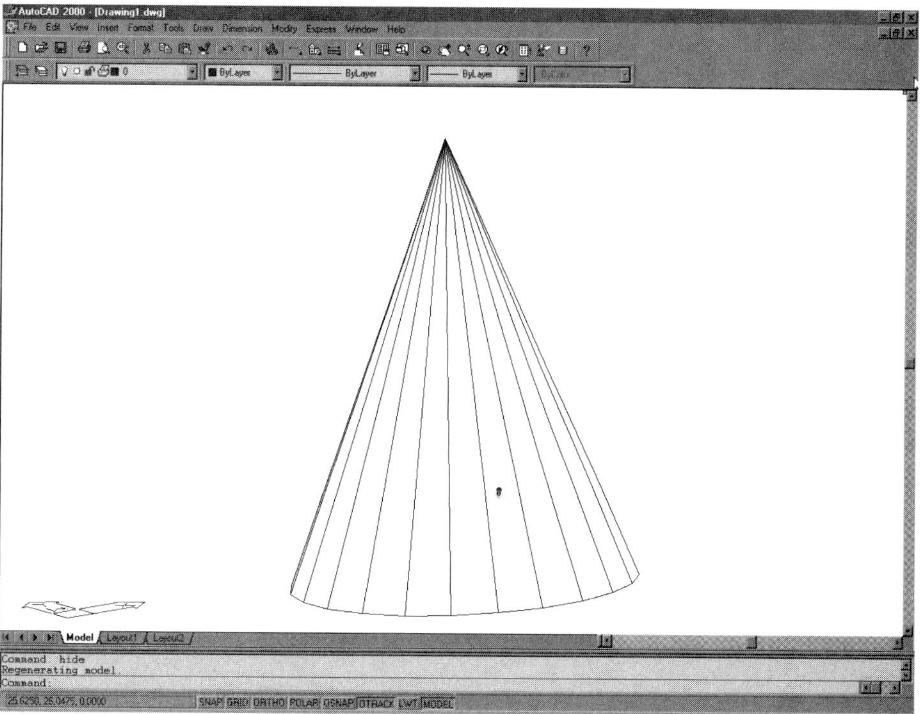

AutoCAD 2000 - [Drawing1.dwg]
File Edit View Insert Format Tools Draw Dimension Modify Express Window Help
ByLayer
ByLayer
ByLayer
Model
Layout1
Layout2
Command: hide
Regenerating model.
Command:
25.6250, 26.0475, 0.0000
SNAP GRID ORTHO POLAR OSNAP OTRACK LWT MODEL

Figure C2.3

Thermal Expansions of Materials

Creating Objects with Volume

HINT

If you press an incorrect button or key at any point during this project, simply press the **escape** key once to clear the current command/action and then enter the correct one.

Start the AutoCAD program:

Left-click on the **Start** button.
Scroll to **Programs.**
From the side menu, select **Applications-CDD.**
Left-click on **AutoCAD 2000** to run the program.
When the Startup box appears, click **OK** to begin the AutoCAD drafting environment.

Step 1: Creating the Objects

1. In this Drafting/Design Project, you analyzed the volume of some three-dimensional objects. In this lab, we will begin by drawing two objects that have volume: a cube and a cylinder.
2. Find the **Draw** button at the top of your AutoCAD screen. Left-click on it and scroll down the pull-down menu to the very last option, **Solids.** When the side menu appears, find and left-click on the **Box** option.
3. You will return to a blank AutoCAD screen. Move your crosshairs to a place in the bottom left portion of your drawing window and left-click to begin drawing your cube.
4. Look at the command line at the bottom of the screen and find the word "Cube" in brackets in the bottom line of text. Words that appear in brackets in the command line are options within the main command. The main command here is "box" and one of the options is "cube." To access `[Cube]` type **C** then **enter.**
5. At the command line, type a value of **4** and press **enter.** AutoCAD calculates the dimensions of the cube for you, and a two-dimensional outline will appear on the screen.
6. Next you will create a cylinder. Once again, left-click on the **Draw** button at the top of the screen. Scroll down to **Solids** and left-click on the **Cylinder** option from the side menu.

7. Place your crosshairs anywhere in the right-hand portion of the drawing screen and left-click.
8. The command line now instructs you to specify a radius for the base of the cylinder. Type **1** and press **enter.**
9. Next you must specify the height of the cylinder; type **4** and then **enter.** A circle appears, indicating that you are looking directly at the bottom of the cylinder as in Figure C3.1.

Figure C3.1

Step 2: Viewing Volumetric Shapes and Attaching Materials

1. Click the **View** button at the top of the screen. Scroll down the menu to **3D Views** and select the **SW Isometric** option.
2. Access the **View** menu again, but this time scroll down to **Render** and left click the **Materials** option from the side menu. Materials are images or shading that you can add to your three-dimensional objects to give them a specific look, like metal, wood, or glass.
3. The Materials Dialogue box will appear, as in Figure C3.2.

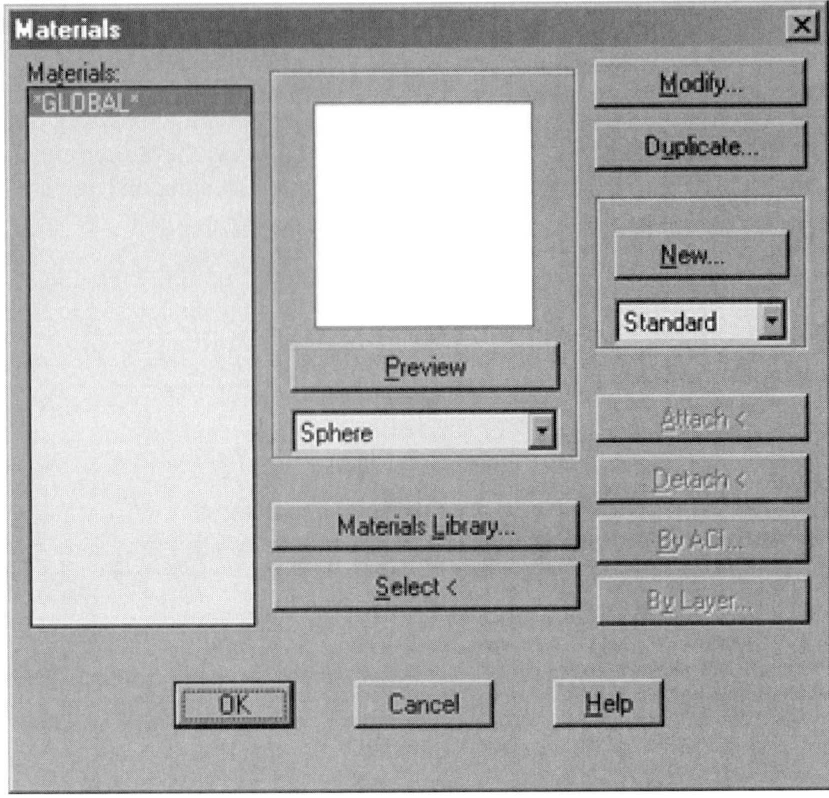

Figure C3.2

4. Left-click on the **Material Library** button located in the middle of the box. The Materials Library dialogue box will now appear (see Figure C3.3).

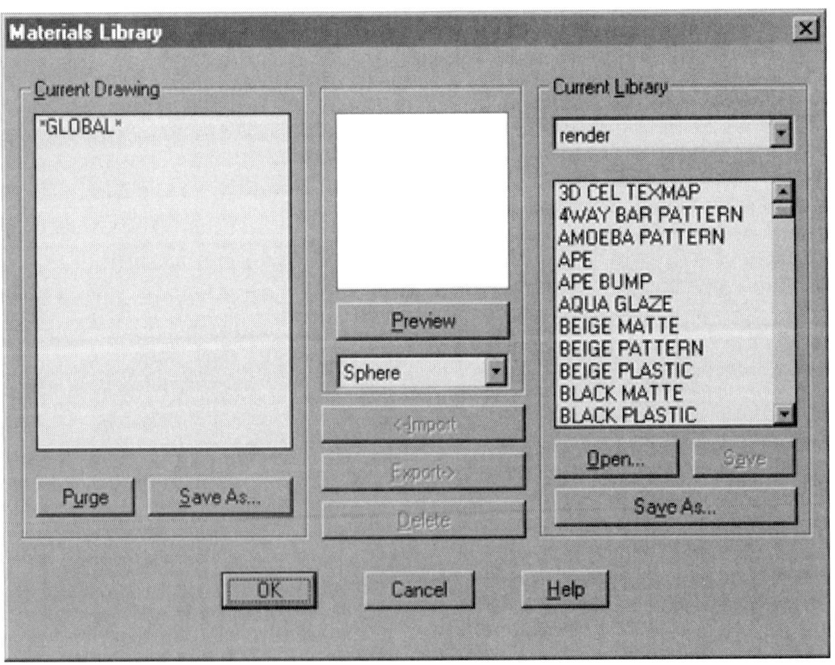

Figure C3.3

5. On the right side of the Materials Library box is a listing of the material types that you can add to your shapes. Using the sliding bar, scroll down

to the material named **COPPER** and highlight it. Once it has been highlighted, move your cursor to the **Import** button and click. You will notice that the word COPPER now appears on the left-hand side of the Materials Library box also.

6. Now return to the listing of materials and scroll down to **OLD METAL** and highlight it. Click on the **Import** button again so that OLD METAL also appears on the left side of the box.
7. Click **OK.**
8. You have now returned to the Materials Dialogue box and will see that you have imported the materials COPPER and OLD METAL into it. Highlight the imported material **COPPER** by clicking on it.
9. On the right-hand side of the box you will find the **Attach** button; left-click on it. The attach option returns you to the AutoCAD drawing screen and waits for you to select the objects to which you wish to apply the selected material. Place the pickbox on top of one of the lines making up the cylinder and left-click. When the object is selected (it will appear dashed), press the **enter** key.
10. Once again, you are returned to the Materials box. AutoCAD allows you to attach any additional materials to your objects before closing this box. Highlight the material OLD METAL and press **attach.**
11. This time, use the pickbox to select the cube and then press **enter.**
12. Click **OK** to close the Materials box.
13. Type the command **render** and press **enter.** The RENDER dialogue box will appear; notice that many options are available to you when rendering objects. However, at this time we will not explore these options. Press the **Render** button. The screen will refresh to show the volumetric objects you created, with the materials attached to them as in Figure C3.4.

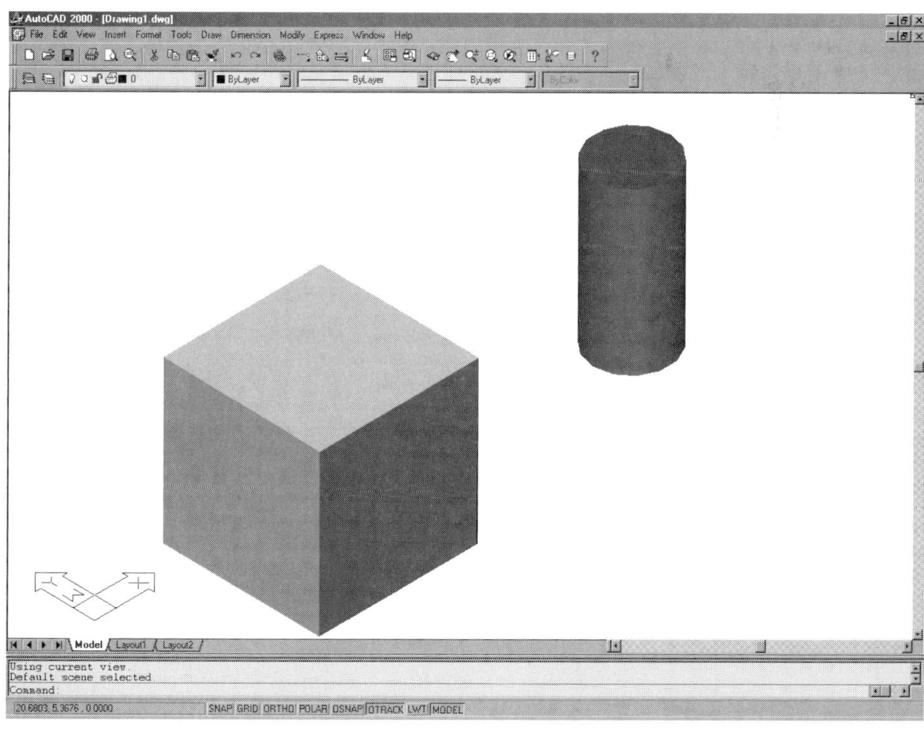

Figure C3.4

Gear Systems

Generating Gears for Visual Analysis

HINT

If you press an incorrect button or key at any point during this project, simply press the **escape** key once to clear the current command/ action and then enter the correct one.

Start the AutoCAD program:

Left-click on the **Start** button.
Scroll to **Programs.**
From the side menu, select **Applications-CDD.**
Left-click on **AutoCAD 2000** to run the program.
When the Startup box appears, click **OK** to begin the AutoCAD drafting environment.

Step 1: Drawing a Gear

1. You will begin by drawing the basic outline of a gear and then will add the specific characteristics of the teeth. Type **circle** then **enter.**
2. With your mouse, move the crosshairs to the middle of the AutoCAD drawing screen. Left-click to place the center of your circle.
3. The command line, located at the bottom of the screen, asks you to `Specify the radius of circle or [Diameter]:`, type **2** and press **enter** to complete the circle.
4. You will need two more circles to complete the outline of the gear. Instead of drawing new circles, you will use AutoCAD to alter the existing circle to create the new ones. Type **offset** and then **enter.** The command line reads: `Specify offset distance or [Through]:`. Ignoring the `[Through]` option, type **.3** (note the period before the number in this and other values) and press **enter.**
5. You must now tell AutoCAD which object to offset. Moving your mouse, place the pickbox so that it is completely on a part of the black line making up the circle and left-click. The circle will appear dashed, signifying that it is selected, and the usual drawing crosshairs will appear. Place the crosshairs so that they are outside of the circle and left-click.
6. A new, larger circle will appear. Press **enter** to finish the offset command.
7. Use the offset command again to create the third circle. Type **offset** and then **enter.**

8. Type **1** as the offset distance and **enter.** With the pickbox, select the inner circle by left-clicking.
9. The new circle needs to be smaller than the original, so place the crosshairs inside the circles and left-click. Type **enter** to finish the command, creating three concentric circles as in Figure C4.1.

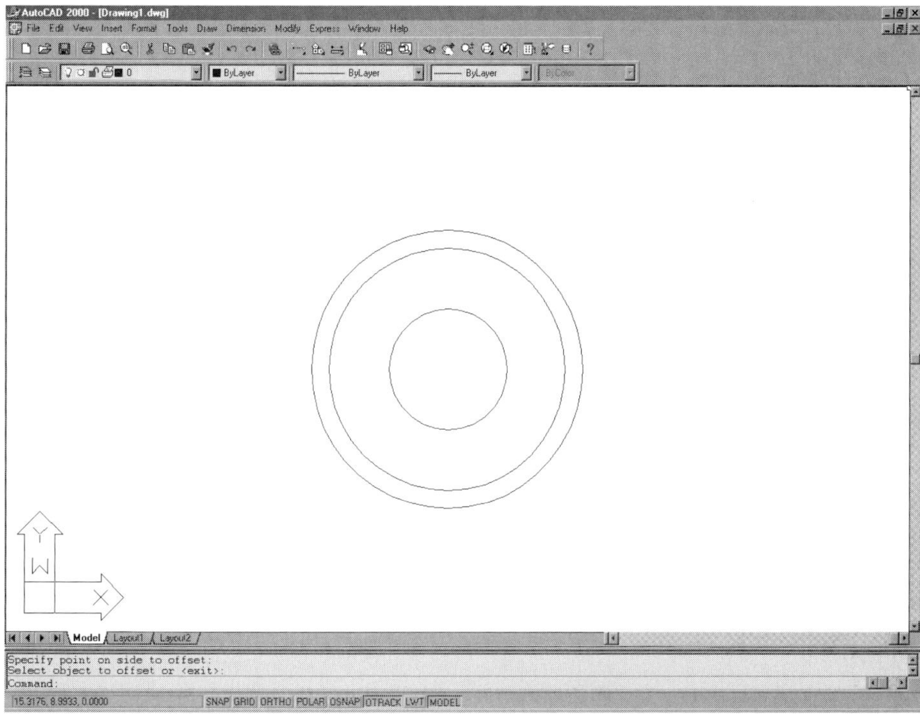

Figure C4.1

Step 2: Adding Teeth to the Gear

1. Type **line** then press **enter.** To begin drawing a line you must first specify a start point for the line. In this case, the first point of your line should be located at the center of the circles. (Notice that all three circles share a common center point.) Type **cen** (for center) and press **enter.**
2. Place the drawing crosshairs directly on one of the circles and left-click. Move your mouse around the screen. You should see a line connecting the crosshairs to the center of the circles.
3. Now, press the **F8** key. This function key allows you to draw straight horizontal or vertical lines easily. Move your crosshairs around the screen to see how this works.
4. Move the crosshairs to the top portion of the drawing screen, directly over the circles. Left-click to complete your vertical line and then press **enter** to exit the line command.
5. You will use the offset command to begin creating the first tooth of the gear. Type **offset** and then press **enter.**
6. Specify a distance to offset by typing **.25** and pressing **enter.**
7. The pickbox will appear in the AutoCAD drawing screen. Use it to select the vertical line you have just drawn by clicking on it. The line will become dashed signaling that it is selected.

8. First, using the crosshairs, left-click any point to the right of the line. Use the pickbox to select the original vertical line again but this time left-click a point on the left side of the line. Because you have already specified the offset distance (in this case, .25), it doesn't matter how close or far from the line you click, it only matters in which direction you wish to offset. Press **enter** to leave the offset command.
9. Type **erase** and press **enter**. Use the pickbox to select the middle vertical line; when it is selected, press **enter.** Because you only used this line as a guide to create the other vertical lines, you need to erase it from your drawing.
10. Type the command **trim** and press **enter**. Move your pickbox so that it is over the outermost circle and left-click. The outer circle will become selected. Now, use the pickbox to select the next smaller circle. When both have been selected, press **enter** to move on.
11. You will now use the pickbox to shorten or trim your vertical lines to meet the selected circles. We will work on the outside initially. Place the pickbox on one of the vertical lines, making sure you are on the outside of the largest circle and left-click. Do the same for the other vertical line. Notice how the line shortens itself to conform to the outer selected circle.
12. Before exiting the command, trim the same two lines, but this time shorten them the other way, to the inner selected circle. Pick on the vertical lines making sure you are inside the selected circles. (Caution: Do not trim the lines between the two selected circles.) The lines will shorten again leaving only a portion between the two outer circles. Press **enter** to exit the command.
13. To make the gear look real, you will also need to trim one of the circles. Type **trim** and **enter.** Use the pickbox to select the two shortened vertical lines and press **enter** when they are selected.
14. Now use the pickbox to left-click on the largest circle both to the left and to the right of the vertical lines. Notice that the circle has been shortened to leave only an arc connecting the two vertical lines. These three lines make up the first tooth of the gear as seen in Figure C4.2. Press **enter** to exit the command.

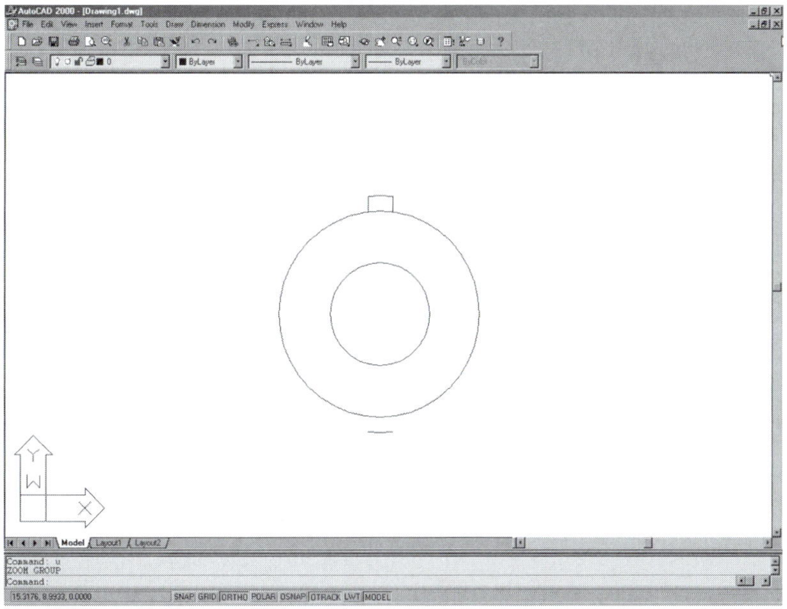

Figure C4.2

15. Type **array** and **enter.** Using the pickbox, select the two vertical lines and the top line that is connecting them. When selected, press **enter.**
16. Type **p** and **enter.** You are now asked to `Specify center point of array:`, by the AutoCAD command line. The center of the array will be the center of the circles, type **cen** and press **enter.** To select the center of the circles, place your crosshairs over one of the circles and left-click.
17. AutoCAD will next ask you to `Enter the number of items in the array:`. The number entered here determines the number of teeth to be included in the gear. Type the number **18** then **enter.**
18. Press **enter** two more times to finish out the array command and all of the teeth will appear around the gear as in Figure C4.3.

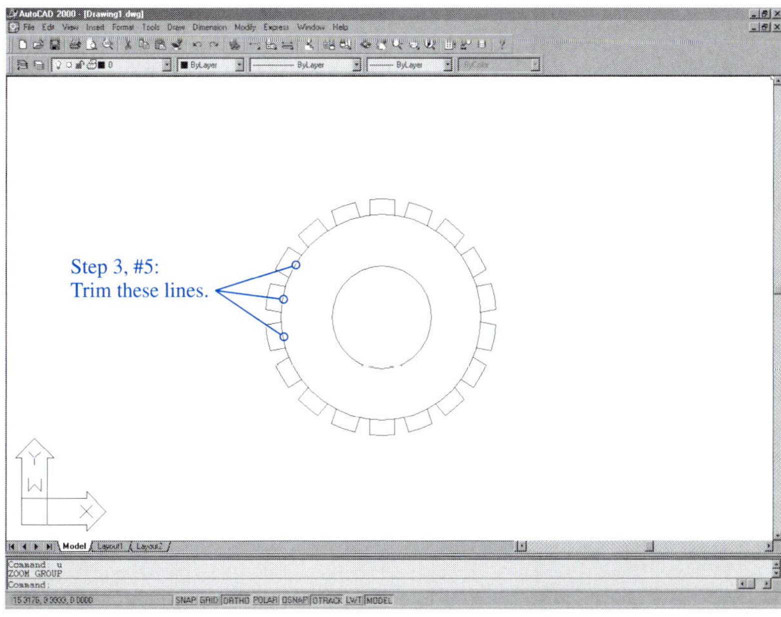

Figure C4.3

AutoCAD

Step 3: Adding a Third Dimension to the Gear and Displaying It

1. To depict the gear accurately, we must first remove some of the extraneous lines that are included in the current representation. Type **trim** and press **enter.**
2. Using the mouse, place the pickbox in the upper right-hand corner of the drawing window and left-click.
3. Moving your mouse away from this point creates a rubberband box. This dashed box is used for simultaneously selecting numerous objects without having to pick them individually.
4. Pull the rubberband box so that it includes all of the lines making up the gear and left-click again. All of the lines will now appear dashed indicating that they are selected. Press **enter** to continue.
5. Use the pickbox to trim the parts of the circles that run through the bottom of the teeth. (Refer to Figure C4.3.) Left-click on the parts of the circle to be removed. Repeat this step until all 18 teeth have been completed and press **enter.**
6. Type the command **region** and press **enter.** As you did previously, locate the pickbox in the upper right-hand corner of the drawing window and left-click to start the rubberband box. Drag the crosshairs so that all of the objects are within the box and left-click again to select them. Press **enter** to finish.
7. Type **extrude** and press **enter.** Using the pickbox, create a rubberband box that will select all the lines comprising the gear. Press **enter** once you are finished selecting.
8. If you look down at the command line, AutoCAD has asked for the desired height of the extrusion. In this case the height value will be the thickness of the gear. Type **.5** and then press **enter** twice.
9. Type the command **subtract** then **enter.** Place the pickbox over any line making up the toothed portion of the gear and left-click to select it. Press **enter** to continue.
10. Use the pickbox to select the inner circle and press **enter.**
11. Steps 7 and 8 of this process gave the thickness, and steps 9 and 10 created a hole in the center of the gear. Now, find the **View** button on the top toolbar, and left-click. From the pull-down menu, select **3D Views** and then **SW Isometric.**
12. Type **hide** and **enter.** The gear is now complete and is a fully realized three-dimensional model, as seen in Figure C4.4.

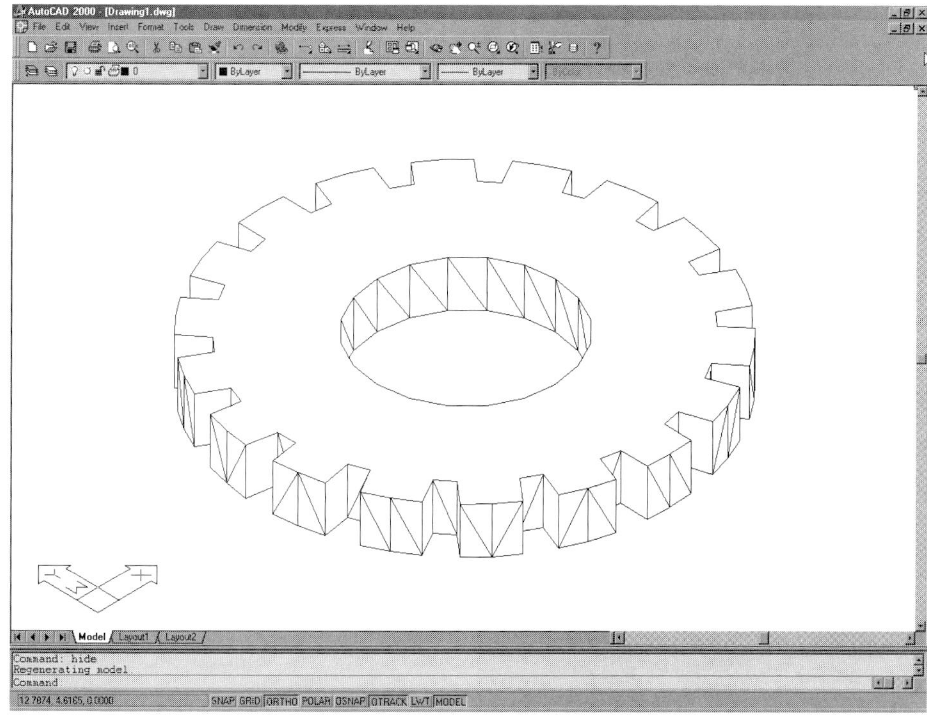

AutoCAD 2000 - [Drawing1.dwg]
File Edit View Insert Format Tools Draw Dimension Modify Express Window Help
ByLayer
ByLayer
ByLayer
ByColor
Model
Layout1
Layout2
Command: hide
Regenerating model.
Command:
12.7874, 4.6165, 0.0000
SNAP GRID ORTHO POLAR OSNAP OTRACK LWT MODEL

Figure C4.4

Center of Mass

Translating Center of Mass Concepts into an AutoCAD Environment

HINT

If you press an incorrect button or key at any point during this project, simply press the **escape** key once to clear the current command/action and then enter the correct one.

Start the AutoCAD program:

Left-click on the **Start** button.
Scroll to **Programs.**
From the side menu, select **Applications-CDD.**
Left-click on **AutoCAD 2000** to run the program.
When the Startup box appears, click **OK** to begin the AutoCAD drafting environment.

Step 1: Drawing a Three-Dimensional Sphere

1. Using the mouse, locate and left-click on the **Draw** button (located towards the top of the screen) to access the Draw pull-down menu.
2. Scroll down to the last selection on the menu, **Solids.** When the side menu appears, left-click the option named **Sphere.**
3. You will return to the blank AutoCAD screen. Center the drawing crosshairs on the screen and left-click to begin drawing the sphere.
4. The command line (located at the bottom of the AutoCAD screen) asks you to `Specify radius of sphere or [Diameter]:`. Type **1**, then press **enter** to finish the command. Your screen should now resemble Figure C5.1.

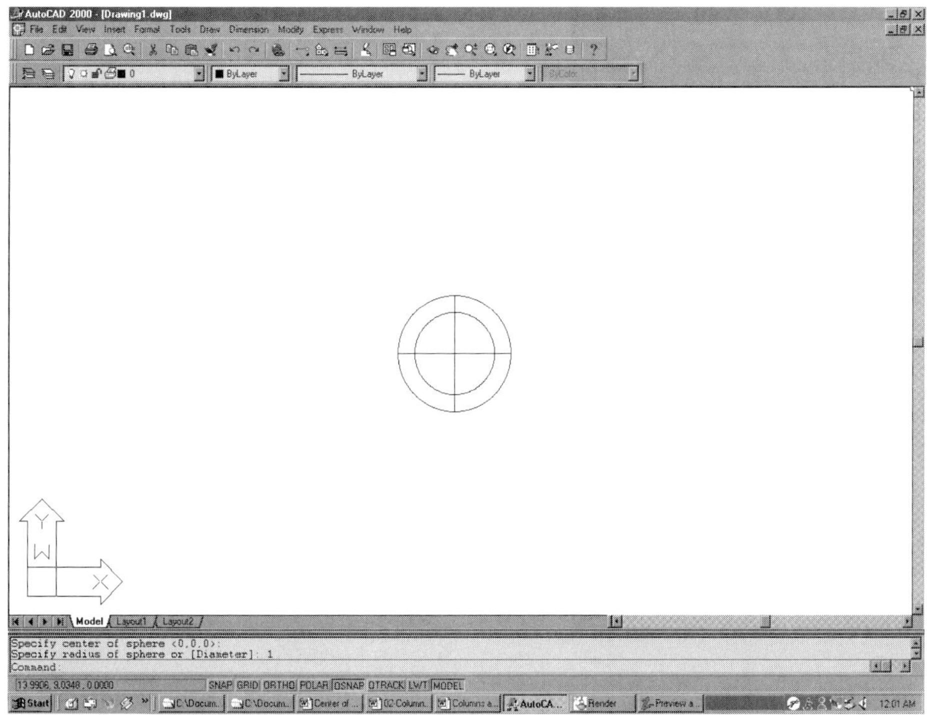

Figure C5.1

Step 2: Copying and Scaling to Create Two New and Different Masses

1. Type **copy,** then press **enter.** The command line now asks you to `Select objects:`. Using the mouse, place the pickbox (which has appeared in place of the crosshairs) over one of the black lines making up the sphere, and left-click on it. Press **enter** once the sphere has been selected (selected objects will appear dashed).
2. Now press the **F8** key. This function key will lock the direction of movement to be completely horizontal or vertical. In other words, no diagonal movement will be permitted.
3. Left-click a point anywhere inside the sphere to use as a starting position for copying.
4. Another sphere will appear. Use the mouse to drag the sphere to a position on the far right of the drawing screen, being careful not to let it disappear from the window. When you are satisfied with its location, left-click to end the command.
5. Repeat the copy command to create a third sphere on the far left of the screen.

Step 3: Scaling Objects

1. Type **scale** and press **enter.**
2. Using the pickbox, select the sphere furthest to the left on your screen, then press **enter** or right-click.
3. AutoCAD now prompts you to `Specify base point:`, which is used as the stationary point in scaling. Type **cen** and **enter,** to keep the center point of the sphere in line with the center of the other spheres.

4. To pick the center of the sphere, place the crosshairs close to or on any of the lines making up the simple sphere shape and left-click.
5. Moving the mouse around the screen allows you to expand or contract the size of the sphere arbitrarily. To specify an exact amount to scale, type **.5** and press **enter.**
6. Now practice this scaling technique on the sphere to the right. Instead of scaling the sphere to half of its original size (.5), type **2** to double its size.

Step 4: Viewing the Spheres in a More Realistic Way

1. Press the **View** button (located in the menu bar at the top of the screen) to access the View pull-down menu. Scroll down to **3D Views** and select the **SW Isometric** option.
2. The screen will refresh with a fuller representation of the spheres. (*Note:* The *x*-axis has been shifted to an angled position for viewing purposes. The spheres are still in line with each other.)
3. Type **hide** then **enter** to achieve an even more accurate three-dimensional representation of your models, as in Figure C5.2.

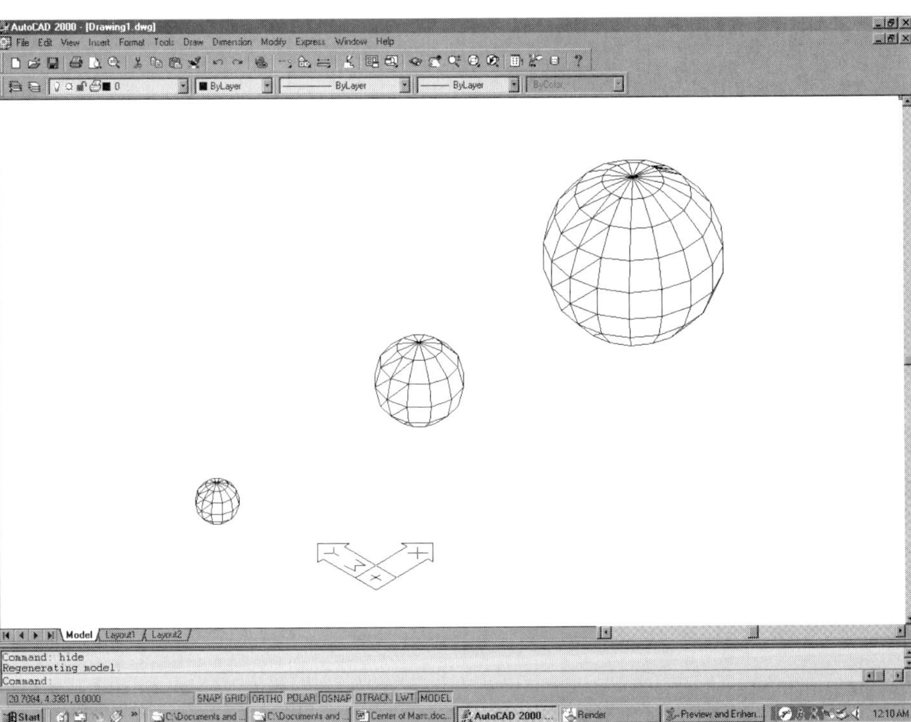

Figure C5.2

Fluids and Piping

Drawing a Three-Dimensional Section of Pipe

HINT

If you press an incorrect button or key at any point during this project, simply press the **escape** key once to clear the current command/action and then enter the correct one.

Start the AutoCAD program:

Left-click on the **Start** button.
Scroll to **Programs.**
From the side menu, select **Applications-CDD.**
Left-click on **AutoCAD 2000** to run the program.
When the Startup box appears, click **OK** to begin the AutoCAD drafting environment.

Step 1: Constructing the Basic Shape of a Pipe

1. Before starting to draw, go to the **View** button located at the top of the AutoCAD window and left-click. Scroll down to **3D Views** and left-click the **Front** option from the side menu.
2. Type **circle** and **enter.** Next, locate the crosshairs in the center of the drawing screen and left-click to specify the center point of the circle.
3. The command line located at the bottom of the screen instructs you to `Specify radius of circle or [Diameter]:`, type **1** and press **enter.** This circle will serve as the outside diameter of our pipe.
4. Again, type **circle** and press **enter.** Now, type **cen** and press **enter.** Move your drawing crosshairs so that they are very near or on top of the first circle, and left-click when you are satisfied.
5. Type **.9** as the radius of the second circle and press **enter.** A new, slightly smaller circle will be drawn. Notice that both of the circles share the same center point because we used the **cen** subcommand (Figure C6.1).

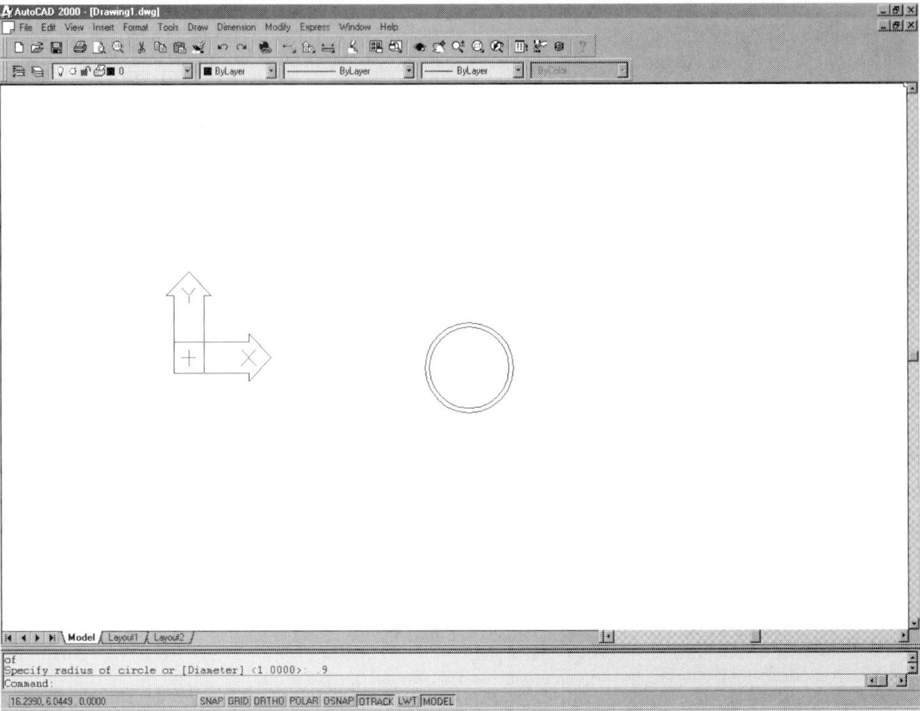

Figure C6.1

Step 2: Adding a Third Dimension to the Pipe

1. Type the command **extrude** and press **enter.** You will see that the pickbox has taken the place of the usual drawing crosshairs. Use the pickbox to select each of the two circles by left-clicking on each. The circle is selected when it changes from a solid to a dashed line. Use the same technique to choose the other circle, and when both are selected press **enter.**
2. The command line now prompts you to `Specify height of extrusion or [Path]:`. Type in a value of **10** and press **enter.** Press **enter** once more to finish the command. Although you are unable to see it at this time, the extrude command has taken the two flat circles and has turned them into three-dimensional cylinders.
3. Use the inner circle to cut out a hole in the center of the solid form. Type **subtract** and press **enter.**
4. Use the pickbox to select the outer circle, making sure that the pickbox doesn't accidently overlap the inner circle as well. Misplacing the pickbox may cause AutoCAD to select the wrong circle. When the outer circle becomes dashed, press **enter.**
5. Now use the pickbox to select the inner circle. Once again, be careful not to overlap the other circle. Once selected, press **enter** to finish the subtract command.

Step 3: Viewing the Section of Pipe in All Three Dimensions

1. Left-click on the **View** button and scroll down to **3D Views.** When the side menu appears, find and left-click on the **SE Isometric** option. The object will change viewing angles so that its true shape is displayed.
2. To view your pipe as a three-dimensional object, type **hide** and press **enter.** Your pipe should look the same as Figure C6.2.

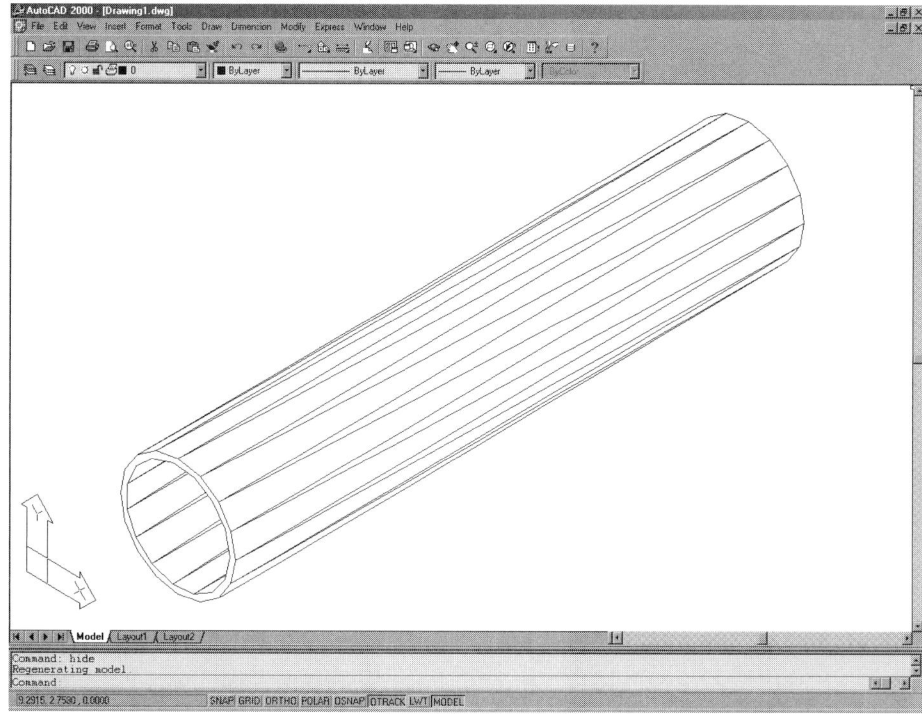

AutoCAD 2000 - [Drawing1.dwg]
File Edit View Insert Format Tools Draw Dimension Modify Express Window Help
ByLayer
ByLayer
ByLayer
Model Layout1 Layout2
Command: hide
Regenerating model.
Command:
9.2915, 2.7530, 0.0000
SNAP GRID ORTHO POLAR OSNAP OTRACK LWT MODEL

Figure C6.2

Strengths of Materials

Graphing Functions Using AutoCAD

HINT

If you press an incorrect button or key at any point during this project, simply press the **escape** key once to clear the current command/action and then enter the correct one.

Start the AutoCAD program:

Left-click on the **Start** button.
Scroll to **Programs.**
From the side menu, select **Applications-CDD.**
Left-click on **AutoCAD 2000** to run the program.
When the Startup box appears, click **OK** to begin the AutoCAD drafting environment.

Step 1: Drawing the Coordinate Axes

1. Type **line** and press **enter.** Using your mouse, place the drawing crosshairs in the top-center portion of the drawing window. Left-click to begin drawing the line.
2. Press the **F8** key. This function key constrains the cursor to drawing only straight lines. Move the crosshairs toward the bottom of the screen so that a vertical line is created. Left-click again to choose the other end-point of the line, then press **enter.**
3. Type **line** and press **enter.** This time draw a horizontal line that intersects the lower portion of the vertical line. Move the crosshairs slightly to the left of the vertical line, making sure that the new line crosses over the vertical line, and left-click.
4. Drag your mouse to the right side of the screen and left-click again to end the line and then press **enter**. These two lines will serve as the coordinate axes, as seen in Figure C7.1.

Figure C7.1

Step 2: Drawing the Function

1. The function you will be graphing is $y = 2x + 1$. The first step in constructing this function is creating guidelines.
2. Type **offset** and press **enter.** Next, type a value of **1** and press **enter.**
3. The pickbox will appear on your screen. Move your mouse so that the pickbox is directly over the horizontal line and left-click. Note that the selected line changes from solid to dashed.
4. Once the line is selected, move the crosshairs so that they are above the horizontal line and left-click. A new line will be created above the original line.
5. The crosshairs will again change back to the pickbox. This time select the line you have just offset. Move the crosshairs above the newly selected line and left-click. Repeat this step as many times as necessary to reach the top of the drawing window (four or five more times).
6. Before exiting this command, use the pickbox to select the vertical line. Move the crosshairs this time to the right of the vertical line and left-click. Press **enter** to finish the offset command. Your screen should look like the one in Figure C7.2.

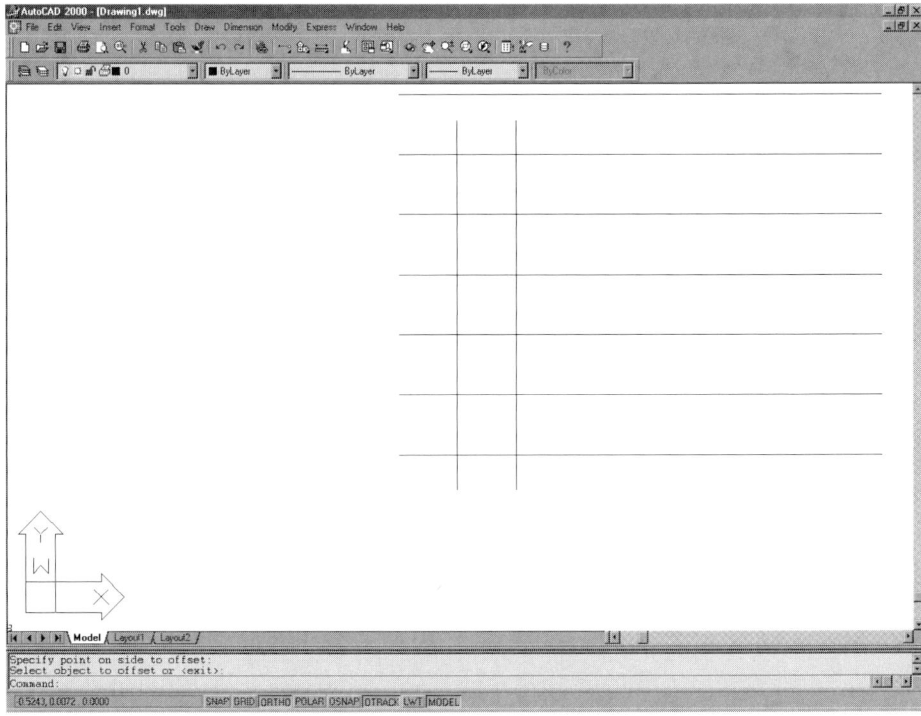

Figure C7.2

7. Returning to our function, $y = 2x + 1$, we see that we have points at (0,1) and (1,3). We will now draw a line that connects these points to begin graphing our function.
8. Type **line** and **enter.** Remembering that the bottom horizontal line is the x-axis and the vertical line farthest to the left is the y-axis, locate the point (0,1).
9. Type **int** for intersection (this command selects a point at the intersection of two lines) and press **enter**. Place the crosshairs over the point (0,1) and left-click to start your line. (*Note:* You may see a yellow "X" appear at the intersection of the lines. This is AutoCAD's way of confirming that you have found the intersection of the lines.)
10. If you move the crosshairs around the screen, you will notice that your movement is confined to a horizontal or vertical direction because the F8 option is still in operation. Because the function $y = 2x + 1$ is a diagonal line; we will want to release this option by pressing **F8** again.
11. Now, locate the point (1,3). Type **int** and **enter** again then left-click at the intersection of those lines to create a portion of the function. Press the **enter** key to move on.
12. To extend the line representing the function to include more than just these two points, type **extend** and press **enter.** With the pickbox, select the horizontal line closest to the top of the screen, then select the line representing the x-axis, and press **enter** when finished. These two lines are the lines that the function will meet once it is extended.
13. Next, we extend the function past the point (1,3). Using the pickbox, select the function line close to the point (1,3). Note: you must left-click on the line itself. Notice how the line has stretched itself to meet the top horizontal line. Now to extend the function back beyond (0,1), use the pickbox to select the function line close to the point (0,1) and press **enter**.

14. To clean up the graph, we must erase the guidelines. Type **erase** and press **enter.** With the pickbox, select each of the guidelines, being careful to leave the *x*- and *y*-axes and the angled function line, as in Figure C7.3. Press the **enter** key when all of the guidelines have been selected.

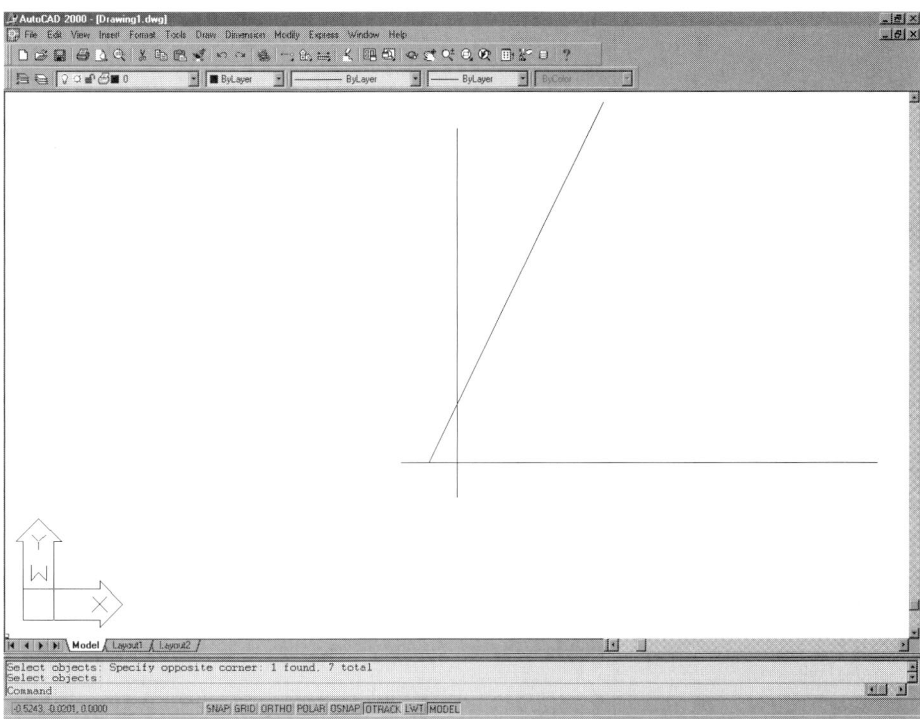

Figure C7.3

Step 3: Labeling the Axes

1. Now we will place text on the graph to label the *x*- and *y*-axes. Type **text** and press **enter.**
2. We begin by labeling the *y*-axis. Using the crosshairs, select a point near the top of the vertical line and left-click. (*Note:* Don't worry if the placement is not exact, you will be able to move the text later to put it in a better location.)
3. Type **.5** as the height of the text and then press **enter** twice. You will notice that a symbol that looks like an elongated "I" will appear on the screen—this is the text cursor. Type **y** and press **enter** twice.
4. Type **text** and press **enter.** To add the label to the *x*-axis, place the crosshairs near the right-hand end of the *x*-axis and left-click. Press **enter** twice and the same text cursor will appear again. Type **x** and press **enter** twice again.
5. You may not have been very accurate at placing your labels. To fix this problem, type **move** and press **enter.** Use the pickbox to select the text you wish to move and press **enter.**
6. The AutoCAD command line instructs you to `Specify base point or displacement:`, use the crosshairs to pick a point very near the text. Now if you move the crosshairs around the screen you will find that you can move the text anywhere you want. Left-click a point that puts the text closer to the axis. Repeat this command for the other axis label, if necessary, so that your drawing looks like that in Figure C7.4.

Figure C7.4

Elevations

Manipulating Right Triangles for Use with Elevations

HINT

If you press an incorrect button or key at any point during this project, simply press the **escape** key once to clear the current command/ action and then enter the correct one.

Start the AutoCAD program:

Left-click on the **Start** button.
Scroll to **Programs.**
From the side menu, select **Applications-CDD.**
Left-click on **AutoCAD 2000** to run the program.
When the Startup box appears, click **OK** to begin the AutoCAD drafting environment.

Step 1: Drawing a Right Triangle

1. Begin by using the line command to construct the three sides of a triangle. Type **line** and press **enter.**
2. Using the mouse, place the drawing crosshairs in the center of the screen and left-click to pick the starting point of your line.
3. There are two ways to finish drawing the line. You may pick another point with the crosshairs, or enter a value using the keyboard. Entering a value is more accurate than just picking points for your lines at random, and is the recommended approach.
4. Type @**3,0** (holding down the shift button while pressing the 2 key gives you the @ symbol) and press **enter**. Notice that AutoCAD computes a straight line for you.
5. You can draw the other sides of the triangle without typing the line command again, because AutoCAD allows you to draw connecting lines until you exit the command. Type @**0,4** and press **enter**. The upright leg of the triangle is now drawn for you.
6. Next type **close** and press **enter** twice. The close option draws a connecting line for you, completing the triangle, as seen in Figure C8.1.

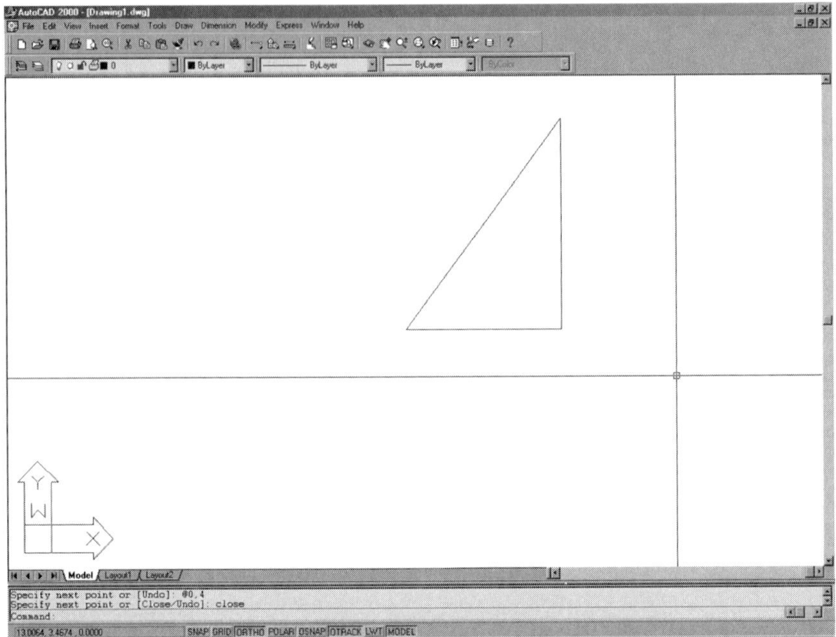

Figure C8.1

Step 2: Constructing Mirrored Copies of the Elevation

1. Type the command **mirror** and press **enter.** The command line (located at the bottom of the AutoCAD screen) asks you to `Select objects`:. Notice that the drawing crosshairs have been replaced by a box called the pickbox. Move the pickbox to a position that is directly over one of the lines making up the triangle and left-click. The line has been selected when it becomes dashed.
2. Again, place the pickbox over one of the other lines and left-click. Do this again on the last line, so that all the lines making up the triangle are selected, and then press **enter.**
3. Next, we must pick a point to begin mirroring. Locate the crosshairs just to the right of the triangle and left-click. When you move the crosshairs around, a mirrored copy of the triangle appears and rotates around the point that you just picked. Because we want the new triangle to be vertical and not at an angle, we must do one more step.
4. Press the **F8** key. This key restricts movements to those along the *x*- or *y*-axes. Move your crosshairs to the top of the screen over the triangle and left-click. Press **enter** once to finish the mirror command.
5. Repeat these steps to mirror the triangle in another direction. Type **mirror** and press **enter.** Use the pickbox to select the original triangle, just as you did before. Press **enter** when all three lines are selected.
6. Use the crosshairs to pick the starting point of the mirror, slightly below the selected triangle.
7. Using your mouse, move the crosshairs to the right side of the screen. You will be able to see the mirrored triangle appear upside-down under the selected triangle. Left-click when the new triangle is shown to be upside-down and press **enter** to finish the command. Your screen should look similar to Figure C8.2.

AutoCAD

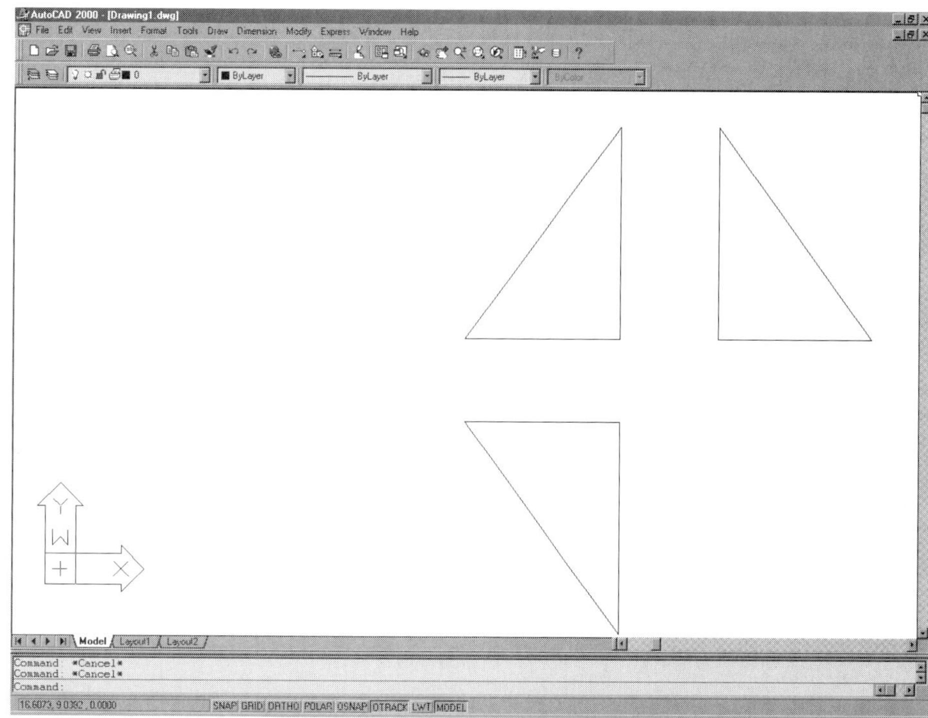

Figure C8.2

8. If any part of one of your triangles is cut off, type **zoom** and press **enter.** Then type **all** and press **enter** again. This command will cause the view to zoom out so that all of the lines are shown completely in the drawing screen.

Torque

Drawing and Attaching Materials to a Three-Dimensional Beam

HINT

If you press an incorrect button or key at any point during this project, simply press the **escape** key once to clear the current command/action and then enter the correct one.

Start the AutoCAD program:

Left-click on the **Start** button.
Scroll to **Programs.**
From the side menu, select **Applications-CDD.**
Left-click on **AutoCAD 2000** to run the program.
When the Startup box appears, click **OK** to begin the AutoCAD drafting environment.

Step 1: Constructing the Beam

1. Go to the **View** button located on the top toolbar of your AutoCAD screen and left-click on it. A pull-down menu will appear, scroll down to **3D Views** and left-click on the **Front** option. Choosing this view will make it easier to see our three-dimensional beam later on.
2. Our strategy will be to draw a two-dimensional representation of the beam and then use AutoCAD's 3D operations to make the beam a solid object. First, go to the **Draw** button and left-click.
3. The menu will open; left-click on the **Rectangle** option. You will be asked to use the drawing crosshairs to pick the first corner of the rectangle. Locate the crosshairs near the center of the drawing window and left-click to pick the first corner.
4. As you begin to move the crosshairs to the lower right-hand corner of the screen, you will see that a rectangle is being stretched from the beginning point (the point that you have just picked) to the ending point (the intersection point of your crosshairs).
5. Left-click an ending point when you have a medium-sized rectangle, as in Figure C9.1.

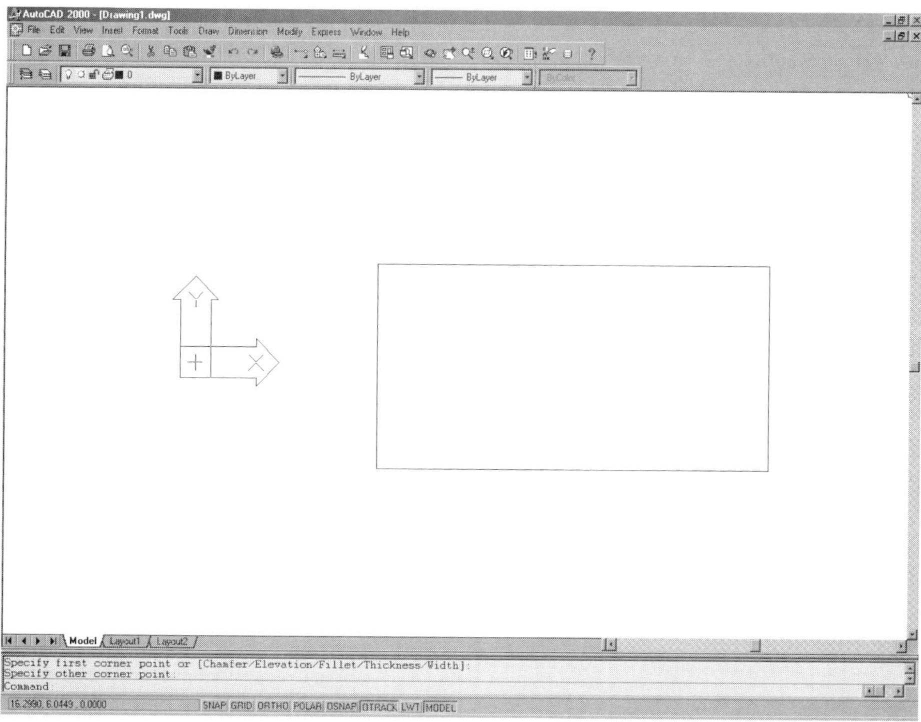

Figure C9.1

6. To make the rectangle three-dimensional, use the extrude command, which creates depth for two-dimensional objects. Type **extrude** and press **enter.** The command line (located at the bottom of your screen) asks you to `Select objects:`. With the pickbox that has taken the place of the crosshairs, left-click over any of the lines that make up the rectangle. The rectangle will be selected when it appears as a dashed line. Press **enter.**
7. Now you must enter a number that tells AutoCAD how long you want your beam to be. Type **25** and press **enter** twice.

Step 2: Viewing the Beam in Three-Dimensional Space

1. Click on the **View** button at the top of your screen. Find **3D Views** once again but this time select the **SE Isometric** option.
2. The beam is now in a three-dimensional orientation but still does not appear solid. To give the beam a solid appearance, type **hide** and press **enter.** Your beam should now look like Figure C9.2.

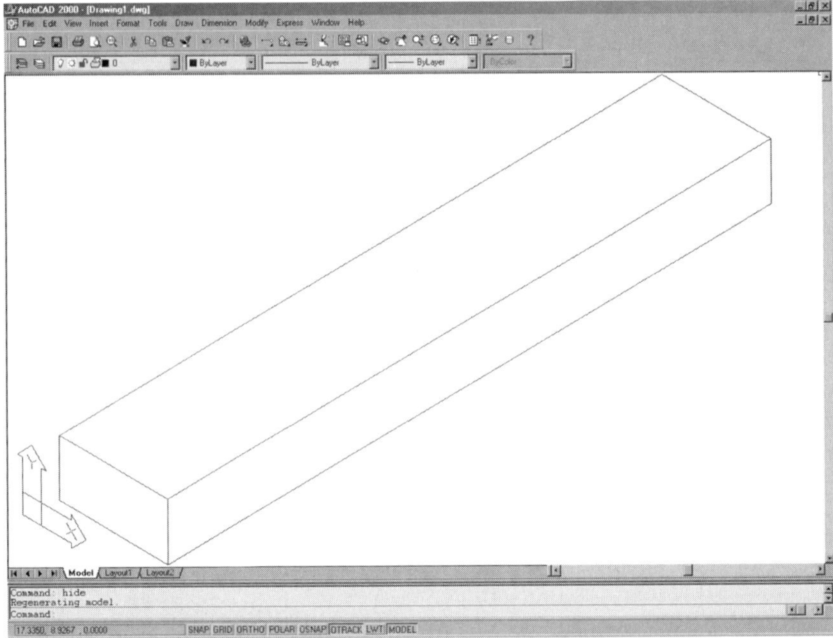

Figure C9.2

Step 3: Attaching a Material to the Beam

1. Left-click on the **View** button and scroll down to the **Render** option. Find **Materials** and left-click on it.
2. The Materials dialogue box will appear in the center of your screen. You will use this tool and the Materials Library box (Figure C9.3) to make the beam look as if it were made of wood.

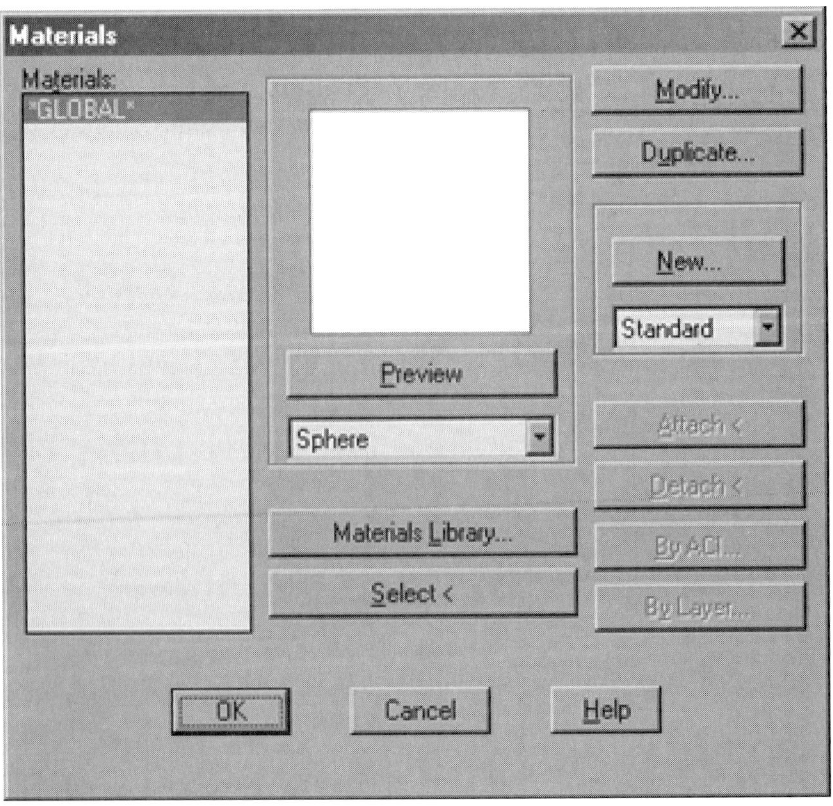

Figure C9.3

AutoCAD

3. First, find the **Materials Library** button in the middle of the box. Left-click on it. The Materials Library dialogue box will appear on top. If you look to the right side of the box you will notice a listing of colors and patterns as in Figure C9.4. This is the list of materials that AutoCAD supplies to apply to rendered objects.

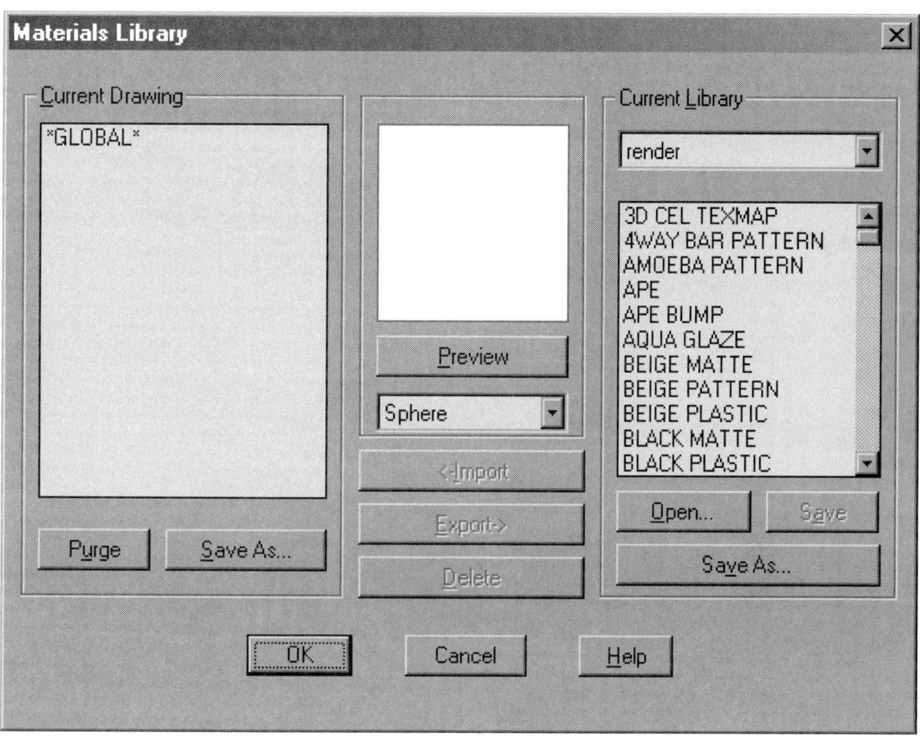

Figure C9.4

4. Scroll down almost to the bottom of the list, where you will find seven different types of wood patterns to choose from. Find **WOOD – WHITE ASH** and left-click on it to highlight it.
5. Now, find and left-click on the **Import** button located in the middle of the Materials Library box. Press the **OK** button to continue.
6. Now that you are back in the Materials box, find the wood material that you have just imported and left-click on it to highlight it once again. Move to the right side of the box and left-click on the **Attach** button.
7. AutoCAD will return you to the drawing window and ask `Select objects to attach "WOOD - WHITE ASH" to:`. Using the pickbox, select any of the lines that make up the beam. Press **enter** when the beam is selected.
8. Press **OK** in the Materials box to finish.

Step 4: Rendering the Beam and Revealing Attached Materials

1. Type the command **Render** and press **enter.** When the **Render** dialogue box appears you will see many options. You need change only one of the settings to render the object as a wood beam.
2. At the top of the render box (Figure C9.5), find the **Rendering Type** pull-down menu. Left-click on the small downward arrow (▼) to open up the menu. Change the setting from **Render** to the one directly below, **Photo Real.** This will improve the quality of the displayed graphics, making the wood beam look more realistic.

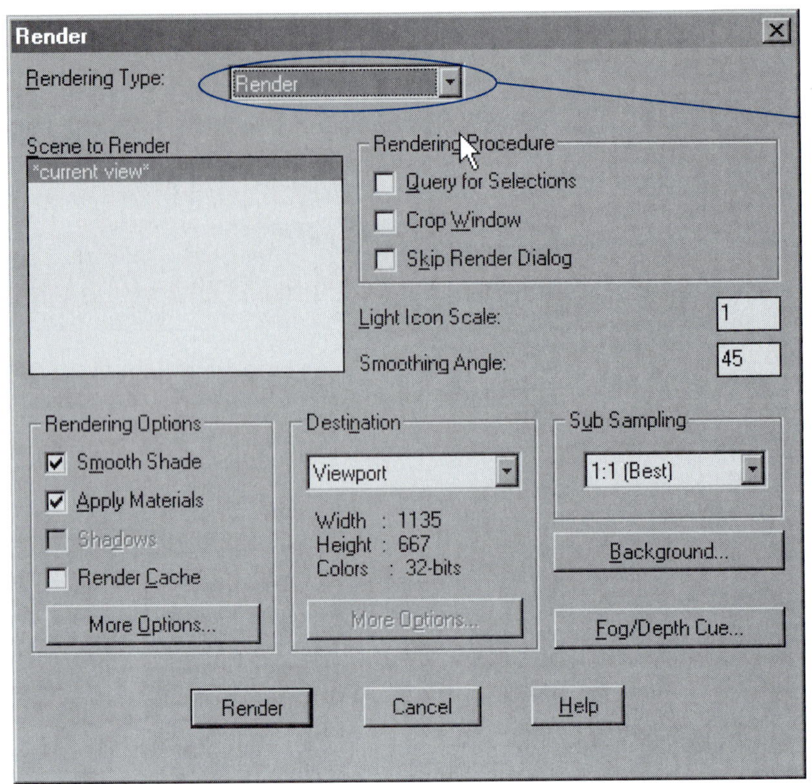

Figure C9.5

3. Press the **Render** button at the bottom of the box to render your wood beam. It should look like the beam in Figure C9.6.

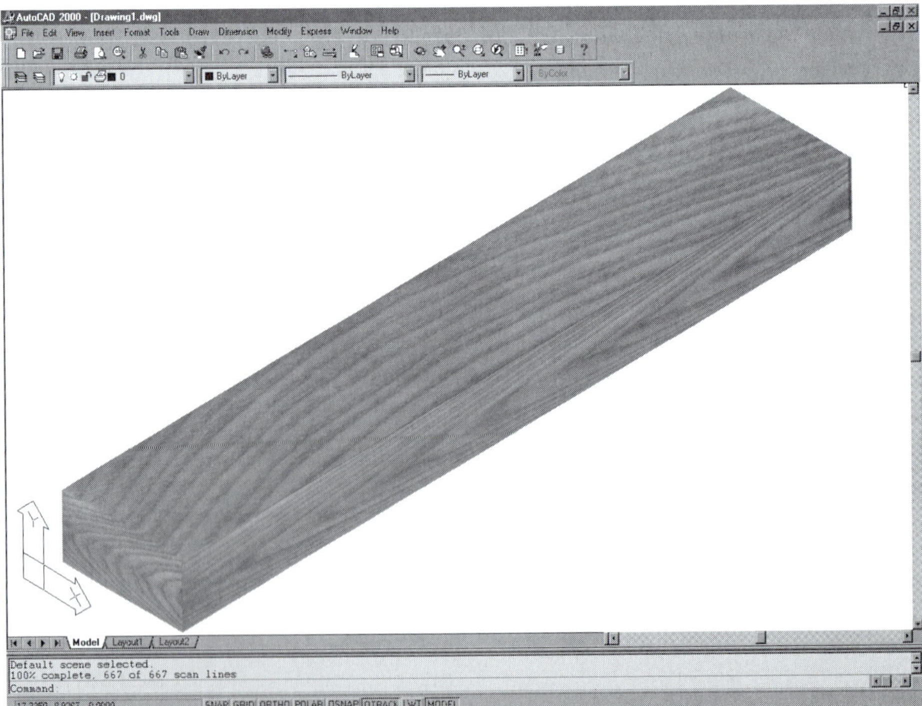

Figure C9.6

AutoCAD

Independent Drafting/Design Research

Using AutoCAD Commands More Effectively

HINT

If you press an incorrect button or key at any point during this project, simply press the **escape** key once to clear the current command/action and then enter the correct one.

In this project, you are challenged to independently explore several more-advanced AutoCAD commands. This lab encourages you to think about how to explore and gain familiarity with a new drafting software program. Although drafting and design courses will guide you through a selection of the most common commands and applications associated with a particular software package, there is no replacement for independent exploration.

Start the AutoCAD program:

Left-click on the **Start** button.
Scroll to **Programs.**
From the side menu, select **Applications-CDD.**
Left-click on **AutoCAD 2000** to run the program.
When the Startup box appears, click **OK** to begin the AutoCAD drafting environment.

Exercise 1: Drawing Simple Shapes

In the drafting and design industry, most of the drawings produced in AutoCAD start with the creation of a simple shape like a line, circle, or polygon, which is then manipulated to meet a specific design requirement.

Command 1: The Line Command

1. Access the **Draw** pull-down menu by left-clicking the **Draw** button (located at the top of the screen). The first option on the menu is Line; activate the command by left-clicking on the word **Line.**
2. The first step in creating a line segment, or sequence of line segments, is to select a starting point on the screen to begin the line. Use the crosshairs to pick a starting point for your line by left-clicking in the drawing window.
3. If you move the crosshairs around the drawing screen you will notice that a starting point for your line is fixed at your chosen point and that a "rubberband line" connects your start point to the crosshairs. The rubberband line is how AutoCAD previews a line segment.

4. Find a point on the screen and left-click to choose a second point for your line. You will see that a line appears. Because you are still in the line command mode, your crosshairs continue to pull a rubberband line. AutoCAD will continue to draw connecting lines until you tell it to stop drawing by pressing the **enter** key.
5. Select a few more endpoints for your connecting lines and then press **enter** to end the line command.
6. Before we begin drawing a different shape, there are a few more important tips to be aware of when using the line command. Access the line command through the **Draw** menu. Pick a starting point by left-clicking, and try to draw a horizontal or vertical line. You will see that it requires a great deal of patience to create perfectly straight lines in this manner. AutoCAD offers a shortcut.
7. Press the **F8** key. This function-key option constrains AutoCAD to draw lines and other shapes along the *x* (horizontal) or *y* (vertical) axes only. You determine whether the line is drawn horizontally or vertically by moving the crosshairs in the appropriate direction. To turn off this option press F8 again. Draw several horizontal and vertical lines using this option. Experiment by drawing a rectangle.
8. Press **enter** to end the line command. At this point your screen may be filled with lines. To clear the drawing screen, go to the **File** button on the top toolbar and left-click. Scroll down to **Close** and left-click. A small box will appear in the center of your screen asking if you would like to save your changes. Click **No.** The current AutoCAD drawing screen will disappear but the AutoCAD program will remain active.
9. Return to the **File** button and select the first option, **New,** from the menu. When the Startup box appears, press **OK** to create a new drawing screen.
10. Access the line command again. (It doesn't matter if you are still using the F8 option or not.) Use your crosshairs to draw two connecting lines. Look at the bottom of the screen to find the AutoCAD command line. It reads: `Specify next point or [Close/Undo]`:. The command line displays text to prompt you regarding what you need to do next within a specific command. (The bottom line is always the most current line of text.)
11. The text given in brackets, `[Close/Undo]`, represents options that you can choose instead of, or in addition to, the regular command, `Specify next point`. The capital letter (the "C" in Close and the "U" in Undo) is the letter you type to choose an option.
12. For now, type **u** and then press **enter** (note that you needn't type it as a capital letter). The undo option will undo or delete the last line segment that you've drawn. The undo command is very useful, as it lets you change your mind if you don't like something you have drawn. Redraw the line segment so that you again have two lines on your screen.
13. This time type **c** and press **enter** to access the Close option. You will notice that AutoCAD has taken the last endpoint drawn and connected it to the start point of the first line drawn. By drawing two line segments you have easily completed a triangle. AutoCAD automatically exits the line command because it assumes that you are finished drawing the shape.
14. There is one more useful operation to learn while working with the line command. AutoCAD allows us to invoke a variety of subcommands while inside of a command. The first one we will look at is the **end** subcommand.

NOTE

If you do not see a yellow box around one of the endpoints, you have probably not placed your crosshairs on top of a line or close enough to an endpoint. If you retry these steps and still do not see the small yellow box, contact your instructor. An internal setting may not been configured properly for the computer on which you are working.

15. To begin, access the line command. Next, type **end** (for "endpoint") and press **enter**. This tells AutoCAD to start the line at the endpoint of an existing line. Place your crosshairs on top of one of the lines making up the triangle.
16. Note that a yellow box appears at one of the endpoints of the line under the crosshairs. This yellow box indicates which endpoint AutoCAD will select. AutoCAD's selection is based on the nearest endpoint of the line on which you are working.
17. Using the crosshairs, move around the triangle to test the end subcommand. Decide which endpoint to choose and left-click to pick a starting point at that endpoint. (If you are currently using the F8 option to draw only horizontal and vertical lines, release it by pressing F8 again.)
18. By invoking the endpoint subcommand you have not changed how the line command works, you have only used it to specify a place to start your line. Draw a few more connecting lines, making some of the lines cross each other. Before exiting the line command, type **mid** and press **enter.**
19. The midpoint (mid) subcommand allows you to pick the exact midpoint of a line segment. Move your crosshairs along some of the lines. A yellow triangle will appear when you are close to the midpoint of a specific line. Again, the yellow triangle signifies that you are about to pick the midpoint of that line.
20. Locate the midpoint on one of your lines and left-click to select it. Press **enter** to end the line command.
21. Start a new line. Before selecting your first point, type **int** (intersection) and press **enter.** The intersection (int) subcommand allows you to choose the intersection or crossing point of two or more lines. Find two intersecting lines and place your crosshairs over the intersection. This time a yellow "X" will appear to denote the intersection you are about to choose. Pick that point by left-clicking and draw a few lines. Press **enter** when you are finished.
22. When you have completed a drawing and are ready to begin another, you must close the current drawing window and open a new one. Go to the **File** button and click on the **Close** option. In this case, choose **No** in response to saving your changes. Access the **File** pull-down menu and choose **New,** then press **OK** in the Startup box.

Command 2: The Circle Command

1. Choose the circle command by accessing the **Draw** pull-down menu and scrolling down to the **Circle** option. There are several different choices for types of circles that can be drawn. This example will focus on the first option (Center, Radius).
2. Left-click on the **Center, Radius** option. The first step in drawing the circle is to choose a center point, or starting point, for the circle. Locate a point in the center of your screen and left-click to begin drawing. When you drag your crosshairs around the drawing screen, an outline of a circle is drawn. This circle outline serves the same purpose as the "rubberbanding" in the line command. The farther you move from the center of the circle, the larger the circle, and the closer to the center you move, the smaller the radius of the circle.
3. Left-click another point to create a circle that doesn't quite fill up your screen. After the circle has been drawn, AutoCAD will automatically exit the command.

4. Access the circle command again. Before selecting a center point for the new circle, type **cen** and press **enter.** The **cen** (center) subcommand is comparable to the **end, int,** and **mid** subcommands you examined in the section on Line commands. Place your drawing crosshairs over the line making up the circle. A small yellow circle will appear at the center point of the existing circle. When the yellow circle appears, left-click to choose the center.
5. A "rubberbanding" circle will appear to indicate your new circle. The command line offers a number of options for how to draw this circle. You may simply left-click a point to make a new circle, as in Step 3. Another choice is to invoke the `[Diameter]` option by typing D and pressing enter. Finally, we can consider the number inside the carets (< >), which represents a size value for the circle. (Although this concept is not obvious at first, it becomes clear upon review.)
6. The number that appears inside the carets is the size of the last circle drawn (the only existing circle on the screen). If you were to press enter now, the new circle would be drawn to the same size as the existing one. To create a circle of a different size, enter a new value at the command line. Type **1.25** and press **enter** to create the new circle. Notice that both circles share the same center because you used the cen command.
7. Access the circle command. Before selecting the center point, type **qua** and press **enter.** Qua, another drawing subcommand, is useful when you want to identify a particular quadrant of a circle. (Recall that a quadrant is a fourth of the circle.)
8. Locate your crosshairs over a quadrant of one of your circles; you will notice a small diamond appear at the quadrant. When you see the diamond, left-click to start your circle at that quadrant. Look down at the command line and see that the value you specified (1.25) now appears between the carets.
9. Type **.25** and press **enter.** A small circle will be drawn at that quadrant. Continue to draw circles of the same size as the other three quadrants of your circle. It is not necessary to type .25 each time, simply press **enter.**

Command 3: The Rectangle Command

1. Clear the drawing window by closing the current screen and starting a new drawing. Access the **Draw** pull-down menu. Scroll down to the **Rectangle** option and left-click. Left-click a point to start your rectangle.
2. Move your crosshairs around the screen. You will see a rubberband rectangle being created. Drag the crosshairs and left-click to confirm the opposite corner point of the rectangle. It is much easier to draw a rectangle in this manner than to draw four connecting lines.
3. Access the rectangle command again. Use the **end** or **mid** subcommands to create adjoining rectangles. If you pull the crosshairs to create a rectangle inside an existing rectangle, the rubberband rectangle may not show. You will have to use the crosshair lines to judge the size of rectangle you want to draw. Practice drawing rectangles using the end and mid subcommands.

Exercise 2: Modifying Objects

Command 4: The Erase Command

1. At this point you should have a few rectangles drawn on your screen. Left-click on the **Modify** button on the menu bar at the top of the screen. Find and left-click on the **Erase** option. Instead of starting a new drawing, you will simply erase the present objects.
2. There are three ways to use the erase command. First, place the pickbox over one of the lines making up a rectangle and left-click to select the rectangle. The rectangle will become dashed signifying that it is selected and is ready to be erased. Press **enter** to erase the rectangle.
3. Invoke the **Erase** command again. This time, move the pickbox to a point in the upper right-hand corner of the drawing screen and left-click. Move the pickbox to the lower-left corner of the screen. A dashed rubberband rectangle will appear. This is a selection box. Instead of using the pickbox to individually select objects to erase, you can use the selection box to erase, more than one object at a time.
4. It is important to learn about another aspect of the selection box before you use it to erase the rectangles. Press **escape** twice and then access the erase command again. (Escape is always used to exit a command.)
5. Place the pickbox in the lower left-hand corner of the screen and left-click. Move your mouse to the upper-right hand corner. This time when you drag the selection box it appears as a solid box rather than a dashed box as before. The solid box option has a specific purpose. Press **escape** twice. The two types of selection boxes have the following applications:

   (a) A selection box pulled from right to left (which appears as a dashed line) will select anything that the box overlaps.

   (b) A selection box pulled from left to right (which appears as a solid line) will only select objects enclosed fully inside the box.

   Practice using both kinds of selection boxes to erase your rectangles.

AutoCAD

Command 5: The Copy Command

1. Draw a line anywhere on your screen. Left-click on the **Modify** pull-down menu and then choose the **Copy** command.
2. To copy an object, you must first select it. Use any of the selection options learned previously to select the line (remember that the line will become dashed when it is selected), then press **enter.**
3. Looking at the Command line you will see that AutoCAD asks you to: `Specify base point or displacement, or [Multiple]:`. To specify a basepoint or displacement, use the crosshairs to pick a point on the screen. It best to pick a point near the object that you are copying.
4. Move your crosshairs around the screen to see that a copy of the line follows them. To make a copy of the original line, left-click a point. Practice this command, selecting basepoints for copying in different places in your screen.

Command 6: The Move Command

1. The **Move** command works exactly like the **Copy** command, except that it only moves the line and does not make a copy of it. Access the move command by left-clicking the **Modify** button and then selecting **Move.**

2. Select the line you wish to move and left-click.
3. Pick your basepoint or displacement with the crosshairs and move the line. When you have found a good location, left-click to confirm the move.

Command 7: The Rotate Command

1. Access the rotate command by choosing **Rotate** from the **Modify** pull-down menu. To begin rotating an object, you must first select the object. Select only one object.
2. Before selecting a basepoint to start rotating, type **end** and press **enter.** The same subcommands may be used for the Modify commands as for the Draw commands. Place your crosshairs over an endpoint of the selected object and left-click. Move your crosshairs around the screen and you will see that the line is rotating around the point you have just picked.
3. Locate the point to which you want to rotate the object and left-click. A copy is not made of the line; it is only rotated to another angle.

Command 8: The Trim Command

1. Clear your screen by erasing all the objects. Draw a few horizontal and vertical lines using the **F8** option. Make some of the lines intersect.
2. Go to the **Modify** button and left-click on the **Trim** command. Using a selection window, select all the lines on your screen.
3. The command line directs you to `Specify object to trim:`; find an overhang on one of the overlapping lines and use the pickbox to select the line you wish to trim (shorten) so that it will be flush with the crossing line.
4. The trim command is very easy to understand with some practice. Trim some of the other crossing lines for practice.

AutoCAD

Command 9: The Extend Command

1. Extending a line is the opposite of trimming one. Access the **Extend** command from the **Modify** pull-down menu.
2. To extend a line you must first select lines that are boundary edges (look down at the command line). Boundary edges are lines or objects that you want another line to abut.
3. Using a selection box, select all the lines on your screen to be your boundary edges. When all the lines are selected, press **enter.**
4. The command line will now prompt you to `Select object to extend:`. Place the pickbox over any of your lines and left-click to begin extending. To extend a line in a specific direction, it will be necessary to select the end of the line that you want to extend.
5. You can use the **Extend** command to create corners, as in a rectangle, and to extend a line past a corner. Practice extending your lines until none can be extended.

NOTE

If the line does not extend, you must address one of two possible problems. Either your pickbox is not close enough to the end of the line you want to extend, or you have not identified a perpendicular or boundary edge in that direction for your line to abut.

Appendix D: Instructions for Information Technology Lab Projects

1 Prime Numbers and Computer Encryption Codes
2 Converting from Decimal to Binary
3 Permutations and Combinations
4 Logical Reasoning
5 Tracking Profits
6 Corporate Optimization
7 Memory Fields and Matrices
8 Fiber-Optic Cables
9 The Next Generation of Computing
10 Independent Information Technology Research

Prime Numbers and Computer Encryption Codes

Sieve of Eratosthenes Overview

Named after the Greek mathematician who invented it, the algorithm known as the Sieve of Eratosthenes is a method for taking all numbers up to a defined maximum and running them through a filtering process to isolate the prime numbers. The algorithm works well on computers and is commonly used to test computer chip processing and code execution speeds.

Key Definitions

Integer—Any positive (e.g., 5, 20) or negative (e.g., −5, −10) whole number or zero; distinguished from a fraction.

Prime Number—An integer that is evenly divisible only by itself and 1 (e.g., 7 is a prime number, 10 is not).

Multiple—A number that is a product of two specified numbers (e.g., 10 is a multiple of 5; 8 is a multiple of 4).

Drawing and Chart Creation with Microsoft Word

What makes a software product successful? Good marketing, filling a niche, and excellent functionality all contribute. One lesser-known software success factor is customization. Behavioral research shows that allowing users to customize software provides them with a sense of ownership, which directly affects user attitudes and long-term productivity with the product.

In this project, you will create a logic flowchart of the Sieve of Eratosthenes. To complete the project, you will explore customization features within Microsoft Word. Microsoft Word is a word processing software application bundled within the Microsoft Office product family. Word is one of the most commercially successful word processing programs ever released. To complete the Sieve of Eratosthenes flowchart, use the symbols and annotation functionality provided in Microsoft Word's *drawing toolbar*. The drawing toolbar lets you enter circles, squares, and general polygons into Word documents. You will enter and annotate drawing objects to demonstrate the decision structure and logic flow of the Sieve of Eratosthenes.

Flowchart Legend
Use these symbols to create the flowchart.

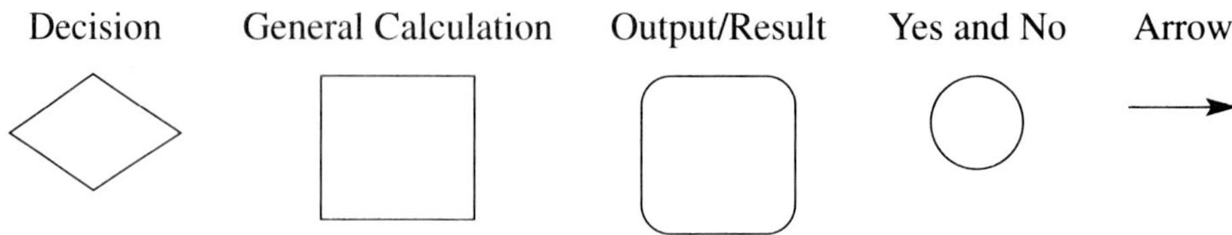

FAQ: Symbols and Shapes

Q: How do I activate the drawing toolbar?
A: Left-click the **View** menu then select **Toolbars** | **Drawing** (**View** | **Toolbars** | **Drawing**).

Q: How do I insert a shape into my Word document?
A: Insert shapes by left-clicking the shape symbol on the drawing toolbar, then positioning the shape in the Word document.

Q: How do I position a shape once it is in the Word document?
A: Using your mouse, left-click and hold the shape. Once selected, move the shape by moving the mouse. To move shapes gradually, select the shape (left-click), then simultaneously use the **Ctrl** and arrow keys to gradually position the shape.

Q: How do I select and position multiple shapes?
A: To select multiple shapes, hold down the **Shift** key, then select each shape. Once selected, move multiple shapes with simultaneous use of the **Ctrl** key and arrow keys.

Q: How do I insert text into a shape?
A: Right-click the shape and left-click **Add Text** from the pop-up menu.

Q: How do I resize shapes?
A: Left-click the shapes to display the highlighted outlines. Slowly move the mouse around the shapes to display the bidirectional arrow cursor. Left-click, hold, and drag the mouse inward or outward to resize the shapes.

Q: How do I create diamond and rounded rectangle shapes?
A: The drawing toolbar offers many shape styles. Left-click **AutoShapes** from the drawing toolbar then select **Basic Shapes.**

Q: How do I change the font size of text within a shape?
A: Slowly right-click the shape. Select the text inside the shape, then change the font size and style with the **Formatting** toolbar. Ensure that the **Formatting** toolbar is visible through the **View** menu command (**View** | **Toolbars** | **Formatting**).

Develop the Sieve of Eratosthenes flowchart given in Figure D1.1.

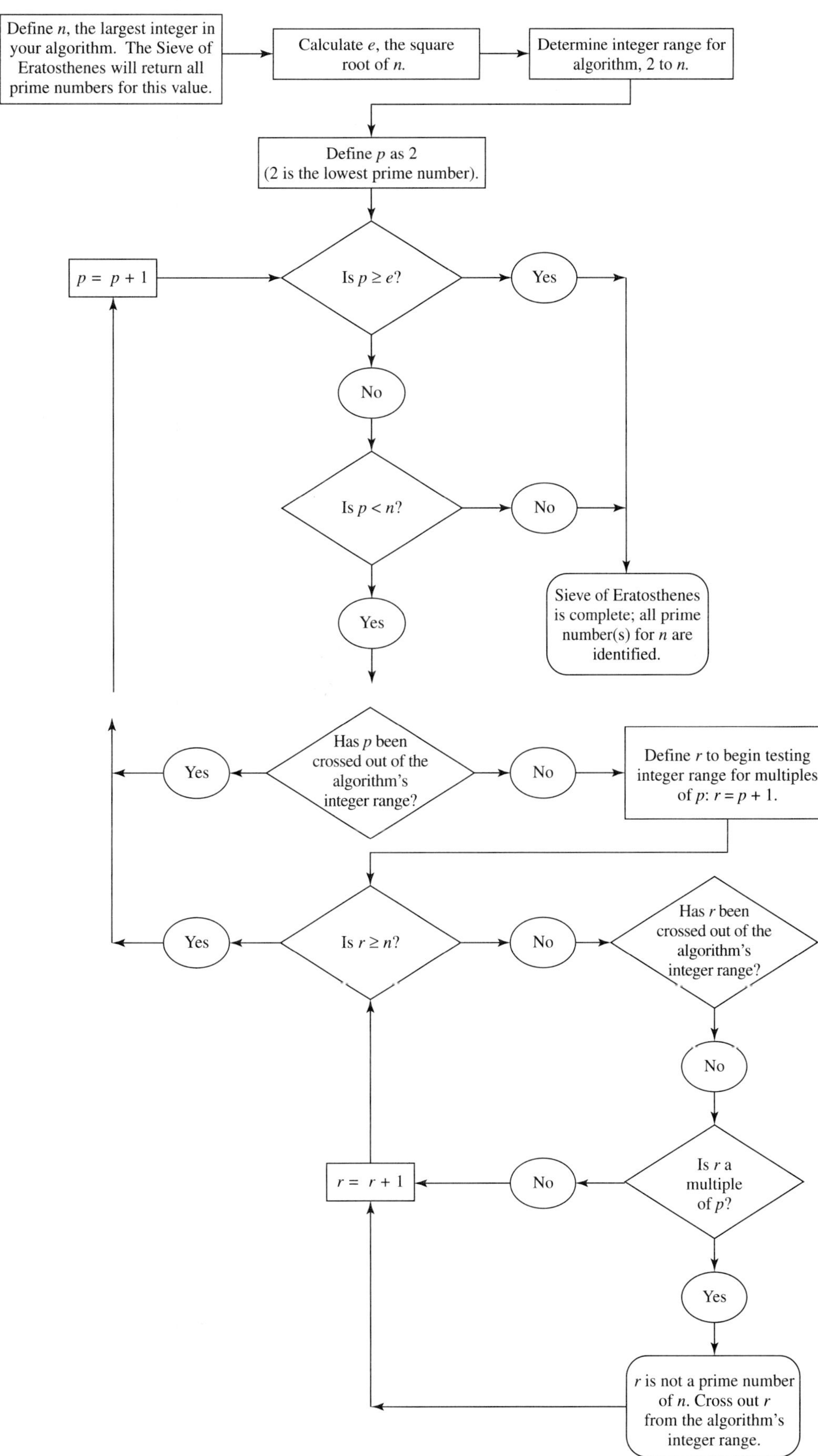

Figure D1.1 Logic flowchart using the Sieve of Eratosthenes

Converting from Decimal to Binary

Overview

In this Information Technology Lab you will practice translating decimal numbers into binary, and will learn to convert the binary information given into a computer code.

Decimal to Binary: A Computer's Perspective on Base 2

For computers, the binary number system (base 2) is more efficient than the decimal number system (base 10).

- In contrast to the decimal system, binary does not require the use of large addition and multiplication tables. Binary calculations repeat operations very quickly, making the binary number system more efficient to use than base 10.
- A decimal system requires more than two values of voltage, magnetism, or signal. Because binary uses only two values of this type, it makes it possible to design computer hardware that is more resistant to noise.

HINT

If you need help to work Assignment 1, review Information Technology Project 2, *Converting Decimal to Binary*.

Assignment 1—Translate Decimal Numbers into Binary

Decimal 8 is binary _______.
Decimal 5 is binary _______.
Decimal 34 is binary _______.
Decimal 10 is binary _______.

Assignment 2—Translate ASCII Character Codes to Binary Notation

The development of standards in information technology helps to prevent the reinvention of common procedures, and promotes compatibility across the broad spectrum of computer types, operating systems, and software applications. One of the best-known standards is ASCII text. ASCII (pronounced "askey") is the common text code used for microcomputer equipment. Computers can only understand numbers, so an ASCII code is the numerical representation of an alphanumeric character.

ASCII is an acronym for American Standard Code for Information Interchange, proposed by the American National Standards Institute in 1963. In short, ASCII character codes represent alphanumeric symbols. Each alphanumeric symbol is assigned a unique character code. The following table lists character codes 0–127.

Code	Char	Code	Char	Code	Char	Code	Char
0		32	[space]	64	@	96	`
1		33	!	65	A	97	a
2		34	"	66	B	98	b
3		35	#	67	C	99	c
4		36	$	68	D	100	d
5		37	%	69	E	101	e
6		38	&	70	F	102	f
7		39	'	71	G	103	g
8	**	40	(	72	H	104	h
9	**	41	)	73	I	105	i
10	**	42	*	74	J	106	j
11		43	+	75	K	107	k
12	.	44	,	76	L	108	l
13	**	45	—	77	M	109	m
14		46	.	78	N	110	n
15		47	/	79	O	111	o
16		48	0	80	P	112	p
17		49	1	81	Q	113	q
18		50	2	82	R	114	r
19		51	3	83	S	115	s
20		52	4	84	T	116	t
21		53	5	85	U	117	u
22		54	6	86	V	118	v
23		55	7	87	W	119	w
24		56	8	88	X	120	x
25		57	9	89	Y	121	y
26		58	:	90	Z	122	z
27		59	;	91	[	123	{
28		60	<	92	\	124	|
29		61	=	93	]	125	}
30	-	62	>	94	^	126	~
31		63	?	95	_	127	

Each character is denoted by its numeric symbol. For example, 90 equals capital Z, 119 equals lowercase w.

As another example, consider the code string 80 114 111 106 101 99 116. Using the table, we see that 80 = "P", 114 = "r", 111 = "o", 106 = "j", 101 = "e", 99 = "c", and 116 = "t". Therefore, the character code string 80 114 111 106 101 99 116 spells out "Project".

Converting ASCII Codes to Letters, Words, and Base 2 Numeric (Binary) Representations

1. What is the alphanumeric equivalent of the character code string 105 84 84?
2. What word is obtained by translating the character code string 83 116 117 100 101 110 116?
3. What is the binary representation of the ASCII notation for the word "cats" (without the quotation marks)?
4. When alphanumeric 123 is converted to character code notation, what would be the base two (binary) representation for the character code sequence?
5. True or False: character codes represent numbers and letters exclusively. Provide examples to validate your answer.

Permutations and Combinations

Overview

Electronic and paper documents in which data are stored and manipulated using rows and columns are called *spreadsheets*. Calculations ranging from a corporation's Profit and Loss Statement to complex scientific calculations carried out at the forefront of technology are handled efficiently by spreadsheets. One software package commonly used to create electronic spreadsheets is Microsoft Excel. In this Information Technology Lab, you will use Microsoft Excel to create a workbook with spreadsheets that will calculate the factorials, combinations, and permutations that were the topic of Information Technology Project 3.

Project 1—Finding Factorials with Microsoft Excel

Milestone 1—Create a New Spreadsheet

Task 1a. Open Microsoft Excel
Open Microsoft Excel in the Programs menu found under the Start button. You should see a blank spreadsheet as in Figure D3.1.

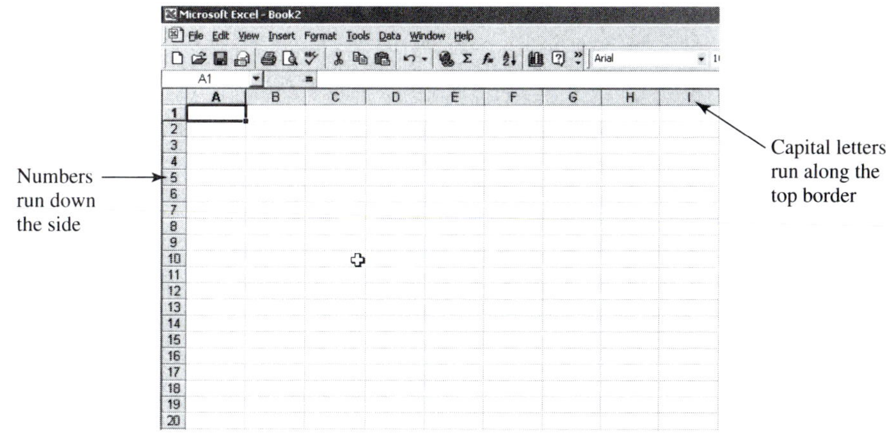

Figure D3.1 A New Microsoft Excel Spreadsheet

IT

The capital letters that run across the top border and the numbers that run down the left-hand side are used to identify the cells in the spreadsheet. For example, the cell "A1" is the first cell in the top, left corner. "A2" is the cell directly below it, etc. Cells can contain numbers, letters, formulas, or any other data that you wish to enter.

> **HINT**
>
> To move between cells in the spreadsheet use the Tab key, the arrows on your keyboard, or your mouse.

Task 1b. Enter Column Headings into the Cells

Enter the letter *n* in the cell A1 and the expression *n*! in the cell C1. The letter *n* is a heading that indicates the number for which we are calculating a factorial, and the heading in C1 is the factorial of the number. Because these are headings, you may want to make them boldface.

Milestone 2—Enter Data into the Cells

Task 2a. Enter Numbers 1–20 in a Column

To enter the numbers 1–20, enter the number **1** in cell A2 and **2** in cell A3. Highlight cells A2 and A3, as shown in Figure D3.2, release the button on your mouse, and place your cursor over the small black box at the bottom right corner of the highlighted area. When the open white cross cursor symbol becomes a solid black cross, click and hold down your left mouse button and drag the highlighted window down to cell A21. When you release the mouse button, the column will have "autofilled" with numbers 3–20, as seen in Figure D3.3.

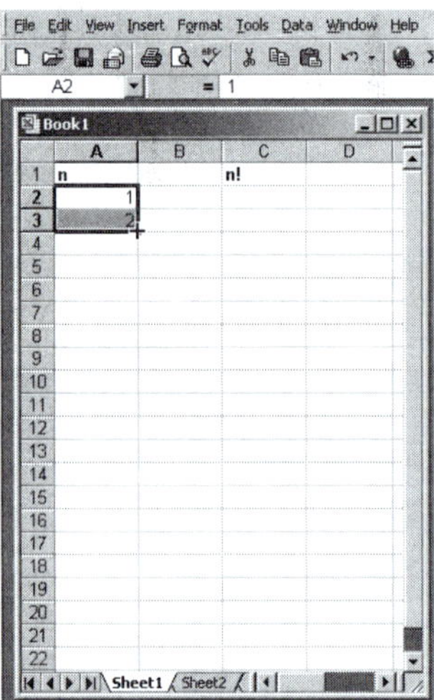

Figure D3.2

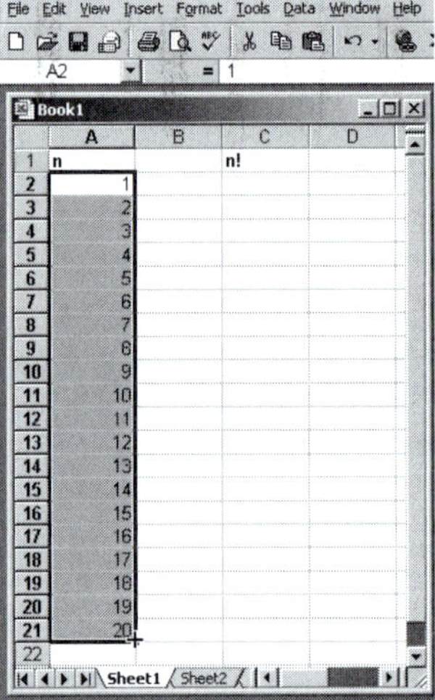

Figure D3.3

Milestone 3—Use Formulas to Calculate Factorials

To calculate the factorials for the numbers 1–20, we could create new formulas in Excel. However, Excel already contains many formulas and it is easier to use the existing menu of options.

Task 3a. Use the Paste Function Submenu

Highlight cell C2. Access the functions menu by left-clicking **Insert** and then choosing Function (Figure D3.4). Left Click on **Function** and the Paste Function submenu will appear. Choose **All** in the left menu and then scroll through the right menu and select **FACT** to choose the factorial function (Figure D3.5).

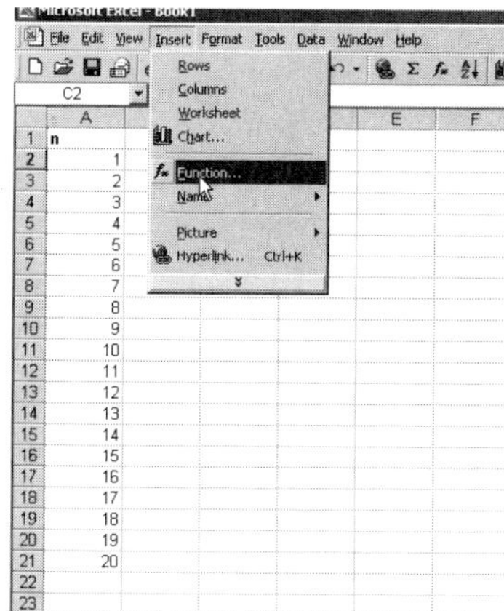

Figure D3.4

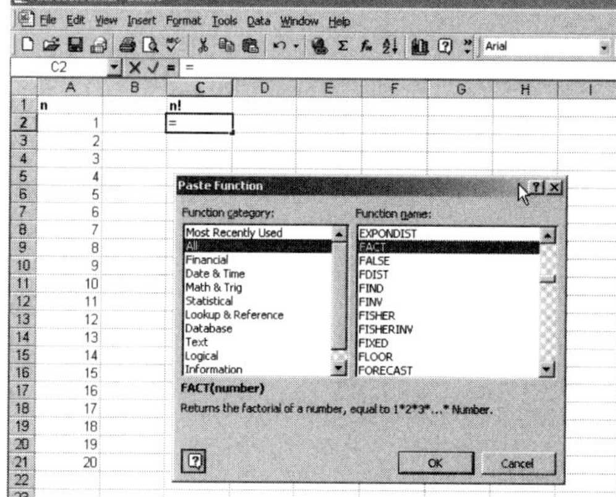

Figure D3.5

Task 3b. Paste the Formula into the Cell

After selecting All and FACT, left-click **OK.** A screen will appear that asks for the number of the factorial we want to calculate. Enter **A2,** the cell location of the first value for which we want to calculate the factorial (Figure D3.6).

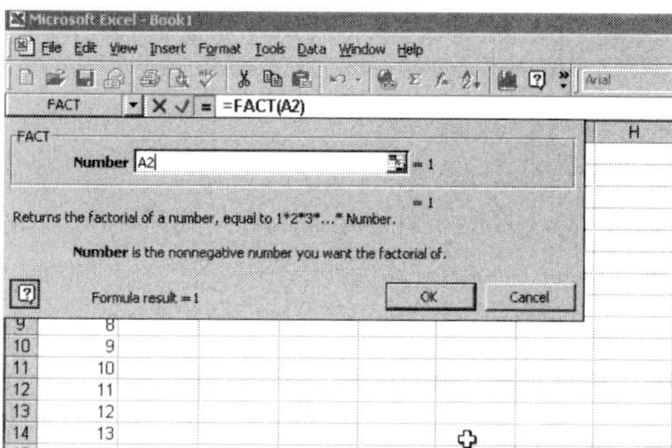

Figure D3.6

Left-click **OK** and the number 1, the result of 1!, will appear in cell C2.

Task 3c. Copying and Pasting Formulas

To calculate the factorials of the numbers 2–20, we will copy the formula used in C2 and paste it into the cells C3–C21. Right-click on the cell C2. Choose **Copy** from the edit command in the top toolbar. Highlight the cells C3–C21. Choose the **Paste** option in the edit command. The factorials of the numbers 1–20 should now appear in the cells C2–C21, as shown in Figure D3.7.

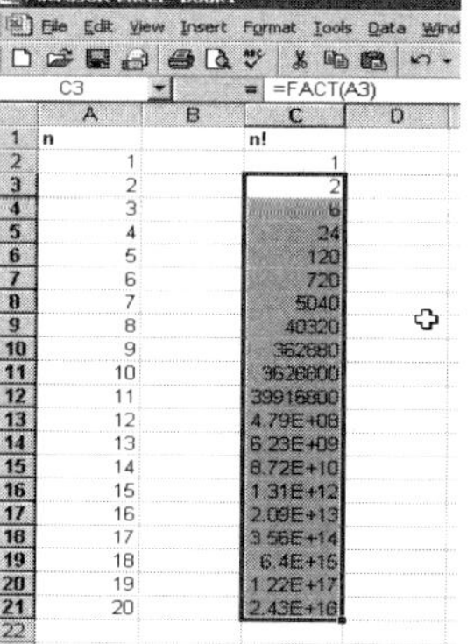

Figure D3.7

IT

Project 2—Calculating Combinations and Permutations with Microsoft Excel

Use a spreadsheet to calculate the number of combinations and permutations of two objects selected from sets ranging from 2 to 30 objects.

1. Open a new Excel spreadsheet.
2. Enter the heading "Number of Objects in the Set" in cell A1, the heading "Combinations" in cell E1, and the heading "Permutations" in cell G1.
3. Type "2" in cell A2 and "3" in cell A3 and use "autofill" to enter the numbers 2–30.
4. The combination function is found in the same menu as was the factorial function used in Project 1. Select cell E2. Choose **Insert** in the top toolbar and select **Function.** In the new submenu that appears, choose **All** and **COMBIN** (the combination function). After clicking **OK,** a new screen will ask you to insert the number of objects in the set, and the number of objects that are to be selected. Enter A2 for the number of objects in the set, and 2 for the number of objects chosen (Figure D3.8).

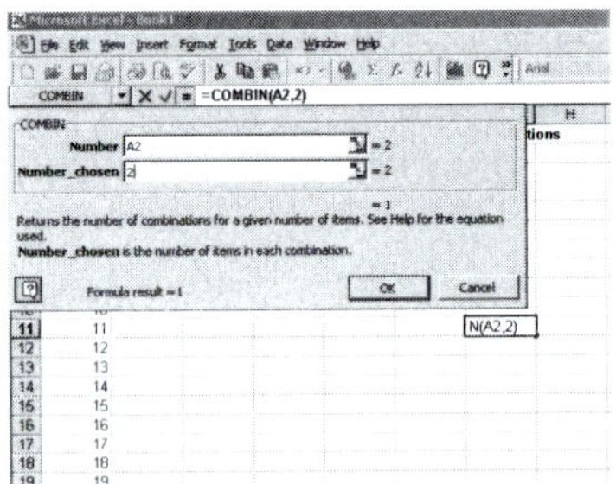

Figure D3.8

5. After clicking **OK,** the number 1 will appear in cell E2 because there is only one possible combination of the two objects.
6. To calculate the possible combinations of two objects drawn from sets that contain 3–30 objects, cut and paste the formula in E2 into the cells E3–E30 using the same procedure as used in Task 3c of Project 1.
7. Choose cell G2 and access the permutation function (PERMUT) in the function submenu. Enter A2 in the number of objects and 2 in the number chosen. After clicking **OK,** the number 2 will appear in cell G2 because there are two possible permutations of two objects.
8. Copy and Paste the function in cell G2 into the cells G3–G30. The number of permutations of two objects drawn from sets ranging from 2 to 30 objects will now appear in the cells G2–G30, as shown in Figure D3.9.

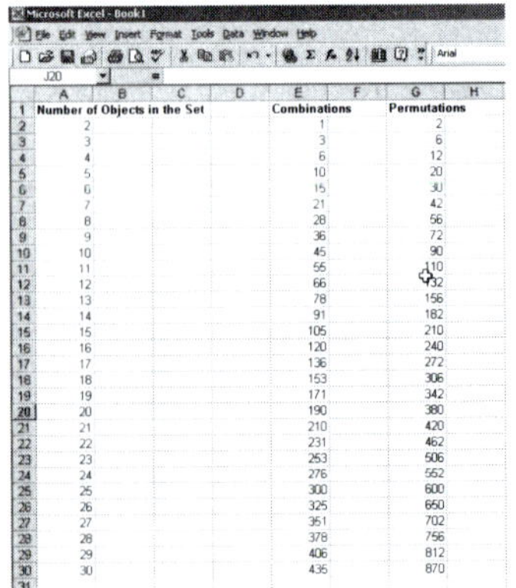

Number of Objects in the Set	Combinations	Permutations
2	1	2
3	3	6
4	6	12
5	10	20
6	15	30
7	21	42
8	28	56
9	36	72
10	45	90
11	55	110
12	66	132
13	78	156
14	91	182
15	105	210
16	120	240
17	136	272
18	153	306
19	171	342
20	190	380
21	210	420
22	231	462
23	253	506
24	276	552
25	300	600
26	325	650
27	351	702
28	378	756
29	406	812
30	435	870

Figure D3.9

Logical Reasoning

Overview

The purpose of this lab is to acquaint you with the basic principles and techniques of the Boolean logic that is indigenous to all computer calculations.

Boolean Logic

Boolean logic is the mathematical study of elements that are evaluated as TRUE and FALSE. Boolean algebra is the study of how to manipulate those evaluations to make a process or calculation easier. Together, Boolean logic and Boolean algebra provide a framework to manage and articulate expressions.

Boolean logic was originally developed by George Boole in the mid-1800s, and provides a mathematical model used in computer science to map out information into bits and bytes. More specifically, the mathematics of Boolean algebra is the theoretical foundation of computer circuit design.

Boolean logic employs a set of simple logic "gates" used to build combinations that implement nearly any imaginable digital component. Gates formed out of transistor switches may implement Boolean AND, OR, NOT, and XOR functions. There are three primary gates, AND, OR and NOT. In evaluating the three primary gates, it becomes easy to interpret each gate based on the operator (AND, OR, or NOT) that denotes each gate's name.

Consider the AND gate, which performs a logical "and" operation on two inputs, *a* and *b*:

Inputs		Output
a	***b***	***Q***
0	0	0
0	1	0
1	0	0
1	1	1

The general concept of the AND gate is that if *a and b* are both 1, then *Q* should be 1.

Now consider the NOT gate, which takes one bit as input (A) and produces its opposite as output (Q):

Input A	Output Q
0	1
1	0

The last of the three primary gates is the OR gate. The concept behind the OR gate is that if a is 1, or b is 1, or both a and b are 1, then Q is 1 as well.

Inputs a	b	Output Q
0	0	0
0	1	1
1	0	1
1	1	1

Searching the Internet Efficiently Using Boolean Logic

The internet is a vast network of databases, file servers, and sparsely annotated web pages. As such, its contents must be searched according to the rules of computer database searching. Much database searching is based on the principles of Boolean logic. Using Boolean logic to search the internet defines a logical relationship among search terms, and adds scope to your search effort. A well-constructed Boolean search expression will help yield two desired search results:

1. Elimination of unrelated/undesired content.
2. The return of relevant, useful information.

Creating a well-designed Boolean Web search is not always simple or easy. Different search engines handle Boolean operators differently. However, any worthwhile search engine will process the three primary logic gates (AND, OR, NOT). Searches are issued through a user-defined *query,* where each query may contain optional Boolean operators.

Boolean Example 1: Using the OR Operator
Desired Search—I want to see information on **cats** or **dogs.**
Boolean Operator Employed—OR
Query—cats OR dogs

Result—Any Web page with information on cats or dogs will be retrieved. This may include Web pages with just cat information, just dog information, or with both. The more keywords we use with OR logic, the more records retrieved.

Search keywords	Results
Cats	502
Dogs	1,302
Cats and dogs	105
Total results returned	1,909

IT

Boolean Example 2: Using the AND Operator
Desired Search—I want to see information on **cats** and **dogs.**
Boolean Operator Employed—AND
Query—cats AND dogs

Result—Only those Web pages containing information on BOTH cats and dogs will be retrieved. This will exclude those Web pages with just cat information, and those with just dog information. The more keywords we use with AND logic, the fewer records retrieved.

Search keywords	Results
~~Cats~~	~~502~~
~~Dogs~~	~~1,302~~
Cats and dogs	105
Total results returned	105

Boolean Example 3: Using the NOT Operator
Desired Search—I want to see information on **cats,** but want to eliminate anything with **dogs.**
Boolean Operator Employed—NOT
Query—cats NOT dogs

Result—Only those Web pages containing information on cats are returned. Clearly, this eliminates any pages with just dog information, but also eliminates those pages where "cats" appears with "dogs." Because "dogs" was prefaced with the NOT operator, any "cats" Web pages are excluded if they contain content on "dogs."

Search keywords	Results
Cats	502
~~Dogs~~	~~1,302~~
~~Cats and dogs~~	~~105~~
Total results returned	502

Putting Boolean Logic to Work

Use Boolean logic expressions to do online internet research. The objectives of your project are twofold.

1. Identify which Boolean expressions deliver the best results for your defined criteria.
2. Determine which internet search engine provides the most accurate and relevant search results for your Boolean expressions.

Use Boolean expressions to perform three searches in each of the following categories. Use the expressions as given for each category.

Automobiles
General Subject—Automobiles
Boolean AND—Automobiles AND Ford Dealerships
Boolean OR—Automobiles OR Dealers
Boolean NOT—Automobiles NOT Cars

Great Lakes
General Subject—Great Lakes
Boolean AND—Great Lakes AND Zebra Mussels
Boolean OR—Great Lakes OR Lake Erie
Boolean NOT—Great Lakes NOT Zebra Mussels

Jazz Musicians
General Subject—Jazz Musicians
Boolean AND—Jazz Musicians AND Charlie Parker
Boolean OR—Jazz Musicians OR Acoustic
Boolean NOT—Jazz Musicians NOT Rap

Computer Components
General Subject—Computer Components
Boolean AND—Computer Components AND Dell
Boolean OR—Computer Components OR Hard Drives
Boolean NOT—Computer Components NOT RAM

Olympic Sports
General Subject—Olympic Sports
Boolean AND—Olympic Sports AND Lake Placid
Boolean OR—Olympic Sports OR Hockey
Boolean NOT—Olympic Sports NOT Hockey

U.S. State Capitals
General Subject—U.S. State Capitals
Boolean AND—U.S. State Capitals AND Sacramento
Boolean OR—U.S. State Capitals OR Capital Buildings
Boolean NOT—U.S. State Capitals NOT Hawaii

Outdoor Recreation
General Subject—Outdoor Recreation
Boolean AND—Outdoor Recreation AND Camping
Boolean OR—Outdoor Recreation OR Hunting
Boolean NOT—Outdoor Recreation NOT Hunting OR Camping

Operating Systems
General Subject—Operating Systems
Boolean AND—Operating Systems AND Microsoft
Boolean OR—Operating Systems OR Unix
Boolean NOT—Operating Systems NOT Macintosh

Internet technology evolves daily. Web sites and Uniform Resource Locators (URLs) change constantly. To complete the project, you must select three from the following nine major search engines:

Yahoo Search Engine—http://www.yahoo.com
Web Crawler—http://www.webcrawler.com
Hot Bot—http://www.hotbot.com/
Ask Jeeves—http://www.askjeeves.com/
Microsoft Network—http://www.msn.com
Alta Vista—http://www.altavista.com/
Google—http://www.google.com/
Excite—http://www.excite.com
Yahoo—http://www.yahoo.com

Task Outline

1. Identify three search engines and complete the four searches for each subject.
   (a) Complete the four searches for each of the three subjects. You should run a total of twelve searches.
   (b) Record the records or pages returned for all searches.
2. Analyze the cumulative results of all twelve searches.
3. In terms of your search subjects and search engine used, answer the following questions.
   (a) Which Boolean expressions delivered the best results for your defined criteria?
   (b) Which internet search engine provided the most accurate and relevant search results for your Boolean expressions?
   (c) How many total results were returned for your second search?
   (d) Which Boolean expression returned more results, AND or OR? What is the logic behind this result?

Tracking Profits

An Overview of Corporate Profit and Loss

In the final analysis, determining the profit or loss of a company always concludes with one of two possible outcomes. The company realizes a profit; it earned more than it spent. This is known as being *in the black.* Alternatively, the company experiences a loss. When a company has spent more than it earned, it is said to be *in the red.*

Although it seems easy on the surface, many factors must be considered in determining whether a company has been profitable. Some of the questions that must be answered are: What was the total dollar amount spent on capital investments? How much revenue did the organization bring in? Is the company a non-profit? What new tax laws affect this business model? Because no two organizations are exactly alike, a company's profit or loss is determined on a case-by-case basis.

Microsoft Excel Overview

Microsoft Excel is a component of the Microsoft Office software suite. This spreadsheet application is used for accounting, financial reports, statistical analysis, and reporting. Microsoft Excel applications are developed from three primary objects: workbooks, worksheets, and cells. These objects form distinct one-to-many relationships, where one workbook can hold many worksheets, and one worksheet can hold many cells. Typically, a single workbook encapsulates one to three worksheets, and each worksheet represents a user-defined matrix of cells.

Project Outline

In this project, you will gain basic familiarity with Microsoft Excel and learn how to create a profit and loss statement. Your assignment is to create an Excel application that calculates the profit or loss of your chosen research company. By law, the U. S. Securities and Exchange Commission (SEC) requires that P & L information be readily available. You may have the necessary P & L data for your research company. If not, develop your Microsoft Excel application with the sample data provided.

To complete the assignment, implement your Excel application following the four project milestones:

1. Create and save a new Microsoft Excel workbook.
2. Insert revenue and expense data into the Excel worksheet.
3. Program Excel formulas to compute total revenue, total expenses, and profit or loss.
4. Save your work and review the profit or loss results.

Sample Project Data
Company Name—Malabar L.L.C.
Core Competency—Pharmaceuticals/Stem cell research

Revenue—$457,393,400
Private Donations—$1,500,000
Government Grants—$2,500,000
Payroll Costs—$3,523,500
Research and Development—$168,110,000
Stock Buy-Back Initiative—$38,391,469
Dividends Paid—$12,493,294
Taxes Paid—$118,140,000
Operating Expenses—$594,786

Milestone 1—Create and Save a New Microsoft Excel Workbook

Task 1a. Open Microsoft Excel

Using the Windows Start Menu, open Excel via the Run command.

1. Left-click the Windows **Start** button.
2. Left-click **Run.**
3. Type the word **Excel.**
4. Left-click **OK.**

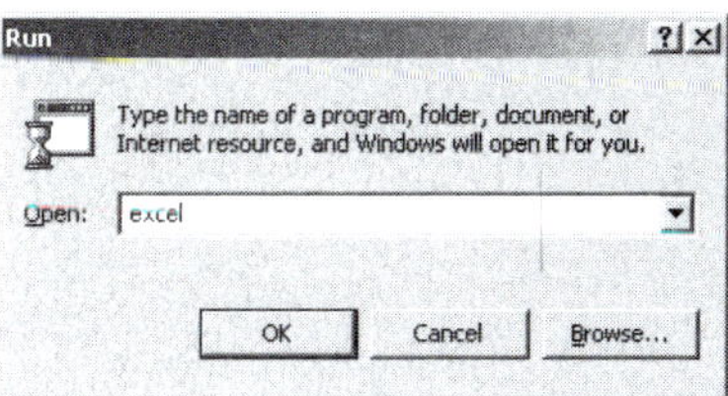

Figure D5.1 Loading Microsoft Excel from the Run Command

Task 1b. Identify and Save Excel Workbook

After the Excel workbook finishes loading, immediately save your new workbook. To save the workbook, click the **File** | **Save** menu command inside Excel. Specifically, move your mouse to the top left corner of the screen, click the **File** menu, and then click the **Save** menu item.

Milestone 2—Insert Revenue and Expense Data into Excel Worksheet

Task 2a. Identify Worksheet Cell Orientation

Each cell in a worksheet is uniquely identified by a specific Column and Row coordinate. For example, cell A1 is the first cell in Column A. Cell D4 is the fourth

IT

cell down in Column D. Figure D5.2 displays cells A1–D4 with each cell's unique coordinate typed in.

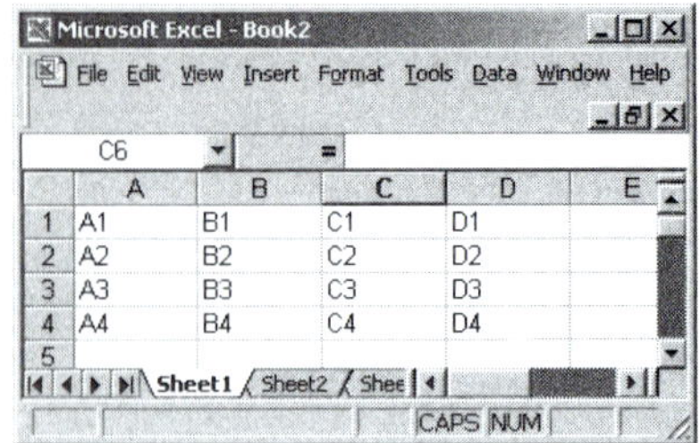

Figure D5.2

Task 2b. Identify Revenue and Expense Cell Ranges

Profit or loss is the difference between the sum of revenues and the sum of expenses. For this project, we will allocate three cells (B1–B3) to compute total revenue, and eight cells (B6–B13) to compute total expenses. Cell B4 will compute total revenue; cell B14 will compute total expenses. Use cells A1–A14 to describe adjacent B1–B14 cells. Use cell D6 to compute the difference between total revenue (B4) and total expenses (B14).

Task 2c. Insert Revenue and Expense Data into Excel Worksheet

Your Excel worksheet should look similar to Figure D5.3.

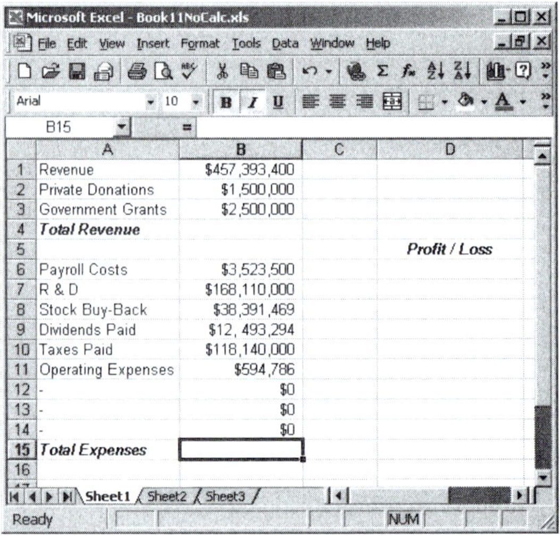

Figure D5.3

Milestone 3—Program Excel Formulas to Compute Total Revenue, Total Expenses, and Profit or Loss

You will program three simple formulas to determine company profit or loss. To create an Excel formula, select the cell to hold the formula and type the necessary calculation into the cell. The formula bar textbox directly above the Column headings should display the formula as it is typed into a cell. After the formula is typed, press the **enter** key.

Task 3a. Type the Three Functions Necessary to Compute Profit or Loss

Cell	Formula (type this into cell, exactly as shown)
B4	=SUM(B1:B3)
B15	=SUM(B6:B14)
D6	=(B4-B15)

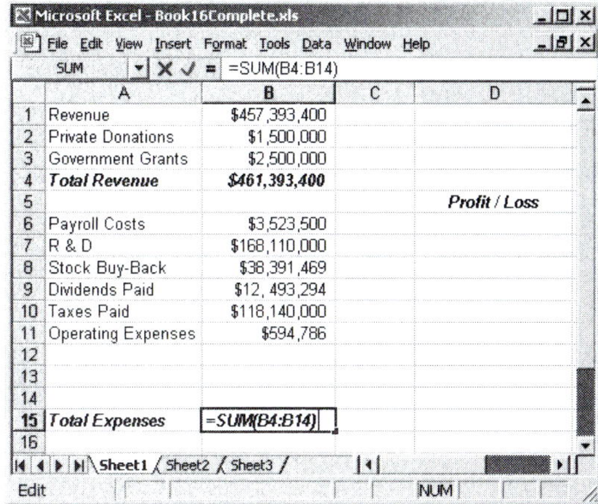

Figure D5.4 Typing the Total Expenses Formula into Cell B15

Milestone 4—Save Work and Review Profit or Loss Results

Press Ctrl+S on the keyboard or use the **File** | **Save** menu command. With company data entered, cell ranges defined, and range functions programmed, you are able to see the profit or loss calculation. The profit or loss cell, D6, will be black or red depending on the outcome of profit or loss, respectively. Experiment with revenue and expense values to dynamically change SUM formulas and profit or loss calculations.

Corporate Optimization

Optimization Overview

An old adage in business is that "past results indicate future performance." While this adage may hold true in human resources or project management, today's digital marketplace is more dynamic, faster-paced, and based on up-to-the-minute information. For the successful organization, effective analysis of data models and industry trends is vital for any measure of success in the new economy.

Consider another old business adage: "If it ain't broke, don't fix it." Is this statement true? It depends. Subscribing to the adage may get your product shipped, but it may not ship for long. For a company to remain competitive, it must regularly assess itself and determine what resources (*in what quantities*) produce the best overall gain. This assessment process is based on the mathematical concept called optimization. In mathematics, optimization involves varying one or more independent variables and monitoring the response of the dependent variable(s). Consider the following business scenario illustrating optimization.

Term	Resource	Allocation	Result
Q1, 1995	Advertising	$10,000,000	4,255 new customers
Q1, 1996	Advertising	$15,000,000	5,103 new customers
Q1, 1997	Advertising	$5,000,000	1,221 new customers

The dependent variable, new customers, is effectively monitored against its independent variable, allocation of advertising funds.

Corporate Optimization Analysis in Action

In this project, you are challenged to conduct a corporate optimization analysis and make a recommendation based on your analysis. To do this, implement the project following these key milestones.

1. Choose a company.
2. For your company, identify the dollar amounts for general line-item profit and loss calculations. These may include revenues, taxes, payroll costs, advertising, operating expenses, or any other relevant data found in researching your company's balance sheet.
3. Locate four consecutive quarters' worth of data for your company balance sheet.
4. Plot the profit or loss balance sheet into Microsoft Excel.
5. Use Microsoft Excel to build a graph representing the profit (or loss) of your company over the four quarters of data.
6. Using optimization, make recommendations to improve the profit for your company.

Milestones 1–3—Independent Research

Use the internet to gather balance sheet data for four consecutive terms for your company.

Milestone 4—Plot Profit or Loss Balance Sheet into Microsoft Excel

Task 4a. Open Microsoft Excel
Using the Windows Start Menu, open Excel via Run command.

1. Left-click the Windows **Start** button.
2. Left-click **Run.**
3. Type the word **Excel.**
4. Left-click **OK.**

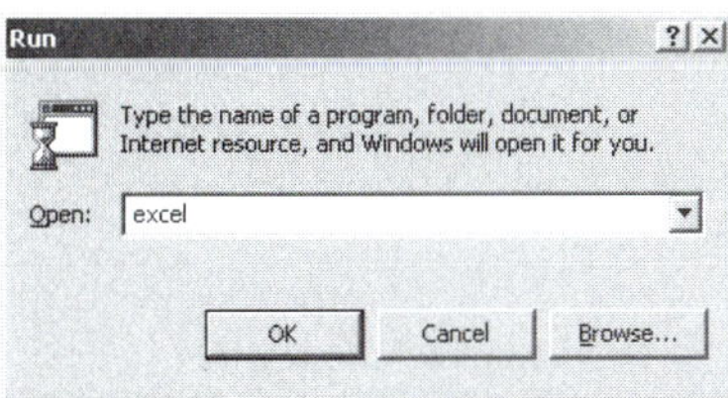

Figure AD6.1 Loading Microsoft Excel from the Run command

Task 4b. Identify and Save Excel Workbook
After the Excel workbook finishes loading, immediately save your new workbook. To save the workbook, click the **File | Save** menu command inside Excel.

Task 4c. Insert Four Consecutive Terms of Data in Excel Worksheet
Applying calculations to Excel worksheets requires you to identify the cell range to calculate, and type the calculation expression into a cell. Figure D6.2 shows the addition formula for a range of three cells. Your completed worksheet should look similar to the one in the figure, which shows that the total revenue formula for Q1, 1998 has been typed into cell B6:

IT

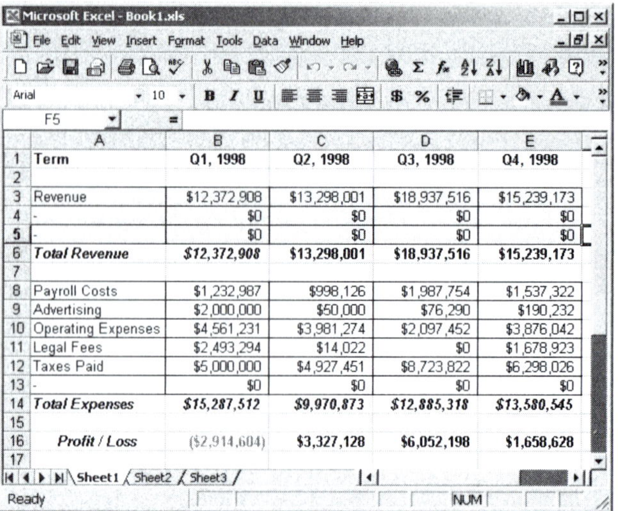

	A	B	C	D	E
1	**Term**	**Q1, 1998**	**Q2, 1998**	**Q3, 1998**	**Q4, 1998**
2					
3	Revenue	$12,372,908	$13,298,001	$18,937,516	$15,239,173
4	-	$0	$0	$0	$0
5	-	$0	$0	$0	$0
6	***Total Revenue***	***$12,372,908***	**$13,298,001**	**$18,937,516**	**$15,239,173**
7					
8	Payroll Costs	$1,232,987	$998,126	$1,987,754	$1,537,322
9	Advertising	$2,000,000	$50,000	$76,290	$190,232
10	Operating Expenses	$4,561,231	$3,981,274	$2,097,452	$3,876,042
11	Legal Fees	$2,493,294	$14,022	$0	$1,678,923
12	Taxes Paid	$5,000,000	$4,927,451	$8,723,822	$6,298,026
13	-	$0	$0	$0	$0
14	***Total Expenses***	***$15,287,512***	***$9,970,873***	***$12,885,318***	***$13,580,545***
15					
16	***Profit / Loss***	($2,914,604)	**$3,327,128**	**$6,052,198**	**$1,658,628**
17					

Figure D6.2

Creating formulas with Microsoft Excel can be both simple and complex. Accessing the Help menu inside Excel provides you with contents, an index, as well as search capabilities. For more information about using the Formula Palette or creating more complex functions, use the Help menu. In the preceding example, profit/loss is calculated with addition and subtraction functions such as these: =SUM(B8:B13), =(B6-B14).

Milestone 5—Use Microsoft Excel to Build a Graph

Graph creation in Excel is handled through Excel's Chart Wizard. The Chart Wizard is a powerful tool that makes the creation of a colorful, dynamic chart easy to accomplish. The wizard walks you through four sequential steps, including selecting a chart type, determining the chart's data source, configuring chart options, and determining the chart's location. Of these four steps, only the second step, determining the chart's data source, is actually required. Default options are supplied for the first, third, and fourth steps; however, you should experiment with these three options to create the most professional and representative chart for your data.

Task 5a. Highlight Profit/Loss Cell Range

Highlighting your cell range prior to activating the wizard is an effective shortcut to selecting a chart's data source (second step of the wizard). Left-click, hold, and drag your mouse across the range of profit/loss cells. This hold-and-drag mouse technique is called lassoing. At this point, all four profit or loss cells should be outlined together.

Task 5b. Activate Chart Wizard

With the cell range highlighted, open the Chart Wizard from Excel's **Insert** | **Chart** menu command. Specifically, move your mouse to the top left corner of the screen, click the **Insert** menu, and then click the **Chart** menu item.

Task 5c. Complete Steps 1 and 3 of Chart Wizard

Because we have predetermined the data source for our chart, you need not manipulate any of the information in the **Data** range section of Step 2. Steps 1 and 3 define the chart's style, labeling information (including axis), and general visual format. Supply this information. Figure D6.3 shows Step 2 of the Chart Wizard.

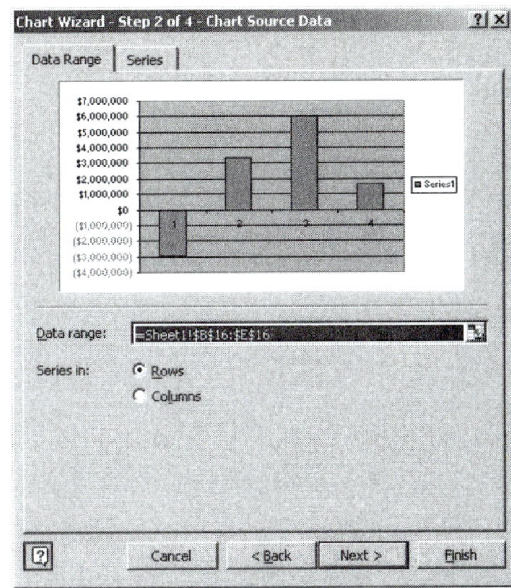

Figure D6.3

Task 5d. Position Chart in your Worksheet

After completing the Chart Wizard, you may need to move the chart to an unused portion of the Worksheet. To move the chart, left-click it and hold, then move the mouse to position the chart.

Task 5e. Customize Chart

Once the chart is on the Excel worksheet, you may go back at any time and reconfigure the properties that define the chart (for example, the chart's title, axis labels, or style). To reconfigure chart properties, left-click the white box encompassing the chart, then select either **Chart Type** or **Chart Options** from the popup menu.

Milestone 6—Using Optimization, Make Recommendations

Task 6a. Manipulate Independent Variables and Monitor Dependent Variables

Corporate optimization often involves analyzing expenses (independent variables) to monitor positive and negative effects on profit (dependent variables). Identify independent variables that can be optimized to affect profit. Change several independent variables and monitor the effects on the company balance sheet. Notice how the graph changes dynamically to indicate such changes. Change three independent balance sheet variables to monitor effects on profit. What effects stand out?

Task 6b. Answer Questions

1. What is the dependent variable for the exercise?
2. Looking across all four quarters, what is the largest independent variable?
3. Using corporate optimization analysis, what five recommendations can you offer to increase the profits for your company? Why?

Memory Fields and Matrices

Overview

Understanding and maintaining a computer's memory is important in ensuring that the machine runs efficiently. In this project, you will research a number of terms that are associated with computer memory and use Microsoft Word to summarize your findings. Then you will perform operations to help improve the memory of your computer and find the amount of memory occupied by several files.

Assignment 1—Computer Memory Terminology

Execute the necessary research to find the meaning of each of the following terms, and then summarize your findings in a Microsoft Word document:

- hard drive
- floppy drive
- RAM
- ROM
- virtual memory
- cache
- sector
- primary storage
- secondary storage

Assignment 2—Perform Disk Defragmentation and Disk Cleanup

Problem 1: Perform a disk defragmentation on one of your hard drives.

Disk Defragmentation

Over time, the files on your hard drive can become spread over many areas of the disk, rather than being located in one large but compact area. A badly fragmented hard drive can cause applications to run more slowly and can even affect the ability of an application to run at all. A system tool known as Disk Defragmentation can be used to defragment a disk drive when this problem occurs.

This utility is accessed through the Accessories and System Tools subdirectories of Programs, as seen in Figure D7.1.

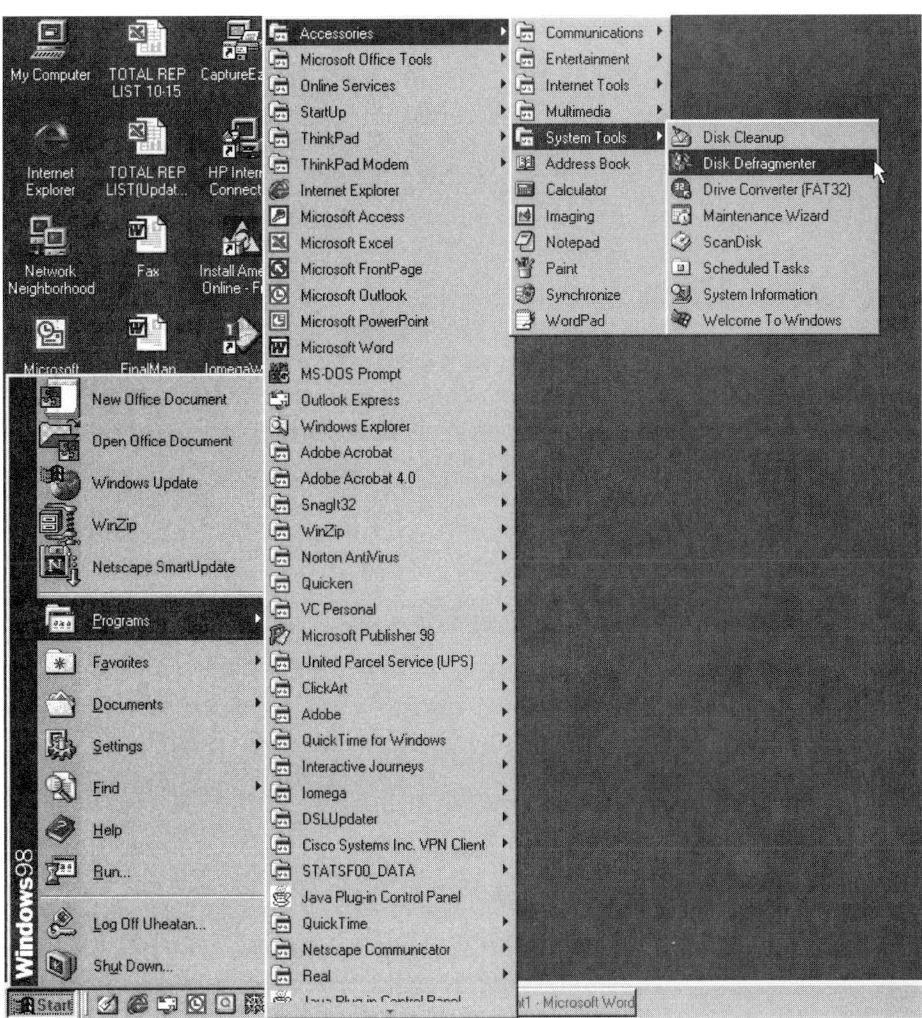

Figure D7.1

To begin the defragmentation process, you must first choose which drive(s) you wish to defragment, as shown in Figure D7.2.

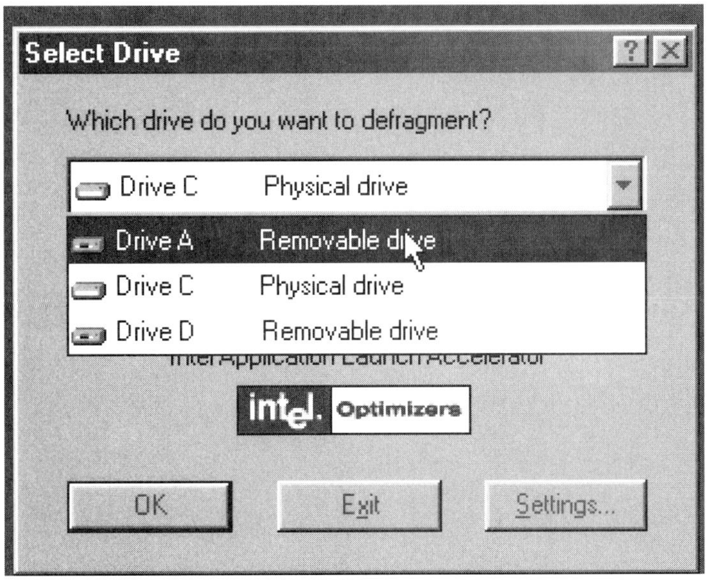

Select Drive

Which drive do you want to defragment?

Drive C Physical drive

Drive A Removable drive

Drive C Physical drive

Drive D Removable drive

intel. Optimizers

OK Exit Settings...

Figure D7.2

Problem 2: Perform a disk cleanup on one of your hard drives.

Disk Cleanup

All computers have a quantity of virtual memory that is used when running applications, surfing the internet, and so forth. When this virtual memory is exhausted, the computer will inform the user that there is not enough virtual memory to run the current application. Virtual memory can be freed by eliminating the temporary files that are occupying this memory. The Disk Cleanup utility can be used to eliminate these temporary files.

Like the Disk Defragmentation feature, this utility is accessed through the Accessories and System Tools subdirectories of the Programs folder, as indicated in Figure D7.3.

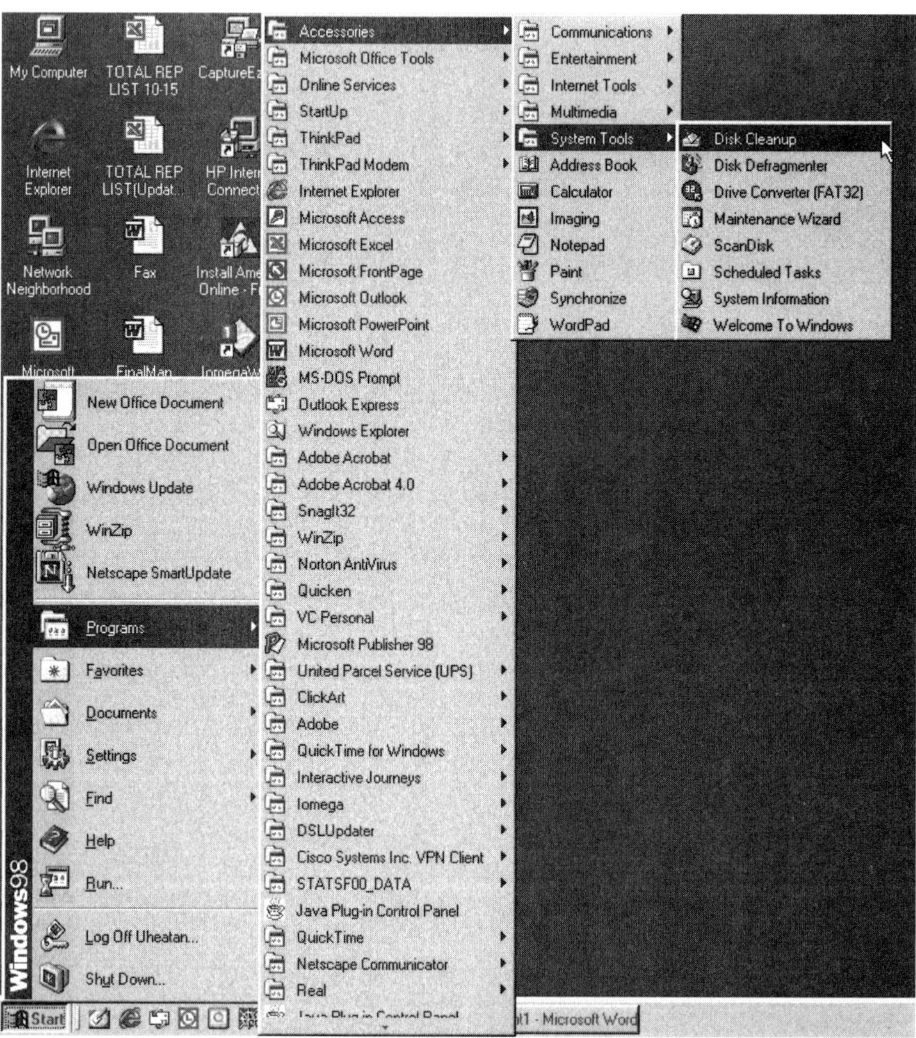

Figure D7.3

Fiber-Optic Cables

Overview

As discussed in Information Technology Project 8, fiber-optic cables are an extremely efficient method of transferring information. In this Optional Lab, you will compare the speed of fiber-optic cables to that of their predecessor, the electrical wire. After completing your research, you will use Microsoft Word to summarize your data, using both text and pictures.

Research

Use the internet or another resource to identify the speed(s) at which information is transferred through fiber-optic cables and electrical wires.

Documenting Your Research

To complete the project, create a documentation report in Microsoft Word. Construct a Word document that contains both text and images. Your document should be set in 12 point Times New Roman font, and have justified margins. The following summary lists five Microsoft Word procedures necessary to complete the report requirements.

1. Creating a new Microsoft Word document
2. Formatting document text
3. Displaying document images
4. Sizing and positioning document images
5. Using textboxes

1. Creating a New Microsoft Word Document

Using the Windows **Start** Menu, open Word via the **Run** command.

1. Left-click the Windows **Start** button.
2. Left-click **Run.**
3. Type **winword.exe.**
4. Left-click **OK.**

Figure D8.1 shows how to load Microsoft Word from the Run command.

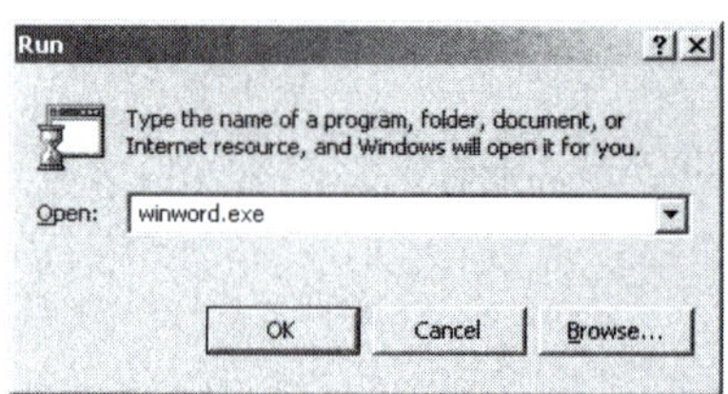

Figure D8.1

HINT

In computer-related training documents, the "pipe" keyboard character (|) is often used to distinguish elements and folders in the Windows Start menu. The pipe is also used to differentiate items in drop-down menu commands and Windows directory paths. In this project, we will use the pipe character to define navigation paths in the Windows Start menu and application menu commands.

2. Formatting Document Text

The bulk of your work will be typing the research information into your Word document. Be sure to save your work often with Word's **File | Save** menu command. Document text may be formatted before, during, or after typing is complete. Nonetheless, use Word's **Formatting** toolbar to format document text according to the report requirements. Ensure that the **Formatting toolbar** is activated and visible through Word's **View** menu command, (**View | Toolbars | Formatting**).

It is recommended that you highlight each report paragraph and the contents of each textbox, and apply the required formatting, as illustrated in Figure D8.2.

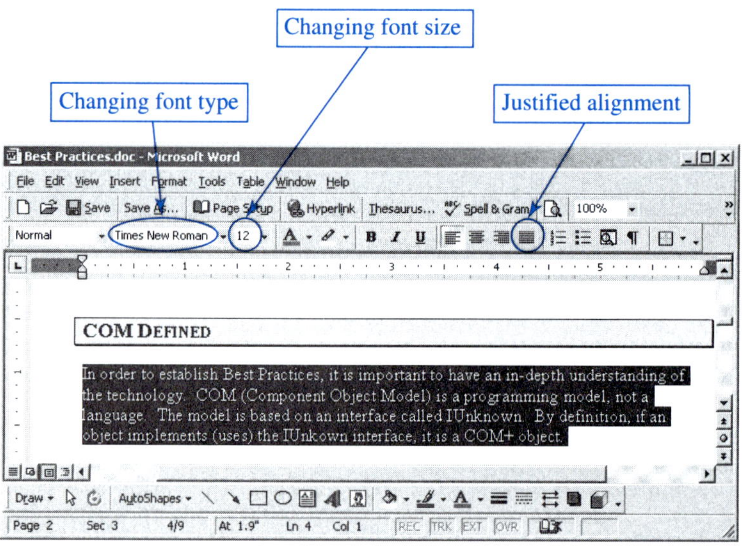

Figure D8.2

3. Displaying Document Images

Images are inserted into Word documents through two procedures. First, identify the image name and where it is stored on your computer. Second, use Word's **Insert | Picture | From File** menu command. Figure D8.3 shows Word's Insert Picture menu command in action, with three image file types (.jpg, .bmp, .gif) available to select from the C:\ directory.

IT

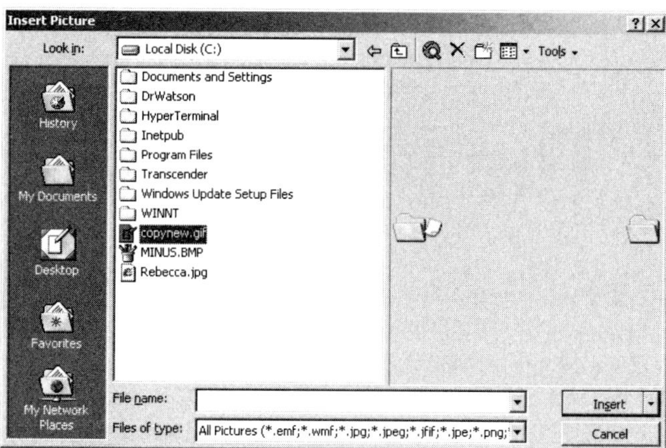

Figure D8.3

4. Sizing and Positioning Document Images

To Size an Image—Left-clicking an image will display a black border outlining the image. Along the border are eight resizing tabs displayed as small black squares. The eight resize tabs are positioned geometrically along the four corners and four center points of the image outline. Move the mouse to one of the eight resizing tabs and notice the mouse pointer change to display a bidirectional arrow cursor. To resize an image, left click and hold the bidirectional arrow cursor, dragging it inward or outward to resize the image.

To Position an Image—Position the mouse over the image. Left-click, hold, and move the image with the mouse.

5. Using Textboxes

Images are an important aspect of any well-designed report; however, inserting an image into a Word document often skews paragraph text and makes image annotation difficult. A solution to this is using Word's **Textbox** feature. The textbox's biggest strength is its versatility in positioning a block of text anywhere on the document. Once a textbox is created, it may be positioned (by dragging) to any specific location in the document. Textboxes are especially useful when used in conjunction with images. For your report, include at least one textbox describing each image you insert.

To Insert a Textbox—From Word's menu bar, use the **Insert | Text Box** menu command. Activating the menu command changes the mouse cursor to *crosshairs*. Click or drag in your document where you want to insert the textbox. Textboxes are resized and positioned like images. To add text to a textbox, left click the mouse inside the textbox. To modify textbox properties, right click the textbox border and select **Format Text Box. . .** from the pop-up menu.

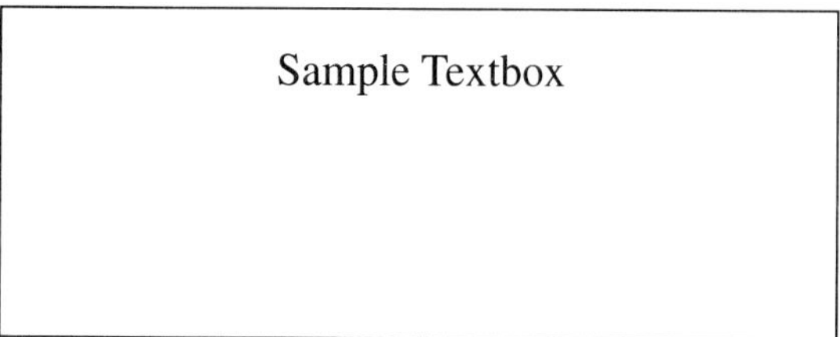

The Next Generation of Computing

Overview

In this lab you will research the fundamentals of a computer microprocessor (central processing unit), and learn the differences between microprocessors currently available for today's computers. After completing your research, you will use Microsoft Access to store your information in a database.

Beginning Your Research

Execute the research necessary to identify a minimum of four of the listed properties for each of the six following microprocessors.

CPU	Number of Pins	Clock Speed	Level-2 Cache	Memory	Warranty	Price
AMD Duron						
Celeron						
Pentium						
AMD Athlon						
Pentium 2						
Pentium 4						

These microprocessors represent a small selection of the computer processing units (CPUs) available on the market. You are encouraged to research CPUs based on current industry trends and information availability. Your considerations may include not only the latest *types* of available microprocessors, but also the available *search techniques.* A good starting point is to conduct a search on microprocessors from a major internet search engine (see the list of search engines in Appendix D-4).

Documenting Your Research

To complete this project, create a small database using Microsoft Access. Construct an Access database that contains both a database table and a database report. The following summary lists five Microsoft Access procedures necessary to construct the data table and report.

1. Creating a new Microsoft Access database
2. Creating a new database table
3. Entering research data into the database table
4. Creating a new database report
5. Printing the report and submiting it to instructor

HINT

In computer-related training documents, the "pipe" keyboard character (|) is often used to distinguish elements and folders in the Windows Start menu. The pipe is also used to differentiate items in drop-down menu commands and Windows directory paths. In this project, we will use the pipe character to define navigation paths in the Windows Start menu and application menu commands.

1. Creating a New Microsoft Access Database

Using the Windows **Start** Menu, open Access via the **Run** command.

1. Left-click the Windows **Start** button.
2. Left-click **Run.**
3. Type the word **msaccess.exe.**
4. Left-click **OK.**
5. As Access opens, a dialog box appears requiring you to determine which Access file to open. Select the **Blank Access database** radio button to create a new database.

Figure D9.1 shows how to create a blank Access database from the opening dialog prompt.

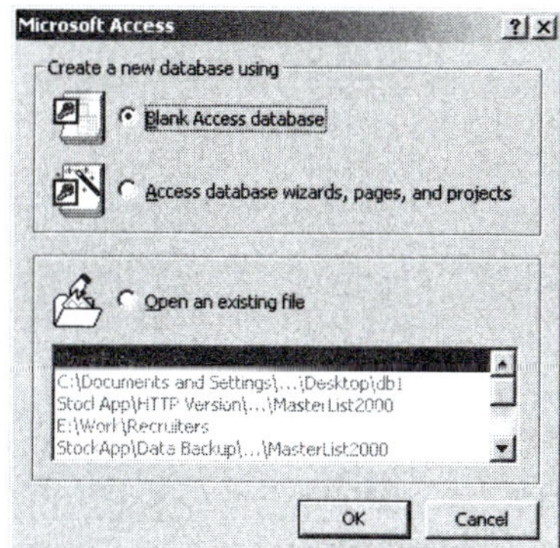

Figure D9.1

2. Creating a New Database Table

To create a new table, follow these steps.

1. Click **Tables** under **Objects,** and then click **New** on the Database window toolbar.
2. Double-click **Design View.**
3. Define each of the fields in your table. The database table will hold seven fields: CPU, Pins, Clock Speed, Level-2 Cache, Memory, Warranty, Price. In the Design view, the database table should look like Figure D9.2.

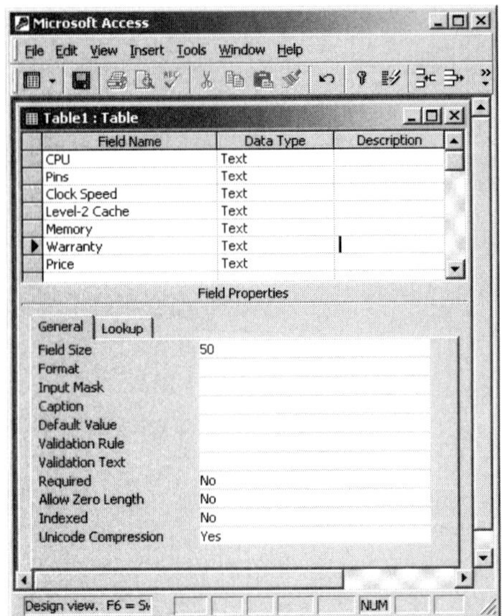

Figure D9.2

Click **Save** from the **File** menu, saving the table as Table1. Click **Yes** when Microsoft Access asks you whether to define a Primary Key for your table.

3. Entering Research Data into the Database Table

To enter data into a table, the table must be in Datasheet view. Tables are created in Design view; data is entered in Datasheet view. Access Datasheet view by selecting the **View | Datasheet View** menu command. In Datasheet view, Access tables are represented with columns and rows. For each row, enter the data acquired in your research. Figure D9.3 shows fictitious data entered into the Datasheet view of Table1.

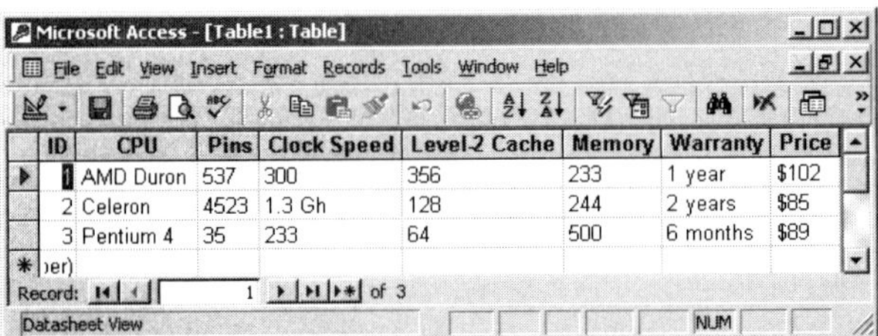

ID	CPU	Pins	Clock Speed	Level-2 Cache	Memory	Warranty	Price
1	AMD Duron	537	300	356	233	1 year	$102
2	Celeron	4523	1.3 Gh	128	244	2 years	$85
3	Pentium 4	35	233	64	500	6 months	$89

Figure D9.3

Click the **File | Close** menu command to close Table1.

4. Creating a New Database Report

To create a new Microsoft Access Report, follow these steps.

1. In the Database window, click **Reports** under **Objects.**
2. Click the **New** button on the Database window toolbar.
3. In the **New Report** dialog box, click the wizard that you want to use. A description of the wizard appears in the left side of the dialog box.
4. Click **OK.**

Figure D9.4 shows how to define Table1 as the data source for the Access Report Wizard.

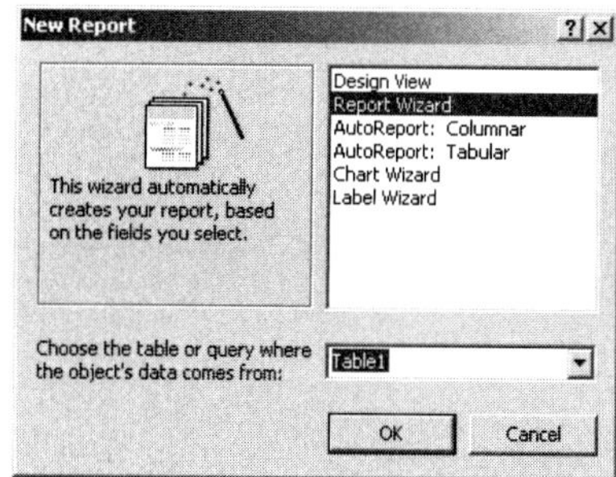

Figure D9.4

Using the Report Wizard

There are six steps to complete in the Access Report Wizard. The first step requires the user to submit the table fields that are to be used in the report. All fields are required. Double-click each field in the **Available Fields** box, thus transferring each available field to the **Selected Fields** box. Click the **Next** button to advance to Step 2 of the wizard.

Navigate through each of the remaining five steps of the Report Wizard by clicking the **Next** button. This procedure accepts the formatting default values of the Report Wizard. After the **Finish** button is clicked, the Report Wizard is finished and the completed report is presented on the page.

5. Printing the Report and Submitting it to Your Instructor

Print your report from the **File** | **Print** menu command.

Independent Information Technology Research

Overview of HTML

In this project, you are challenged to learn the basics of the Hypertext Markup Language (HTML), to construct a Web page that displays the information obtained during your independent research.

The breadth and reach of the internet is global. Why has it spread so far and fast? One major reason is that creating basic Web pages with HTML is easy and straightforward. Unlike some technologies, HTML has a low learning curve. HTML's ease-of-use allows home users and businesses to create a Web presence without high entry barriers and development costs.

A Web page is a text file composed of HTML tags and regular text.

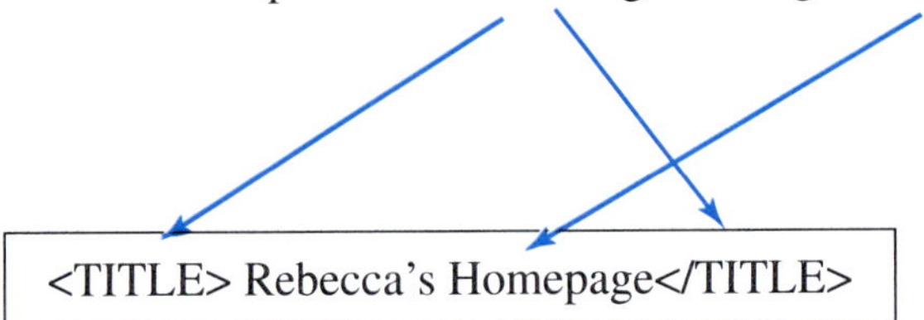

The markup language provided by HTML is a way to embed special tags that describe the structure and formatting of a document. HTML has a collection of tags used by Web authors to design Web pages. The preceding example illustrates the <TITLE> tag, which defines a title for a Web page.

HTML tags are used in pairs, with a starting and an ending tag. Start tags and end tags contain the same text; however, end tags provide closure of the HTML statement with the forward slash character (/). All HTML tags use these delimiters. The opening caret or less-than sign (<) is the delimiter to start an HTML tag. The closing caret or greater-than sign (>) is the delimiter to close an HTML tag. Although HTML is not case sensitive, it is recommended to type all HTML tags and attributes in uppercase letters.

Consider this HTML statement that creates a hyperlink to Lycos.com:
<A HREF="http://www.lycos.com">Lycos</A>

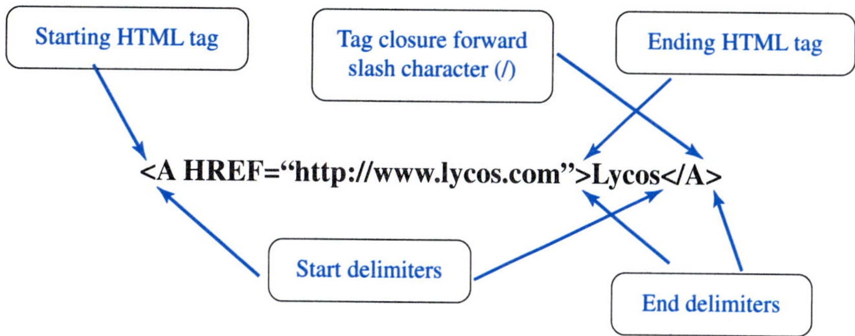

Only two HTML tags are necessary to define an HTML document. These are the <HTML> and <BODY> tags. An entire HTML document should be enclosed between an <HTML> tag (to open it) and an </HTML> tag (to close it). The entire content for any HTML document occurs in the body section, which is enclosed between <BODY> and </BODY> tags.

The basic structure of an HTML file should be:

<HTML>
<BODY>

(*Content, text, images and links reside here within the* <BODY> *tags*)

</BODY>
</HTML>

With this understanding of basic HTML structure, review these common HTML tags used to format and display text.

Tag	Function
<FONT> </FONT>	Add text to a Web page
  (No closing tag needed)	Force a line break
<H2> </H2>	Apply a heading to a Web page
<CENTER> </CENTER>	Center text or elements within the page
<B> </B>	Boldface text
<TITLE> </TITLE>	Provide a title for a Web page

Note: The <TITLE> tag does not format text; however, standard practice is to use the <TITLE> tag to label and classify all HTML documents.

Saving Documents as HTML to Use in Web Pages

As mentioned, HTML pages are text files formatted with HTML code and given the .htm filename extension. To create a Web page, create a new text file then save it with the Web page filename extension, .htm. To edit a Web page, change the extension from .htm to .txt.

To change a filename extension:

1. Locate the file in Windows Explorer.
2. Left-click the filename once.
3. Slowly left-click the filename again.
4. Retype the filename extension (replace .htm with .txt).
5. Press the **enter** key.
6. Click **Yes** on Windows file rename confirmation prompt, as seen in Figure D10.1.

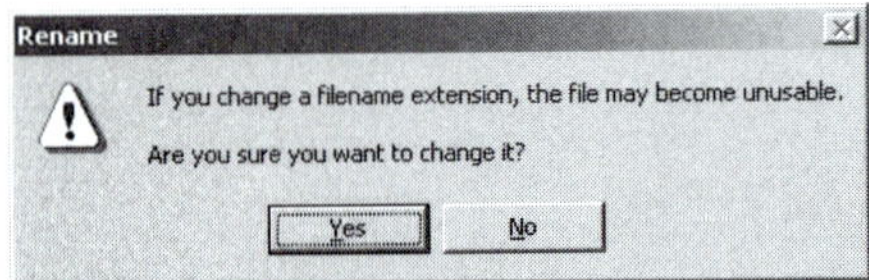

Figure D10.1

If filename extensions are not visible when viewing files, you must configure Windows to display them. Follow these instructions to view filename extensions.

To show all filename extensions:

1. In **My Computer** or Windows Explorer, click the folder you want to look at.
2. On the **View** menu, click **Folder Options.**
3. Click the **View** tab, click to clear the **Hide file extensions for known file types** checkbox.

Assignment 1—Creating a General Web Page

In this assignment, you will use Windows Notepad program to create a new HTML document. Windows Notepad is a text-editing program native to all Windows operating systems.

1. Left-click the Windows **Start** button.
2. Left-click **Run.**
3. Type the word **notepad.**
4. Left-click **OK.**
5. At this point, a blank Windows notepad screen will appear. (Figure AD10.2).

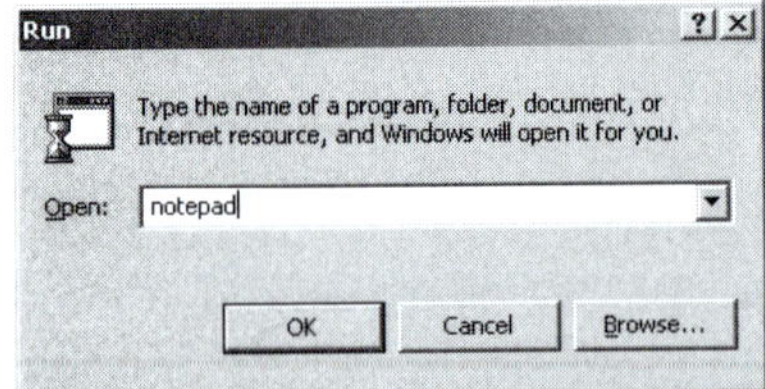

Figure D10.2

6. Type in the HTML code shown in Figure D 10.3.

IT

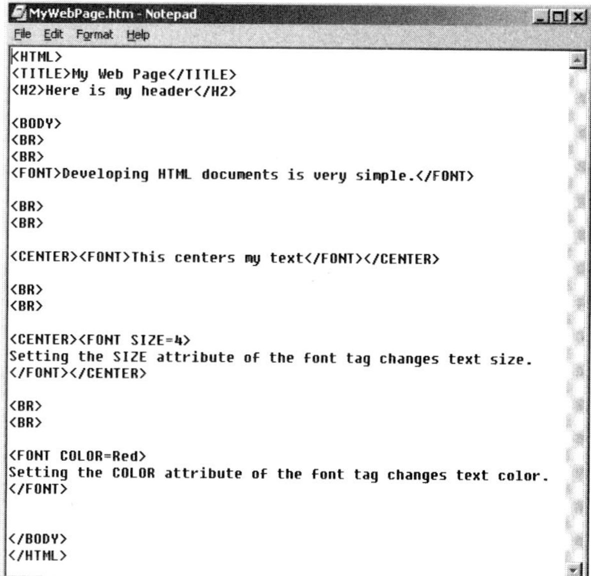

```
MyWebPage.htm - Notepad
File Edit Format Help
<HTML>
<TITLE>My Web Page</TITLE>
<H2>Here is my header</H2>

<BODY>
<BR>
<BR>
<FONT>Developing HTML documents is very simple.</FONT>

<BR>
<BR>

<CENTER><FONT>This centers my text</FONT></CENTER>

<BR>
<BR>

<CENTER><FONT SIZE=4>
Setting the SIZE attribute of the font tag changes text size.
</FONT></CENTER>

<BR>
<BR>

<FONT COLOR=Red>
Setting the COLOR attribute of the font tag changes text color.
</FONT>


</BODY>
</HTML>
```

Figure D10.3

7. Save your work with the **Save As** menu command in Notepad's **File** menu (Figure D10.4).

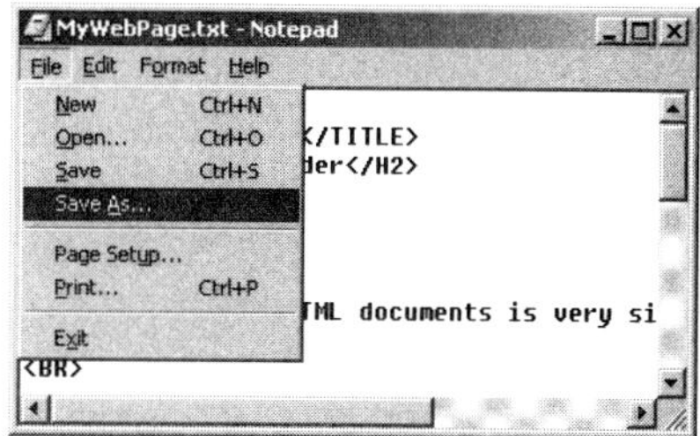

Figure D10.4

8. Save the file as "C:\WebPage.htm" (without the quotation marks). Be sure to set the **Save as type** to **All Files *.*** as seen in Figure D10.5. If the file already exists, click **Yes** for Windows to overwrite the existing file.

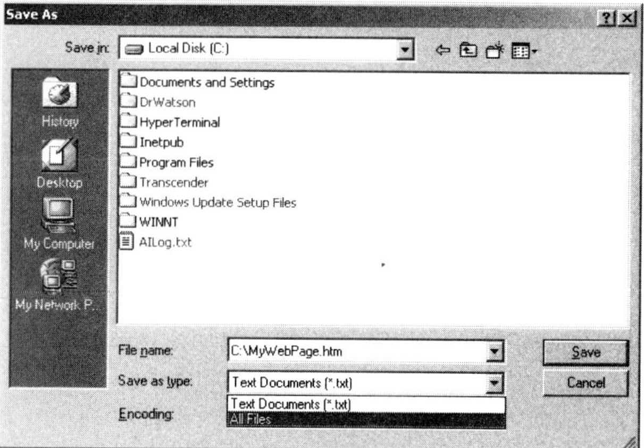

Figure D10.5

9. To view the HTML page, repeat steps 1–4, but type "C:\MyWebPage.htm" (without the quotation marks) instead of "notepad."

Assignment 2—Creating a Web Page Documenting Your Research

1. Use the development approach outlined in Assignment 1 to create your research Web page.
2. Name your Web page after the subject of your research. Be sure to include .htm as the last four letters of your filename to ensure that a Web document is created. For example, MyResearch.htm.
3. Use the HTML <CENTER> tag and the COLOR attribute of the <FONT> tag for creativity and presentation display options.
4. Center your research project subject inside the <H2> </H2> tag for display at the top of the page.
5. Include all pertinent research data inside the Web page.
6. Separate unrelated lines with the <BR> tag. Two consecutive <BR> tags create about 1/2 inch of white space.

IT